"VASLAV NIJINSKY, the greatest male dancer of all time, had a meteoric career which lasted in all just ten years and ended abruptly when he was declared insane. . . . He was only twenty-nine when he was forced to discontinue his profession. The five years he danced in his native Russia and the five years abroad, in Europe and North and South America, were sufficient to establish him as among the immortals of the dance.

〰〰〰〰〰〰〰〰〰〰〰〰〰〰〰〰〰〰〰〰

"I have told the story of this career—its origin, its great ten years, and its ending . . ."

—Romola Nijinsky

Are there paperbound books you want but cannot find in your retail stores?

You can get any title in print in **POCKET BOOK** editions. Simply send retail price, local sales tax, if any, plus 35¢ per book to cover mailing and handling costs, to:

MAIL SERVICE DEPARTMENT
POCKET BOOKS • A Division of Simon & Schuster, Inc.
1230 Avenue of the Americas • New York, New York 10020

Please send check or money order. We cannot be responsible for cash.   *Catalogue sent free on request.*

Titles in this series are also available at discounts in quantity lots for industrial or sales-promotional use. For details write our Special Products Department: Department AR, POCKET BOOKS, 1230 Avenue of the Americas, New York, New York 10020.

NIJINSKY

by

Romola Nijinsky

His Wife

Foreword by Paul Claudel

A KANGAROO BOOK
PUBLISHED BY POCKET BOOKS NEW YORK

NIJINSKY

POCKET BOOK edition published February, 1972 .

3rd printing......................October, 1977

This revised POCKET BOOK edition is printed from brand-new plates.
POCKET BOOK editions are published by
POCKET BOOKS,
a Simon & Schuster Division of
GULF & WESTERN CORPORATION,
1230 Avenue of the Americas,
New York, N.Y. 10020.
Trademarks registered in the United States
and other countries.

ISBN: 0-671-81836-8.

This POCKET BOOK edition is published by arrangement with
Simon & Schuster, Inc. Copyright, 1934, by Simon & Schuster, Inc.,
a division of Gulf & Western Corporation. Copyright renewed, ©,
1961, by Romola Nijinsky. All rights reserved. This book, or portions
thereof, may not be reproduced by any means without permission of
the original publisher: Simon & Schuster, Inc., 1230 Avenue of the
Americas, New York, N.Y. 10020.

Printed in the U.S.A.

To the Memory of

FREDERICA DEZENTJE
WITHOUT WHOSE AFFECTION AND FRIENDSHIP
THIS BOOK COULD NOT HAVE BEEN WRITTEN

ACKNOWLEDGMENTS

I WISH to thank Madame Karsavina, Messieurs Legat, Fokine, Bolm, and Professor Roerich, for much valuable information and kind help. Also Mr. Lincoln Kirstein, the editor of *Hound and Horn,* for his immense labour and patient researches into the history of ballet.

Finally, I would like to thank Mr. Arnold L. Haskell, the well-known English *balletomane* and critic, and Mr. Warren Zambra for their practical help in preparing this book.

ROMOLA NIJINSKY

CONTENTS

FOREWORD   xi

PART ONE

1. MY FIRST ENCOUNTER WITH THE RUSSIAN
   BALLET   3

2. THE CHILDHOOD OF VASLAV NIJINSKY   15

3. THE IMPERIAL SCHOOL OF DANCING   24

4. NIJINSKY AND THE MARIINSKY THEATRE   38

5. THE RUSSIAN RENAISSANCE   46

6. THE FIRST PARIS SEASON   63

7. THE FRIENDSHIP OF SERGEI DE DIAGHILEFF
   AND VASLAV NIJINSKY   79

8. NIJINSKY'S BREAK WITH THE MARIINSKY
   THEATRE   96

9. NIJINSKY AS CHOREOGRAPHER   119

10. *L'APRÈS-MIDI D'UN FAUNE*   143

11. *JEUX* AND *SACRE DU PRINTEMPS*   154

12. NIJINSKY'S MARRIAGE   175

PART TWO

13. THE BREAK WITH SERGEI DE DIAGHILEFF   217

14. PRISONERS OF WAR   235

15. "LENT" TO AMERICA   255

16. THE NEW YORK SEASON   274

17. THE AMERICAN TOUR   289

18. SPAIN AND SOUTH AMERICA   311

19. HOME IN ST. MORITZ   336

20. *MARRIAGE AVEC DIEU*   348

    EPILOGUE   365

A 16-page photographic insert
appears between pages 178 and 179.

FOREWORD

RIO DE JANEIRO *is the only big city of my acquaintance that has not succeeded in turning out Nature. You are plunged in the sea, the mountains, the virgin forest that tumbles down into your gardens from all sides, intrudes its mangoes and palm-trees into the houses, escorts the tramlines with its clear waters, leaves on the rotten gateways of the negro laundries patches of bougainville and spiced greenery. The popular quarter itself dances and canters all the way down to its meeting with the ocean, over the hills that are the last stirrings of the mountain. And from wherever you may be, from the hotel terraces or the windows of drawing-rooms, you have only to raise your head to see all kinds of peaks and strange horns wrapped in the dark mantle of the forest, Tijuca, Gavea, Campo dos Antes, Corcovado, and the Profile of Louis XVI. Always behind you stands waiting something immense and black, something fresh and brilliant, and with one bound you are in it.*

It was there that on the stage of a theatre for me undistinguishable—through a mass of unimportant plasterwork—from an esplanade of the forest, I saw, for the first and last time, Nijinsky. We had already reached the third year of the war; he himself had just escaped from a concentration camp, and for me, the acute accents of the little orchestra which under Ansermet's baton was addressing the backcloth through the curtain wave mingled simultaneously on that strange antarctic shore, with the noise of the ocean flinging its prodigious fireworks against

*the breakwater of Beira Mar, and that of the ever present
cannonade over there. I was like someone who is about
to enter a ballroom from the outside, throws his cigar one
way, and casts a final glance the other way towards the
horizon where a dreadful moon is spreading its blaze
behind a curtain of poisoned vapours. The storm had
thrown up between Copacabana and the Sugarloaf the
gaily-painted vessel of the Russian Ballets, and I was
invited to take my ticket like those one-time emigrants
going to applaud some exile from the Royal Opera on a
chance stage of Coblenz or Spa.*

Nijinsky appeared.

*I had never had much taste for the conventional art of
ballet such as it is practised, sometimes with an idiotic
perfection, in more than one State Theatre, or by the
sinister Pavlova—any more than for the prowess of singers and violinists. Beauty is a thing that responds rarely
to a search. It is natural that sham artists, irritated at the
capricious and divine generosity of inspiration, should try
to replace it with superstitious execution of a mere formu-
la, and by that frenzied labour to which the mocking lips
of the Latin Janus have attached the epithet improbus.
But the crown of France is not won by breaking stones,
and merit will never merit grace. So I was one of those
who have never prized any other dance than that of the
East, in which the feet rarely leave the ground, and which
is either a discourse whose phrases, starting from the
central twine of muscles and entrails and addressing by
means of the body that revolves all the points of a cir-
cumference, spread themselves out through the joints
right to the extremity of the phalanges, the slow manifestation or, on the contrary, the instantaneous discharges
of a complete movement—or else the untiring answer of
the apparition to a verse a hundred times caught up and
repeated by the flute and the drum.*

*Nijinsky brought with him something else; the feet have
at last quitted the ground. He brought the leap, that is
to say, the victory of breath over weight. Just as the
singer or the actor, by the movement of his arms, merely
increases the swelling of his chest that is being lifted up*

filled with air, so the dancer's inspiration, and that urge of our desire towards life are strong enough to detach him from the earth, all it remains is a springboard triumphantly trodden by his feet. It is the possession of the body by the spirit, and the utilisation of the animal by the soul—again, and again, and once again shoot up, great Bird, to your encounter with that sublime defeat. He falls again, as a king comes down, and once more he darts away up like an eagle, and like an arrow snapping from the crossbow of its own accord. For a second the soul carries the body, this vestment becomes a flame, and matter has passed. He traverses the stage like lightning and hardly has turned away, when he is back on us like the thunderbolt. It is the great human Creature in its lyric state, interrupting our savage dance like a god. He paints our passions on the canvas of eternity, he takes up each of our most vulgarized movements, as a Virgil does with our words and our images, and transposes them into the blessed world of intelligence, of power, and of the upper air. Even in "Scheherazade" when the negro, doubled up like a spring, runs over, or rather measures —with those ten electric points at the end of those arms no longer arms, but at once lips, a greedy tongue, and a spirit—a body ideal round the half-visible real body of the beautiful woman, the gesture, potentially lubric, takes on an unspeakable dignity and grandeur.

And that "Après-midi d'un Faune"—ah what loveliness, what joy, what a poignant melancholy. It took place both in Sicily and on that abandoned terrace in the middle of the virgin forest that my friend Milhaud knows well, near a great overflowing basin beneath a wall of green stones, and the flaming moon among the leaves like the cymbals in every gap of the orchestra.

Once Nijinsky consented to accompany me to the Legation, and I could see him at close quarters. He walked as tigers do, it was not the transference of an inert mass from one position of balance to another, but the supple alliance with weight, like a wing on the air, of all that machine of muscles and nerves, of a body that is not trunk or statue, but the complete organ of power and movement. There was no gesture so small—the one, for example, when he turned his chin towards us, when the little head swung round suddenly on that long neck—that Nijinsky did not execute with glory, with a vivacity both ferocious and suave, with overwhelming authority. Even at rest, he seemed to be imperceptibly dancing, like those sensitive vehicles that used to be called "eight springs." There was a green half-light in the dining room, and the sun of midday with the intermittent cry of cicadas reached us dulled by the mango trees, there was a green shade on the cloth between the fruit-dishes and the silver service, a gleam of emerald played in the glass salad-bowl among the fragments of ice. And Nijinsky spoke to us of the great work he had completed during his years of internment in Hungary. He had found a way to write down and annotate dance as they do music. It was true. The book exists, and Madame Nijinsky tells me that it is being translated.

And now over the divine dancer's face there is a black evil. He is somewhere in Switzerland and I am at Los Angeles and Madame Nijinsky is sitting beside me in the hall of this hotel and showing me strange drawings. They are human faces and the great Sylph's own portrait drawn with trajectories that cut across one another. At the meeting-place and heart of circular forces and algebraical whirlwinds rises a head made of interfering lines. It is as if the man was made, limbs and face, of a knot of movements distributed and recovered round him by the dancer; function of a number, intoxicated center, realisation of a soul in the explosion of a spark.

Greetings there where you are, Nijinsky, God be with your darkened soul. Over the forbidden threshold where those two intertwined sisters, admiration and pity, meditate, and remember, prayer can still find a way. . . .

PAUL CLAUDEL

Translated by Lord Derwent

Part One

be reached the highest ... But this daring ambition almost caused his death. One day in the classroom,
where dancing was forbidden, waiting for the teacher,

Chapter One

MY FIRST ENCOUNTER
WITH THE
RUSSIAN BALLET

EARLY in the spring of 1912 I was invited to attend the first performance of the Imperial Russian Ballet in Budapest. The city was in a great state of excitement. Fantastic tales of the glamorous, exotic beauty, and of the attainment of great heights of artistic achievement, had preceded this unique company, which was a part of the Imperial Theatre of St. Petersburg.

I recalled that in my childhood I had once seen a performance by former dancers of the same Imperial Ballet, and above all I remembered the imperceptible smoothness and fragile elegance of the *prima ballerina* Preobrajenskaya, as delicate as a Meissen figurine. For her partners she had the two dashing Legat brothers, Russia's foremost dancers, complete technicians of their time. So now I expected to see an equally enchanting performance.

The brilliant audience which gathered in the Municipal Opera House to welcome the Russian artists, who had already taken Paris and all Western Europe by storm, was formed of the *élite* of the then prosperous Hungarian capital. The people of Budapest were rich, critical, and intelligent. With all the pride of a small capital they maintained a running competition with Vienna. They expected a great deal. Budapest was willing to be shown, but it insisted on the most capriciously high standards. As soon as the orchestra struck up the first few bars of the overture, everyone felt that the strange, powerful, alluring music was the composition of a great master. And then,

3

as one ballet followed the other, we were transported from
the tall red temple of Egyptian stone to the cruel luxury
of a Persian harem and to the endless barren Tartar
steppes. A magic hand lavished upon us the inexhaustible
variety of gorgeous colours. It was a riot of hitherto unknown colours: purples, greens, of unthinkable depth.
Oranges, all enveloped in the golden barbaric art of
Byzantium. The very soul of each country and period was
revealed. The exquisite art of the dancers was indescribable. The audience sat awe-struck and breathless.

The impressions of that first ballet performance were
so overwhelming, it was difficult to grasp and appreciate
the greatness of the individual dancers themselves. Even
the smallest rôle was portrayed by an artist who was a
star in his own right. This was the policy of this astonishing company. The fact that an equal number of male
dancers shared with the women important and dominating
parts in the performance was also most unusual at this
time. We soon understood how this remarkable company
had been able to resurrect the long-lost art of the ballet,
and raise it to hitherto unknown heights, wherever they
had appeared before.

On leaving the theatre, I learned that the brightest star
of the company had not been able to appear this evening
because of a slight indisposition. I determined to attend
all their performances. The next evening found me again
at the theatre. The programme was composed of
Cléopâtre, Schumann's *Carnaval,* and *Prince Igor.* Once
again the audience was a brilliant one. Seeing *Cléopâtre*
a second time, I was better able to appreciate the perfection of Astafieva, Fedorova, and Bolm's dancing. The
scenery used for Schumann's *Carnaval* was a heavy velvet
curtain of royal blue, painted with beautiful garlands of
roses. The costumes were of the lovely Biedermeier period. The audience instantly grasped its light-hearted
gaiety. The scene changed. Pierrot, Papillon, and Pantalon
flirted and swept across the stage, like so many little
whirlwinds. Suddenly a slim, lithe, cat-like Harlequin took
the stage. Although his face was hidden by a painted
mask, the expression and beauty of his body made us all

realise that we were in the presence of genius. An electric shock passed through the entire audience. Intoxicated, entranced, gasping for breath, we followed this superhuman being, the very spirit of Harlequin incarnate; mischievous, lovable. The power, the featherweight lightness, the steel-like strength, the suppleness of his movements, the incredible gift of rising and remaining in the air and descending in twice as slow a time as it took to rise—contrary to all laws of gravitation—the execution of the most difficult pirouettes and *tours en l'air* with an amazing nonchalance and apparently no effort whatever, proved that this extraordinary phenomenon was the very soul of the dance. With complete abandon the audience rose to its feet as one man, shouted, wept, showered the stage with flowers, gloves, fans, programmes, pêle-mêle in their wild enthusiasm. *This magnificent vision was Nijinsky.* My one desire, from that moment on, was to know more about the extraordinary manifestation of art embodied in this entire company, and the individuals who had succeeded in creating it.

It was not very difficult for me to carry out my plan. My mother, Emilia Markus, was the foremost dramatic actress of Hungary. She kept open house, and it was customary for eminent foreigners to visit her home and pay their respects. I immediately got in touch with some music critics and a group of advanced painters and sculptors to obtain an introduction to some member of the Russian Ballet. I succeeded in discovering that one of my compatriots was a friend of Adolf Bolm, the Russian character dancer. He took me back stage and presented me. Bolm was not only a powerful dancer, but very sociable, extremely cultured, well-read, and musical. He was the son of the concert master of the Imperial orchestra. We entertained him, showed him Budapest, and through him I made the acquaintance of many members of the company with whom he seemed to be very popular. I could find no opportunity to meet Nijinsky, nor was I certain whether or not I wished to know him. His genius swept me off my feet, but at the same time I had an uncanny feeling of apprehension. Bolm spoke of him in the highest terms, almost as a priest might speak of divinity.

After a week of triumphant success, the Imperial Ballet journeyed westward on their tour, carrying with them the heart of another conquered city. How I longed to be with these people always, and to follow them all over the world!

During the following months I abandoned my training for the theatre with the celebrated French actress Réjane, and, carried away by a greater ambition, I worked diligently to become a dancer.

Around Christmas, when the Ballet visited Budapest a second time, I was at home for the holidays. I spent most of my time with Bolm, and made friends with others in the company, especially with their teacher, Enrico Cecchetti. He loved to call himself "the King of the pirouettes," and he never tired of talking of the time, some fifty odd years ago, when he was the Don Juan of Rome and the Idol of the Italian capital. He would pose with great pride whenever he told tales of his youth. "For thirty years I have been teacher and coach of the *greatest* and *best* dancing school in all the *world:* the Imperial School of Dancing in St. Petersburg," he would assert with great eloquence and true Italian fervour. The *Maestro* (as everyone called him) was not only the perfect teacher, but also the jealous guardian of the pure, classical traditions of the Ballet. Among his pupils he counted such dancers as Pavlova, Karsavina, Mordkin, Bolm, and Nijinsky. I soon discovered I could win his heart through flattery. I had a genuine admiration for him and a very real affection, but I had to use him in order to achieve my purpose—to become permanently attached to the Ballet.

During their stay in Budapest, I was present at every performance, at every rehearsal, and, by very special permission, at the classes of the *Maestro.* These classes were compulsory for each member of the company. The first thing every morning, wherever they happened to be, was a class with Maestro Cecchetti, just as though these artists were still students at the academy in St. Petersburg.

It was a strange sight to see these Russians in their high patent leather boots and fur caps going along the gloomy corridors of the Royal Opera House, which was their home during this second visit. On their arrival, the monotonous, dull routine of the musty old building was instantly changed into a vibrant, pulsating, feverish activity. One of their own famous conductors, Pierre Monteux or Inglebrecht, immediately took possession of the orchestra. It was astonishing how contagious was their spirit. Whoever came into personal contact with them—musicians, electricians, stagehands, dressmakers, hairdressers— all displayed unsuspected gifts in their respective fields, as though working under a spell.

While a rehearsal was in progress on the stage, in the dimly lighted auditorium, in the midst of a group of men, stood a figure of medium height; his hat drawn down over his ears, his coat collar turned up. Simultaneously he gave orders to the chief electrician, conferred with the conductor of the orchestra, was interviewed by three reporters, and discussed business matters with the administrative secretary. He seemed to be a real authority in every branch of the organisation. His mere presence made one feel that he was not only a versatile and gifted director, but also a *grand seigneur*. Everyone obeyed him blindly. This man was Diaghileff—Sergei Pavlovitch Diaghileff, the master magician of the Russian Ballet.

At rehearsals I always hid in some dark corner of the theatre, fearing that if I attracted attention I might be sent away. On this occasion I happened to be sitting in the back of the house with a newspaperwoman, who had come to watch rehearsals. She raved on and on about Nijinsky. Impatiently I interrupted her pæans by saying, "If you really know this 'wonder' so well, then please introduce me to him at once." We went over to the group of men where Nijinsky was conversing with Diaghileff. It was an exciting moment. One would never have thought that this unassuming young man, with his Tartar face and the appearance of a Japanese student in his badly fitting European clothes, was the same being as the marvellous apparition the whole world had learned to admire. The introduction actually occurred. In the ensuing conversation there was a bit of confusion, which was greatly aided by the diversity of languages spoken. Nijinsky misunderstood my identity, and thought I was the *prima ballerina* of the Hungarian Opera, whose name had been brought into the conversation at that moment. As time went on and I grew to know more and more about Nijinsky, I learned that it was probably due to that error on his part that he greeted me with so charming and respectful a bow. For many, many times after that first introduction I was introduced to him, and never was there more than a polite, fleeting acknowledgment and never by any chance did he recognise me.

Meanwhile, at my mother's home, we entertained the Russian artists lavishly. They had all been our guests except Diaghileff and Nijinsky, who were unapproachable. Bolm never left my side. As usual, he was my source of information, and from him I knew all the inside stories of the company. We spoke a great deal of Nijinsky, and of the young girl who bore such a close resemblance to him —his sister, Bronislava. She possessed the dreamlike quality and the lightness of Pavlova, together with the overpowering acting ability of her brother. To see the two of them dancing together was an unforgettable experience. Then there was the glamorous Matilde Kshessinskaya— favourite of the Tsar, the whole Imperial Court, and idol of the intellectual and artistic world of St. Petersburg. She was continually surrounded by a special bodyguard. The strangest and most contradictory rumours were abroad concerning this lovely woman and great dancer. She had a magnificent country estate, a palace in town where she maintained a court like a Grand Duchess. Her receptions were unequalled in luxury. Even in comparison with the wealth of the times, her priceless collection of jewels caused comment. Whenever she appeared on the stage, she wore real diamonds and emeralds, as large as walnuts. Although she was a member of the most exclusive Court in the world, this magnificent woman was very generous and tender-hearted to everyone. She had an open purse as well as an open heart, and no one who came to her for help went away unrequited. According to gossip, in his bachelordom the Tsar of all the Russias was ignorant of all but a strictly celibate life. The wise Court chose the glorious and distinguished Kshessinskaya to convert His Majesty. She succeeded splendidly, we are told; slightly better than the Court would have wished. But those who were instrumental in staging this love-affair always knew how to correct the pranks of fate. So on one cold, wintry morning the motor-car of the Imperial favourite skidded, and, due to this unfortunate accident, the expected royal baby never saw the light. In later years Kshessinskaya's name was linked with that of the Grand Duke Vladimir, the powerful Commander-in-Chief of the entire Russian Army. The wagging tongues maliciously quoted that the gold borrowed from France to buy new cannon went into the coffers of the *ballerina*. Her influence at Court and in theatrical circles was omnipotent. No one dared contradict her, not even Count Fredericks, the Court Minister and most intimate friend of the Tsar. Kshessinskaya was at home in all the intrigues of high politics too. But she did not want to be left out of the tours of the Imperial Ballet abroad. She quickly understood that the tours were not undertaken purely from artistic impulses, and that they had a far-reaching political significance, and served to bring a friendlier relationship between foreign countries and Russia much more quickly than any diplomatic stratagems. Even Diaghileff, the absolute ruler in the company, treated Kshessinskaya with distinction, except in artistic matters, where he never loosened his iron grip.

These exuberant personalities were something entirely new to us. The better we came to know them, the more evident it became that it was impossible to get to know them at all. Contrary to all European theatrical customs, their private affairs never interfered with the rigid discipline of their work. Everyone was fascinated by them. Even the serenity of the old, jovial porter at the stage door was disturbed. This enormous, lumbering old fellow, who was called "Tiny" by everyone, had, for forty-five years, guarded his post at the stage door, quietly

smoking his pipe, totally unconcerned by what was going
on inside the Opera, impervious to the famous artists and
unusual personalities that passed him at the door. He
came at a certain hour, left at a certain hour, smoked
his pipe, and remained in his shell. He was *blasé*. But
these Russians did something to him. No matter how
many hours earlier than his appointed time he arrived,
he was always too late, and the dancers were working
at high speed. Finally it became a race with the inevitable. He never won. While other artists turned around
in their beds, the *Maestro* had already shouted himself
hoarse in his classes. From eight in the morning until two
in the afternoon the *Maestro* exercised his pupils in separate groups. Those who had not worked late the evening before were in his first class, as well as those whom
he thought less perfect in technique. He grouped his pupils according to artistic capacity. Thus he kept the later
period, from twelve to two, for his star pupils—Karsavina,
Kshessinskaya, Nijinsky. Simultaneously rehearsals were
in progress on the stage from ten in the morning until
the late hours in the afternoon. It was a mystery when
the dancers could find time to rest or sleep. *Maestro,*
greatly flattered by my constant presence in his classes,
encouraged my dreams to become a dancer, in spite of the
fact that I was already seventeen years of age. He
thought that with great perseverance he could yet make
something of me, and I sat day after day respectfully
watching him teach. Bolm wanted to teach me too, but,
realising that it was practically impossible for me to join
them, he advised my mother to send me to the Wiesen-
thal sisters in Vienna. They were members of the Imperial Opera at Vienna, who, under the influence of
Isadora Duncan, had become concert dancers. The
thought of having to study with them was very distasteful to me. I was interested in the Russians, and especially
in Nijinsky. I used to watch him closely at dinner. He
listened to the gypsy music and seemed to observe the
people with an aloof, distant air. His half-closed eyes
gave an extraordinary, fascinating expression to his face.
His features were decidedly Mongolian, and the almond-

shaped eyes were a dark brown, although on the stage they seemed a dark blue or green. He was of medium height and very muscular, but on the stage he seemed tall and slender. Even his physical being seemed to change according to the part he danced. The fact that he never greeted me on passing my table infuriated me, and one day I boldly ran after him in the corridors of the Opera and asked him for his autograph. He stopped and gave it to me with a charming smile, but from the way he looked at me I knew that he didn't recognise me. I wondered why. Occasionally I caught his eyes resting on me, but as soon as I looked at him he quickly turned his glance elsewhere.

I was determined to find some way by which I would be able to stay with them. *Maestro,* who by that time was my sworn ally, advised me to speak to Diaghileff, but somehow I was afraid of him. I really wanted to ask Nijinsky to help me, but Bolm said, quite casually, that even members of the Ballet could not approach him. He was always followed by Vassily, his valet and Diaghileff's faithful slave; never spoke to any one of them except at, and about, their work. And I had heard enough gossip to know that Diaghileff kept an impenetrable Chinese wall around Nijinksy. I could not understand this strange air of isolation around Nijinsky, but I realised one thing very clearly: I would have to proceed with the utmost caution. Nobody noticed my adoration for Nijinsky. I learned later that the company thought that, apart from my artistic admiration for the Russian Ballet, I was interested in Bolm. I was very fond of him as a friend and admired him as a great artist. It remained for *Maestro* to notice, even before I myself was aware of it, that I was in love with Nijinsky. For one morning he arrived at *Maestro's* class earlier than usual. I knew that I would have to leave the rehearsal hall, and got up to go. As I passed the *Maestro,* he whispered, "Beware, Nijinsky is like a sun that pours forth light but never warmth." His prophetic words came back to me in later years.

They left for Vienna, and I followed them. For weeks every ticket had been sold in advance. The same excitement prevailed in Vienna as in Budapest. The Court, society, the world of art, and the great public eagerly awaited their arrival.

To enter the Opera House during rehearsals, even for a member not actually working on the stage at the time, was impossible, according to the very strict (military) regulations. But why was my godfather head of the Imperial Family's archives and the confidant of Franz Joseph? To help me. And why was my brother-in-law the first Wagnerian star of his day? To serve me, of course. So, therefore, I set them to work and obtained a special permit to allow me to come and go as I pleased.

The opening was a command performance. Even the Emperor, who was already very old and led a retired life, made an unusual exception and appeared. The seventy-five most important members of the reigning house of Hapsburg fought bitterly between themselves for places in the three archducal boxes. Even the *loges* of the Imperial suite were crowded with eager Hapsburgs, and the ladies- and gentlemen-in-waiting had to content themselves with whatever orchestra stalls they could get.

The press everywhere was unanimously enthusiastic. Only one critic, Ludwig Karpath, the influential Hungarian musical critic, dared lift an opposing voice. A real intellectual, intimately connected with the Wagner dynasty, he had a fighting spirit, and the profound conviction that, for the healthy development of art, opposition was always essential. He could not bear to have the Russian Ballet's supremacy pass absolutely unquestioned, more for its sake than any carping notions of his own.

Nothing could escape the attention of Diaghileff. Yet, unapproachable as he was, and offended as he might have been, he granted Karpath an interview as soon as he asked for it.

Hard as it was for Karpath to ask for a meeting with Diaghileff after his attack, he did it only for my sake. The large, corpulent man could never forget that I had once rendered him a small favour in Marienbad years ago. I had seen his childish terror of the darkness, and I offered to accompany him through the forests at night to his hotel, some distance away. My whole destiny was changed through this small incident.

I was neither awed nor embarrassed when we went to see Diaghileff. I was determined to obtain my point, and, when my mind was definitely set, nothing and nobody mattered.

Diaghileff received us in the middle of the afternoon, in an empty public reception-room of the Hôtel Bristol. As soon as he entered we felt his dominating personality. We expected a cold, resentful reception. But Diaghileff, who with every gesture and word expressed at the same time the superiority of an emperor and an irresistible charm, confused both Karpath and myself by the warm interest he took in our requests. He made us feel absolutely that nothing interested him more than my intention to become a dancer. With conscious magic he led the conversation around, so that, without Karpath noticing it at all, he made me speak, against my will; apparently a young society girl had come to the great artistic organiser with a request. In reality, two powerful enemies had crossed swords for the first time. Diaghileff held the thing I most wanted—Nijinsky. And he sensed at once, with his fine instincts, however subconsciously, the approaching danger. I just as quickly realised that he wished to read my mind. Karpath was completely unaware of the fine covert duel that was being fought between and behind words, and mostly in thought. And by this time Karpath was entirely lost in admiration for Diaghileff.

"I think Bolm is wrong in advising you to go to the Wiesenthals." One thought seemed to follow the other, aloud. "The ideal thing for you would be to become a pupil of the Imperial Dancing School in St. Petersburg. But of course it is not feasible, even with the greatest possible pull for you are not a Russian, and you are long past the required age." He paused. "I think the best thing for you to do would be to take private lessons from Fokine in St. Petersburg."

With apparent joy I jumped at the idea.

"I would love it." I misled him deliberately. "It has always been my dream to go to Russia."

He then asked my impressions of the different ballets and the artists of his company. My answers must have been correct. He smiled approvingly. During all this time I felt that gradually I was falling under his spell. I tried to fight against his almost hypnotic power. With a desperate effort I began to rave about Bolm as a man, not as an artist, like any stagestruck girl would. And then Diaghileff, with unexpected strategy, turned and asked, "What about Nijinsky?"

Without hesitation I answered, "Oh, Nijinsky is a genius. As an artist he is incomparable. But somehow Bolm is more human to me"—and I continued my extravagances about Bolm. By this time he was convinced of my good faith, and then said the fatal words:

"I will speak to Maestro Cecchetti. He has taught all our greatest artists. I am sure he will take you as a special, private pupil. This way you will have not only a marvellous teacher, but also the possibility of travelling with us and closely studying our work."

I thanked him gratefully, and so our interview ended. I had won my first battle. I could scarcely believe I had succeeded in fooling such an inconceivably clever man as Diaghileff.

The same evening, when I went back stage, *Maestro* greeted me from afar with enthusiastic gestures and loud shouts of Italian joy.

"Sergei Pavlovitch has decided that you should study with me. I am overjoyed, *bambina*. I will make you work frightfully hard, *cara mia*. But you will see in a few years what a dancer I will make of you." He embraced me and kissed me on both cheeks. He always liked to kiss young girls; when he was enthusiastic and excited he would rub his small fleshy hands, and in high spirits he always talked about his youth, when all the women in Rome were in love with him. After a few details of past love-affairs, we finally settled when and how I would start to study. I was to join them on the 4th of February in London.

When I left the Opera House, I did not walk; I flew to my brother-in-law and my sister to tell them of my good news. Eric was won over entirely by the Russians.

And he was very difficult to convince, being himself a great artist; but after the first night not only did he go to every performance, but he watched the rehearsals as well. He had never seen so great and finished an artist as Nijinsky work so hard every day. When I told him my good luck, he heartily congratulated me, and said it was a rare chance, and that it was the opinion of the ballet-master of the Hofoper that from the point of view of classic Italian ballet the technique of the Russians was so perfect that not even the Italians outdid them, after hundreds of years of tradition. It was the quintessence of the classic school.

After a few days the Russians left Vienna. On the 4th of February, 1913, I began to work enthusiastically under Maestro Cecchetti in London, where I joined the Russian Ballet. From that moment my whole life was consecrated to its art; but the centre of my interest was Nijinksy, his past, present, his personality, and his genius.

Chapter Two

THE CHILDHOOD OF VASLAV NIJINSKY

NIJINSKY was born in the City of Four Hundred Churches, Kiev, in South Russia, on the 28th of February, 1890, according to the Russian calendar.

He was christened Vaslav, and baptised some months later in Warsaw in the Roman Catholic faith, which was his mother's. His mother, wishing to save him from future military service in the Russian troops of the army, had him christened in the Polish capital, so she could obtain a certificate from there. She even went so far as to give

a false date—1889—as the year of baby Vaslav's birth,
because children born in that year were privileged in the
order of their military service.

Vaslav's parents were both of Polish origin. His father,
Thomas Nijinsky, a handsome, dark, temperamental,
high-strung, and ambitious young man, was already a
dancer of the fourth generation in a family in which the
art of dancing and technique was handed down from father to son, as in the dancing dynasty of Vestris and
Petipa.

Thomas Nijinsky lived and danced in Russia, where he
was both famous and popular, but on account of his Polish
descent, and because he did not graduate from the Imperial Schools, he could never obtain his greatest desire,
which was to become a member of the Imperial Theatre.
This was the tragedy of his life. Thomas Nijinsky was a
perfect classical dancer, a master technician, and, according to Vaslav, surpassed even him in technique. He was
an excellent acrobat, had a superb *ballon,* and was splendid also in character parts. Thomas had his own troupe,
and danced with them all through Russia, and even
ventured as far as Paris in the late 'eighties, for the
International Exhibition, to perform at the Olympia. This
was the first time a Russian dancer had appeared in the
Western metropolis.

While touring the Polish provinces of Russia, he met
one day, in Warsaw, Eleanora Bereda, a student of the
Warsaw School of Dancing. She was a beautiful, delicate
girl, with blue eyes, golden hair, and a perfect body. She
had a sweet, placid nature, and was the daughter of a
well-to-do, religious, cultured, but conservative gentry family. On her mother's side her ancestors came from the
Transylvanian nobility. Her father, a wealthy Polish land-
owner, led the life of a country gentleman, and, after
gambling away everything he owned, shot himself. Her
mother died of grief shortly after, and the orphans were
taken to an uncle in Warsaw. This uncle, the president
of the Polish State railways, took complete charge of the
children and wished to bring them up according to his
ideas. Eleanora, being the oldest, mothered her brothers

and sister, and everything went well until one day Eleanora suddenly declared her overwhelming desire to become a dancer. This conservative and deeply religious family was scandalised at the thought of having one of their kin on the stage. But Eleanora would not abandon her idea, so she was disinherited. She struggled along, and without any help from her family developed into the most exquisite type of character dancer.

Thomas Nijinsky fell violently in love with her. His fierce, passionate love-making frightened the quiet girl, and, though she was flattered by the courting of the famous dancer, she was not in love with him. He would never have succeeded in his persistence had he not terrified her by threatening to kill himself if she refused him. Panic-stricken, the young girl finally consented.

The first few years of their married life were fairly happy. She was a sensitive and affectionate woman, a dreamer. After a little while she sensed that this violent, impetuous man was not only a gifted dancer, but possessed an artistic spirit and an enchanting personality. Eleanora became deeply attached to him.

Thomas, not being a member of any theatre, had no permanent residence. So, wandering from city to city, they had to exercise their beloved art and earn their livelihood as best they could. The Nijinskys, with their troupe, crossed all the Russias, from the Baltic to the Black Sea, from Poland to the Caucasus, from Siberia to Turkestan.

One day, while travelling in the Caucasian wilderness on the Grusinsky road, the military highway which leads to Persia, an accident befell them which cast the shadow of a later tragedy on the little family. It happened between Tiflis and Vladikavkas, somewhere in a small mountain village in the midst of great forests, where they had stopped for the night. The troupe's wagon halted by an inn, where there was a stable, a tavern, and rooms for travellers. During the night, after they had retired, the inn was attacked and raided by bandits. Their savagery, cruelty, and the suddenness of their onslaught had a terrifying effect on the young expectant mother. Eleanora lost her power of speech for three days.

Her first baby, a boy, was born soon after. He was named Stanislav. The sturdy, muscular, fair-haired little baby resembled his mother. Already, in his infancy, he showed an unmistakable predisposition for music and dancing. A year later Vaslav was born. He was the image of his father. He had a dark complexion and big brown eyes. His mother danced on the very evening of his birth, an hour before the baby's arrival. So he was a real child of the stage. From the moment of his birth he was engaged in the service of the art whose priest he was to become.

Eleanora, who was very religious, took the children to church whenever the family went. Those churches, with their big, bulbous, glittering towers, the deep, sonorous chimes and mellow bells, the gloomy scent of incense, the colourful painted walls, the golden icons, and the richly robed, jewelled, long-bearded popes, made a profound impression on the already vivid imagination of the baby, Vaslav.

Endless travelling was their life. There were interminable coach rides through immense fields of wheat, of golden corn, vast plains, endless steppes, dusty roads, highways deep in mud, mountains, valleys. Summer and autumn merged into snowy winter, and still the troupe moved like a small dark ribbon in a borderless land, covered with deep snow, under a grey, monotonous, leaden Russian winter sky. In rain or sunshine, day and night, night and day, the troupe moved on. Under the blazing summer sun, in the snow storms and bitter blizzards of hard winters this heroic little group of artists slowly fought its way through the most hidden and forgotten corners of European and Asiatic Russia. So little Vaslav learned to know and love Russia.

There was no end of interesting variety for the children of the Nijinsky family. They very seldom stayed in any place longer than a month. They moved on from city to city, through villages, where at the entrance a toll-gate was invariably thrown open by scrutinising, furry Cossacks or uniformed guards, to whom passes had always to be shown and money paid.

Then came their temporary home, always an inn or some hostelry, bleak rooms with paraffin lamps that usually smoked terribly, and big porcelain stoves on which the children loved to sit or sleep amid the smell of vodka and the sweet hum of the samovar.

From the moment of its arrival in a new place the troupe was busy day and night. They had to be artists, stagehands, all at once. First the scenery was unloaded, then costumes and properties and personal belongings. Then came rehearsals with the local musicians, who were not, as a rule, accustomed to accompany ballet-dancers, sometimes culminating in fights and tears. Eleanora tried to keep the children close to her, in the dressing-room or behind the scenery. She thought it was safer for them. But the boys ran out in the streets, played about the theatres, whenever they became tired of watching their parents. To the children, the elders when dancing suddenly became knights and princesses, nymphs and fauns. The children could not distinguish between reality and fairy-tale, for the ballets they saw seemed more real to them than life itself.

They ate and slept in the theatre, in some corner of the stage, or on the laps of their parents in the mail coaches. Sometimes they passed nights with *moujiks* in their carved wooden huts, when no inns could be found. During their travels they saw marvellous countries and cities, many tribes, many different customs, costumes, dances, and songs. The songs and dances of all Russia became their nursery rhymes. And in this infinitely colourful, varied environment little Stanislav and Vaslav grew up. A little girl, Bronislava, was added to the family circle.

Vaslav could only faintly remember the events of this period. As he said himself, "My mother could probably recall when I cut my first tooth, but hardly the time when I began to dance." However, he did recollect distinctly when he appeared in public for the first time—at the age of three. His father composed a *pas de trois* for the child prodigy, a sailor dance, which little Vaslav executed with his brother and tiny sister. He was intensely proud of this little sailor dance.

Thomas soon discovered that among his gifted children Vaslav had the greatest talent, and began to instruct him. In these early dancing lessons Thomas taught him the most elementary steps and the five positions. Vaslav enjoyed these lessons immensely; and always begged his father to show him new steps whenever he had the time. His father did not believe in too rigorous a training for a child so young. From this time on the children often appeared in the ballets.

Thomas Nijinsky's passion for his wife faded. While travelling in Central Russia he met a young dancer, a Jewess. Soon afterwards he had a violent love-affair with the girl. Eleanora, full of affection and devotion to her husband, noticed his unfaithfulness, but she could do nothing but bear her sorrow in silence. The girl joined their troupe and they went on dancing from one place to another.

Eleanora had engaged a *nana* for her three children, and one day, in Warsaw, where Thomas at the time was *maître de ballet,* when she had to go to a rehearsal she left the children under her care. An organ-grinder stopped under the window. Stanislav, climbing up to the sill, leaned out curiously, lost his balance, and with a scream of terror fell out of the third floor. His fall was stopped by the railing of the balcony on the first floor. His father heard the cry, the confusion of voices, the shrieks of the *nana,* and, rushing out on the street, saw his eldest son in the perilous position. He rushed up and rescued him from death. But the shock and the concussion of the brain which the child must have suffered had sad consequences. His development halted. This strong, physically healthy little fellow never advanced any further mentally.

Eleanora imagined also that the shock she had received when the bandits attacked them in the Caucasus was partly responsible for Stanislav's mental illness. She was heartbroken, and Thomas, deeply grieved, tried every doctor he could find, in every city where they performed, in the hopes of finding some cure. When the boy became worse, he was taken to a specialist in St. Petersburg in order that he might secure the best treatment that the capital could afford, and to do this the family settled there permanently. The tragedy which had befallen the little family, instead of bringing the parents together, further estranged them. Thomas was increasingly irritated that in spite of his success he could not enter the Imperial Theatre. The continual silence and sadness of his wife depressed him, and the gap between them widened. The final break came when his mistress was with child, and he asked his wife to divorce him so that he could marry the girl. It is a peculiar strain in Russian men that they feel it a duty, if a woman bears them a child, to marry her and legitimise the child, in spite of the tremendous difficulties that the Orthodox Church puts in the way of divorce. Eleanora, a devoted Catholic, could not and would not divorce him. She refused once and for all, and Thomas, exasperated, left his family.

An accident in which he broke his leg prevented him for a long time from dancing and hindered him from providing for both his families, though for a few years he supported them as best he could. The small amounts he used to send his wife arrived more and more irregularly, and finally they stopped altogether.

Eleanora, bereaved, stood in the world alone with three small children. One of them was seriously ill, needing constant care. She had now no income except the occasional meagre salary she earned by giving dancing lessons, or here and there by an infrequent appearance. Stanislav's accident made it clear to her that she could not leave her children alone in the care of *nana;* to pursue the career of a dancer, which demanded constant practising, rehearsing, and concentrated interest, became impossible. The only alternative was to find some occupation which would allow her to stay with her family. As a young girl she ran away from her family to become a dancer. Now she decided to sacrifice her dancing for the sake of her children.

She rented a flat and opened a *pension*. By letting rooms and cooking for her boarders she earned a modest living for herself and her children. She did all the manual work herself, but in spite of it she could barely succeed in getting along. Vaslav was always around his mother, never leaving her side, a real mother's boy, helping her in the kitchen and wherever he could in her daily work. He watched over the place when she went in the morning to the markets. Vaslav was her only assistant, as Stanislav was sick and Bronia a baby.

But this housework had its joys, too, for the little boy. The final clearance of the dishes in which mother cooked was always left to him. Vaslav, who was very fond of sweets, greatly enjoyed cleaning out the kettles in which she previously had prepared the different icings and chocolate creams. He became a connoisseur of cooking himself.

Her good cooking soon made the place popular, but Eleanora, incorrigibly good-hearted, could never insist when one of her guests failed to pay her. During these early years Vaslav was accustomed to being her defender, opening doors watchfully, arguing with tradesmen creditors, looking over the bills that were delivered and which Eleanora was often unable to pay. They were always forced to economise to the last extremity. Small Vaslav made an early acquaintance with the sad and difficult side of life, and his mother confided her troubles in him.

Summer càme. The heat in the city was unbearable. Eleanora decided to send the children to the country, but, with little money, she boarded them with peasants, paying almost nothing.

An entirely new life opened for Vaslav. All day long he was free to play hide-and-seek in the fine, fresh hay, or walk with a band of boys in wide poppy-fields, or bathe in the little brook near the village. The children loved to stage cock-fights, but on one occasion Vaslav was attacked by one of the angry fowls. The rooster cut his forehead wide open with its beak. The child, bleeding, ran home crying, where the kind peasant woman wiped away the tears and cured the wound. But the mark on his forehead remained forever.

It was the busiest time of the year for the peasants: the harvest season. They rose before dawn to go out into the dew-wet fields to cut wheat, rye, oats, and millet, put it on big crosses, and to pray for clear dry weather. When the corn was high, the children ran delightedly through the stiff green plants, like an army of soldiers at attention. In the evenings, groups of workers, coming home from the fields, sang enchantingly the beautiful folk-songs in three or four repeating tunes. The boys followed behind, trying to imitate their carriage, their walk, and their songs. The long twilight fused into the high starlit nights when the harvesters returned to their village. In these surroundings Vaslav learned the appreciation of simple lives, their joys and values, their sorrows and hardships, the inevitability of death. Here for the first time Vaslav came into close contact with the omnipotence of Nature. He worked in the fields with the *moujiks*. At first it seemed easy enough, but he soon found out that work in the fields was not merely fun, but hard and tiresome labour. The young boy's sensitive soul understood under what burden the peasants had to toil, how miserable was their fate in famine if bad weather killed their crops. This boy, the son of trouping parents, who in their constant travels could never set root in a single spot, found now the tie which bound him to his country, his race, his tradition. When the summer passed, and Vaslav returned to the city, he carried in his heart an eternal love for Russian soil.

No matter how hard she worked, Eleanora could never make a sufficient living. The children grew and needed some education. So she went even so far as to humiliate herself by asking help from her husband. Thomas met the situation with an embittered spirit. His artistic ambitions were unfulfilled. His accident had made his long years of work, his assiduous studies, his successful past, seem futile. In this mood he advised his wife that, everything taken into consideration, it would be much wiser for the children not to follow in their parents' footsteps. He suggested to Eleanora that the best thing to do would be to apprentice both boys to some tradesman—for instance, to a watchmaker. He argued that a watchmaker who knew his work could always make an honest living and have a more or less secure existence, compared to the life that might fall to the lot of even the greatest dancer. No, his sons should not go through this suffering.

For Eleanora, his decision was a terrible blow. She was, after all, deserted by her husband; she had given up her beloved art for the sake and future of her children. All for what? To make tradesmen of them. Nevertheless, on the advice of the doctors, she gave Stanislav a trial in a watchmaker's shop. First the child seemed interested, but after a few weeks he became restless, irritated, and had to give it up. Eleanora and the physicians now realised that Stanislav would never be able to do even manual work.

To take the burden of Vaslav's education from her shoulders, and to fulfil her long-cherished dream, she took the seven-year-old boy, at the beginning of the autumn, to the Imperial School of Dancing. She presented him to qualify for the required examination. Although the board of examiners found that the little boy was remarkably fit, and showed a marked disposition for dancing, nevertheless they refused his entrance on account of his youth. They told his mother to bring him back two years later.

The next years passed in a continuous effort to make a living. The only brightness on their horizon was the possibility of Vaslav's entering the Imperial School.

Chapter Three

THE IMPERIAL SCHOOL OF DANCING

AT LAST the day arrived when Vaslav could enter the Imperial School of Dancing. The Imperial School and Theatres were a familiar topic in the Nijinksy household. How often had the children heard that their father could never dance amid these splendours, merely because he had had his dancing education in Warsaw. It was the dream of every child who was ambitious to become a dancer to be a pupil of the Imperial School. Tales were told about the difficulty of being admitted into the school, its discipline, the incessant study, its luxurious surroundings, the Court performances, the feasts, with the great Grand Dukes and even the Emperor himself.

Russians have always loved dancing, as the mural paintings representing scenes of dancing, dating from 1071, on the Cathedral of Santa Sofia in Kiev, and in the Pitchersky Cathedral prove. The Greek Orthodox Church has always violently condemned dancing, but in spite of their steady opposition, lasting throughout the ages, the love for dancing flourished among the *moujiks* as well as in Court.

In the seventeenth century, ballet was introduced to this barbaric, semi-Oriental country by the Tsar Alexis Mihailovitch, the second Romanov ruler, at his wedding festivities. He was the first to create a permanent theatre and ballet. Foreign ballet-masters were engaged, and soon produced native instructors. The successors of Alexis Mihailovitch followed in his footsteps in sponsoring the art of dancing.

Peter the Great took a personal interest in it by composing ballets and by dancing in them himself and ordering his Court by ukase to do the same. With the help of his prisoners, the Swedish officers, he taught his Court. The first serious attempt to organise a school of dancing had been started in 1735 by the Tsarina Anna Ivanovna on the request of Christian Wellman, the teacher of gymnastics at the Imperial Cadet School. He was permitted to take twelve poor boys and girls and train them as professionals. The Tsarina was so pleased with the results that she took all the expenses of their education and maintenance upon the State and allowed them one of her palaces. The first director was Landet, a French ballet-master, and the children were supervised by the widow of a Court coachman. This was the humble beginning of the famous Imperial School of Dancing. But the great task of civilising this immense empire was carried out by Catherine the Great. She reorganised the school in 1779 on the model of the Imperial Cadet Academy, from which the *Corps des Pages,* the Imperial bodyguard, was formed. She built the first stone theatres and opened them to the great public.

Tsar Paul united the Imperial School with the Smolny Institute, which was the most exclusive school of the empire, and, as it was a convent, the clergy opposed the union, but in vain.

At this time, Charles Louis Didelot, the French ballet-master, was invited. We can consider him the father of the Russian ballet. He was the one who emphasised the importance of systematic training, and of the true dramatic spirit: "A true dancer must be also a good actor and a poet at heart." He was strict, almost a fanatic, but, thanks to him, the school produced outstanding dancers and the ballet took the prominent place in Russian art which it never lost until the Revolution. He was for twenty-eight years the director of the Imperial School, a favourite of the Tsar, and, thanks to him, the century-long opposition of the time had to cease. He was the first to invite foreign *ballerinas* to dance at the Mariinsky Theatre, and so St. Petersburg became acquainted with the art of Taglioni, Elssler, and others. His successors tried to keep up this spirit, and ten years later the French dancer Marius Petipa succeeded him. Petipa, whose inventive genius was inexhaustible during the sixty years he was a member of the Imperial Theatre, composed sixty ballets, reconstructed seventeen, and supplied thirty-seven operas with ballets. Petipa not only created a rich repertory for the Mariinsky Theatre, but also developed and enlarged the vocabulary of the dance by innumerable new steps.

The tales which were circulated about the Imperial School were founded on truth. The exclusiveness of the institute, and its close contact with the Court, gave it a halo. As the *Corps des Pages,* the pupils of the school were part of the Imperial household, and belonged to a privileged world.

In this superb school of art the dancing was taught by

the best masters for eight years. Based on military principles, the school was run with an iron discipline that was never slackened. The supreme head of the school was the director of the Imperial Theatres.

The moment a child was admitted, the parents virtually relinquished all rights, and the pupil was formally "adopted" by the Tsar.

A rigorous physical examination made by doctors and the ballet-masters decided which of the children could be taken for a two years' probation, during which time they still lived at home but were otherwise supplied with everything by the Imperial School. Usually several hundred applied, but only six to ten were taken. If they proved to have adequate disposition during the two years, they were taken permanently into the school, and at graduation became automatically members of the Mariinsky Theatre.

The Imperial School was installed in a huge early baroque palace between the Nevsky Prospekt and the Fontanka River, in the middle of the most exclusive district of St. Petersburg, on Theatre Street. It was simply furnished, but this palace of the eighteenth century, with its panelled walls, huge rooms, big crystal chandeliers, exhaled an atmosphere of luxury.

The school had its own chapel, with big choir and yellow and white marble pillars, where divine service was held on Sundays and holy days; its own infirmary, with doctor and nurses in constant attendance, where the children had to undergo an examination every Saturday during the eight years; and its own theatre, where the annual examination took place, and which they shared with the pupils of the dramatic school. Their dormitory was spacious—big enough for forty, and only occupied by twenty-five. Each pupil had his own numbered cubicle, over which his own icon was hung. One of the five governors, who had the supervision of the pupils, slept at the end of the dormitory. They had a special bathing establishment on the premises, where every Friday the boys received "Russian baths," and a chiropodist attended to their feet, which were nursed with almost religious care.

At the preliminary examination on the 20th of August, 1900, when Vaslav was presented, he was chosen with five others from among a hundred and fifty boys. He was very shy and timid, and could hardly answer the examiners, so much the luxurious surroundings impressed him. But Nicolai Legat, the famous solo dancer, who was among the examiners, noticed his extraordinary thighs and well-developed body, and insisted that he should be taken.

Vaslav had never known such luxury: six changes of underwear; three uniforms, a black for every day, dark blue for the holidays, grey linen for the summer; two overcoats, the one for the winter with heavy astrachan collar; patent leather boots, and pumps for home. The uniforms were like those of the Cadet School, with high velvet collar, on which a silver lyre, the insignia of the school, was embroidered. Their caps were like those of the Army, with the Imperial Eagles on them. Vaslav was extremely proud when for the first time he could parade in his new clothes. But perhaps the greatest joy was when he received his dancing kit and shoes. Vaslav was meticulously neat, and took great care of his wearing apparel. He always looked clean and well groomed.

For Vaslav, the change was tremendous. He had hardly ever been away from home and his mother's care, and the classes seemed very difficult to him, as the pupils had also to study the regular subjects of an ordinary school. In all subjects unrelated to art, except mathematics and geometry, Vaslav was not good. From the first moment he entered the school his five classmates began to tease him, mocking at his Mongolian features and almond-shaped eyes, and gave him the nickname "Kitajec" (Chinaman). This nickname hurt Vaslav, as the Russo-Japanese War did not make the Mongols popular in Russia. In everything Vaslav shared the life of the other pupils, except in food, as in the first two years he had to bring some from home. His mother was not able to supply him with the same delicacies as the others. But Vaslav did not know the feeling of envy; he always offered to share the little presents he received from his teachers or elder pupils with the others.

One person alone was able to pierce the wall of Vaslav's reserve—his master, Nicolai Legat. He was not only an extraordinary dancer, but a fine teacher with a charming, gay personality and great understanding. From the first second he laid eyes upon Vaslav he knew that he had found something in him which could be developed, under proper conditions, into great art. Vaslav loved to study with him. Those lessons seemed like holidays. As soon as he entered the dancing-room he seemed to throw off his shyness and enter his natural atmosphere. With worshipping admiration and blind obedience, he executed with infinite ease the steps Legat with great patience showed to his pupils. Out of these lessons a mutual sympathy grew which lasted ever after. And Vaslav told me later that he owed all to Legat's untiring tutoring. Even his fellow pupils were entranced as soon as Vaslav began to dance, and very soon the rumour was spread in the Imperial School that a new star was rising. Only Vaslav seemed ignorant of the fact.

After the two years of probation were over, in 1902, Vaslav was permanently admitted to the Imperial School. Now he became a boarder. At first he missed his mother tremendously, but now the serious study of art had begun. From the first year on, the pupils were used in the ballets and operas at the Mariinsky Theatre as walkers-on, or in small parts. The boys loved to go to the theatre, to which they were taken under the supervision of the governor on duty, in special landaus belonging to the Imperial stables. The pupils had their own dressing-room on the fifth floor of the Mariinsky Theatre, where they were supposed to stay while not busy on the stage, but Vaslav always found a way to escape and to hide himself in the wings to watch his ideal, Chaliapine. It was he who made a lasting impression on young Vaslav's imagination, and whom he ardently desired to follow. He watched his every movement and studied his make-up, and very soon was able to make up with such amazing virtuosity that his teachers were surprised. It was in *Aïda,* as one

of the negro boys, that he first stepped on the stage of
the Mariinsky Theatre. Often he took part also in the
operas, and, as he was extremely musical, soon knew
them by heart. He was cast as Gottfried, Prince of Bra-
bant, Elsa's brother, in *Lohengrin,* and was very proud
of his first solo part.

Vaslav, like his parents, was brought up in the Roman
Catholic faith, and was profoundly religious, but somehow
already, at this age, he could find God's presence everywhere, and, as the majority of the pupils were of Greek
Orthodox faith, he attended their services in the school
chapel, which he loved for its golden altar and huge yellow
marble pillars. Father Vassily, the pope of the school, had
always a kind word when Vaslav bowed before him, in
spite of his different faith. And Vaslav admired his dignified carriage and his glittering gold cross.

Vaslav adapted himself well to the daily routine. At
7:30 the bell was rung by the usher, and the pupils had
to get up. This was a difficult moment for Vaslav, as he
loved to sleep, and tried to snatch a few more moments
of extra rest. Then they went to the wash-house, which
was a feature of the school. Round the walls were placed
the lockers of each boy, and in the middle of the room
there was a large circular copper basin, to which a fountain supplied the tepid water. Within fifteen minutes,
they had to pass the governor, waiting for them at the
door of the dining-room, which was opposite the dormitory. Here the boys had to give up their handkerchiefs
every morning, to be exchanged for clean ones. Before
starting breakfast, one of the older boys said grace. A
simple Russian breakfast of coffee, tea, rolls, and butter
was served. The children were allowed to eat as much
as they wanted, and the nourishment of the school was as
good as that of the Imperial family, who often sent them
delicacies from their estates.

After breakfast they formed a crocodile, and accompanied by a governor, went for a walk until nine o'clock,
either on the Nevsky Prospekt or to the Kasansky Sobol.
The well-mannered, uniformed children were known and
liked among the inhabitants of the capital.

Then, upon their return, lessons followed. Vaslav quickly became a good piano player, and in his free hours played in their rest-room for his classmates.

At ten the dancing classes began, and lasted daily until noon. The school had several large dancing-rooms, where the floor was sloped like that of the stage and made of soft pinewood.

The boys came attired in their regular dancing costumes to the classroom: black trousers, white shirts. Those who excelled in their dancing were allowed to water the floor.

At noon, a light luncheon was served, and, after, the children had one hour's rest. From one to five they devoted their time once more to the regular subjects.

Then a large dinner followed, of several courses, after which they rested or played games. The most popular was the Russian national ball game called *lapda,* in which Vaslav excelled; as he did in fencing. Other forms of sport were at the time strictly forbidden, as they might develop the muscles in a different way than that required for dancing.

They would have ballroom lessons with the girls, and during those classes innocent flirtations naturally started, and, as all communication was strictly forbidden, the children used to hide their *billets doux* in secret places, such as under the leg of the piano. If discovered, they were punished, and dessert was withheld. All the boys had their platonic sweethearts except Vaslav, who already at the time had only one real love—that for the dance.

Among all the lessons except that of the classical dance Vaslav loved best that of pantomime. It was taught by the great mime Guerdt himself, who admired Vaslav's ability, and proudly told his colleagues at the Dramatic Theatre: "Russia's coming great actor is a pupil of the dancing school, the little Nijinsky."

In the classes for "make-up" Vaslav was greatly interested. In a large room which was fitted out like a theatrical dressing-room, with adequate red and green lighting effects, mirrors and tables, the pupils had to study the anatomy of their faces, the effects of the colour and lines, and how to create a characteristic make-up.

Vaslav was indeed a strange child. He did not mix with the other frolicking pupils unless expressly called by them, as by this time he had become used to being ignored by his classmates, who were jealous of him. Silently he meditated in a corner or invented some prank. He was mischievous by nature, and whenever there was fun he was the schemer, and on such occasions his suggestions were gladly accepted. In fact, he was always involved as ringleader in all the pranks which arose. He painted the chair of the professor of mathematics with ink; he distributed sneezing-powder in the class. Only at the dancing lessons they could not drag him into any insubordination. Those lessons and the stage were sacred to him. In his studies he was slow, and the teachers, who did not quite understand his psychology, thought him lazy; for this he was often deprived of sweets or of his vacation. Vaslav patiently submitted, and passed the hours locked up in the room specially kept for this "detention." The walls were covered by the photos of ballet-masters and great dancers of past centuries, and Vaslav was greatly absorbed in studying their gestures and costumes, and did not realise that he was actually punished.

The superintendent of the school often complained to Vaslav's mother about his laziness, and she pleaded with him, with tears, to be more diligent. Her boarding-house was not prospering; she lived in constant poverty and need of money. She was forced to pawn her most cherished belongings. Slowly everything she owned found its way to the pawnshop, and never to return. And, when everything seemed to be at its worst, an unexpected blow staggered the poor woman; Vaslav was suspended from school as punishment for his latest trick.

One day, when the boys had to go to the theatre, they took along in the bus their toy bow and arrow. Vaslav was an excellent shot, and, aiming through the window, unfortunately hit the tutor in the eye, who, infuriated, asked for the culprit. Vaslav stood up and confessed the crime, and his expulsion followed. His mother wept bitter tears; her most beautiful dream shattered, her hopes crushed, the immediate need to feed another hungry mouth was a real catastrophe for her. The transition from the luxurious comfort of the school to the bourgeois flat, smelling of cooking, from the life without worries to one of want, deeply impressed the sensitive Vaslav. He met the neighbours with a sense of humiliation and shame. They all knew he was expelled from school. Vaslav noticed that among them was a too conspicuously dressed woman, smelling of cheap scent, laden with vulgar laces and ostrich feathers, who visited them constantly, especially at meal-times. She drank Eleanora's tea, ate her food, and gossiped, gossiped continuously.

The days were filled with constant fear of creditors, and the possibility of being turned out of the flat. One day Eleanora had to meet an unavoidable debt; she needed five roubles. But she had nobody to ask except the friendly neighbour. She had to make a terrible effort to go through the ordeal to ask for this loan. Vaslav was in the room when she explained the pressing situation. The woman listened with attention and interest, like an understanding soul, but, when Eleanora finally brought her request, she sighed, began to cry how sorry she was, and refused. With words of consolation, she sailed out of the flat. Eleanora burst out crying as the door closed behind her. So they would be without any food for the children! Vaslav, huddled in a corner, watched the scene motionless. Now he realised his mother's situation, her sorrow, and he made up his mind to work and study, to make a great effort to become a great dancer, so that soon he could be of help to her.

The disciplinary measure was rescinded, and Vaslav returned to the school. From that day on he kept his promise to himself and studied assiduously. Soon he became the pride of his masters. Two years after Vaslav's admission, Bronia became a pupil of the school.

However thrilling the participation in the performances at the Mariinsky, it could not be compared to the Court performances. Everybody, from the *maître de ballet* to the footmen, was agitated on such occasions. The children were told not to forget the rigid etiquette of the Imperial Court. As they were taken over in their carriage, they were deeply impressed by the fact that soon they would be face to face with the Tsar of all the Russias, their master, their "Little Father." The palace gates were thrown open; the guards saluted; inside more soldiers, Kammerjunkers.

As they entered the ballroom they were for a second blinded by the splendour of it, filled with the members of the diplomatic corps with their satin ribbons, smothered under the jewelled orders, the gold of their uniforms reflecting in the crystal lights. The children were nervous at the sight of the audience, their Majesties, their Highnesses, and their "suite." But, as soon as the first bars of the music were played, all went smoothly. When they danced, they were in their own atmosphere. After the performance, the Tsar and Tsarina spoke graciously to them, gave them presents, and served cake. Those who danced exceptionally well received a distinction in the form of some jewellery, and one evening Vaslav, as he moved up to kiss the hand of the Tsar, after finishing his solo, was presented by the Court Chamberlain with the gold watch with the initials of Nicholas II. This was the highest sign of His Majesty's pleasure to a pupil of the Imperial School.

It was much less terrifying to dance in the palace of the Grand Duke, where there was no royal restraint, and after their dance they were allowed to sit on the laps of their Imperial Highnesses and play with their glittering jewels and decorations.

Vaslav's talent developed with astonishing rapidity during these years. His fame was thoroughly established in the school, and his inherent natural gifts exceeded those of anyone in the annals of its history. Vaslav was full of energy and ambition to perfect himself; he was never satisfied, and as he felt that pirouettes did not come to him quite as easily as jumps, he decided to practise them until he reached the highest grade. But this untiring ambition almost caused his death. One day in the classroom, where dancing was forbidden, waiting for the teacher,

Vaslav began to pirouette and to make *tours en l'air*.
He was so engrossed in his practising that he did not pay
sufficient attention to the benches. He landed with full
force against one, and injured his abdomen dangerously.
For three months he lay between life and death, flat
on his back in a hospital, but his rugged constitution
finally pulled him through. After a long enforced rest,
Vaslav resumed his study, and progressed with unfaltering
certainty to his ultimate brilliance of technique. Outside
events rarely penetrated the walls of the school. In calm
seclusion, well protected, these hothouse plants developed
undisturbed. After the lost war with Japan, however, revolution swept over Russia. On the 9th of January, 1905,
Vaslav was quietly walking with his school books under
his arm toward his mother's apartments when suddenly
he was confronted with a tidal wave of swarming people,
who were running like furies to the Winter Palace. The
demonstration was led by Father Gapon. Vaslav was carried away with the mob, which pressed around him with
terrific force. He tried to get out, but struggled in vain
against this flood of humanity. When the rushing crowd
came close to the palace, a squadron of mounted Cossacks, armed with their terrible knouts, charged. The wild
onrush stopped suddenly; stones and bricks flew in the
air. The snorting, plunging horses dashed into the mob.
The knouts fell on heads and backs like a hailstorm.
Women screamed, men shouted, children cried. Vaslav
tried to shield himself with his books, and, bending down,
he suddenly felt a terrific pain, and the running of his
own warm blood over his face. With wild strength one
of the Cossacks had cut him on the forehead. The deep
gash left a scar, next to the one the rooster had inflicted.
This scar always reminded him of that dreadful scene,
the merciless attack of the Cossacks on the weaponless,
starving people who were asking for bread. Vaslav became ever after that brotherly toward his fellow men,
and began to understand the suffering of the masses.

Late in January the strikes of the terrible year of revolution came to a head. The national revolt had been violent, but little report of it managed to creep into the

fastness of the Imperial Dancing School. Even the Mariinsky Ballet Company, usually so loyal to the Court, which supported and protected them, had been infected by the contagion of unrest that was everywhere in the air. Fokine, Pavlova, and Karsavina presented certain claims for the improvement and maintenance of the standards of the company in October of 1905, and with great gallantry and courage attempted to stop a performance of Tchaikovsky's *La Dame de Pique* as a sympathetic strike.

The revolt failed. The republic proclaimed at the mass meeting of the 16th of October fell. The three great dancers, deserted by the majority of their colleagues, who refused to strike and signed a declaration of loyalty, awaited dismissal and arrest.

In the school there was an unknown atmosphere of tension. The corridors were quiet. The governors seemed preoccupied. The older boys were worried and even the little ones knew that an aching suspense paralysed the nation. A revolution was momentarily expected. But, in spite of it, the lessons, the practice, the rehearsals, continued. Only one morning Serge Legat, Nicolai's brother, did not appear. Nor did he ever teach again.

Serge Legat had somehow signed the declaration of recantation, against his will. Already in a highly strung state of mind from a desperately unhappy love-affair with Marie Petipa, the great *maître de ballet's* daughter, he was plunged into the abyss of grief and shame at what he considered to be the betrayal of his friends. Perhaps Vaslav did not know then that he had raved all night: "Marie, which is lesser in the eyes of God, that I should take your life or mine?" He did not learn until much later that they had found him in the morning with his throat slit by a razor.

Vaslav went on studying, practising ceaselessly. His progress was amazing, and he was cast in quite important solo parts, the first time in the ballet *Paquita,* when he danced the mazurka. It was a great moment for the young pupil to be rehearsed by the great Petipa himself with the members of the Mariinsky Theatre, as if he were their equal. More parts followed . . . and then, in 1906, Obouchov, who was now Vaslav's teacher, reported that he could teach him nothing more, as he surpassed his masters in their art.

His success was such that the director of the school offered to make him a regular member of the Mariinsky Theatre two years before graduation. It was an unheard-of event, without any precedent in the history of the school. Vaslav was extremely proud and exuberantly happy, but he begged to be allowed to finish his classes and to graduate at the regular time. So for two more years he remained, at his own request, at the school. But the Mariinsky Theatre made a lot of use of his talents, and gave him in 1907 the important part of the Marquis in *Pavillon d'Armide*. The graduation performance usually took place in the Mariinsky Theatre, and on that night the house, with its blue velvet curtains and upholstering, its gilt plaster and heavy pyramids of hanging crystal, was filled with the *élite* of St. Petersburg society. Mozart's *Don Juan* ballet was chosen for the occasion, and Vaslav had the distinction of appearing on the same bill with such artists as Obouchov and Legat. His partner was Ludmilla Schollar.

Vaslav's success was immediate and overwhelming, his happiness great. His fellow pupils, the artists of the Mariinsky, surrounded him, congratulating, and he could only smile with tears in his eyes when Petipa patted him on his shoulder. Then his idol Chaliapine arrived and embraced him. Turning towards Petipa, he said, "Did I not tell you years ago that he would be the pride of Russia?" And then, kissing Vaslav on both cheeks, continued, "Slavuska, just go on dancing like you did to-night."

In a few days he had to leave the Imperial School, which had been his home for eight long years, where he could devote all his time and energy to his beloved art. As usual, the last days were passed in fêting the graduate. As the last day arrived, Vaslav went from room to room saying farewell to those familiar places. Finally he went to the chapel and knelt before a golden icon, the image of the Saviour, thanking Him for his blessings throughout those years of study, and praying ardently for His divine protection in the coming years, so that he should become not only the glory of the Mariinsky, but a true servant of God.

Chapter Four

NIJINSKY AND THE MARIINSKY THEATRE

IN MAY 1908 Vaslav graduated with distinction from the Imperial School and automatically became a member of the Mariinsky Theatre.

The Imperial Opera House of St. Petersburg, officially known as the Mariinsky Theatre, was named in honour of the Tsarina Maria Feodorovna. Like the other Imperial Theatres of St. Petersburg and Moscow, it belonged to the Tsar, and was supported by him under an annual subsidy of two million gold roubles. It was under the supervision of a Minister of the Court, who was directly responsible to the ruler for the management of the Imperial Theatres and Schools.

About one hundred and eighty dancers in all, male and female, including soloists and *prima ballerinas,* comprised the *corps de ballet.* All had to be graduates either from the St. Petersburg or Moscow Imperial School. Upon graduation a dancer became first merely a member of the *corps de ballet,* later a *coryphée,* a *sujet,* then a *prima ballerina,* and, highest of all, a *prima ballerina assoluta,* or, if a man, *soloist to the Tsar.*

All the dancers had to proceed, if possible, through this grading, and parts were assigned according to ability.

Their term of service extended, from graduation, for twenty years, after which, even if they were at the height of their careers, they had to retire on a small pension for life. This rule was only broken in exceptional cases. If the dancers were of unusual merit, they were retained as teachers in the Imperial School. The Mariinsky and the school were intimately connected. The same iron rule dominated both. The time for rehearsals, the order of a performance, were published in an official notice hung on a board in the theatre every Monday morning, and the more important members were notified by a letter and printed schedule.

Into this institution, with its glorious traditions, Vaslav entered at the age of seventeen. The *balletomanes,* who had recognised his extraordinary talent and predicted for him a great future, hailed his *entrée.* He made his début in the ballet of Mozart's opera, *Don Juan.* It was an unforgettable moment in both Vaslav's and Eleanora Bereda's lives.

He was rapidly given more important parts, and danced regularly now, as her partner, with the *prima ballerina assoluta* Matilde Kshessinskaya, as well as with the *prima ballerinas* Preobrajenskaya, Pavlova, and Karsavina. The expert public of St. Petersburg sat spellbound before this slim, light child who floated, hardly touching the ground, and who executed the most technically difficult steps without any effort. They saw in him the reincarnation of the classical style of Noverre, the leaps of Vestris, the ethereal qualities of Taglioni, and the fire of Camargo. Even Petipa, who had seen the great dancers of the last century, was amazed that so many gifts had been showered on one human being. And soon Vaslav was called *"Le Vestris du Nord."*

His days were spent in exercises at the Mariinsky Theatre, rehearsals, performances, and lessons. with Maestro Cecchetti. The old Italian's idea of a good dancer was more a human machine, with sinews hard as wires, muscles like steel springs, the heart an inexhaustible pump, rather than a human body which might tire. But Vaslav never failed to learn from him, and his supreme

standard of technical perfection was the greatest incentive
for an artist of Nijinsky's calibre.

But in spite of this he found time for himself. He was
passionately fond of literature. His great favourites were
Shakespeare, Ibsen, Chekhov, but above all Tolstoi, who
cast a spell over him. They were similar in their essential
nature, not only in their love of mankind and of the soil
and soul of Russia, but in their conception of art to lift
humanity and serve God. On free evenings he often went
to the opera, especially to hear Moussorgsky and Wagner.

In spite of the fact that Vaslav was acknowledged by
his teachers, fellow artists, and the public, and was aware
of his own talent and capacity, he yet felt there was
something unattained, something lacking in his art. The
perfection of his technique did not satisfy him. It had
been developed for many centuries, so that now it shone
brilliant as a diamond. But it was not enough to transpose
music into terms of the dance. Dancing had an independent function, which it had as yet never fulfilled. He
applied this technique, of which he was a master, and its
musical accompaniment, not as a pretext for display or
as parallel accents, but as a dominating entity.

Vaslav spent a great deal of time in museums and
picture galleries, especially the Hermitage. He was a great
admirer of Holbein and Dürer, but most of all he was
drawn to the Italians of the Renaissance. He studied
their masterpieces carefully, particularly Leonardo, Ra-
phael, and Michelangelo. He realised that harmony and
beauty of movement were of supreme importance, and
that technique existed only to enable the artists to express
their conceptions more perfectly. From that day on Vaslav
put this lesson into his dancing. The amount of pirouettes
and *entrechats* were no longer so important to him as the
harmony of movement, even if it required less bravura.
The effect on his dancing was subtle and compelling, and
the audience was conscious of the change, even if they
could not define it.

Vaslav used to take long walks by the side of the canals
in the evening, when he was free. The fog enveloped the
houses, the walls of the bridges, in a luminous haze; a

mysterious twilight, hooded from the sun, a time for calm meditation. The idea of the Preaching Monk, which he recalled from his early childhood, returned to him from time to time. To follow a pure, ascetic life, to teach the masses, to seek truth, were all singularly fascinating to him. But each time his overwhelming love for the dance conquered.

Shortly after Vaslav had left the school his mother moved into a larger apartment, in a more select neighbourhood. This was more expensive and far above their means, but they had to live up to the standard of a member of the Imperial Theatre. Vaslav had lived magnificently for eight years at the Tsar's expense. It was a change to have graduated from the school, where everything conceivable had been provided without thought of money, and now to have to live and support brother and sister on sixty roubles a month. Clothing and food and labour, however, were comparatively inexpensive at this time in Russia. Eleanora engaged a servant. The apartment was cosy and meticulous. Vaslav inherited from his mother her neatness, sense of order, cleanliness. He always looked tidy and well groomed, even after several hours of strenuous exercises.

Eleanora Bereda was an excellent cook, and prepared all of Vaslav's food herself. She adored him as her favourite child, and this was reciprocated by Vaslav. Even in later years, when they were parted from each other, no matter how exhausted he was, he would send her a note every day, though he disliked writing and never wrote to anyone else.

Saturdays and in the summer months Bronia returned home from the Imperial School. In these times Vaslav continued the lessons he began to give her in former years. So, almost unconsciously, she absorbed his creative spirit, his ideas, his sense of form.

The only shadow over their tranquil lives was the incurable illness of Stanislav. His mother kept him at home, nursing and watching the boy, who, though most of the time passive and obedient, was mentally undeveloped. His blank face would light up with joy whenever Vaslav danced a little for him in the apartment. Stanislav was extremely good-looking, like his mother, with fair hair and blue eyes, slightly taller than Vaslav, for whom he had a real adoration. Anything that Vaslav suggested to him he would do, and when he became excitable a word from Vaslav would quiet him.

During one of the holidays, when they were all at home, dining, Stanislav became excited. They tried to calm him as usual, but they failed, and when Eleanora sternly commanded him to behave himself he hurled a knife at her. Vaslav, with his incredible swiftness, grasped his hand in time and mastered him.

But after this scene they decided to carry out the advice of the doctors, who knew Stanislav might at any moment become dangerous, and confine him in an asylum. A cruel moment for all of them! Vaslav took all the necessary steps to have his brother placed in the best State institution they could afford, and afterwards on every Sunday, accompanied by his mother, visited Stanislav, bringing little presents for him and his nurses.

Vaslav took every tragedy in his life placidly, with a seeming outward indifference. Inwardly he felt it more deeply than the others, with an almost Oriental fatalism.

Vaslav did not go to the cafés and music-halls with the other boys. His life was wholly divided between his mother and his art. At the Mariinsky he was liked, always quiet, polite, and reserved, and his colleagues as well as his superiors respected him in spite of his youth. The *prima ballerinas* not only liked him as a superb partner, but because he had agreeable manners and was easy to work with. Even the male dancers had a kind word to say for him, and he was universally liked, without malice or envy, with only one exception—Anna Pavlova, who at the time had already achieved the grade of *prima ballerina*. She was an exquisite dancer, with a matchless technique which almost attained the perfection of Kshessinskaya. The fact that she was able to revive the long-gone charm of Taglioni gave her an outstanding position at the Mariinsky Theatre. One evening, after completing a *pas de deux* with Vaslav, noticing that his shouted name recalled him oftener before the curtain than her, she fainted back stage in an uncontrollable fit of jealousy and resentment. Vaslav, ignorant of envy, pitied her.

The generous Kshessinskaya, always anxious to help, entertained lavishly in her hospitable house, where Vaslav met Prince X. He was a well-bred aristocrat, with delightful manners and decadent tastes. He surrounded himself with the most attractive young men of the fashionable regiments and the *Corps des Pages,* and lived in a surfeited atmosphere of semi-degenerate indulgence. X took a great liking to Vaslav as soon as they were introduced, and constantly invited him to his palace. He was seventeen years old, and for the first time he saw *life.* Now that he was a part of these receptions and not merely a decorative ornament, there was a fascination in walking up a flight of heavily carpeted stairs, passed on by one footman to another, until one was announced into the big bright room blazing with lights. Yet amid all the laughter and complete abandon there was never a woman to be seen. They would go to the fashionable restaurants, like Medved or Cubat, to social gatherings, and everywhere gaiety reigned, champagne and gold flowed—Vaslav never drank, but his nature, full of mischievous charm, made him, even in these male gatherings, an agreeable companion and not a spoil-sport. A sentimental intimacy between X and his friends was taken for granted. The young men were closer to each other than mere friends. Nothing that he saw seemed particularly unnatural or abnormal to Vaslav. Before, he had known only school. Now, this must be the way the rest of the world chose to behave.

Eleanora did not oppose these sorties. She thought that after the isolation of school the time had come for Vaslav to know life. Of course, neither she nor Vaslav in their innocence understood the meaning of X's affection.

During Carnival there was the great *bal masqué* at the Mariinsky, where the *élite* of St. Petersburg appeared. It was the event of the season. Everybody was costumed and wore masks. Vaslav was requested by X and his friends to wear a lady's costume of the eighteenth century. Considering this a prank, he put on a dress of that period, with all the jewellery and laces, and with great ability he mimed a lady of the Rococo. He looked as if he had walked out of a Watteau, assuming the very air of the eighteenth century. Nobody could have told that this charming masquerader was not really a girl. For Vaslav this was all only a part to play, but not to the others, and only later was he shocked into regretting his perfection and his innocence.

X one evening offered at another of his innumerable parties an unusual attraction by inviting a group of the loveliest Vengerkas[1] of St. Petersburg to amuse his young friends, if any of them should happen to take a fancy to such an unfamiliar mode of distraction.

Vaslav was frightened by the intrusive manners of these women, but respecting womanhood deeply, even in these caricatures, and not wishing to offend them, he humoured them in their desires. He never had any false fear of sensuality, and his dancing often showed a deep intuition of the passionate. But he who until now had had no association with women was, after this first experience, profoundly hurt in his soul. He shrank even from the memory of this evening.

Vaslav's fame grew greater from day to day, and his father, who had all these years been separated from them, touring Russia with one ballet company after another, began to hear of his son's achievement. One day he expressed the desire to see him. At first, Eleanora, with a heart full of bitterness, tried to prevent the meeting. But Vaslav tenderly persuaded her to grant Thomas's wish. He loved his mother deeply, and naturally resented his father's behaviour towards her, but, after all, he, the son, had no right to judge. So, after considerable coaxing, she let him go.

It was at the time of the summer vacation, and Thomas Nijinsky was in Kazan. It was momentous for Vaslav to make the acquaintance of his father, whom he could only vaguely remember. As he had only a little money to

[1] In Russian, Vengerka means a Hungarian woman, but, since almost all prostitutes in Russia were Hungarian, the word became synonymous with cocotte.

spend, he did not travel all the way from St. Petersburg
to the interior by train, but went as much of the way as
he could by steamboat down the Volga to reach Kazan.
He had not left the capital, except for brief excursions,
since he was six years old. His early childhood journeys
all over the empire were as unreal as dreams.

Now the vast stretches of country unfolded themselves
before him endlessly, and for hours he stood at the rail
of the boat watching the flow of the majestic river, the
ever-changing panorama of its banks, cities, villages, with
the bulbous golden church towers between the poplars,
the white shining loneliness of isolated monasteries, and
the roll and shimmering wave of the cornfields.

So, slowly, Vaslav approached his father, whose loss
may well have caused the tragedy of his life. It was a
great moment for both of them when they finally met.
Vaslav, at this time, was physically almost the image of
his father, and Thomas Nijinsky saw himself completely
in the dark, lithe youth, who had fulfilled his own most
cherished hopes. Perhaps as an artist he felt an unconscious pang of jealousy, but at the same time he was
exuberantly proud of his famous son. His conscience was
burdened with his neglect and injustice, as he faced the
boy who had become the provider and protector of his
family. But Vaslav had no word, no gesture of reproach.
He smiled his irresistible, charming smile, expressed his
respect for his father, and his gratitude for the talents he
had transmitted to him. For Vaslav knew then that the
amazing power of being able to jump so high, to float in
the air, and to descend more slowly than to rise, he
inherited from his father.

The few days they spent together in Kazan were very
happy. They became great friends as Vaslav told his father all about himself, the work at the Mariinsky, his ideas,
and his life. They danced for each other. Thomas was
literally speechless when he realised that Vaslav's dancing
revealed what was the hopeless dream of most dancers,
the quality of genius. As a parting gift Thomas gave his
son a pair of cuff-links. Vaslav always wore and treasured
highly these inexpensive gold buttons set with some semi-

precious stones from the Urals—his father's only present
to him. Thomas promised to come the following winter to
St. Petersburg to see him dance at the Mariinsky, but fate
decided otherwise, and they never saw each other again.

Chapter Five

THE RUSSIAN
RENAISSANCE

IN THE winter following this trip Vaslav
met the person who played the most important part in his
life, both as an artist and as a man—Diaghileff.

Sergei Pavlovitch Diaghileff was widely known among
the artistic and intellectual circles of the Imperial Theatres, and in the social and political life of St. Petersburg.
Ever since he first appeared on the horizon he had started
a powerful irresistible artistic movement. Sergei Pavlovitch
was the son of Paul de Diaghileff, a general in the Russian Army, who belonged to the nobility, and was a great
amateur of music and the owner of large distilleries. Sergei
Pavlovitch was born on the 19th of March, 1872, in
Nijni Novgorod, where his father was stationed at that
time. His mother was a musician with an agreeable
voice, and often sang for charity. Sergei Pavlovitch was
brought up very carefully on his father's estate among
the gentry of the land, and later in Perm. His mother and
aunt and the ever-faithful *nana* guarded him. Discipline,
and the motto *Noblesse oblige,* were the chief factors of
his childhood. His parents kept open house in their large
home in Perm, and it was run as a kind of local Medicean
palace, with great luxury and real Russian hospitality.
Sergei Pavlovitch attended the gymnasium at Perm, with

little interest in his school work after the excitement of the evenings at his parents' home. He was surrounded by a military aristocracy, with the constant factor of serfs in obedience.

Sergei Pavlovitch was an extremely gifted and clever boy, and soon became the pride of the *lycée* of Perm, but had a very patronising attitude towards his classmates and even professors, as he knew the importance of his own family and how anxious they were to be invited into the Diaghileff mansion. So Seroja, as he was called, instead of using his brilliant mind, simply took his school years easily by copying his classmates' work and bossing them. His tendency to enchant, and then make use of the talents of others, could already be noticed; also the streak of cruelty in his nature if anybody dared to resist his wish. He expected everybody to serve him blindly. He had the real nature of the Russian autocrat. He could make anybody suffer without even wincing and then walk away with a smile. At home he was cherished and spoiled. He had elegant clothes and was carefully groomed—more like a little prince than a son of the gentry.

His aunt exerted a very great influence on Sergei Pavlovitch's life. This remarkable woman, who excelled in the handicrafts in which all Russian women are gifted, organised the first art schools for the peasants on her estates.

Sergei Pavlovitch's father wished him to become a soldier like himself, but his aunt gave him the strength and the encouragement to choose for himself another career.

Diaghileff, even at a very early age, was a dandy. His charming, extremely personal manners elegantly suited him, and when he talked he gestured with one hand and snapped the fingers of the other, a trick learned from some grown-up whom he admired.

Sergei Pavlovitch came to St. Petersburg to finish his education at the Mai School. It was the first time he had been to the capital, but he soon felt he had lived there all his life. His manners were not of the provinces, but of the world. His uncle, the Minister of the Interior, gave him the immediate *entrée* into Court Society. Letters of introduction brought him in contact with Walter Nouvel, a young man of good family and of his own age, with musical interests, who was the centre of a small circle of painters and writers, and far more to his liking than the official society. Nouvel introduced him to Alexandre Benois, a young painter of French descent, who later became his close friend and adviser. A world-wide authority on the eighteenth century and a great connoisseur of painting, he was later to design so many of the famous settings for the Ballet Russe. Already considered by official circles as the most suitable head of the Imperial Museum of Art, the Hermitage, his fame was well established. Nouvel, Benois, Filosovov, Diaghileff's cousin, and other young artists and students of art soon became very good friends and were constantly together, hearing the latest music, seeing the latest paintings, and discussing the latest ideas from Paris. They formed, indeed, as he later called them, a *laboratoire artistique,* and, without the others being conscious of it, Diaghileff came to assume very quickly, in his delightful, gracious way, the leadership of the little circle, and to direct and control their artistic destiny with a guidance as insinuating as it was strong and directed. It was Benois who knew painting, who knew the museums as if they belonged to him, and he gave to Diaghileff the rich accumulation of his taste and information whenever the impulse or the opportunity offered itself.

Diaghileff attended the University of St. Petersburg. He was a brilliant student, but his private fortune obviated the necessity of any profession. His inherited love of music impelled him to take courses in harmony at the Conservatory of Music under Rimsky-Korsakov, and he became a real virtuoso of the piano, and since he had an agreeable baritone voice, of which he was inordinately proud, he studied singing. He tried every means to determine for himself some definite artistic vocation. In the second year of his studies he went so far as to compose a fragment of an opera in the manner of Moussorgsky, whom he passionately admired, and whom he felt he had, in a way, discovered. But when it was given an audition to the circle of friends, Filosovov, Benois, and Nouvel told him frankly that it was pastiche. That they were correct in their judgment is supported by the words of his teacher, Rimsky-Korsakov, who some three years later, at his graduation, said: "Do whatever you want, Seroja, but promise me never to become a composer." And so Sergei Pavlovitch abandoned any idea of becoming a musician, yet he understood music and had a clear musical judgment. The painters said he was always a dilettante in the plastic arts, but in music he knew his ground, just as it was said of Disraeli that the writers called him a good statesman, and the statesmen a good writer.

Diaghileff quickly assumed the exquisite life of the capital. His less sophisticated new friends were scarcely used to the scale of his life. He behaved as a *boyard* in his little court of friends, encouraging, condemning, putting one unsuspected talent next to an unknown gift, planning and making himself known in the right places. Perhaps Diaghileff's most individual power was in being able to pursue an idea, to slave for it, to accomplish it after terrific labour, and then suddenly to turn on it, profane and degrade it. In personal relationships he was always dependent on mastery. It must be he who was the direct inspirer, the power that set creation in motion.

At this time Diaghileff encountered a young Jewish artist, shy, proud, sensitive, and extremely gifted. He had a wonderful talent for stage decoration, and Sergei Pavlovitch, with a suggestion here, a word of admonition, drew him into the circle. His name was Leon Bakst. At the time of his meeting with Diaghileff he was already well known in his own right, a *protégé* of the Grand Duke Vladimir, through whose influence he had been commissioned by the Government to make paintings for the Ministère de la Marine. He had graduated from the École des Beaux Arts of St. Petersburg and he had returned from studying in Paris with the Finn painter, Edelfeld. His real master, however, was Vroubl, from whom Bakst took his colours, his wild palette, and made a bold innovation by introducing them to the stage. It was Vroubl's idea to abandon the *constructed* scenery, and to treat the whole

stage, not as an artificial reality, but as a living picture.
Bakst was a member of the School of St. Petersburg, as
others have been members of the Tuscan, the Roman, or
the Venetian School. It was in opposition to the School of
Moscow, which was less refined, less Western, than the
painting of the capital.

Diaghileff would defend and praise Bakst, and, when
his success seemed too assured, he would apply the nee-
dles of distrust: "Oh, yes, I think Leo does enchanting
things—such colour, such taste, and so delightfully *dé-
modé.*" Maybe he would merely infer that Bakst had
always been a good decorator, even when he'd first discovered him, but that there were others with equal talent.

Diaghileff was clothed in a worldliness which it was
impossible for him to discard. He, Nouvel, Bakst, and
Benois often drove out to Tsarskoe-Selo for picnic excursions. They would embark on a hot summer day from
the sweltering city, the carriages full of hampers of food
and wine. They would pass through the broad alleys of
Orienbaum, Nouvel whistling a tune from last night's
opera, Benois on the lookout for a château at the end of
a little lake, a bit of Marly-le-Roi set in Peterhof. And
when they arrived and spread the cloth out on the grass,
Diaghileff could only smile a little weakly, helpless in the
open air, wishing for the proper table and chairs, white
linen and wine buckets, to which he was accustomed.

At this time Diaghileff, finished with his study of law
and music, started on his first trip to the West. But for
Diaghileff this tour was not, as with other young men,
only a finishing school. For him it was the first taste of
what could be done in the wide world, of what *he* could
do.

The great excitement of the *fin de siècle, l'art pour l'art,*
was at its height, and at Dieppe in 1894 he met Jacques
Émile Blanche, the portrait painter, and the young Englishman whose contributions to the *Yellow Book* made
the name of Aubrey Beardsley famous. The watering-
place, populated half by English artists and society, half
by Flemish and French people on a holiday, had its casino
and *plage*, and here the young Russian, more French

than the French, promenaded, and watched and listened. There others were amused and impressed by his facile manners, his dandy's air, masking, under the Western veneer, the unquenchable, smouldering fire of the unaccountable Slav. His Russian friends nicknamed him Chinchilla, from the single white strand in his hair.

When they asked him little questions about Russia, he answered with a mysterious hesitancy. He would never deny or affirm the flattering rumours that always seemed to follow him. Perhaps he was indeed the illegitimate son of a Romanov; perhaps not. Who could tell? He soon became an accomplished boulevardier, and loved Paris with a comprehensive passion, and an intensity only possible in an adopted Parisian.

With a grand gesture he commissioned Blanche to paint portraits of his cousins, and returned to the Court Society of St. Petersburg determined not to practise law, or go into Government service, but rather to organise young Russian artists into a more self-conscious group, in opposition to the Academic School, which sent exhibitions of their historical canvases all over the empire, and hence were known as *peripatetics*. Diaghileff had seen the Impressionists in Paris, and realised that there was a rich vein of Russian fantasy that could be drawn upon.

He began to go back and forth regularly from St. Petersburg to Moscow, bringing the artists of one city into contact with his friends of the other. In the capital he kept a permanent table at the Hôtel de Europe for the pleasure of his circle, Bakst, Nouvel, Benois; Roerich, the painter and Tibetan scholar; Maliavin; the great designer Golovin; the critic Ossovsky; Prince Argoutinsky-Dolgorukoi, a cultivated amateur; and General Brezobrazov, the leader of the Mariinsky *balletomanes,* an old soldier who made a study of ballet technique and who knew the shapes of the legs of each *ballerina* far better than his strategy or ballistics.

Although Sergei Pavlovitch had little appreciation for the charm and beauty of women, he always found time to lavish attentions upon the important social leaders of art and society. His charming manners were irresistible, and his power grew by seducing with his enchanting smile the omnipotent ladies of St. Petersburg. He always found time to turn up at the right place for tea, to kiss the hands that held the most possibility of power, to say a few amusing words, and to leave for the palace before they'd hardly known he'd come or gone. He was laying his foundations sensibly.

In Moscow he had a similarly representative and powerful group of friends on whom he could depend. There was the Court painter Serov, and Korovin, the stage designer; there was the chief critic of the Moscow Press, Kashkin, and, by no means least, two rich merchants, Ostrukov, and the caviar and fish magnate Sava Mamontov, who supported Chaliapine and built handsome theatres from which started the Arts Theatre of Stanislavsky. The movements which Diaghileff inspired, and the theatres of Stanislavsky, were the two greatest single facts of the Russian Renaissance, developing out of the art and tradition of the Imperial Theatres.

Inspired by his impressions which he received on his trip to the West, Diaghileff organised the first exhibition of contemporary French and English painters at the private galleries of the Musée Stieglitz, and in 1897 made his official début as an "organiser" in the world of art. The official critics flattered it with their most violent disapproval. Society, however, on whom Diaghileff leaned always the most heavily for his support, began to come in considerable numbers and made it a social success.

The attacks of the critics by no means discouraged Diaghileff, and the following year he arranged at the same small museum a show of Russian painters, young and old—Benois, Maliavin, Vroubl, Repin, Serov, Somov, Korovin, and Levitan.

The name of Sergei Diaghileff began to be mentioned more and more frequently in the circles which moved around the activities of the artistic interests at the Imperial Court. It was arranged that this young aristocrat, who was already Kammerjunker, should somehow be attached in a semi-official capacity to Prince Sergei Volkonsky, the new intendant of the Imperial Theatres, and advise him on special novelties in connection with the staging of opera and ballet.

Diaghileff was also entrusted with editing the official *Annual of the Imperial Theatres,* a traditional survey which covered the entire yearly activities of the five theatres in Moscow and St. Petersburg. It had formerly consisted merely of programmes, notes, and photographs, plainly bound in dark brown buckram stamped in gold. Now, unasked, Diaghileff enlarged its format to a quarto, had it beautifully printed and lavishly illustrated with many photographs, scenic and costume designs, costing something over thirty thousand roubles, which effectively exhausted the moneys of the survey.

His activities at the Imperial Theatre by no means took up all his time or fulfilled his ambition. Now, in 1898, with the financial aid of Princess Tenishev and Mamontov, he founded the magazine of art and letters, *Mir Isskoustvo (the World of Art),* upon which he spent most of his own fortune. This journal was exceptionally brilliant both in its presentation of material and its list of contributors. He invited the best-known painters to illustrate it.

Diaghileff had been restricted enough under official discipline to know what unconditional freedom meant to an artist or a writer, and he gave absolute liberty to the people whose work he commissioned. It included not only his familiar circle of painters and musicians, but also such writers as Dostoievsky, Merejkovsky, Turgenev, Chekhov, and Leo Tolstoi.

Sergei Pavlovitch had the courage—many people considered it the effrontery—to question the æsthetics of Leo Tolstoi in an exciting literary controversy which brought him a great number of new readers. He was so convinced of his opinions that he actually went down to Yasnya Poliana in an effort to argue with the old patriarch. Tolstoi, as can be imagined, hated the dilettante from St. Petersburg, who must have seemed to him the personification of everything he most opposed.

In the fine arts the magazine became the semi-official organ which particularly defended and furthered the work of those artists who expressed fantasy or archaism, such as

Nicolai Roerich's Scythian researches, Benois's revival of
the eighteenth-century baroque of Potsdam and Versailles,
and Bakst's Orientalism. They were all of them passionately united against the hard, generally accepted natu-
ralists. The best of the young painters soon left their easels
and began to design and paint stage scenery, a most
valuable and popular method of propaganda for the new-
er spirit.

Now Diaghileff began to organise exhibitions under the
auspices of the *Mir Isskoustvo,* and in 1899 he imported
from Paris a great show of the Impressionists. This was
his first real contact with the French galleries and patrons.
The extraordinary success of this exhibition was of historic
importance for the future of Russian painting and for the
stage design of the world.

Diaghileff did not co-operate very well with Volkonsky
at the Imperial Theatres. He saw no reason why his
friends, who were, after all, the best painters in Russia,
should not be commissioned to do scenery, and for this
reason he independently asked Benois to design Delibes's
ballet *Sylvia* in an entirely new production, which was a
deliberate break with nineteenth-century perspectived
scenery. *Sylvia* was never permitted to be shown. Diaghileff hated the petrified bureaucracy that encumbered the
management, and he was not particularly tactful in his
expression of it. Finally Volkonsky, in 1901, irritated beyond measure, asked him to resign. Diaghileff refused and
was summarily discharged under the preposterous Article
III of the Imperial code, by which the discharged servant
is never again permitted to enter Government service.

To the stupefaction of everyone, not more than a week
later Taniev, an important official, nominated Diaghileff
for another position at the Ministère de la Cour, although
the Tsar always disliked him personally, and told his
cousin, the Minister of Commerce, that he'd "one day
play him a dirty trick." All this time he kept up his editorial activities on *Mir Isskoustvo,* he constantly visited the
studios of new artists and new writers, and attended every
concert of modern music. With Nouvel, who was always
absorbed in music, he helped in 1901 to found the So-

ciety for Evenings of Contemporary Music, and presented for their initial Russian performances the French moderns of the day.

Mir Isskoustvo, the shows of painting, the evenings of music, led to a great deal of talk in the capital. Diaghileff, who was conceded by the artists at first as a charming, helpful Mæcenas, but a dilettante, very soon showed that he was anything but that. He had the uncanny gift of discovering talent in absolutely unknown young people. And he was always untiring and ready to sacrifice all personal advantages to secure opportunities for them. Now, in his tastefully furnished, elegant apartment in the Zamiatin Peroulok, he kept open house, and it became a custom for the progressive artists to come in at night after the theatre or concert. In these informal gatherings around Diaghileff's hospitable table was founded that nucleus of the artistic movement which so profoundly affected the art of the twentieth century.

Watchful for every possible development of art he penetrated into the remotest provinces in an effort to secure the best paintings, which he knew hung, unknown to connoisseurs and collectors, on the walls of old country estates, for a retrospective exhibition of native Russian art. Wrapped up in a greatcoat lined with nutria, he was driven over the long country roads to the big mansions of governors of the provincial districts, who were so impressed by his official air that they thought he might be a *chinovnik,* an envoy of the Tsar, on a secret mission. From rooms where the plaster was falling from the ceiling, from attics and old closets where the paintings hung loose in their frames, and from cellars where the damp had mildewed the canvas, he brought together a great collection of historical material, which made a great impression when they were well hung in the old Tauride Palace in 1903. Nobody had realised that this kind of traditional painting was so rich in Russia. The result of the trip was a magnificent iconography of Russia of the first historical importance, which he later offered to the Government as a permanent collection, an idea which was turned down, and in the later disturbances many country estates were burned and the pictures forever lost.

On his return he had said, "The era of summing up the past has arrived. . . . I am deeply convinced we are living at a great historical moment. The time has come for a new culture, to be raised by ourselves, but one that will eventually thrust us in our turn aside." So strong was the influence of this national exhibition that a group of painters actually started a *Patiomkin tendency* of intense Slavic inspiration, named after Catherine's great Minister who tried to maintain the Russian Empire as an organic, indigenous whole.

Mamontov, who had supported *Mir Isskoustvo* in 1904, had, however, suffered great financial losses. Diaghileff, who loved the magazine, made every effort to save it. He had spent a great part of his own capital to continue its publication, but its expense was crippling, and he was forced to discontinue publication.

About the year 1906 Diaghileff started to interest his French friends in securing an invitation from the Salon d'Automne to have Russian painters exhibit in Paris. It meant a great deal of diplomacy through the Foreign offices of France and Russia, and in the official circles of the French artists. But Diaghileff was a master in pulling all the necessary strings, and he never failed to obtain what he wanted. Fortunately, his artistic integrity was such that neither personal ambition nor advantage could tempt him. This was Diaghileff's greatest virtue.

For the first time Paris saw at this exhibition the work of Russian painters and sculptors. Every school of Russian painting was represented, from the earliest icons to the fantasies of the most advanced Impressionists. Leon Nikolaevich Bakst was commissioned to redecorate the Salon d'Automne, which he did charmingly, with an arrangement of lattice-work like a winter garden. Bakst had designed ceiling decorations for great houses in Paris and Moscow. The Grand Duke Vladimir, through Diaghileff's secret urging, commissioned decorations for ballets at the Hermitage Theatre, and he had designed the scenery and costumes for the classical season of the

Hippolytus and the *Œdipus* at the Alexandrinsky Theatre. He was himself a member of the Salon d'Automne, and for his services to French art was decorated with the Legion of Honour. The patrons included the Grand Duchess Maria Pavlovna, a great patroness of Russian painters and wife of the Grand Duke Vladimir, and the Countesse de Greffuhle. The success of this exhibition was colossal. Diaghileff's star rose higher and higher in the sky of artistic Europe.

Encouraged by his reception of the year before, he organised in Paris in 1907 a series of five *Concerts Historiques* of Russian music. As usual, Diaghileff secured the patronage of many eminent people. The programmes were composed of music from Glinka to Scriabine, from Borodin to Balikierev, Moussorgsky and Rimsky. Before these auditions Russian music meant only two names to the French: Tchaikovsky and Rubinstein. Scriabine and Rachmaninov appeared as pianists, and his *chefs d'orchestre* included Nikisch, Rimsky-Korsakov, Glazounov, and Chevillard. The success of the orchestral season surpassed even the exhibition of painting. Diaghileff's ambition became greater. Now he wanted to show the Russian operas, and again he succeeded. In 1908 he brought Russian opera to Paris, presenting for the first time *Boris Goudounov* and *Ivan the Terrible,* with Chaliapine, Smirnov, Lipkovska, and Baklanov, from the Imperial Opera, to a dumbfounded Western world. Benois was made artistic director.

Diaghileff, the amiable dilettante, had become the invincible magician. He was highly praised by the Imperial family, the Court, the Society of Paris and St. Petersburg; and the artists considered his judgment infallible. His position was now impregnable. Then the innumerable intrigues against him began. Everybody in an artistic position of importance imagined that he would be displaced by him. The curator of the Imperial Museums, the director of the Hermitage, the intendant of the Imperial Theatres, all formed a secret alliance, which was readily joined by those whose mediocre talents had been ignored by Diaghileff. The head of this Anti-Diaghileff

League was General Teliakovsky, the new intendant of the Imperial Theatres, who had followed Volkonsky. He was an inoffensive man and a satisfactory director, who even introduced reforms at the Imperial Theatres by encouraging Russian painters and musicians. But he was by nature unimaginative. Teliakovsky, cunningly, had his spies at Diaghileff's gatherings, and as soon as they heard of an idea he quickly tried to realise it. Teliakovsky was too weak to hold such an important position, and he tried to humour everybody, from the Court Ministers to the public, the critics, the singers, or *prima ballerinas,* the Grand Dukes, and above all the mighty Kshessinskaya, which was difficult enough, as each had contradictory aims and objects.

Vaslav had heard of Diaghileff's artistic gatherings. He knew many members of the Mariinsky Theatre who frequented them. He had even met Diaghileff, *en passant,* during a performance. One day Bakst asked Vaslav to accompany him to one of these reunions. From that day on started the collaboration, which gave so much to art, and created the deep affection of these two remarkable men. Although Diaghileff was twenty years older than Vaslav, he immediately found the way through the boy's reserve, and won his friendship, which, in spite of all misunderstandings and quarrels, Vaslav unalterably kept for him. Diaghileff was at once attracted by his strong, resilient body, by the subtle, elusive combination of a boy's bearing with a feminine softness, and by the steady, glowing power which was the chief force of his character.

As Vaslav later told me, "Among all the people I have ever known, Diaghileff, of course, meant the most to me. He was a genius, the greatest organiser, discoverer, and developer of talents, with the soul of an artist and a *grand seigneur,* the only man with universal talent that I could compare to Leonardo da Vinci." And in a way Vaslav was right. Diaghileff was a real man of the Renaissance. He was not a musician, yet he sang a little and played the piano well; he was no artist, yet he drew a little; he was no dancer, yet he knew dancing in its most perfected style. In short, he knew enough of everything to make his authority respected in each field, and he had the added alchemy of perception, of suggestion, which drew out of everyone his greatest possible energies. He was, in the best sense of the word, a dilettante, but the dilettante raised to the nth power, the dilettante all-power-ful, the dilettante whose career was the furtherance of other more intense talents. Not only in Russia at this time, but later in France, Italy, Spain, the artist benefited by Diaghileff's wonderful gift of right advice. Ravel, Picasso, Marinetti, Derain, Gontcharowa, Albeniz, and an endless number of others were revealed through him to the public and themselves.

Vaslav loved to attend the evening gatherings, where he soon felt quite at home, and very soon these revered artists who were present not only had discussions with, but came to listen to, this inspired youth. Diaghileff's affection for Vaslav was profound, and he soon felt that he was not only a prodigious dancer, but a seeker after new forms and new ideas. Diaghileff now spent a great deal of time with Vaslav, and he took him to visit the studios of painters, to the Hermitage, to private collections, and to concerts. He advised him on the choice of reading and in all other matters. His influence over Nijinsky by no means pleased Teliakovsky's group, and malicious gossip began to be circulated about these inseparable friends. But nobody could dissolve the bond between them. They were united in a common aim—to raise Russian art to the highest peak. Diaghileff's was the guiding hand, by which Vaslav could develop and reach his ultimate height as an artist, a dancer, and a creator.

Vaslav was naturally greatly interested in all Diaghileff's undertakings, and he was overjoyed at his success. One day, in the early winter of 1909, he came to him with a proposition. "Sergei Pavlovitch, why not form a troupe from the Ballet of the Mariinsky Theatre and take it to Paris? Don't you want to show the world what we dancers can do?" For a moment Diaghileff was taken aback, then he began to think. Vaslav was perfectly right. Western

Europe had great music, great painters, great theatres. But Russia was the only country to possess in this century a great ballet and great dancers. Diaghileff was convinced, and so the Russian Ballet was born to Western Europe.

But to take it to Paris was another matter, and almost impossible to carry out on account of the insurmountable obstacles. There were the immemorial traditions of the Mariinsky to break down, permissions to obtain from the Tsar, and the endless routine of referring requests from one office to another, the question of precedent and assent, and there was, finally, the essential subsidy to be granted by the Imperial Government.

But Diaghileff was not the man whom obstacles could frighten. On the contrary, the greater they were the more he was determined to overcome them, and so he started at once with his marvellous ability to organise and to attack the several roads which led to the possible realisation of his ambitious scheme. His influence at Court, through his uncle and the intimate friends of his father, was already at work. The Grand Dukes he knew well, also Count Fredericks. And the critics, Rimsky-Korsakov, Serov, who was the portraitist of the Imperial family, and last, but not least, Kshessinskaya, the favourite, all made their utmost efforts to further his wishes. Before Teliakovsky and his group could realise what was happening, Diaghileff had obtained the order of the Tsar to take the Ballet to Western Europe. The Foreign Office instructed the Ambassador in France, Isvolsky, to offer him every available help. At this time the alliance between Russia and France was pending, and Count Fredericks made a special point of the fact that a visit of the Russian Ballet to France would strengthen the diplomatic and political relationship between the two countries. He placed at Diaghileff's disposal a subsidy large enough to cover the expenses of the project, and the Hermitage Theatre was put at their disposal for rehearsals.

Benois, Bakst, Prince V. N. Argoutinsky-Dolgorukoi, an expert in the antique, N. N. Tcherepnin, the composer and conductor of the Mariinsky orchestra, General Brezobrazov and Valerian Svetlov, two *balletomanes* and critics of dancing, met constantly, an unofficial committee, in Diaghileff's flat, with its walls hung with unfinished drawings from *Mir Isskoustvo,* and piles of music all over the shelves, and over their tea they discussed what they would do. They agreed that they wanted above all to show Russian ballets. There was *Konick Gorbunchok,* a Petipa creation of the mid-nineteenth century, with a Russian libretto and music by Pugni. Without a word, Diaghileff strolled over to the piano and started to play the banal, empty measures. *Konick* was never mentioned again. They thought of the *Sleeping Beauty.* It was a perfect example of Russian *mise en scène* of the classical period, with a wonderful chance to show off the dancers' technical virtuosity, and the pretty Tchaikovsky music. But it had a Perrault story, and, besides, the French called Tchaikovsky the Russian Massenet. There was *Giselle,* the historic rôle of Taglioni, and Bakst insisted on the inclusion of the old ballets with white *tutus.* Pavlova would be a perfect *Giselle.* But it was too long, and perhaps Paris knew it too well.

There was the *Swan Lake.* That would be better. It was definitely old-fashioned, but it was a masterpiece of Petipa. Benois would paint a new curtain for it and design the new dresses. What else? Fokine's *Pavillon d'Armide.* It was in a way still in the old tradition a *ballet d'action,* but with a very great difference. There were *ensembles,* variations, *pas de deux,* but a solid consecutive action of mimed interludes that held the dramatic narrative together. The story was no longer a mere pretext for dances.

To demonstrate something of Russian national dances, Diaghileff decided to use the second-act scenery of Glinka's *Rousslan and Ludmilla,* for which Korovin had painted a great mediæval hall as a setting for a *divertissement,* to be called *Festin.*

While Diaghileff was arranging the programme, assigning the designs for scenery, selecting the music, the group of artists set out with feverish enthusiasm to perfect the chosen repertoire. He invited Tcherepnin and Cooper, the two eminent conductors of the Mariinsky Theatre, to

join them. Then Diaghileff selected the dancers. The first
one to be asked was the *prima ballerina assoluta,* Matilde
Kshessinskaya. Then he invited from the Mariinsky company as well Thamar Karsavina—who held the same rank
of *prima ballerina* as Anna Pavlova—Sofia Fedorova,
Baldina, and Smirnova, fine classical dancers, and the
male soloists, Mihail Fokine, Adolph Bolm, Monakov,
Bulgakov, Kshessinsky, Matilde's brother, and Vaslav
Nijinsky. Diaghileff used his free hand lavishly. He would
select the best dancers of all the Imperial Theatres, not
only from St. Petersburg. So he invited from the Bolshoi
Theatre in Moscow, Mihail Mordkin and Theodor Koslov,
and the *prima ballerina* Koralli.

Everything was proceeding smoothly. Every possible aid
had been given to him, when suddenly an incident occurred which threatened the very life of the undertaking.
The mighty Kshessinskaya did not like Diaghileff's idea
of giving prominent rôles to Koralli. She told him so.
Diaghileff in turn made it clear to her that he would not
tolerate anyone interfering with his functions. Kshessinskaya immediately went to the Grand Duke Vladimir, the
Tsar's uncle, her very intimate friend at that time. A few
weeks before their planned departure the authorities withdrew the subsidy from Diaghileff's troupe.

It was a terrific blow, but as the authorisation to use
the dancers was not withdrawn, Diaghileff acted quickly
to accomplish his plans and rented a small theatre on the
Ekaterinsky Canal and continued his rehearsals there.
He immediately got in touch with his influential friends
in Paris, and they arranged to subscribe enough money
to pay for the rent of the Châtelet Theatre. Gabriel
Astruc, the French impresario, managed the business and
interested Sir Basil Zaharov, while the Comtesse de
Greffuhle, Robert Brussel, Boni de Castelane, Polignac,
and Misia Edwards sponsored the enterprise.

Finally, the great day of departure arrived, and when
the troupe boarded the Paris-bound express the platform
was full of well-wishers. Vaslav's mother came down to
see him off. Many of the noblemen who had estates in

France were accompanying the Ballet. The train left the St. Petersburg station with a flutter of waving hands behind, bearing unsuspected to the great audiences of the West the most powerful Russian invasion the modern world had known.

Chapter Six

THE FIRST PARIS SEASON

In Russia the spring had hardly touched the trees, and the long train rolled along through the vast winter-killed fields and an occasional town. This was the first time Vaslav had left Russia. As the train rushed through Germany he was fascinated by the sense of order and routine shown by the well-kept roads that ran parallel to the tracks, the canals, the neat clean towns, all the methodical arrangements of signals, conductors, and guards.

The windows of the cars were filled all the time by the faces of the young Slavs, staring out at the unfamiliar neatness of the trim East German towns. Absorbing with their eyes the fleeting landscape, they talked endlessly in their soft Russian tongue of the reception they might expect in Paris, of the merits of the French dancers.

With every minute that brought the train closer to Paris, Vaslav's curiosity and excitement rose. Suddenly, faint as in a dream, upon its hill stood Sacré Cœur, and the towers and blurred rooftops of Paris came into focus. "You see, Slavushka," pointed Chaliapine, "that is Montmartre, and there, where my finger points, you can faintly see, towards the left, the Tour Eiffel. Yes, that's it." The long journey was actually over. This was Paris at last.

"Gare du Nord." A few more minutes and the train stopped. Under the great dome of the station the platform was full of waiting Russians who came to welcome the Imperial Ballet. Vaslav and the rest of the dancers were completely bewildered by the noise and excitement, the eternal shouting of the blue-shirted porters in a strange language.

Vaslav wanted to drink in every small detail of this most famous city in the world. He turned left and right to catch sight of the line of the atticked roofs, the full boulevards and avenues, their names as familiar as his own from the history, novels, plays, and the newspapers he had read. It was the first day of May. Fragrant spring air charged the atmosphere of the city with delicious electricity, which cannot be found anywhere but in Paris. As the coach rolled along the avenue, they passed by the grand façade of the Opéra, its flight of steps, the Carpeaux dancers, the columned balcony arcade, and above, the dome, crowned by a lyre. Here the traditions of the antique French dance were still maintained, here the words of Noverre were living precepts, and the name of Gætan Appolon Balthazar Vestris was still alive.

Not far along the Avenue de l'Opéra they stopped at a small, unpretentious hotel, the Hôtel de Hollande, which no longer exists. After a short rest, they went straight to the Châtelet Theatre, where they were to give their performance and where Vaslav exercised under Maestro Cecchetti.

The Châtelet, owned by the City of Paris, was a huge, shabby, old-fashioned house, consecrated to spectacles of old-fashioned popular appeal, *Around the World in Eighty Days,* with great scenic effects, fires on the stage, storms, and hurricanes. When Vaslav was shown into the huge auditorium, it was dark and dusty. He said it looked like a lake without water. Neither Vaslav nor the rest of the company saw anything of Paris for the next few weeks, except the buildings that bordered their drive from their hotels to the Châtelet. The constant rehearsals worked them up to fever pitch. The Russian conductors, Tcherepnin and Cooper, took charge of the famous

Colonne orchestra, and endless rehearsals were necessary to acquaint the French wood-winds and brass with the amazing new sonorities, which at first seemed almost incomprehensible to them.

Maestro Cecchetti was stricter than ever, and, in spite of the fact that the dancers had innumerable rehearsals with and without the orchestra, he never allowed them to miss a lesson. His classroom was filled with admiring French and Italian dancers, and friends of his who marvelled at the wonderful discipline and technique of his *pupils* of the perfection class.

Diaghileff invaded the musty hall with an army of carpenters, decorators, and electricians. They had to construct an entirely new floor on the stage—of pine, the elasticity of which is most suitable for dancing—which covered over the orchestra pit and eliminated the first rows of stalls. The columns and balustrades were re-covered in new velvet, and green potted plants were placed in the corridors. Diaghileff had brought a complete technical staff with him and the mechanic, Valtz from Moscow, supervised the traps and elaborate changes of scenery required in *Armide.* Everything proceeded rapidly. He was here, there, and everywhere, behind the scenes, in the lobby, in the orchestra, advising and supervising.

Astruc, the indefatigable impresario, had asked young Jean Cocteau to write and illustrate a booklet announcing the coming marvels. Auguste Rodin, Odilon Redon, Marcel Proust, Jean-Louis Vaudoyer, Reynaldo Hahn, Gerard d'Houville, la Comtesse de Noailles, Jacques-Émile Blanche, Robert Brussel, José Maria Sert, by their talk, threw the artistic and literary circles of Paris into a ferment of anticipation.

And in this Tower of Babel Vaslav, as often as Fokine could spare him, exercised without allowing himself to be disturbed, unaware even of his surroundings. Whenever there was a free moment amid the din, Vaslav escaped from the glaring, shifting lights, the crashing chords, the calls of the stagehands and the electricians' signals, into a dark, quiet corner of the big stage, where, unobserved, for two or three minutes he could repeat an *entre-chat royal*,[1] or a *grand fouetté à la seconde*.

Vassily, Diaghileff's faithful valet, once a servant on his father's estate, who had found himself in trouble and been pardoned through Sergei Pavlovitch's good offices, watched over Vaslav like a nurse, keeping the curious at a distance. Vassily was a real Russian *moujik,* crop-headed, with a heavy beard. Erect and sinister, almost always silent, without a trace of servility, he knew how to command respect by his dark presence. He seemed to know everything that was going on without ever being told, and he would have committed murder for Diaghileff without a tremor. Like a shadow, he was omnipresent, hovering over Vaslav except when Diaghileff appeared. Then he would vanish, only to be mysteriously at hand whenever his master needed him. He was in charge of the small dancing-shoes which were especially made for Vaslav by Nicolini of Milan. They were of soft kid glove-leather, and he used from two to three pairs each ballet, for his feet when dancing swelled and split the thin hide. Vassily always stood in readiness with half a dozen pairs of shoes and a flat surface where Vaslav could scuff the soles with powdered rosin.

The preparations were so intense that no time could be spared even for meals. Therefore Diaghileff ordered food to be brought over from Larue's famous restaurant. Larue had once been the Tsar's chef, and he loyally maintained that French and Russian cooking could not be surpassed. The platters of caviar, the heaps of blini, the tureens of borscht, carried over from Larue's by the waiters, in the restaurant's silver service, were set around on upturned boxes of props and costumes, and the dancers ate on the stage, barely taking a bite between steps.

Finally the great day of the *première* arrived, and, as before a great storm, there was a torpid calm. Paris has seldom seen such an audience as came into the revivified Châtelet on the evening of the 17th of May, 1909.

---

[1] The *entre-chat* is a step of crossing the feet in mid-air a number of times. *Entre-chat dix* (ten times) has only been performed in modern times by Nijinsky.

Pavillon d'Armide, Festin, and *Prince Igor* were on the programme. The bells in the corridors rang, the house lights started to dim. People left off talking to each other. A few late-comers rushed in, amid half-breathed apologies. Tcherepnin appeared from under the stage, stepped upon the podium, his baton acknowledging the perfunctory applause. A tap on the music-rack, and he began the opening strains of his own *Pavillon d'Armide.*

Vaslav had absolutely no idea what was going on on the other side of the asbestos curtain. As usual, he had arrived at the theatre with Vassily around seven o'clock and had gone straight to his dressing-room, changed into his practice costume, and gone on the stage to exercise for an hour. This he had done invariably all his life before each performance. After this, he went in to make up.

Nobody was ever allowed to enter his dressing-room, and it was an unusual event if even Diaghileff was permitted. The greatest possible order was maintained there, for Vaslav was scrupulously neat. His costumes were already hung up and prepared, his dancing-shoes lined up in one row on the floor. On his dressing-table, in military precision, was set out his make-up—sticks of Leichner grease paint, from the darkest to the lightest.

His make-up took him almost half an hour, and he did it with enormous care. Indeed, only Chaliapine knew as well as he did how to make up. Often, when inventing a new character, Vaslav would ask the professional advice of Bakst or Benois. When he was finished with this the hairdresser came in and affixed his wig and head-dress with glue, so that no leaps could dislodge it. Then clever Maria Stepanovna, the wardrobe mistress, entered to inspect his costume and see if anything needed a needle and thread. In many of his rôles, notably in *Spectre de la Rose* and *Faune,* he had literally to be sewn into his clothes.

All this happened in silence. Vaslav, from the moment he had entered his dressing-room, had no other thought than his part. He was already in its mood, and disliked anyone to speak to him.

Bakst and Benois, with Diaghileff, had the artists pass

in review before them on the stage, to see if they had
been made up and costumed as they had been instructed.
For each ballet they had to conform to the wishes of the
designer, and no variation was tolerated. The chief stage
manager was responsible for seeing that they did not wear
rings or other personal jewellery, or anything not indicated for the costumes, and especially no pins. These
rulings were strictly upheld.

This was the first time that Paris was prepared to watch
a whole evening of ballet divorced from opera or spoken
dramatic interludes.

Fokine had created Vaslav's dances with a great display
of technique. They were stylised into the essence of behaviour at the Sun King's Court. The mimed action was
fluent, stately, and human. From what Vaslav told me
later, the instant he began to dance his first variation a
murmur went through the public which almost terrified
him. The audience burst into an unceasing storm of applause after his first *tour en l'air*. He sensed the complete
abandon of the public in response to his performance.
When he leaped off the stage, there were resounding cries
for *"Encore, bis, bis, bis"*; but the rules of the ballet
rigidly forbade any artist appearing except when his part
called for him.

The *entr'acte* was applauded wildly through, without
a stop in the bravos. Robert de Montesquieu, with his
white gloves and gold-handled cane, waved again and
again over the audience. Paris was stupefied and transported.

The uproar was terrific; the critics were almost hysterical. They crowded the stage in a mad, breathless
excitement. But Vaslav did not know of all this, as he
was changing in his dressing-room.

He took off the necklace which Benois had designed
for him, little realising that he had set a fashion. At first
the jewelled collar had rested low on the top of his satin
coat. Thinking the line was bad, he raised it, so that it
formed a choker around his neck. Cartier was quick to
perceive the innovation, and the great ladies of Paris and

London for the next two seasons wore collars of black moiré and diamonds, pearls and brilliants, *à l'Armide*.

From the parterres of Versailles to the steppes of Central Asia! The prelude of the Polovetsian dances from Borodin's *Prince Igor* swarmed over the violins, and the stage revealed the round hide tents of a Tartar encampment, with Roerich's gold and smoky russet sky. Lines of women in baggy trousers circled, trailing dusky veils. Fokine's wonderful choreography was the perfect equivalent, in its asymmetrical cadences, of the counterpoint of chorus and orchestra.

Le Festin was an arrangement calculated to show the entire troupe in national dances, orchestrated from the work of several composers. It opened with the march from Rimsky-Korsakov's *Coq d'Or;* then dances from *Lesghinka* by Glinka, *The Golden Fish* by Tchaikovsky, a Glazounov czardas, a Moussorgsky hopak, a Glinka mazurka, a Tchaikovsky trepak, a *pas classique hongrois* by Glazounov, and a stirring finale taken from Tchaikovsky's Second Symphony. Vaslav danced a *pas de quatre* with Adolf Bolm, Mordkin, and Koslov, which created a furore of enthusiasm.

Only at the end of the performance, when Diaghileff opened the door to the stage, the "sanctuary," to his friends, the *élite* of Society, the artistic circles of Paris, did Vaslav realise that something quite unusual was going on. He was surrounded by an increasing crowd of marvellously bejewelled ladies, men—everybody asking questions which he could not understand, as he did not know a single word of French. Nouvel and Gunsburg did their best to answer for him. Overwhelmed by all the questions, the flattering hands, the terrific rush and enthusiasm of people who wanted to meet him, shake his hands, touch him, even look at his shoes, he became violently embarrassed and fled into his dressing-room. Vassily guarded the door. Diaghileff went on to a big party with his friends and sponsors, but Vaslav begged to be excused, and, completely bewildered, drove back through the lamp-lit streets to the hotel, leaving the streets crowded with the enthusiastic audience, loath to go home.

As he hated to get up early, Sergei Pavlovitch break-
fasted in bed, receiving the reports of his secretaries,
dictating his correspondence, reading the telegrams of congratulations. Diaghileff had the blinds always drawn, and
the electric lights burning brightly, even if it were midday,
like an old Marquise afraid of the daylight. He spoke
on several telephones at once, and worked untiringly with
his technical staff and his friends, with rarely a free moment, as he had not only to supervise everything to the
smallest detail in connection with the Ballet, but he also
had pressing social obligations; patrons and patronesses
to call upon, respects to pay to the Grand Duke, and the
thousand small attentions whereby he maintained the
large circle of his supporters.

Vaslav, the morning after the *première,* dressed as usual
and wanted to go down to the Châtelet to practise, but
while he was putting on his suit his door was forced open,
in spite of the ever-watchful Vassily, and an excited band
of strange, gesticulating men stormed the room. At first
Vaslav thought: "My God, even in France it is like Russia. The police are searching the suite for political reasons." But not at all. They were only reporters and
photographers, who tried desperately to explain to Vaslav
that he was indeed the sensation of Paris, that the cultivated audience of the town already named him *Le Dieu
de la Danse,* and that by this time he was world-famous.

Soon Diaghileff, Bakst, and the rest came over from
their rooms and rescued him, explaining the whole story,
after which he docilely posed for the cameras. Vaslav was
exuberantly happy that the reception in Paris had been
so immediate and so warm, that they understood and
loved his art so well.

Diaghileff and the dancers were fêted wherever they
chose to appear. However, Vaslav very rarely accompanied them, as he disliked to alter the routine of his
day the very slightest.

In the morning, after a few cups of tea, he would go
down to the theatre for a lesson with Maestro Cecchetti.
A rehearsal with Fokine was followed by a late lunch
around four o'clock with Diaghileff at Larue's, where

Bakst, Benois, Gunsburg, and the more intimate of the
balletomanes always gathered. Their crowd enlarged from
day to day, for every one of the friends brought friends
of his—French and English musicians, painters and actors, Gunsburg, his international banker friends, and
Nouvel, his statesmen and diplomats. In this way Vaslav
met everyone of importance in the international world—
constantly observing, but keeping silent.

After lunch he went for a drive in the Bois, usually
with Nouvel or Bakst, up under the great lindens and
horse chestnuts, past the lake with the children sailing
their toy boats, past the parasols and gay tables of
Armenonville, and back slowly, with the long shadow of
the Arc de Triomphe behind them, to the hotel, where
Vaslav's *masseur* rubbed and relaxed his muscles for an
hour, and then he went to sleep for another hour in a
darkened room. At half past six he was awakened by
Vassily, and they would leave for the Châtelet and the
evening's performance.

The other novelties of the season were *Cléopâtre, Les
Sylphides,* and *Les Orientales.*

While *Pavillon* showed unmistakable signs of the new
spirit, and demonstrated Fokine's real power, it did not
include the sensational innovations of *Cléopâtre. Une Nuit
de Cléopâtre* had been originally prepared for the Mariinsky stage, after the well-known story of Théophile
Gautier, where the Queen seeks a night's lover who is
willing to die at dawn. Fokine, who could only accomplish a little of what he wanted on the stage of the Imperial Theatre, was constantly asked to produce ballets
for charity, where he had absolute freedom to do as he
wished and the pick of the ballet company. So for a single
charity performance he re-studied *Cléopâtre,* rifling the
Imperial costume wardrobes for new costumes. Spears
formerly held in Petipa's old *Fille du Pharaon,* a helmet
or a shield from *Aïda,* a few dresses from *Eunice,* combined with a little paint and thread, looked admirable.
Arensky's music he had re-orchestrated, introduced bits of
Liadov, Glazounov, Rimsky-Korsakov and Tcherepnin,
and made out of the ballet an actual danced tragedy—

not a pantomime, but a drama where words were gestures
and the chorus group movements. Instead of the faces of
the dancers being set in rigid smiles, they actually moved,
gave expression to desire and grief.

For Diaghileff, Bakst now designed entirely new costumes and a huge architectural scene. The magnificent
setting, with its splendid colouring, brought the atmosphere
of Egypt, with a perfect understanding of the mood—an
Egypt realistic, fantastic, that immediately acted on the
audience like a light, delightful narcotic. The music carried them further into the Egyptian mood, and when the
dancers appeared the audience was completely prepared
to receive the impression which the artists wanted to
create. Between great red gods which framed a high hall
was a court of a temple. At the back, through other
columns, was a glimpse of the glistening Nile.

Vaslav, a young soldier, and Karsavina, a slave-girl, a
veil carried between them, enter the temple in a dance
which is a *pas de deux,* not of conventional supported
adagio, but love. The Queen was carried in on a palan-
quin which could have been a painted mummy-case. Set
on the floor, her wrappings were whirled off her by slaves.
A black panther of a man crouched under her divan,
aching to kill the young warrior who came out of the
temple shadows to her with helpless attraction. Cleopatra's
part was mimed, not danced, in a semi-stylised manner
—not rigid, but reminiscent of the hieroglyphics.

Ida Rubinstein's beauty and magnificent body fitted this
part perfectly. The little slave-girl, which was danced by
Karsavina, alternating with Fokina, carried the action to
the point where Nijinsky made his entrance with infinite
verve and *élan.* There was a dark rout of negroes, a sway-
ing dance of heavy Jewesses with swinging ornaments,
and finally a wild bacchanal of Greek captives in an
ecstasy of Dionysian frenzy, led by Karsavina and Pavlova
—here only a dance in a ballet, but whose substance
Pavlova lived on for years later in her Bacchanal.

The freedom of the use of the whole body, the actual
flesh seen through slashed silk trousers, the breasts tossing
under their gold nets, the hair loose, the great leaps of the

Ethiopians, the intense drama and the quickening *tempo* to the climax, was an achievement which is a chapter heading to any history of dancing in our time.

The evening began with *Les Sylphides* (in which Vaslav danced with Pavlova and Karsavina), the enchanting evocation of Taglioni's classic style which Fokine had designed as a monument of formal choreography to music by Chopin. Benois had given the dancers long Victorian *tutus* and frail white diamanté wings and set it all against a mournful, romantic scene of a deserted, ruined holy place. Vaslav's conception of this part was to impersonate Chopin. Therefore he brought out the very essence of Slavonic languor and softness.

In his blond wig, the curls down to his shoulders, in white tights, *crêpe de Chine* shirt, and black velvet *gilet*, Vaslav danced like a body without weight, so that whenever he came down one had the feeling he was already on his way up—like a rubber ball, the harder bounced, the higher it rises. He floated, literally floated, and for a second stopped in the air. His unbelievable capacity of almost flying stupefied the audience and his *entre-chat dix* was another miracle. No one could achieve more than six *entrechats,* or on rare occasions, eight.

From front stage to back stage, he covered the whole distance in the air at a single bound, and left them gasping. Never stopping for a second—for even in his pauses he re-echoed the preceding movement—he made the audience feel as if this preceding movement and the one to come were fused in a thrilling whole. Vaslav never stopped to make a preparation before executing a leap, however difficult it might be, as the other dancers did. He explained to me later that dancing should be as simple as one breath taken after another, and, though every step is a separate action, it must seem to be the natural and harmonious consequence of all previous action. Thus his dancing had an unending, constant weaving rhythm, which gave to the spectators an inexpressibly wonderful sense of beauty.

His *entre-chat royal* caused a furore among the dancers

and ballet experts. But his technique was so perfectly understood that he never made it felt.

Vaslav had a perfectly proportioned body. He weighed almost one hundred and thirty pounds. His legs were so muscular that the hard cords stood out on his thighs like bows. With his unusually powerful arms, controlled by the highest technique, he could pick up and lift his partners with such ease that it seemed as if he only held a doll of straw. He did not, like the other male dancers, support the girl with both hands on her hip, but with one single arm he raised her straight from his side.

His hands, when not in a *danse de style,* when the costume and manner were not dictated by its nature, were always held with the fingers close together, in a simple natural way. He told me that one must always watch children if one wishes to learn the proper way of using hands beautifully, because children are always unself-conscious. One never sees a baby extending its little finger when raising its hand. Everything in his dance was worked out to the minutest detail.

When the last ballet of the evening had been danced, the audience stood up and applauded in swelling, ecstatic thunder. The curtain went up again and again, but the performers, according to their rules and traditions, never took a separate bow, but received their ovation in the position in which the curtain found them. Vaslav always made his bow in keeping with the style and mood of the particular ballet in which he happened to be dancing.

While Diaghileff was embracing Karsavina or congratulating Bolm, amid the hubbub of excitement as the artists and spectators mingled to discuss their impressions and the stagehands busily removed the scenery, Vaslav imperturbably continued dancing in order not to come abruptly to a full stop, just as a horse is trotted up and down with decreasing momentum after a race gradually to calm its quivering muscles. Then he hurried off the stage, brushing by the other excited dancers, past Diaghileff, into his dressing-room.

The day's routine usually ended in a big dinner, but

very often a group of them went to the Café de la Paix. Sometimes they played an interesting game to amuse themselves, each one guessing the profession or occupation of a chosen passer-by. Bakst gained his impression by the face and head; Benois from his clothes, shoes, the colour of his cravat; Vaslav from the stranger's bodily movements; and Diaghileff from a general impression. To verify the guesses, Bakst was sent after the stranger to ask him!

Every morning Diaghileff showed Vaslav the sheaf of newspaper and magazine criticisms, which he collected with considerable care. The eulogies naturally pleased Vaslav, but they never went to his head. He always remained the simple, modest boy he was. But there was one criticism of which he was enormously proud. This was the quotation by a journalist of a criticism of the great Vestris, the idol of France, by Beaumarchais, the author of *La Mariage de Figaro,* now referring to Vaslav: *"Il faisait oublier le comble de l'art par la plus ingénieuse négligence."*

The Russian Opera was performed at the Châtelet, on alternate nights with the Ballet, *Boris Godounov, Ivan the Terrible,* and *Prince Igor.* Chaliapine, Smirnov, Kastorsky, Chernov, Lipkovska, Petrenko, Zbrouevska, were the stars of the company, which had its own superbly trained choruses. The effect on the audience and musicians of Paris was only second to the profound impression of the Ballet. Vaslav, like a child absorbed, watched Chaliapine every time he sang, either from the auditorium or behind the scenes, and afterwards he would frequently join Diaghileff and the rest for supper. Chaliapine, who called Nijinsky "Slavushka," had a Chinese servant who adored Vaslav and always let him into the master's dressing-room.

Vaslav was always fascinated by Bakst's constant sketching, on menus, marble-topped tables, napkins, or scraps of paper. He started himself to draw, at first a little timidly, until Bakst told him he had a real talent for it undeveloped. But Diaghileff would not hear of his doing this. "Let him alone, Levoushka," he would say; "don't distract him. He's got enough to do as it is, with his dancing." Bakst and Diaghileff, accompanied by their Parisian friends well acquainted with the peculiar specialties of Paris, would make occasional sorties on the town, late, after supper, but Vaslav was always left behind safe in the hotel, with Vassily to watch over him. But they never treated him like a child, nor patronised him in the manner of older men. They respected his opinions and his presence and adored his gifts. The Ballet company was proud of him in a curious, detached way, for they only saw him when he worked on the stage with them.

Vaslav had very little idea of the sophistication of the capital. He arrived in Paris with only a blue and a brown suit, besides his costumes. Brought up on clean tap-water, he drank out of the faucet in France and came down with a terrible attack of typhoid fever, so that he was unable to finish the season. Sergei Pavlovitch had no faith in French doctors, and he was fortunate in being able to call in Dr. Botkin, the Tsar's personal physician, who happened to be in Paris at the time. Botkin was just able to pull him through, but Vaslav had been terribly sick. When he had made a thorough physical examination, Botkin went to Diaghileff and told him there was something curious about Vaslav's glands. "Sergei, take care of him—there's something about it I don't like." But no one gave it any attention at the time, and Vaslav was soon on the road to recovery.

The Paris season was over. The troupe packed up, made arrangements for shipping scenery, trunks, and costumes, and anticipated the still greater honours and welcome which awaited them in St. Petersburg, the triumph accorded to the return of a victorious army.

Diaghileff decided to go on a well-earned vacation with Vaslav and Bakst to Karlsbad.

Vaslav enjoyed Karlsbad, with its hills, excursions into the pine forests, and the little Russian church. The place reminded him of Narzan, in the Caucasus, which was a similarly smart Russian resort. They had pleasant rooms with balconies looking down from a hill-top. Vaslav didn't take the cure. He did absolutely no work for two months, no exercises, only massage. After two or three weeks of rest they went down to Venice.

The beautiful trip through the Tyrol and over the Italian Alps pleased Vaslav, and he was up early and would not move away from his window till bedtime. They stopped at the old Hôtel des Bains at the Lido, and as soon as they were settled Benois took Vaslav all over the city, into every church, palace, museum, and private collection he knew, explaining the paintings and architecture, and Vaslav in his turn took them down to the beach for a swim. He was an excellent swimmer, and could do all manner of tricks, including pirouettes, under the water. With Benois, they dragged Bakst into the Adriatic, enjoying tremendously his terror of the sea. Diaghileff never went near the sea. His hatred of water nearly amounted to a phobia, and in his suite at the Lido the curtains were always drawn on the windows that gave out on the lagoons.

They had a marvellous time in Venice, sightseeing and swimming all day, and talking with new friends all night. Shortly after their arrival a large circle of new acquaintances was formed around them. D'Annunzio had known Diaghileff, and joined them whenever he could. The first time the poet met Vaslav he was already far gone in his royal mania, and turned to him, saying, "Pray dance me something." As soon as he understood the imperative quality of the remark Vaslav was quite angry, and answered quickly, *"Please write me something."*

But after the first meeting he became friendly and congenial, and there was no hitch in their friendship.

Isadora Duncan was also in Venice, and Vaslav met her for the first time at a crowded party in the palace of the great Italian beauty and queen of Roman society, the Marchesa Casati; the beautiful eccentric, who had made her début in Rome by driving into a ballroom in a chariot drawn by lions, with a live snake as her main costume.

Isadora Duncan did everything she could to be with
Diaghileff, because she hoped he would engage her to
play parts similar to those mimed by Ida Rubinstein. But
Diaghileff, with his consummate tact, always avoided
every possible encounter in which she might force him
into any definite answer. Not only did he avoid meeting
her personally, but also refused to express an open opinion of her style of dancing. He was indeed relieved that
Vaslav could speak nothing but Russian, because the
latter would have told her or anyone bluntly what he
thought of Duncan. Vaslav was only silent because he
never understood the questions, and they were never
translated to him.

Isadora Duncan did not conceal from anyone her desire to sleep with every famous man she met, since she
wanted to have children by them, to help propagate another artistic generation. Naturally she asked Vaslav to
create with her a dancer, and when Diaghileff, very much
amused, translated her invitation to him, he merely
smiled.

They knew Duncan had no basic knowledge of the
technique of the dance, and, although she produced something entirely new in our time, her execution betrayed her
secret and her weakness. She was an amateur. It went so
far, in their unshakable opinion, that whenever they saw
something bad, poor in execution or taste in dancing or
opera, whereas they had formerly dismissed it by saying
"C'est du Munich," they now said *"C'est du Duncan."*

They enjoyed the parties and the gay company, but
they mostly loved to sit by themselves on the Piazza San
Marco, in front of the Confiserie of Floriani, eating *gelati*.
In the evening the piazza was full of people listening to
the band concerts, and Vaslav, watching the wheeling
pigeons and the different types of passing Italians (officers gracefully corseted with slender effeminate waistlines,
capes swishing in the breeze, black eyes snapping brilliantly; swarthy skinned women gesticulating) composed
their criss-cross movements into dances. Perhaps it was
here that he first thought of composing choreography himself.

At the end of August they had to return to Russia, as Vaslav's leave was up. With regret they left Venice, but they were proud and happy on their triumphant return to St. Petersburg.

Chapter Seven

THE FRIENDSHIP OF SERGEI DE DIAGHILEFF AND VASLAV NIJINSKY

THE NEWS of the Ballet's tremendous success and Nijinsky's personal triumph in Paris had of course preceded them. St. Petersburg received the conquerors with open arms; the papers were full of them, and they could really say about the Paris season, *"Veni, vidi, vici."* At the station Vaslav was met by his mother and his sister Bronia. Eleanora Bereda could scarcely believe that it was her Vatza of whom she had read so much, and she kept sobbing and laughing at once, and talking to him all the time. The first days passed in feverish excitement. There was so much she had to be told about Vaslav's success, about the trip, about Paris and Venice.

When the rehearsals began, Vaslav reported at once at the Mariinsky. Baron Fredericks expressed to him the satisfaction of the Court and himself, congratulating him on his success and thanking him for the service he had rendered Russia through his dancing. His colleagues received him with cheers, but soon his life came again under the iron discipline and rules of the Imperial Theatre, with its exclusive and expert audiences, whose tickets had actually been handed down from generation to generation.

This was Vaslav's third season at the Mariinsky since his graduation. More and more parts were assigned to him after the Parisian success.

Giselle was a famous French ballet, after a poem of Théophile Gautier's, with music by Adam. The choreography was arranged by Koralli, and it was performed for the first time on the 28th of June, 1841. It was Carlotta Grisi's most famous rôle, and ever since it has been the most exacting and desirable of the classical dancer's parts —almost a Hamlet of the ballet. It was a perfect vehicle for Pavlova. She danced a young village girl who, betrayed by a Prince in disguise, goes mad and commits suicide. Anna Pavlova was magnificent in this exhausting tragic *pas seul,* a heroic Ophelia of the dance, a wonderful example of technical virtuosity combined with an overwhelming dramatic intensity. It was her favourite part.

In the famous second scene, when we see her grave, and the Prince scattering blossoms on it, kneeling and offering prayers for her resurrection, Pavlova emerges from the damp ground like a ghost of frightening beauty as she subtly casts off the veils of death and floats about the stage like a creature without bodily weight, to dance her *pas de deux* with the Prince.

Pavlova's performance was perfect. Since she had a proprietary interest in the ballet she resented so much the more Vaslav's phenomenal success as the young Prince. That a male dancer should be applauded, called for again and again and showered with flowers like a *prima ballerina assoluta,* was an unheard-of event.

Vaslav thought very highly of the art of Anna Pavlova. He found her technique matchless, her attitudes and arabesques extremely beautiful, and he loved to dance with her. Her lightness and exquisite frailty appealed to him. He enjoyed dancing with her at the Mariinsky, where she fulfilled herself as a lyric poet of the ballet, and, although intensifying her emotion and establishing her swooning style, she could not overdo it there, controlled by the iron discipline and tradition of the Mariinsky, as she later did with her own independent troupe.

Vaslav felt that the quality of their dancing came from the same source, and that in his flying movements, at least Pavlova could give the impression by her lightness that they complemented each other. Their dances together in *Les Sylphides* were of a consummate sympathy beyond description.

Diaghileff, after his return, was fêted as never before. The subsidy withdrawn the previous year was now almost forced upon him. Kshessinskaya invited him often to her palace, and made it quite clear that she wished to be included in the next tour. Diaghileff had been officially approached to bring the Ballet back to Paris the next spring, not to the Châtelet, but to the Opéra itself. His evening meetings were resumed again, and during this winter the unforgettable ballets of *Carnaval* and *Scheher-azade* were created.

Fokine, who always seemed doomed to create his best work outside of the Mariinsky, had been asked to design dances for a ball. The magazine *Satyricon* had arranged an evening party in the Sala Pavlovna, a large public ballroom. The editor Kornfeldt, and his friend the poet Patiomkin, told Fokine that they were calling the party *Carnaval*. Fokine immediately thought of Schumann's enchanting early piano pieces. They translated characteristic bits of Schumann's life and letters to him, as he spoke no German, and he absorbed the atmosphere of the period. Who would do the decorations and costumes? Fokine suggested Bakst, of course. Kornfeldt said he would be perfect, but too expensive. Fokine persuaded him to do it for half his usual fee, and gave him part of his own pay, for which Bakst presented him with a painting. Bakst was enchanted with the idea, and immediately saw costumes of the time of Schumann, the Austrian Biedermeier period of eighty years before. Fokine had only three days for rehearsals, and was forced to practise in a ballroom where the carpenters were pounding all over the floor, preparing the wall decorations.

Diaghileff was right in his judgment about *Carnaval,*

and, when he finally presented it, not a single movement had been changed. Schumann must have visualised movement, composing this piece. It needed great courage to transcribe music written for piano for full orchestra. It was almost sacrilegious and unmusical, and Diaghileff, who was a fine musician, knew this. But if it were done, it must be done, as in the case of *Les Sylphides,* by eminent musicians who would understand the subtlety of Schumann. Diaghileff chose Glazounov for this extremely delicate and difficult task. The score of *Carnaval* proves that Diaghileff was right to entrust the orchestration to him, for he rendered it perfectly. And in spite of the fact that both Liadov and Tcherepnin also collaborated, the final effect was as harmonious as if it had been orchestrated by a single person.

Carnaval is the frame in which these personages appear before us: the sad, heartbroken Pierrot, always teased, always seeking a sweetheart; Papillon, the gay young girl who flirts and plays with Pierrot, who takes her so seriously; Florestan and Eusebius, the one the romantic, the other the stormy, temperamental side of Schumann's own nature; Pantalon, the ancient *beau,* chasing eternally after Columbine; Harlequin, the mischievous; and all the young men and girls laughing, dancing, teasing, flirting. The music and the dance simultaneously express the same idea. In *Carnaval,* as in *Les Sylphides,* movement is for the first time given its due place. Fokine re-created in his choreography the period of Alt Wien. *Carnaval* is a perfect gem among Fokine's ballets. It is harmonious from beginning to end. The Valse Noble, danced by eight couples, remains the masterpiece of the waltz.

Bakst, to whom the scenery and costumes were entrusted, very cleverly chose a curtain as background. This is now a banal form of scenery, for every dancer uses it at recitals, but it was Bakst's innovation. He chose a heavy velvet of royal blue, with a deep and warm hue. On the bottom were painted heavy garlands of leaves and vivid pink bouquets of roses, which contrasted marvellously with the darkness of the velvet. At each side of the back of the stage was a ridiculous and enchanting red and green striped Biedermeier sofa.

The men, in tail-coats of different colours and tall black velvet top hats, lace jabots and white gloves, looked irresistible. The girls swung great panniered skirts of steel-blue taffeta, and wore small velvet bonnets and white kid gloves. They all carried black velvet masks, which they held before their eyes and put on only when they danced. Pierrot appeared in his loose, familiar dress and his endless, huge, white, tragic, helpless sleeves and big ruff of black tulle, and Columbine in her white full taffeta skirt, with garlands of cherries painted on it by Bakst himself, and, in her hair, Karsavina, who created this part, wore also a wreath of cherries. There is Chiarina (Fokina), the coquette, who danced, in a dress sewn with small tassels, with two other girls. Their *pas de trois,* all magnificently performed on points, was one of the most perfect and seductive creations Fokine has ever done. And above all there was Harlequin, mischievous, sly, half cat, half spoiled child, in his white *crêpe de Chine* blouse and huge black neatly tied bow, with his skin tights painted in red, green, and white octagons by Bakst. This needed the skill of a master, because it was extremely difficult to paint the pattern on the leg so that the muscles would not distort it, but the costume was so perfect that every ripple of Nijinsky's leg showed as if the markings were transparent.

Fokine's originality was manifested in more ways than one. His brother was one of the first automobile merchants in Russia, and Fokine was naturally interested in his success. The other dancers were vastly amused at an artist's connection with business. Diaghileff himself never attempted to correct or influence him, and relied implicitly on his taste and ideas. But, when he was designing the brilliant dances for *Prince Igor,* Benois and General Brezobrazov, a little shocked at their violence, approached him with shy, tentative suggestions. They could only ask him to "change it; well, just change—how shall we say it?—a little." They didn't know exactly how to change it, but felt that a difference would help. Fokine flatly re-

fused. He said he knew what he was doing and he would
do it. It has not taken history to tell him how right he
was.

Sergei Pavlovitch did correct him, once. At a rehearsal
of the mimed part of *Coq d'Or,* Fokine had a character
grasp his hand to his side at a reference in the song to
his liver. From the back of the house came Diaghileff's
authoritative voice, "The other side, Michel; the liver's on
the other side."

Diaghileff, ever on the lookout for new dancers to
present, made frequent trips to Moscow, where he was
well known, and acquired Katherina Geltzer and Alexander Volinine, first dancers of the Imperial Opera there.

Among the new dancers from St. Petersburg, Diaghileff
decided to take along Fokina, the wife of the *maître de
ballet,* Biber, Puni, Poliakova, Doubrovska, Loupokhova,
and Loupokhova II, who later became famous as Lydia
Lopokova. They were all graduates of the Imperial School,
fine dancers, and of course a valuable addition to the
troupe.

The only one who had not so graduated was Ida Rubinstein, who was to accompany them on the tour to create
the mimed rôle of Scheherazade, after her success as
Cleopatra. During the whole winter she worked arduously
with her master Fokine. To Kshessinskaya was assigned
the important part of Armide. *Giselle,* although already
in the Mariinsky's classic repertory, was remounted by Diaghileff as the perfect part for Pavlova. But this year she
preferred to tour by herself in Denmark and Sweden,
where the ballet has always been kept on a high standard.
After the first season, impresarios flooded the stars with
separate offers. But most of them realised that the Russian Ballet as a whole was an unparalleled organisation
whose great strength lay in its unity, that their art could
be developed in this way to its highest point and their
individual talents shine best in this frame. Pavlova was
blinded. She was a magnificent dancer, but she loved
personal success more than the perfection of her art in its
entirety. This was the fundamental difference between
Pavlova and Karsavina. The latter always sacrificed her

private ends to that of dancing. Pavlova could have performed a real service to her chosen art by educating the
masses who loved her, instead of following their undeveloped taste. Her scenery and staging in the first years
were mediocre, and with her music she made similar
concessions to public taste. Later on she realised that in
spite of her own marvellous performance she would not
be accepted unless she raised the quality of her production. Then she asked Fokine to compose dances for her,
and Bakst and Benois designed a few *décors* and costumes.

Pavlova as an interpretative dancer ranks with the
greatest. She has her niche safe beside La Sallée, Camargo, and Taglioni, but she never was, in the full sense, fair
to herself. Diaghileff and his colleagues regretted immensely her defection from their company, but they never
forgave her for her prostitution of her own gifts and of
their great art.

Vaslav and Diaghileff, whenever they happened to have
a free evening among the constant duties of the Mariinsky
and the feverish preparations for the next Western season, used to go to theatres and concerts. Ibsen and
Maeterlinck were constantly shown, and the plays of
Maeterlinck appealed immensely to Vaslav. The dreamy,
semi-mystical, illusory sense of reality struck a re-echoing
note in his own nature, and he read many of his books
as well. He always wanted to make a ballet of *Pélléas
and Mélisande*.

One evening they went to a concert given by members
of the composition class at the Conservatory of Music.
On the programme was the first hearing of a short symphonic poem called *Feu d'Artifice*. Its author was a young
man of twenty-six, the son of a celebrated singer at the
Imperial Theatre—Feodor Stravinsky. After the performance Diaghileff called on the young Igor, whose father
he had known and admired, and, to Stravinsky's utter
amazement, commissioned him to write a ballet expressly
for his company.

For a long time Fokine had had the idea of a distinctly Russian story for dancing, founded on native legends.
Fokine told the story of the *Fire Bird* to Benois, over

innumerable glasses of tea, and with every glass he added another embellishment, and every time he repeated the tale he put in another incident. Benois was enthusiastic, and they went so far as to tell Diaghileff and asked who would be a good one to compose the music. Liadov's name was mentioned. "What," cried Fokine, "and wait ten years!" Nevertheless, the commission was awarded to Liadov and three months passed. Then Benois met him on the street and asked him how the ballet was progressing. "Marvellously," said Liadov. "I've already bought my ruled paper." Benois' face fell, and the musician, like a character out of Dostoievsky, added, "You know I want to do it. But I'm so lazy, I can't promise."

Diaghileff thought at once of Igor Stravinsky, and the conferences between him, Benois, and Fokine commenced.

Fokine heard Stravinsky's *Feu d'Artifice* and saw flames in the music. The musicians made all manner of fun of what they considered his "unnecessary" orchestration, and he was touched by, and grateful for, Fokine's congratulations. They worked very closely together, phrase by phrase. Stravinsky brought him a beautiful cantilena on the entrance of the Tsarevitch into the garden of the girls with the golden apples. But Fokine disapproved. "No, no," he said. "You bring him in like a tenor. Break the phrase where he merely shows his head on his first intrusion. Then make the curious swish of the garden's magic noises return. And then, when he shows his head again, bring in the full swing of the melody."

Fokine made the choreography extremely fantastic. The steps are as rich in variation, as light and weird, as the story itself, especially in the solo dances of the *Fire Bird,* which constantly imitate the movements of a feathered creature.

Golovin's scenery of a garden, with the castle of Kotschei in the background, surrounded by trees, is wonderful as in a dream, stylised, but so convincingly unearthly, so sensuous, that one is in another world. The costumes were based on native Russian dress: fur-edged coats, stiff with gold and jewels, and high, embroidered leather boots.

Stravinsky was wild with enthusiasm to compose the music. By commissioning him Diaghileff proved his uncanny gift of the divining-rod again, which sensed talent wherever it lay latent. Just as with Vaslav, he gave Stravinsky an immediate opportunity to unfold his art. He knew at once that he had disclosed perhaps the foremost genius of contemporary music, and for this service alone Diaghileff deserves our lasting gratitude.

Stravinsky threw himself whole-heartedly into the composition, and he had little enough time in which to complete it. He was extremely eager, but, in spite of the awe he had for Diaghileff and the respect held for his elders like Benois and Bakst, he treated them all as his equals. He was already very decided and wilful in his opinions, and in many ways a difficult character. He not only wished his authority acknowledged in his own field of music, but he wanted similar prestige in all the domains of art. Stravinsky had an extremely strong personality, self-conscious and sure of his own worth. But Diaghileff was a wizard, and knew how to subdue this young man without his ever noticing it, and Stravinsky became one of his most ardent followers and defenders. He was extremely ambitious, and naturally understood the tremendous aid it would mean to him to be associated with Sergei Pavlovitch's artistic group.

Vaslav and Igor soon became friends. He had a limitless admiration for Stravinsky's gifts, and his boldness, his direct innovation of new harmonies, his courageous use of dissonance, found an echo in Vaslav's mind. The two of them were the youngest of Diaghileff's collaborators, so they naturally found themselves somewhat together. But Vaslav in a way was more unworldly in the manner in which he lived, and felt that his art was a medium to be used to ennoble humanity. Stravinsky was blunter; he understood the material life, and he was interested in his personal success. His music, his reputation, were important, but his creations are in the largest scale of achievement of our time. And every important work of his, from the *Fire Bird*, through *Petrouchka*, *Sacre du Printemps*, the unproduced *Liturgie*, to *Pulcinella*, *Apollon Musagète*, *Renard*, the operas *Rossignol* and *Mavra*, and the oratorio *Œdipus Rex*, were first given by Diaghileff.

Vaslav's attachment to Sergei Pavlovitch grew stronger and stronger. They were in complete harmony in their ideas about art. Vaslav more than willingly allowed himself to be moulded like soft wax in Diaghileff's hands. He was the ideal pupil, following his master without resistance up to the point where he no longer needed him, where he had outgrown him. Vaslav's affection for Diaghileff was of a profound order. He implicitly believed in him—his manner of living, his notions of life. He let himself be completely guided by him. Diaghileff, in his turn, cherished and spoiled him in every way he knew, trying to attach him more and more all the time. Diaghileff's boundless admiration for Nijinsky the dancer was even overshadowed by his passionate love for Vaslav himself. They were inseparable. The moments, in a similar mutual relationship, of dissatisfaction and *ennui* which come to others, never came to them, as they were so intensely interested in the same work. To make Sergei Pavlovitch happy was no sacrifice to Vaslav. And Diaghileff crushed any idea of resistance, which might have come up in the young man's mind, by the familiar tales of the Greeks, of Michelangelo and Leonardo, whose creative lives depended on the same intimacy as their own.

The relationship between them was so real that it was therefore universally taken for granted. Diaghileff and Nijinsky were one in private life, and nobody would even have dreamed of inviting one anywhere without the other. Diaghileff's artistic group had always known and accepted his outlook on life. Bakst was the only one who, because of his passion for womanhood, tried the hopeless task of reforming Diaghileff. But Diaghileff was merely amused or annoyed when he listened to Leo Nikolaevich's dithyrambics about women as with words and drawings he undertook to prove to Diaghileff the beauty of those whom he forever shut out of his life.

Diaghileff tried to convince Bakst that there can be no

real artist who has not the characteristics of both sexes; that almost all great genuises in the past were homosexual, or at least bisexual. Normal love, according to Sergei Pavlovitch, was merely a necessity to continue the race—an urge of nature, an animal action deprived of all beauty, and degrading to those who longed for spiritual and æsthetic pleasure; but that love between the same sex, even if the persons involved are quite ordinary, because of the very similarity of their natures and the absence of a presupposed difference, is creative and artistic. Yet Diaghileff was by no means entirely a sensualist. There was a strong æsthetic pleasure in his affection for Vaslav, who always in his art and in his life was able to radiate beauty, to heighten emotion to the point of ecstasy—like tightening the string of an instrument more and more to the moment of snapping, and instead of the expected break, to sweep the other into infinite bliss.

The nearest thing approaching a misunderstanding between them was about his sister Bronia. Diaghileff did not want to include her in the company. She had graduated from the Imperial School with honours, and had already obtained important parts at the Mariinsky. She had in her dancing the same quality as Vaslav: a marvellous technique, a great range of performance, chiselled down to perfection, as well as unusual strength and lightness. In her was combined something of the ethereal charm of a Pavlova, the technique of a Kshessinskaya, a great dramatic gift, and an inherent, overwhelming temperament. Bronia was not only a *ballerina,* but a brilliant actress, and she had all the requirements for a distinguished character dancer.

Diaghileff saw in her the material for quite a remarkable dancer, something new and unusual; but he objected steadfastly that the public always wanted *ballerinas* with sweet and pretty faces, and they would not accept the novelty of her dances unless she was pretty. Bronia had a fascinating face and a beautiful body, but she had nothing remotely resembling a conventionally sweet and pretty face. Vaslav, who loved her, was hurt by Diaghileff's attitude. She took lessons from him privately and learned

a lot by it. There was a perfect understanding and co-
operation between them during these years. She was proud
of her famous brother, knew what a genius he was, and
that she could only improve her own talents by observing
his. They lived with Eleanora in their comfortable apartment. Vaslav was very sensitive to cold, and had influenza
every winter, and it disturbed his mother increasingly, as
she felt that the climate of St. Petersburg was dangerous
for him.

In the early spring they commenced to rehearse the
ballets they already knew and the new creations for
the Paris season. This year, as last, a great retinue was
ready to accompany them West. *Pavillon d'Armide,
Prince Igor, Le Festin, Les Sylphides,* and *The Fire Bird,
Carnaval, Giselle,* and *Scheherazade,* made up the repertory.

They left for Paris with even more excitement than
before. As usual, Nouvel and the other intimates of Diaghileff came along. Vaslav told me he felt like a small
child before an examination. This time they were avidly
awaited in Paris. The Press and the public welcomed them
like old friends. The performances were sold out weeks
in advance. They were met at the station by hundreds of
people eager to make plans for parties and ways to
entertain them. Diaghileff said, "Please, please let them
alone. We came to work, not to amuse ourselves."

The season at the Opéra was to open in May and last
through June. Vaslav was thrilled to perform in the atmosphere where his idols, Noverre and Vestris, had
danced. As before, the practices, rehearsals, and lessons
from Cecchetti continued unabated. There was no time for
anything but the most rigorous preparations. But Paris was
familiar now, and there was no sense of strangeness, no
tension of insecurity as to how the French audience would
receive them. Only now they had to dance better than
ever to maintain the supreme impression of the initial
season.

Diaghileff engaged Pierné, the conductor of the
Lamoureaux concerts and the foremost conductor of
France at that time.

Then came the first performance of *Scheherazade*. This was Bakst's unquestionable masterpiece. Nowhere did he so completely express his creative ideas as in this ballet. He surpassed anything even he had yet done in the incredible luxury of his colour. The scenery had no flats or practicable projections. It was all painted on the vivid walls and ceiling of the harem in motives of green and violet blue, rising from a shrill pink carpet. A voluptuous sensation was suggested by the mixing of these sensuous colours. The effect on the public was the arousing of an immediate excitement. The front of the stage was draped in a gigantic curtain, its folds of varying greens, on which designs of blue and circular patterns of pink were sprayed. Colour had never before been so riotously used. In the blue background were three immense doors of silver, bronze, blue, gold. Huge Arabian lamps swayed from the ceiling squares, and heaps of enormous cushions sprawled all over the stage. The costumes of *Scheherazade* were in the most perfect Persian style. Here again Bakst's profound knowledge of Oriental art manifested itself.

The story by Bakst and Fokine was inspired by the tales of the *Thousand and One Nights,* and the music of Rimsky-Korsakov's greatest symphonic poem admirably suited the action of the story. Rimsky-Korsakov had been a naval officer, and much of it describes the sea, but here the second movement is omitted, as the *tempo* is too slow to be danced, and it would make the ballet too long.

Rubinstein, tall, with movements of a great plastic beauty, was admirable as Scheherazade. Her gestures were a combination of dignity and sensuality, and expressed the essential languors of a woman who demanded sexual satisfaction. The slave, danced by Vaslav, brought out the animal side of human nature—physical love. When all the rest of the harem and the slaves sink exhausted after their love-making, Zobeide leans on the Golden Door, queenly high, like an obelisk, awaiting the expectant joy in silence. A pause, and suddenly a superb, golden animal jumps up to an incredible height from a crouch and with one movement he possesses her. His jump is as a tiger's, once caged, now free for his victim. He bounds with her

on to the divan, for the maddest, fiercest activity of love.
Nijinsky was inexpressibly, voluptuously wild, a cat caressing, a tiger devouring, now at her feet, now at her
breasts and mouth, stroking and exciting her. He would
swing himself, hesitating, from side to side, as a feverish
animal might do, staring at this pale, marvellous woman
whom he so desired with every nerve and muscle in his
body quivering. Whenever the slaves sank, the golden
slave soared up, a self-hypnotised Dervish, spurring the
others by his amazing *tours en l'air,* dominating the orgy.

When the Shah returns, he is the first to see him.
One moment of petrifying fear, then with a leap he is
gone. But he is chased back, flashes through the stage
clad in gold tissue, his jewels sparkling. Struck by the
soldier's sword, his head just touches the floor, then his
whole body shoots into the air, legs uppermost, silvery,
glistening, like a fish tossed on to the sand, the nerves
and muscles shudder all through his frame, and the golden
slave lies dead, on his face.

Nijinsky idealised, even in his make-up, the slave, the
negro. He was painted a wonderful deep prune colour,
with a silvery sheen against which were drawn up his
golden trousers, a luscious contrast of colour and texture.

Scheherazade was a triumph for Bakst, the *Fire Bird*
for Stravinsky, and *Carnaval* for Fokine, and, whenever
he danced any of the three, a personal triumph for
Nijinsky.

To see Nijinsky, perhaps to meet him, to touch him,
was the highest wish of hundreds of society women. And
they devised all sorts of subterfuges to gain their ends,
which were mostly wrecked by the vigilance of Vassily.
On one occasion he was so mobbed he had to seek refuge
in a shop. Only when Diaghileff himself personally
brought somebody to meet Vaslav were his duties relaxed.

Vaslav did not mind his isolation. In fact, he never
noticed it. He never knew Diaghileff consciously submitted
him to the most rigorous seclusion. His mind was too
occupied, his time was too filled by his dancing and the
constant companionship of Sergei Pavlovitch. The intimate

circle of Benois, Bakst, Stravinsky, and Nouvel, whom he saw from day to day, completely satisfied him.

Of course, he was often with Fokine, who had always taken a very active part in the creation of the stories, and their mutual work at the theatre brought them constantly together. Vaslav had the deepest gratitude and admiration for Fokine's genius. Fokine's liberation of the ballet from its rigid classical tradition found its most ardent and revolutionary exponent in Nijinsky. At last, in Fokine's choreography, he could dance with the whole body and express ideas with every possibility of the anatomy. Vaslav had interpreted Petipa's creations to the entire satisfaction of that strict master. All technical difficulties were surmounted by his nonchalant ease. But through the medium Fokine gave to Vaslav he was able to develop his talent, and his latent wish to dance with his complete soul, using every part of his body.

In each part—as an Egyptian slave, as a Russian peasant, as Harlequin, as Chopin's living memory—he had the chance to give a complete and separate impersonation. He was so different in each part that he was almost unrecognisable. Where the essential Nijinsky existed was a constant mystery. His face, his skin, even his height, seemed to change in each ballet. There was only constant his one unmistakable signature, his genius. But one always forgot Nijinsky as a person when he danced. We were put in the true mood of the part. As soon as he appeared on the stage an electric tremor was transmitted to the public, hypnotised by his purity and his perfection. The eyes of the audience followed him from one side of the stage to the other, as if they were helpless, in a trance.

To him, dancing was, of course, more natural than speaking, and he was never so much himself, or so happy and free, as when he was dancing. The moment he stepped on the stage, nothing existed for him except his part. He was never aware of his public, and exulted in the sheer, free joy of movement. But he never tried to stand out and crush the other dancers, or give more importance to his own rôle than the *maître de ballet* had intended. He was always entirely harmonious and re-strained himself, the more to blend in with the *ensemble*. Yet his work was so paramount that, without obliterating the others, he was nevertheless a sun shining stronger among them. As soon as he was on the stage, somehow the other dancers were electrified to their utmost capac-ities. He brought out of them a reflection of his own harmony and beauty, and it was constantly said that the same ballet had never the same intensity when Vaslav was not dancing.

Since he never danced for the sake of applause, and was so sure of himself, he was never subject to stage fright. I once said to him what a great pity it was he could never watch himself dance. He said, "You are mistaken. I always see myself dancing. I can visualise myself so thoroughly that I know exactly what I look like, just as if I sat in the midst of the audience." Unlike many other trained ballet-dancers, he never watched himself in a mirror to correct his faults, but he had an instinct of muscular control and needed no sight to tell him where he failed.

His triumphs never changed him, and he was modest, kind, and reserved. Diaghileff let him meet a number of the French artists who regularly attended the performances —Debussy, Ravel, Guitry, Bourdelle, Blanche, "Sarah," Faure, and Saint-Saëns—and they were always surprised on first meeting this silent, self-effacing boy who only smiled at them.

He always excused himself, through Diaghileff, from the continual round of receptions, luncheons, and dinners. But he made exceptions in the case of Debussy, with whom he loved to dine, and with Jacques Émile Blanche, who had an enchanting house at Passy, where he painted Vaslav extremely well in his Siamese costume of *Les Orientales*.

He also saw much of Jean de Reské. There he could at last communicate with words. De Reské was like a father to Vaslav. He was Polish, and so was Vaslav's mother, and he always claimed him as a compatriot. But Vaslav loved Russia with every fibre of his being, and always insisted on his Russian citizenship. De Reské was a great patriot, and his aristocratic birth, his fame and wealth, assured him an important position in Parisian life. But as often as not Vaslav was alone with him and Diaghileff *en famille*. De Reské saw to it that certain of his chosen friends should meet Vaslav, and he also gave a chance to the creative artists who wanted so much to know him.

At this time an important group of young men, the lions of the *jeunesse dorée* of Paris, attached themselves to Diaghileff, and they followed him all over Paris, like a court in attendance. Their leaders were Maurice Rostand and Jean Cocteau. Later on others joined them, and they kept constantly in touch with all the movements of the *avant garde*. Reynaldo Hahn gave Vaslav an autograph of Vestris, and of all the presents with which he was deluged he cherished this most.

Poiret, who had just opened his new home on the Rue Faubourg St. Honoré in an old palace, gave a fantastic party in honour of the Russian Ballet, with incredible lighting effects and luminous fountains, and even the sands in the garden paths were coloured *à la Bakst*.

Madame de Euphrussy repeated her wonderful *Sylphides* fête of the year before, where the dancers shimmered in the pale moonlight of her midnight gardens. Madame Misia Edwards, the wife of the editor of *Le Matin,* often entertained them. She was a Polish woman and had a great *train de maison*. She was a backer of Diaghileff's, and partly responsible for the assurance of his subsidy.

Another person who was an enormous help to Diaghileff was the Comtesse de Greffuhle. She had tremendous political influence, and was always a staunch and resourceful friend of his. All the others were petted and spoiled, Rubinstein and Benois among the artists, and Bakst among the great ladies and gentlemen of the world of society, happiest when he was in the smartest house. Perhaps he felt this was some compensation for his early difficulties, due to his Jewish descent, but surely he was too great an artist to need such a public acknowledgment. Diaghileff did everything he could to put his collabora-

tors in the limelight, saw to it they were displayed
properly off stage as on.

So, in great work and in the social life of parties and
balls, the season of 1910 passed, with performances every
Tuesday, Thursday, and Saturday. Everyone was overjoyed that their second year proved even more brilliant
than the first.

This year there was an international exhibition in
Brussels, and the Russian Ballet had been officially invited to appear at the Théâtre de la Monnaie, the opera
house of the Belgian capital. After Paris, only a few rehearsals were necessary to accustom themselves to the
new stage and the new orchestra. They were their usual
terrific sensation, and the Court attended each performance, while Vaslav and the rest were presented to
King Albert and his Queen. Here the Ballet separated, most
of it returning to Russia for the vacation.

Vaslav and Sergei Pavlovitch once more left for Karlsbad and the Lido.

Chapter Eight

NIJINSKY'S BREAK WITH
THE MARIINSKY THEATRE

In the early autumn of 1910 Nijinsky
and Diaghileff returned from the Lido to St. Petersburg.
During their six weeks' vacation, Sergei Pavlovitch took
the cure in Karlsbad, and Vaslav had complete relaxation.
Many plans for the next season were formulated.

Diaghileff's position in St. Petersburg was impregnable.
Perhaps now the Intendant Teliakovsky had some justifi-
cation for fearing him. Diaghileff's ideas were accepted

and sought. The Court, the Press, and the artistic world considered his opinions infallible, and it would have been only natural that some great official position should be offered him. After the increased success of the last Paris season, his fifth year of continuous activity in the liaison of French and Russian arts, all manner of rumours went around as to his eventual appointment. He would be nominated as the next intendant of the Imperial Theatre. He would become director of the Hermitage and control the State Museums of Art and Archæology.

As the officials of the Mariinsky felt it necessary to be covertly suspicious or jealous of the ballets Diaghileff's group was creating, there was no possibility of Russia seeing them danced as Paris had, free from the hindrance of traditional restraint.

So the Duke of Aldenburg invited Sergei Pavlovitch to present *Festin, Igor, Scheherazade,* and *Cléopâtre,* just as he had at the Châtelet and the Opéra, but now here in the great Narodni Dom. The capital was naturally eager and enthusiastic, but, unluckily, the big People's Palace was burnt down and all their plans had to be cancelled.

Diaghileff enjoyed being home. Somehow in Russia the organisation, the arrangements, even the creation, seemed to progress more easily. At his evening gatherings, they commenced to formulate the next Paris programme: *Petrouchka, Sadko, Narcisse,* and *Spectre de la Rose.* It was decided to produce the Submarine Ballet from Rimsky-Korsakov's opera *Sadko.* Anisfeld designed the undersea *décors.* He had previously been of invaluable service in the actual execution of all Bakst's designs. Bakst merely made the *maquettes* and the sketches for the scenery. But the carrying out of his *décors,* which were so greatly admired throughout the world, was done by Anisfeld. He made a bold innovation, which revolutionised the manner of scenic painting, by spreading the canvas out on the floor and splashing pots of paint in the proper places, instead of a precise indication with the brush and ruler. His free methods had a great deal to do with the loose richness of the scenery, which was as brilliantly realised as a fine painter's canvas.

Diaghileff also wished a ballet expressly written for the new season, in the classic style, in which both Bakst and Fokine excelled. Bakst had been to Greece in 1905, with his friend, the painter Serov, and memories of the Pheidian period were swarming in his head, bursting for re-creation. Nicolai Tcherepnin, the eminent conductor of the Mariinsky Orchestra, was composing the orchestral score.

Narcisse, Sadko, and *Petrouchka* did not seem wholly sufficient as novelties for the new season, and they were all long spectacular ballets. Diaghileff thought that a short piece was needed to complete the programme— something of the order of the *Princesse Enchantée,* a *pas de deux,* which Vaslav and Karsavina could dance together. An evening's bill was usually composed of one long and two short ballets, Vaslav taking part in two only. *Les Orientales* had been dropped from the repertoire as too old-fashioned, so Diaghileff remembered the suggestion made in Paris the year before of *Le Spectre de la Rose.* Jean-Louis Vaudoyer, the poet, one of the young men in his Parisian suite, had quoted to him Théophile Gautier's lines:

> *Je suis le spectre de la rose*
> *Que tu portais hier au bal.* . . .

The poem, *Loin du Bal,* could be transcribed into an exquisite ballet.

Petrouchka was based on a well-known native folk legend and adapted by Benois, the great connoisseur of Russian folk-lore. Benois was opposing an intense Slavic nationalism to Bakst's internationalism. He was with Stravinsky creating a Russian Ballet for Russians to dance. It was to be more native than *Igor* and less remote. Both Benois and Fokine had seen street-fairs in their childhood, with puppet shows, hung with familiar dancing dolls—the Magician, the Ballerina, the Moor and Petrouchka, Russia's own Pierrot, her Tyl, her Puck—with the attendant hand-organs and trained bears, and ancients from the Caucasus with long beards and strange fur clothes.

All these ideas were developed at Diaghileff's gatherings, and one artist made suggestions to the other—an idea, a touch, a plan—and it was so complete a collaboration that it was impossible to know where the work of one began and the other ended. The creation of this atmosphere of unjealous mutual composition was Diaghileff's great achievement.

Vaslav meanwhile lived with his mother, who was only too happy to have him back home again. She was so bewildered by the way things seemed to happen. She had always felt that her Vatza was going to be a great dancer, but she could hardly connect the overwhelming reports of him with the son she knew. The ballets which had been created for the tour had not as yet been given at the Mariinsky, and Eleanora could only see him in the old repertoire. She adored him, and she said it was like going to church on Sunday to watch him dance as the glory of the Imperial Theatre. When she saw him in *Cléopâtre* and *Les Sylphides,* even though they were hard for her to understand, she nevertheless realised the beauty and exquisite quality of Vaslav's performance, and that he not only danced but acted.

Her boy had created something which she had seen only once before, in Russia's pride and national idol, Chaliapine. Just as she knew instinctively that if one subtracted the voice and orchestration of Boris, Chaliapine's presence on the stage would still be sublime, so she felt that even if Vaslav did not dance, but merely walked or moved across the stage, it would still be the expression of great art.

Stanislav's illness had always been the greatest worry and misfortune of her life, and she could never get over it. Bronia, as a girl, was close to her, but her violent energy almost frightened her mother. Vaslav was always patient, and he gave her all the tenderness and affection for which she longed. And these days were very happy ones for Eleanora. In spite of his work he had considerable time to spend with her, and to spoil her, and he would always go with her whenever she wanted to visit Stanislav.

Vaslav's success continued uninterrupted at the Mariinsky until the fatal evening of his performance in *Giselle,* after which he tendered his resignation. There have been many contradictory rumours about this episode, and there were at least three actual contributory causes for the incident. According to some witnesses, the Grand Duchesses Olga and Tatiana, daughters of the Tsar, were present, and their escort was shocked at Vaslav's costume. Another more persistent explanation was that the Dowager Empress Maria Feodorovna, who was occupying the Imperial box that night, felt that Nijinsky was not sufficiently clad, and passed her displeasure on to her suite. Word was brought to the intendant of the Imperial Theatres, and Vaslav's resignation was requested. But Maria Feodorovna, in later years, on a visit to her sister, Queen Alexandra, in London, was asked by the Marchioness of Ripon, Vaslav's devoted friend, if the story were true. She denied it, and said that she had never made any remark whatever about his costume; she was not even aware of the reason for Vaslav's quitting Mariinsky and attributed it all to a malicious Court intrigue of which she had no knowledge at the time. She was proud that Russia possessed such a dancer, and she personally asked Lady Ripon to tell this to Nijinsky and say how sorry she was for the whole affair.

Giselle, which had always been in the repertory of the Mariinsky, was now presented with the costumes, scenery, and arrangement that Diaghileff had used in Paris. Vaslav's costume, designed by Benois, consisted of close-fitting white silk tights with a black velvet *gilet,* which was the same as he had appeared in at the Opéra. The small slip that male athletes and dancers use had not been included by Benois. According to the regulations of the Mariinsky, all dancers of the company were obliged to wear it to hide their forms. Vaslav, whose only idea was to appear as the artistic personification of Benois's designs, discarded the archaic garment. Although he had obtained permission to do this from one stage manager, Director Kroupensky appeared on the stage and made severe remarks to him about the indecency of his costume, which revealed his form too markedly, and demanded that Vaslav change it immediately. This was just a few minutes before the curtain was raised. There was no time to change the costume, and it was impossible to make their Majesties and the public wait. In any case, Nijinsky did not feel himself at liberty to take off the costume assigned to him by the designer, who was in the audience, unaware of the fatal incident.

Princess Galitzina, an eye-witness, who happened to be sitting in a directorial box, has told me that as soon as Vaslav appeared thus dressed, Teliakovsky jumped to his feet, dashed into the small ante-chamber where he had a desk with bells connected to the back-stage offices, and summoned the stage manager. He was in a frightful temper, and ordered Vaslav to change at once. Vaslav refused. It was the costume which Paris had approved, and he saw no reason now to appear differently. He finished the second act of the ballet as he had commenced. After the performance, Teliakovsky demanded his presence in his box, and, furious, suspended him for a time from the Imperial Theatre as a punishment. This had never before happened in the annals of the Imperial Ballet, and aroused a terrific storm of protest. The papers were full of it. St. Petersburg and Moscow were in commotion.

Of course, Bakst, Benois, and all the friends took Nijinsky's part. The blow hit Vaslav, but it was obviously meant for Diaghileff, who accepted the challenge and persuaded Vaslav, greatly incensed at the preposterous suspension, to send in his resignation from the Imperial Theatre before any official action was taken. After a good deal of discussion, and after Diaghileff had definitely promised to form a permanent organisation where all their artistic dreams could be freely realised, Vaslav agreed to resign.

The Mariinsky was completely taken aback. They had never dreamed of such a contingency. Vaslav had graduated with honours from the Imperial School. His artistic career was assured. He was soloist to the Tsar, the pride of Russia, and a lifelong member of the Mari-

insky Company. That he should voluntarily leave was
unthinkable. They would not allow Vaslav to resign. They
needed him, and, besides, an unheard-of precedent might
be created. Also, they had begun to hear of Diaghileff's
new plans. So they made offers to him which culminated
in a proposal of the highest salary ever paid, even to such
singers as Chaliapine, with similar privileges to appear in
foreign tours, and his performances at home limited to
his desires. It was an unusual proposition for a dancer,
but Diaghileff made it possible for him to refuse.

And when he passed the Russian frontier at Eydtkuh-
nen in the spring of 1911, without realising it, he left
Russia forever. Had he known, he would never have left
it permanently. He believed in, and loved beyond anything, Russia, and wanted to be a part of it.

Eleanora was deeply worried about Vaslav, and did
not at all approve of his leaving the Mariinsky. She knew
Diaghileff, and respected him a great deal. He was always
extremely attentive and courteous to her, but somehow
they were so very far apart, and she always felt shy
when she saw him. But she could hardly set her opinion
against his will. Vaslav wrote her from abroad daily.

It was no simple task that Diaghileff had set himself
in raising and supporting a permanent company. More
than once the difficulties seemed absolutely insurmountable. The Russian painters, musicians, and technicians
could go on working for him. Fokine could go on creating
choreography even if he had his duties at the Mariinsky.
But could he acquire enough dancers who would be free
from the Imperial Theatre for his European seasons? He
began to make offers, higher salaries than had ever been
paid before; the smallest was a thousand francs a month
all the year round.

The great possibilities, the glamour attached to Diaghileff's previous success, tempted many. A number of the
Mariinsky Company were quickly engaged. He also picked
good dancers from Moscow and Warsaw. Bolm came
along. He was an ardent follower of the new movement,
and resigned from the Imperial Theatre to join Diaghileff
permanently, and he soon became an important pillar of

the organisation. Sofia Feodorova, the fine mime Astafieva, Bronia, of course, and others, also joined permanently. Diaghileff achieved a real *tour de force* in getting Kshessinskaya and Karsavina, the greatest *ballerinas* of the Mariinsky, early in the spring. They agreed to make flying trips from Paris to St. Petersburg whenever they had to appear.

The whole winter passed in preparation for the tour; the models for the scenery, the costume designs, were completed before they left for Monte Carlo. As soon as the theatre-managers in Western Europe heard that the Ballet was free to give performances in other months besides June and July, they were flooded with offers. Diaghileff decided that they would appear in Rome for the International Exhibition, then Berlin, Paris, and perhaps London. It was the year of King George's coronation. And, in spite of all the adjustments of personal difficulties, of wounded vanities here, of petty jealousies there, of the threats of a lack of financial support, and all the complications of transportation of a big company by train, with scenery and carloads of luggage, all across Europe, they arrived safely in Monte Carlo.

Here Sergei Pavlovitch intended to take a rest and to prepare the whole programme in peace. He had also in mind, to gain as backing for his company, the high patronage of the hereditary Prince of Monaco, so as to be attached to the Monte Carlo Opera House. They stayed this season at the Monte Carlo Palace Hotel, quite close to the Casino, and usually Sergei Pavlovitch took his meals on the balcony of the Hôtel de Paris. Here he held his round table conferences and very soon became the centre of the artistic and intellectual world, as wherever he went. Stravinsky came all the way from Russia particularly to discuss the score of *Petrouchka,* which was originally intended as four piano pieces, only for concert production. Vaslav and Diaghileff were both enthusiastic over the music, and they were full of ideas about the choreography. Stravinsky had finished the piano score before they left and was now rearranging it for full orchestra.

As usual, the mornings were spent in practising, but

very soon Vaslav complained that he was not used to
working without a coach, that practising alone required an
unnecessary moral effort, and that he unconsciously slipped
into lapses of laziness. He insisted on having Cecchetti,
and so Diaghileff immediately started to pull wires in an
effort to secure him. This was by no means an easy task,
as not only was *Maestro* attached to the Imperial School,
but he also had a school of his own, full of promising
pupils. But Diaghileff finally succeeded in winning him
over, and *Maestro* resigned from the Imperial School,
leaving his own in the charge of his wife, and arrived
in Monte Carlo, sighing, cursing, *"Corpo di Bacco,* I can't
have peace anywhere. Vaslav Fomitch, you don't need
me. Where is the rehearsal room, anyway?"

And so they began to practise in the Palais de Soleil,
a disused theatre. Diaghileff took occasional trips to
Paris, and had long conferences with Gabriel Astruc and
Marinelli, his French impresarios, and Eric Wollheim, who
was to manage the affairs for his first London season.

It was at this time that Nijinsky met the Marchioness of
Ripon. The Marchioness was an extremely interesting and
delightful woman, who was not only one of the most
prominent leaders of London Society of her time, but also
a great patron of the arts. She had organised many special
performances in her London house, as well as in her beautiful country place at Coombe Court, where she received
the leading artists of the world. Through her intimate
friendship with King Edward and Queen Alexandra she
had been able to give a great deal of aid to her friends.
She was an extraordinary personality, kind, helpful, conscious of all the small weaknesses of the society in which
she moved. She went back and forth from Paris to Monte
Carlo, and Sergei Pavlovitch grew more and more dependent on her.

In March of 1911 the Russian Ballet appeared for the
first time in Rome, at the Teatro Costanza. The Russians
were extremely nervous about their Italian reception.
There had been a century-old rivalry between the Italian
and the Russian schools of dancing, and there was a
definitely organised party of opposition which arrived *en*

masse at the *première*. All Maestro Cecchetti's friends had come to the rehearsals.

When an old Italian ballet-master had visited *Maestro* in St. Petersburg, he said: "Yes, your Russians are marvellous, but they have the mannerisms of ducks." He meant that from the Italian point of view their limbs were not flexible enough. For Cecchetti had realised, almost as soon as he had come to Russia, that there was something about the bony structure of the Russians which was different from the more supple Latins, and he based his style on the limitations and possibilities of his new pupils. With that in mind he answered his old friend: "We may dance like ducks. It is of no importance. You dance like frogs!"

On the first night, with the opposition grimly entrenched in the orchestra stalls, the company was pardonably anxious. And when the dancing started the whole audience broke into loud whistling. The hearts of the dancers dropped. It seemed a complete failure, their first. They did not know then that whistling was the Roman mode of applause.

Sergei Pavlovitch used to take Vaslav and Karsavina off sightseeing. He wanted to show them the Coliseum in sunlight and in moonlight, the Catacombs, the Campagna, the Vatican, San Pietro. Cecchetti was almost apoplectic. Sightseeing was all very well for Diaghileff. He didn't have to dance. For dancers it was a rank waste of time. They should stick to the perfecting of their pirouettes and leave antiquity to their old age.

Scriabine, the composer, was also in Rome, giving concerts and piano recitals, with the simultaneous projection of rays of light from an early colour organ; there was Marinetti and the first excitement of his Futurist Manifestos, and they would all investigate the biggest and the smallest and the best restaurants for chianti and spaghetti, and soon learned to wind the limp strands around their forks like natives.

Fokine was busily rehearsing *Petrouchka* in a big hall underneath the stage of the Teatro Costanza. The others had to be shown their dances in detail by the *maître de ballet,* but Nijinsky was so familiar with the vocabulary of the dance that he merely had to be told, and the steps indicated by Fokine's fingers: "Here you do two pirouettes *à la seconde,* then a *tour en l'air,* then a *fouetté* to the right, *pas de bourrée* back, and finish the phrase with an arabesque." Vaslav could retain the directions in his memory, and rehearse whole sequences in his mind. Fokine and Vaslav enjoyed working together, because the one could actually see the designs the other had invented at the very moment of conception.

Unlike playwrights who can write speeches for actors once and for all, and unlike composers who can transcribe in a legible notation for their performers, choreographers not only had to compose ballets, but teach the arrangement of the composition, every time a new ballet is composed, because, although there were several systems of choreographic notation, practically all of them were unintelligible.

Petrouchka was perhaps Fokine's greatest masterpiece, although he didn't realise it at the time, and *Petrouchka* was Vaslav's favourite part. It grew on him as he became more and more used to it; and the longer he danced it the more monumental was his conception. The superb rôle of the marionette called for an unusually gifted dancer to interpret the gay, pathetic, and extremely difficult steps, but Vaslav amplified the crazy doll into the symbol of the spirit of the Russian people, oppressed by autocracy, but resurgent and unconquerable after all its abuse and frustration.

Pavillon d'Armide was still, to all intents and purposes, a *ballet d'action. Scheherazade* was a brilliant excuse for dancing, *Carnaval* a series of exquisitely tender dance scenes; but *Petrouchka* was the first danced drama of our day, and it has parallels, in its combination of music and dancing, with the intention, if not the realisation, of Wagner's music dramas, with their synthesis of action and orchestration.

Petrouchka was twenty-five years ahead of *Scheherazade,* which had been a striking innovation of the year before. *Petrouchka* and Nijinsky's choreography of

L'Après-midi d'un Faune are the greatest steps in the development of ballet since Marius Petipa.

The choreography was extremely complex. The action in the street scene, with its entrances of coachmen and nursemaids, gypsies and mendicants, soldiers and *moujiks,* were not merely round dances, but interlocking patterns of continuous action, against which the tragedy of the Moor, the Magician, the Ballerina, and the Marionette is mimed.

Nijinsky grapsed at once the infinite possibilities of the marionette with the living soul.

As the Magician touched the three hanging puppets they came to life. Nijinsky's Petrouchka made one convulsive movement like dead matter suddenly charged with electricity. This *pas de trois,* danced in a mad *tempo,* is the quintessence of choreographic technique, and, while the face of Petrouchka is blank, his scintillating feet execute steps of incredible virtuosity.

Petrouchka, poor, roughly handled doll, suffers from the Magician, who personifies Autocracy, from the unfaithfulness of the Ballerina whom he loves, and from the maltreatment of his rival, the Moor. Alone in his room, Petrouchka kneels, then whirls round, trying to break through the walls. A series of pirouettes and gestures of the arms is all the movement. But Nijinsky succeeded in rendering so convincingly the sorrows of the ill-treated captive, his utter despair, his jealousy, his longing for liberty, and his resentfulness towards his gaoler, that Sarah Bernhardt, on witnessing the performance, said, *"J'ai peur, j'ai peur, car je vois l'acteur le plus grand du monde."*

When Ellen Terry saw it in England she became Nijinsky's fervent admirer.

When Sergei Pavlovitch had been working in St. Petersburg, there was his own circle of artists and musicians at his beck and call. He could spend as many easy evenings as he wanted over as many leisurely glasses of tea as they could drink, discussing what they would do next season in Paris. But now, actually travelling in Western Europe, everything was different. In Rome he had to be planning for three weeks ahead in Berlin. In Berlin, there was

Paris, not two weeks off. And in Paris there was a packed two months, followed immediately by London. There was not only the worry of arrangements, but the multiple difficulties of securing guarantees.

Stravinsky would dash in, worried and upset because his child had come down with measles and he could not finish *Petrouchka*. Fokine would object that Fokina had not been given the parts she wanted. Suddenly a wire would be brought in from St. Petersburg: Karsavina was not free till next Thursday, and if she arrived in Berlin at 8:30, could they make *Cléopâtre* the last ballet of the performance? If Kshessinskaya was given a bigger part than Kyasht, which would be angrier? Where in God's name were those shoes ordered for Vaslav Fomitch ten days ago? Have they made sure that the width of the stage in Berlin will fit the scenery for *Scheherazade?* Will Sergei Pavlovitch please speak to M. Bakst himself this time, and make sure? We know what happened last time. Will the lights be correct? Do we get new reflectors? Could Monteux have the next orchestra ready in time, adequately rehearsed for the special *tempi* the ballets demanded? It was a terrific strain on Sergei Pavlovitch, but he had his staff of secretaries, *aides,* and assistants, who would execute his wishes and commands in the constant turmoil and confusion of the tours. There was Drobetsky, a charming Austro-Pole from Lemberg. He was married to the dancer Sofia Pflanz, and he spoke Russian, Polish, French, German, and English with ease. He was thin and nervous, with a blond, droopy moustache, and was the centre of the Polish group of the Ballet company. Both the Russians and the Poles had their separate social lives, away from the scenes of the ballet, where they would play cards or dominoes, or go sightseeing, or generally amuse themselves at restaurants and cafés. Drobetsky made most of the salary payments and bought railway tickets. Sergei Pavlovitch drove him nearly crazy. He would never tell him what he had personally arranged, and poor Drobetsky might do all the work over again before he discovered that Diaghileff had already seen to it. The Press would arrive to get information. Diaghileff might refuse to see them, but he would be furious with Drobetsky if he presumed to give any interviews himself.

Then there was a certain courier. He had been an anarchist living in London and he was never allowed to return to Russia. He was hard, direct, and extremely efficient—the advance agent—and could go through any necessary dirty business coolly and never speak of it again. He was a kind of secret agent or spy of Diaghileff's, but, though no gentleman, he was by no account mean or untrustworthy.

Tsauschovsky was the chief electrician and prop man. He had charge of all transportation of scenery and properties and was a superb technician. He had a flat nose, spoke excellent French, and eventually died from an extreme preoccupation with women.

Dmitri Kamuchov had red hair and a beard like a Greek Orthodox pope. He was suave, and spoke all the European languages. He was a kind of maid-of-all-work, good-looking, with excellent manners, and slightly common. And there was Grigoriev, a thin Slav, the typical bureaucratic employee. It was then his job to come in and knock: "M. Nijinsky, Madame Karsavina has just finished her first variation."

A superb wig-maker, who constructed all the elaborate head-dresses for the ballet by himself, always accompanied them. And of course there was Maria Stepanovna, the wardrobe mistress, who was on hand when Bakst was designing his costumes, and who was always consulted on their actual making. It was she who went along with him to choose materials, because, once a dress was made, it had to be reduplicated time and again during the season. The stiff white tarlatan *tutus,* for example, used in *Les Sylphides,* were thrown away as spoiled after each performance. The tights for the dancers were made by Châtelet of Paris, and every so often great crates of ballet-shoes would arrive from Nicolini in Milan. Nijinsky's shoes were now made of special kid by Georges of London.

Diaghileff's chancellor of the exchequer and treasurer of the Russian Ballet was Baron Dmitri Gunsburg, a Rus-

sian Jew of a famous banking house. Part of his large
family lived in Vienna. They were only less important
than the Rothschilds. Gunsburg was blond, with a pale
moustache, extremely well dressed and cosmopolitan, the
soul of kindness and a delightfully gay and entertaining
man. He liked women a great deal, and could never understand Diaghileff's intolerance of them. He would flirt
politely with the girls of the Ballet, but he would never
become in the least intimate with them, treating them
rather as an owner of bloodstock would feel towards his
famous stables. At *premières* he would always send
Karsavina great bouquets, and Vaslav a watch or cuff-
links or a pin. He was devoted to Vaslav. Gunsburg was
slightly terrified of Sergei Pavlovitch, who would say,
"Dmitri, let me have thirty [or forty or fifty] thousand
francs, will you? There's a good fellow." He financed
everything with his own cash, and it was his pleasure to do
so. He always had to have quantities of ready cash, but
he loved to travel with the Ballet, in the heart of the excitement, and it gave him a unique position at home,
backing the Ballet as he did. He would occasionally return to St. Petersburg to attend to his family and his
business affairs, and he was always greeted as the brilliant
financier who preferred to follow in the train of art than
pile up more gold. He was shot by the Bolsheviks in the
early days of the revolution.

In Berlin they presented the Ballet at the Theater des
Westens, which was at some distance from the heart of the
city.

Kaiser Wilhelm announced he would be present at the
première but through his Court Chamberlain he ordered
that the dancers should appear in tights in *Cléopâtre,* for
the benefit of the priggish Prussian Court audience. Diaghileff flatly refused to have the dancers do any such
thing. "Either he will look at us as we are, or we shall
not give the performance." But, in spite of this rebuff, the
Emperor came with his suite, and was so delighted with
the Russians that he had the dancers presented to him
afterwards.

Vaslav was oblivious to most of this. It meant little or

nothing when the gossip was repeated to him later. He met hardly anybody because he was so preoccupied with *Petrouchka,* with Stravinsky and Fokine. Besides, the public of Berlin was not the same to him as the Parisian audience which he loved. But he and Diaghileff were delightfully entertained by the great Herr Doktor Bode of the Kaiser Friedrich's Museum, who showed them the magnificent examples of Italian painting and sculpture which he was collecting for Germany.

Diaghileff, who cordially hated the ubiquitous Prussian efficiency, indulged in the snobbism of pretending to speak only French, although he knew German perfectly well, and he did little to endear himself to the German people, either to the artists or to the *Junkers,* and they had their unconscious and probably unsuspected revenge.

Vassily usually sent their wash out every week. When it was brought back, he sometimes paid cash for it and sometimes did not. It was often forgotten as too small an item to be considered. But in Berlin, instead of sending a bill, which might eventually have been honoured, the laundry sent a warrant officer with a summons. Vaslav was told that the police were raiding their trunks and they were to be arrested as Russian spies. He decided all Germans were secret agents in disguise, and was in a constant state of nerves at what he took to be their unfriendliness.

The little choreographic poem called *Spectre de la Rose,* which was inspired by Théophile Gautier's poetry, became a gem among Fokine's compositions. Merely intended as a *divertissement* to fill out the programme, and hurriedly composed, it was so exquisite that it became a classic.

A young girl returning from her first ball leans against the French window of her room and dreamingly recalls all the pleasant impressions of the evening. She thinks of her ideal, and slowly kisses the rose he gave her, which she was wearing in her bodice. Intoxicated by the spring air, the scent of the rose, she falls asleep on a near-by chair. Suddenly the soul of the rose, an intangible, dreamlike apparition, emerges from the moonlit window, in a single leap behind the dreaming girl, as if blown by a soft caressing wind. Is it the scent of the rose, or the echo of a promising love? We do not know. A slender sexless being, ethereal, soft, enfolding, stands before us. Not a flower, not a human being. Both. You cannot tell whether it is a youth or a maiden, a dream, or a wish, something unobtainable—something we can only sense. Slender and beautiful, like an unfolding rose, the warm smoothness of the velvety purple petals, sensuous and pure at the same time. With infinite tenderness a full moment it stands at the sill of the window. *Le Spectre de la Rose.* Then in its glorious lightness it whirls through space. It is not dancing, nor yet a dream. We feel everything pure, lovely, beautiful. Here reality and vision meet.

With one single leap he crosses the entire stage, bringing us the fulfilment of our dreams; the scent of a blossoming garden on a June night, moonlight, mysterious but so infinitely restful. There he is floating, floating enchantingly. Suddenly he stands behind the girl and awakens her to a dazed, semi-conscious state, where she finds her wishes, her dreams, her love itself, in beauty. He carries her through the ether, enchanting, caressing, loving, offering her with a chaste gesture the essence of love, and revives in her all the happy moments of her inmost feelings at her first ball, and, when she glides softly into the chair, falls at her feet to prove its tender submission. Then, with one incredibly light leap, he rises high in the air and once more dances around her, re-echoing the beauty in its supreme conception. The girl, soft, trusting, slumbers, but the spirit of the rose can only be held for one second against our heart. After conquering the space in which he floats he is again behind the girl as at the beginning. With one soft kiss he gives her a part of the unattainable and then forever leaps into the infinite.

That was the *Spectre de la Rose* that Nijinsky gave to us: the romantic poem of Gautier, the perfect classical *pas de deux* of Fokine, with the soul breathed into it by Nijinsky. This charming variation, this lovely Biedermeier picture of Bakst's, became a very prayer. As Vaslav was told, *Spectre de la Rose* made one want to cry from bliss. He told me, "I wanted to express beauty, purity, love—above all, love in its divine sense. Art, love, nature, are only an infinitesimal part of God's spirit. I wanted to recapture it and to give it to the public so that they may know He is omnipresent. If they felt it, then I was reflecting Him." So he did to all of us who were fortunate enough to see him. We knew that we had not only witnessed an artistic performance, but the communion of an initiate with divinity.

Bakst created the chamber of a young girl, high, fresh, white, and blue. Under a great muslin curtain is her alcoved bed, near to it her embroidery frame; against one wall a pink cretonned couch, a white table, and on it a white bowl of roses. At both sides and at the back huge French windows open to the gardens of night.

Bakst wanted to hang a cage with two canaries in it by a ribbon from the centre to the window. But Nijinsky asked, "How will I ever get in?" Every time the cage was taken down and hung somewhere else, Bakst would replace it almost in tears.

Nijinsky's famous last leap in *Spectre,* in which he crossed the whole stage, from the front to the back, in a single bound, was an astonishing *tour de force.* He became almost annoyed with this part, which he had loved so much in the beginning, as everyone constantly associated him with this leap. That's why he used to say, *"Je ne suis pas un sauteur; je suis un artiste."* After the first performance, Marinelli, the London impresario, asked Vassily to show him Vaslav's shoes, to see whether or not they had rubber soles. Many others inspected the stage for traps or other mechanical contrivances. When he made his entrance back stage, Cocteau and the others watched him carefully, almost as if to find out if he were hiding charms in his shoes to aid him.

At the *première,* Jean-Louis Vaudoyer, the poet who had had the original idea for the ballet, came up to Fokine, its choreographer, almost in tears, from gratitude. He said Fokine had created a perfect thing. It was more Gautier than the poem itself; it was a triumph. Fokine

was a genius. Fokine tried to stop him, deprecated his
own part, reminded him that after all he had also something to do with it. "Nothing," cried Vaudoyer; "all I did
was to introduce Théophile Gautier to Michel Fokine."

At the performances the wings were so crowded with
spectators waiting for the final leap that electricians and
stage hands would storm at people of great importance,
friends of Diaghileff or Astruc, who had been magnetised
by the phenomenon. Finally a special prohibitive ruling
had to be made because the work of the technicians was
seriously impeded.

I did not see *Spectre* back stage until London. I was
surprised when I was asked to get out of the way. Four
men—Nijinsky's *masseur,* Mr. Williams; the chief property
man; Michel, and Vassily—held their eight hands together,
crossed, to form a net, and against this I was astonished
to see Nijinsky land. As he stood there panting under
the hissing Klieg lights, Williams massaged his heart and
Vassily applied wet cold towels under his distended nos-
trils.

Bakst's original design for the costume was done on
Nijinsky himself. He sketched it on the shirt Nijinsky was
wearing. Bakst had painted samples of silk pongee, in rose,
rose lavender, dark reds, and various pinks, and these
were given to Maria Stepanovna to have bolts of the material dyed. Bakst cut the forms of the rose-petals himself.
Some had to be tight, others loose, and he instructed her
just how to sew them on so that the costume was created
anew each time Nijinsky danced. It consisted of a close-
fitting, fine silk elastic jersey, into which Nijinsky was
sewn, covering his entire body, except part of his breast
and arms, where bracelets of silk rose-petals bound his
biceps. This jersey was stitched with rose-leaves, which
Bakst would colour as they were needed. Some were
ragged, as from a dying flower; others were stiff and firm;
while still others curled even from his thighs. And after
every performance Maria Stepanovna would refresh them
with her curling-iron. On his head he wore a close-fitting
helmet of rose-leaves, and the whole effect was an extremely close blending of different reds, rose-violet, pink,

and purple, shading one into another, which is the essential indefinable tint of the rose.

Nijinsky's make-up was conceived to personify a rose. His face was like that of a celestial insect, his eyebrows suggesting some beautiful beetle which one might expect to find closest to the heart of a rose, and his mouth was like rose-petals.

The costume seemed always to disintegrate mysteriously after each time it was used. It was sent up, with the others, to be refurbished, yet somehow or other it was always shorn of many of its petals. This happened again and again. No one could explain it. Maria Stepanovna, intrigued by the affair, made a special investigation on her own account. She found out that Vassily had built himself a house out of the petals of the rose, which he would clip off the costume to sell as souvenirs to the sentimental ladies of Paris, who stormed him with their secret requests. Zenon, Drobetsky, and the rest of the staff called it the "Château du Spectre de la Rose," and told Vassily that he had Vaslav Fomitch to thank for making him a capitalist.

The dancers were not supposed to eat or drink before a performance. But Vaslav, to moisten his lips and throat during a dance, would rinse his mouth with water and orange-juice and spit it out. Cecchetti flew into a violent rage if he caught anybody swallowing a mouthful, and took great delight in telling the story of a dancer who drank black coffee before a performance, and died of heart failure.

When Diaghileff tired of the elaborate food of Larue's or Foyot's, he would take Vaslav, Bakst, Benois, and Stravinsky to the Restaurant Viand in the Rue Donau. It was a tiny place with a single door off the pavement, and two tables on the *rez de chaussée*. Madame Viand was a good French *bourgeoise;* who went herself to *les halles* every morning and picked out the food she would cook. At home, she sat at the *caisse,* with a little stair going up behind her to the two or three private rooms, observing everyone who came and went with the minutest scrutiny. Monsieur Viand was an energetic if

patronising host. He always knew beforehand, and for
years afterwards, exactly what M. Bakst or M. Nijinsky
liked to eat, and one could never order independently,
since he insisted he knew far better than they. He always
said he was the man actually behind the Russian Ballet,
because if they didn't eat food they could digest, they
couldn't dance. But he was terrified of Madame. She was
a remarkable woman, providing superb *merlan, éperlans
frites,* and excellent Vouvray, and Sergei Pavlovitch always asked her advice and opinion on the affairs of the
Ballet and its effect on the people of Paris.

Lady Ripon made a great many of the initial and most
influential arrangements for Diaghileff's first season at
Covent Garden, and Eric Wollheim, a clever and honest
impresario, administered all the actual business. Sergei
Pavlovitch always demanded a cash guarantee of forty
thousand gold francs a night, so that he could be assured
of losing only a minimum amount, and Sir Joseph
Beecham backed the performances.

Lady Ripon knew how to handle Diaghileff better than
most women. She loved Vaslav like a son, and gave him
much solid and lasting counsel. At first he couldn't speak
to her at all, but from the beginning he had a profound
affection for her. She also liked Sergei Pavlovitch and admired him, of course, but she knew very well just how to
make him keep his distance from her affection for Vaslav.
She was Nijinsky's first real friend, apart from Diaghileff.
She had plans for him. She wanted him to marry, and
later, when he did, she was one of the very few who
continued to stand by him. She felt he should be released
from the powerful influence of Diaghileff.

The English audiences had been accustomed to good
dancing. They had taken to themselves Adeline Genée,
a fine classical *ballerina,* whom they adored. They had
seen Anna Pavlova in variety, as well as the enchanting
Karsavina, with her own small troupe. They had read
the extravagant praise lavished on the Russian Ballet by
the French Press, and with their characteristic scepticism
put it all down to the usual Parisian enthusiasm at the
dernier cri. Nevertheless, this time there was an added

note of conviction in the Continental praise, and there were not a few Englishmen who had actually seen the Russians at the Châtelet, the Opéra, at Monte Carlo even, so there was more than a mere rumour that marvels awaited London.

It was the year of the coronation of King George the Fifth and Queen Mary. And for the coronation a gala performance was to be given before a Covent Garden filled with people who symbolised the last great aristocracy of the world. The programmes were to be printed in gold on sheets of white silk.

That foreign artists were commanded to appear at a special coronation performance was very unusual, and the Russians felt a great honour had been bestowed upon them. The Queen Mother of England, Alexandra, was the sister of Maria Feodorovna, Dowager Empress of Russia, and a great friend of Lady Ripon, who had much to do with the actual arrangements of the occasion. The command performance took place in Covent Garden on the 26th of June, 1911. The programme included excerpts from three operas—*Aïda* with Destinn, *Romeo and Juliet* with Melba, *Barber of Seville* with Tetrazzini and McCormack—and our *Pavillon d'Armide* with Nijinsky, Karsavina, Bolm, Cecchetti, Nijinskaya; Tcherepnin conducting the Ballet. Everybody was nervous. It was an unusual experience to dance in so full a blaze. Thousands of lights illuminated the theatre, thousands of opera-glasses darted at them. They could not help being distracted by the audience, the most fantastic ever seen. The whole theatre, decorated with roses, formed a beautiful garden, peopled with gorgeous uniforms and the exotic splendour of the Oriental costumes of the representation of India, Persia, and the Far East. The royal box scintillated with diamonds. The artists all felt that they danced badly.

Chaliapine sang part of his most famous rôle, *Boris Godounov*. Just before he was to go on, one of the chorus from the Imperial Opera in St. Petersburg caused a disturbance (as in a similar incident occurring three years later) saying that the great bass had struck him, and the entire choir refused to appear. Nothing could persuade them to change their minds. They stubbornly would not go on. Meanwhile the new King and Queen of England waited in the royal box, banked with pink roses. Finally Diaghîleff, in utter desperation, by an almost superhuman force of will, ordered the performance to continue, and by threats of group expulsion from the Imperial Theatres forced them to sing.

After the performance the dancers were terribly depressed and disgusted, for nobody from the Court appeared to congratulate or thank them, as was usual in Russia, and they did not even receive a souvenir programme. They had been quite spoiled in Russia, always receiving personal praise from the Emperor and Empress, and costly presents as souvenirs. Diaghileff swore, and then set out to get a souvenir programme for Vaslav.

But, everything considered, the Russian Ballet was a great success in London. The English public was more quiet, courteous, and reserved in its appreciation than the French. Vaslav always felt that in England he could really relax. And the loyalty of the English audience could be depended upon. He knew that if he came back to London at the age of sixty-five, unable to turn a single pirouette, they would still applaud him for what he had been.

Lady Ripon acted as their social manager. She advised them to change their headquarters to the Savoy, which was à la mode. She told Diaghileff which invitations to accept and which to decline. And she arranged enchanting weekends for them at the great English country houses.

Another most charming society hostess became one of Nijinsky's good friends, and wished to have as close a relationship with him as Lady Ripon. She would come to call every morning at the hotel, with her arms full of cut tulips, jonquils, and fresh roses, and look at him adoringly. She was very sweet, and amused him very much. He was extremely fond of her, and she tried to arrange little parties to entertain him. She was sure he was bored, because, speaking no English and little French, he was usually silent. So she asked Harry Melville, the great London dandy of his day, to amuse him. Melville talked delightfully, like a fine French raconteur.

Nijinsky listened attentively, and after a long silence ventured only: *"Little Tich, c'est un très grand artist."* The talk went on and on, and then silence, and again Nijinsky's simple question, comment, and answer: *"Little Tich, c'est un très grand artist. N'est ce pas?"*

In London it was so much easier than in Paris. Lady Ripon would simply say: "I must have Vatza for the week-end," and she would take him on the private days to Hampton Court or Windsor, and leave him to wander in the gardens for a whole afternoon; or to Arundel Castle, England's greatest Catholic house, the Duke of Norfolk's seat.

Chapter Nine

NIJINSKY AS
CHOREOGRAPHER

EVER SINCE his departure from the Mariinsky, Nijinsky's life had passed in ceaseless work, dancing the old repertoire and the numerous novelties across the Continent, on many stages, in many countries. It was a strenuous, difficult life, with constant journeying, new theatres, new orchestras, fresh audiences, which might easily destroy the health of an artist as well as his creative impulse.

But on Nijinsky it had a different effect. His intuitive conception of his art, his associative ideas, were only strengthened as he crossed Europe from one place to another, coming in close contact not only with the artistic past, but also with the living creations of these countries. He silently observed, admired, and criticised what he saw, and lived it. He selected the different lively impres-

sions, strained them through his essential taste, retaining
a great deal and throwing off the surplus.

During these years, when he triumphed all over Europe,
and to all appearances was utterly absorbed in his dancing with the Russian Ballet, a tremendous change took
place in him. He was developing from the graceful,
technically perfect dancer of the classical ballet, which
achieved its brilliance through grace, lightness, and fluent
line of beauty, to the contemplative revolutionary who
wanted to throw over the very attributes which made him
famous. In the early part of 1912, Nijinsky, the interpretative artist, became the creative.

In St. Petersburg it had already been noticed that there
was a different quality in his dancing from anyone else's.
But this was perhaps due more to the supremacy of his
technique and the adaptability of his body. In his Parisian creation one could see more clearly the change which
was taking place in him. He had danced the rôles in
Fokine's ballets with consummate perfection, not only as
Fokine wished and dreamed, but over and above this he
gave a personality, a particular soul, to each part, which
even amazed its choreographer, who recognised that this
indeed was the very character itself. Here Nijinsky first
showed his creative power, and in the summer of 1911, in
Karlsbad, he formulated his initial ideas on *L'Après-midi
d'un Faune.*

Petrouchka, his favourite part, gave him his initial opportunity to show his faculty as an actor. The whole conception of this ballet was nearer to Nijinsky's own ideas.
While he was dancing it, he felt full of a swelling energy,
a latent strength released, a sense of his own individual
capacity for origination, which gave to the part an unusual intensity. Nijinsky was overtaken by an irresistible
urge to create.

Nijinsky felt that the real liberation of ballet had not
yet taken place. Duncan and Fokine had sensed it, but
had failed to carry it out to the full. Both were fundamentally founded on grace and the circular movement,
Duncan without technique, Fokine in its full possession.
Why did they fail? Duncan wished to throw over every-

thing, good or bad, that had ever been done before.
Fokine brought a new impulse into the older conception,
made a step forward, but both missed the essential truth.
Dance is the art of producing and combining movement.
It has not only to express a dramatic action or an emotion, but the movements of the dancer must be each
penetrated by the living idea. The idea underlying, as in
all art, must be the basis also of the art of movement.
There Nijinsky made a very definite distinction between
movement and the dance, which is a combination of
movements. It was clear to him that the first and most
important thing is to express an idea through movement,
as a writer through words, as a musician through notes
on a scale. It is so clear, so simple, that one can hardly
understand why no one, from Noverre to Fokine, discovered this truth before, and as the dancer of the twentieth
century he did not find an adequate vehicle of self-ex-
pression in the technique of the past, just as the accepted
stage language of pantomime was useless to him in comparison with his personal method of conveying his mean-
ings.

The "antique," the "mediæval," the "classic," and the
"romantic" were different schools to Nijinsky.

His conception of the art of dancing was limitless, its
variety of modes infinite. He took his first radical step
by attacking the idea which was closest to most of us, by
rejecting grace, charm, fluency, and the whole classical
technique. He created a new technique and demonstrated
that the classical steps, such as *entrechats,* pirouettes,
tours en l'air, could also be made by eliminating the whole
school based on the five positions. Any imaginable movement is good in dancing if it suits the idea which is its
subject, but it has to be based on some formulated
technique.

Nijinsky, therefore, treated movement literally, as the
poet the word. He eliminated, consequently, the floating,
sinuous gestures, the half-gestures, and every unnecessary
move. He allowed only definitely rhythmic and absolutely
essential steps, as in verse one uses only the words needed
to express the idea, without rhetoric or embroidery for

its own sake. He established a prosody of movement—
one single movement for a single action. He shows this
first clearly in *Faune,* as in all his ensuing creations. He
uses immobility consciously for the first time in the history
of dancing, for he knew that immobility could accentuate
action often better than action itself, just as an interval
of silence can be more effective than a sound. He introduced a new theory in the facts of plastic expression,
which until now he had only sensed and imagined but
had never revealed, for he realised fully that dancing
is not an art of fixed principles but an art which has as
its progressive purpose the expression of human personality and ideas.

Nijinsky revolutionised dancing by bringing it to its
fundamental principles in the use of straight lines and
angles, but only as an opposition to the serpentine and
the spiral, on which all former dancing was conceived.
The straight line was by no means his ultimate aim. It
was merely a form of expression he voluntarily chose to
liberate movement, by proving that any line or angle and
every form can be good in its proper place. His great
innovation lay in that he created an utterly new technique,
which is no less important than the previous ones of the
older schools. In *L'Après-midi d'un Faune,* as in the
Sacre du Printemps, the movements are based on this
technique. The feet are no longer turned out, toe to heel,
heel to toe, as in the classical five positions, but all those
movements of the body and the five positions are reversed. He showed that what might first be thought to be
ugliness and primitivism can be as perfect a form of
expression as the far too easily accepted beauty and
charm. He took crude movements on purpose, to change
our conception fundamentally. Every movement can be
made in the art; all movements are possible if they are
in harmony with the basic truth of the conception, even
in their most violent and dissonant gestures.

Duncan, like Fokine, understood Greece as the gracious
billowy curves of the Parthenon friezes. Nijinsky, with
his *Faune,* took an utterly different view. It is the severity
of Attic carving, the simplicity and faith of the pre-Phei-

dian sculptors against the charm and elegance of Praxiteles, significant character against grace. For Nijinsky, the conception of art is to express the most one can with as few simple, monumental gestures as possible; Pheidias and Michelangelo against Praxiteles and Giovanni da Bologna. The nineteenth-century *maîtres de ballet* were strongly influenced by the Græco-Roman remains, and they entrusted the dramatic part of their ballets into the hands of pantomimists, who acted without dancing, while the *ballerinas* danced without acting. They concentrated on the perfection of their vocabulary of steps, regardless of the idea of the drama or period, *décor* or costume.

Praxiteles, in his stone, concentrated on elegance, grace, beauty equally, regardless of whether or not his subject was divine, human, or demon. Nijinsky always rebelled against this grace of form for the mere sake of grace. To express a literary and a moral idea was his aim, and therefore he brought acting and dancing together through the medium of movement.

Before him, all the stories of ballets through the centuries were placed in settings which explained the dancing. The Court festivals of the Petipa ballets, *Sleeping Beauty, Swan Lake,* later *Armide,* the harem of *Scheherazade,* the bacchanals in *Cléopâtre,* the flirtation of *Carnaval,* all explain that dancing is logical under the circumstances.

Nijinsky for the first time used and treated dancing as an absolute medium, without excuse or explanation, in *L'Après-midi d'un Faune.* The tennis game of *Jeux,* the activity and death of *Tyl Eulenspiegel,* do not call for dancing as a form, and, in spite of this, the drama, with its climax, was expressed clearly through the medium of the dance.

These ideas on the art of choreography were very clear and definite in Nijinsky's mind. They had been developing during the years of his travels, but he did not speak of them, even to Sergei Pavlovitch, who until now had been unaware of Nijinsky's desire to compose. *L'Après-midi d'un Faune* was thought of first while they stayed at the Villa Schæffler in Karlsbad during the summer of 1911.

Nijinsky took for his subject a simple incident from

ordinary life which happens to every human being: the initial awakening of emotional and sexual instincts and their reaction. The day-dreams, the longings, of a modern schoolboy are similar to the half-voiced desires of those primitive creatures, the ancestors of man, part animal, part male human being. A young boy lies half asleep on a hot, suffocating afternoon; the surroundings weigh in upon him, and he has unconscious, imperative desires for which he cannot account but which he wishes to satisfy. Some girls appear, and he tries to caress them. As soon as he becomes more insistent, they take fright and run away. He has himself no idea what has happened. He is hurt and disappointed. An object lost by one of the girls is found by him. He smells its scent, and the person who lost it suddenly appears before him in his imagination. He kisses it, and, by holding it close to him, the associations of the object satisfy the desires of his dream. An everyday incident of fetichism.

This subject Nijinsky took and placed in the period of archaic Greece, connected in his mind with the firm adolescence of art. The little dramatic action in this plastic choreographic poem is expressed through the absolute medium of movement. Should we produce the *Faune* without music, it would be a complete harmonious whole. It requires no accessories. It is explicit in itself.

That he chose this subject to present his ideas and methods in choreographic art can be explained by the fact that he himself at this period went through the first impulses, not only of creation, but of his mature emotional life. Until now he was not awakened. He had been the obedient pupil, then the dancer, always completely and absolutely concentrated on the dictates of his art. All his emotional experiences of everyday life he unconsciously passed through and absorbed into his art. Until now he was an instrument of choreography, essentially and completely (as Pavlova was all her life), but now life and his instincts claimed their due. The experience with X. was superficial. It gave Nijinsky a different outlook on people, on nature. Those with Diaghileff were merely a proof of his devotion and admiration for Sergei Pavlovitch, a gratitude expressed in the way it most pleased Diaghileff. He was always seeking to discover the truth in art and life. In these early years of their friendship Nijinsky was convinced that Sergei Pavlovitch's attitude to life and love was the right one. In artistic questions he was in a position to argue and defend his own opinions, but in life he gave the older man the lead.

Now, for the first time, he felt that perhaps there was something else somewhere, something else different, of which Sergei Pavlovitch was not aware, and could never comprehend. His fallibility began to dawn on Nijinsky. His own impulses were too strong for personal restriction, and had to find some outlet. Naturally, with Nijinsky they found their way through creative expression, and he conceived the idea of *Faune*.

He had thought much about these problems for months and months. Already, when *Narcisse* was produced, he mentioned to Diaghileff that the Dionysian Greece of Fokine was by no means the best period, and rather a decadent one at that. As the idea of *Daphnis and Chloe* came up, he said to Sergei Pavlovitch, "I have in mind a choreographic poem, not a ballet, which I would like to do. My idea of Greece is utterly different from Bakst's and Fokine's." Diaghileff was interested and amused. "Why, Vatza, why not work on it?"

"I have done so," said Nijinsky, "and the whole *œuvre* is already quite clear. Of course, I should like to have the music composed for it."

Diaghileff became enthusiastic, and encouraged Nijinsky, but he wanted to have it produced as soon as possible, in the next season. They began to consider the composers from whom they could draw, so that one could be commissioned to do the music. Sergei Pavlovitch wanted to know all about his plans for *Faune,* but Nijinsky insisted that he would show him only at the rehearsals, because otherwise he would not understand what he was trying to do. So Diaghileff began to go through the literature of music after Nijinsky explained to him his ideas of Greece. Hours and hours they spent at the piano, but they totally failed to find what they wanted. Finally there was

Debussy's *L'Après-midi d'un Faune*. Nijinsky was enchanted. Yes, the feeling, the atmosphere, was exactly
what he wished, but the music was too circular, too soft
for the movement he had conceived. In everything, except
its lack of angularity, it was the very thing he wanted,
so finally, *faute de mieux,* he decided to use it, realising
that the musical movement would not be the same as his
own plastic expression. The piece was composed in 1891,
after the Eclogue of Mallarmé, so naturally it could not
echo the ideas that Nijinsky wanted twenty years later.
But the underlying feeling was the same. The criticism
that the choreography and the music were in angular and
circular opposition, later voiced in the press, was correct,
and known from the first by Nijinsky. But no existing
piece was more suitable, and there seemed no time to call
in a composer. Sergei Pavlovitch went over to see
Debussy, whom he had known ever since the musician's
visit years before to Russia, and Debussy was delighted
that a work of his should be used, and gladly gave his
permission.

The coronation season was over. The troupe split up,
departed, and went on their vacations back to Russia.
Diaghileff had had many conferences during the season
with Bakst and Fokine, to whom he wished to entrust
the novelties which were contemplated for the coming season. The company by this time was firmly established, and
it was sufficient to send Nouvel or Drobetsky to Russia
and Poland to make offers for Diaghileff for new members
of the Ballet.

Fokine, until now, had been absolute *maître de ballet.*
The ballets, apart from the ones of his own designing,
were all of the classical period. Diaghileff, in the coming
season, was making two distinct innovations—the introduction of Nijinsky as a choreographer, and a foreign, a
French, composer in the person of Debussy. Also a Jean
Cocteau–Madrazo–Reynaldo Hahn ballet was contemplated—the East Indian legend of the Blue God.
Maurice Ravel was composing the music for *Daphnis and
Chloe.* The single Russian novelty in sight was *Tamara,*
after the poem of Lermontov, for which Balakierev had

written a symphonic poem many years before. Bakst adapted the poem for the ballet, designed the marvellous costumes and scenery, and, of course, Fokine the choreography. Fokine was not aware that Nijinsky was intending to compose on his own. Except for Diaghileff and himself, nobody knew. Sergei Pavlovitch thought it would be better to wait, and break the news to Fokine when he came back from Russia with his new creations. Diaghileff knew that he would be extremely upset when he heard that his supremacy as a composer would be challenged. Up to now, for a century, a country, a company, had had only one *maître de ballet*. It was natural, therefore, that the change should displease Fokine, who was at the height of his artistic career at this very moment, particularly with his individual temperament. But Sergei Pavlovitch was fearless when he had an idea, and he took it on himself to break the news. Finally he would understand and, being a great artist, he would in time see the necessity of different composers for the development of their art. The greater difficulty would be to appease Fokina, whose influence on Fokine was great. Fokina had a prominent part in the ballet, and she was a very excellent dancer of her type. But many of the misunderstandings which arose could be accounted, according to Diaghileff, to Fokina's influence.

The creation of *Dieu Bleu* and *Daphnis* necessitated Diaghileff's constant presence in Paris, and he decided to spend a greater part of the summer there. This idea was welcome to Nijinsky, as he wished to compose and finish *Faune* before they started the autumn tour, for which Diaghileff had already signed contracts for Germany, Austria-Hungary, and Monte Carlo, as usual, before going to Paris.

To retain the troupe was not possible, and Nijinsky did not even consider it necessary for the early rehearsals, but he needed one artist on whom to compose, and Diaghileff requested a dancer of the company, Alexander Gavrilov, to give up his vacation and remain in Paris.

Gavrilov was young and enthusiastic. Shortly after he had been graduated from the Imperial School in 1910, he had left the Mariinsky to join Diaghileff. He had heard

so much of them, and as soon as he met Diaghileff, Fokine, and Vaslav, the combination of their talents opened
utterly new vistas of dancing for him. He was glad to
stay. It was a hideously hot summer, Nijinsky took
Gavrilov down to the café in the basement of the Châtelet,
and over a couple of bocks explained with great excitement just what he wanted him to do.

Every day, at the top of the dusty old Châtelet, in the
rehearsal room, they worked on *Faune*. The only other
person there was the pianist. Not even Diaghileff was
admitted. Here Nijinsky composed, with Gavrilov as his
material, as a sculptor works his clay. Each fragment was
worked out and indicated by Nijinsky, then expressed by
Gavrilov. Nijinsky would demonstrate, Gavrilov imitate,
and very often whole phrases were rejected, or completely
changed in movement. Every single day for two months
they worked in the heat and dullness of a Paris summer.
Occasionally in the evening they took a drive around the
lake in the Bois, or dined at the Château de Madrid, or
went to little hidden places in the forests of Saint Cloud
and Meudon, and sometimes they visited Maurice Ravel
at Montfort.

The late summer finally arrived, and Nijinsky, with
Diaghileff, departed for their beloved Lido, to spend
three solid weeks in freedom and relaxation. *Faune* was
completely ready. Now, at last, Nijinsky had peace of
mind. He realised, though, that to teach the troupe his
new creation would be sure to present extreme difficulties,
as it demanded an utterly new technique.

The days slipped by, and in the first week of October
they joined the troupe, which had gathered under Grigoriev in Dresden. Most of them had come back from
Russia, and were full of news about what was going on
at home, and how envied they were by their fellow
dancers.

Bronia arrived. She had spent the summer with her
mother in St. Petersburg. Eleanora was well, and happy
about the success of her children, but she was longing for
Vaslav. Alone in the capital she led a quiet life, for the
first time without financial worries, and with leisure.

Vaslav at once made arrangements for his mother to come, and thought the best place for her to join them would be Monte Carlo. Eleanora would love the Riviera, and there he would have more time to be with her.

They had before them a long list of engagements—Dresden, Leipzig, Prague, Vienna, Budapest, before going in March to Monte Carlo. Maestro Cecchetti arrived, sunburned and in high spirits after the summer spent in Italy, and he was greeted with the usual enthusiasm, and had to listen to all the vacation stories of each member, to which he lent an ever willing ear.

One day, during a rehearsal in Leipzig, word came that Thomas Nijinsky had died suddenly of pneumonia in Kharkov. Nijinsky had not seen his father for many years, but it was a distinct shock to him. He had always hoped that some day they could be together. He took the news calmly, the troupe, as they heard of it, coming to him to show their sympathy. Nijinsky was sitting in the dimly lighted auditorium watching the rehearsal as Bolm, having some free moments, came down and expressed his regrets over the sad tidings. Nijinsky thanked him, looked up, and smiled. Bolm was amazed at this, and decided he must be heartless. Only years later, when Vaslav's long illness began, we learned that this peculiar outward expression, a smile at sad news, or weeping at joy, may indicate the exact reverse of the true psychological reaction.

This year the Berlin performances took place at the Kroll Opera House. They were held in a festival atmosphere, and Berlin turned out, friendly and appreciative. The Kaiser himself was their principal patron. The director of the Imperial Berlin Museums told Sergei Pavlovitch that on one occasion, when some matters connected with the Museum were discussed at a Cabinet Council, the Kaiser held forth on dancing, and actually showed the assembled Ministers some of the steps in his favourite ballet. He then proceeded to say:

"Gentlemen, there is more beauty in this Russian Ballet than in all our Museums from the cellar to the roof."

And the Kaiser gave strict orders that the directors of

all the Imperial Museums should come and see the Ballet.

Karsavina made flying visits from St. Petersburg, and this tour was carried out chiefly without Kshessinskaya. Bronia travelled with the other girl dancers, and received the same treatment as they did. She seemed to be happy and satisfied. Vaslav did not want to give her an exceptional position, in order not to destroy the discipline of the troupe, and thought that when the time came for her to be a *prima ballerina assoluta,* she would get the privileges which were due to her rank.

But some of the remarks of the other dancers began to impress Bronislava Fominichina's mind. Why did not Vaslav Fomitch travel with her? Why did she not stay in the same Palace hotels as her brother? Why did she not accompany her brother and Sergei Pavlovitch at their different receptions? Whenever other members of the troupe were asked, not only Karsavina and Vaslav, but of course Bronia was taken along.

Whether or not she realised at this time the exact nature of the friendship between Nijinsky and Sergei Pavlovitch is hard to say. She must have known Diaghileff's admiration and jealous guardianship over Vaslav Fomitch. All this time Vaslav was trying to persuade Diaghileff to give her the parts she deserved through her talent. Diaghileff had opposed her as long as the ballets called for sweet and pretty *ballerinas,* but, now that *Petrouchka* and other creations came up, where art, and not the idea of a pretty face, was important, Bronia began to be cast as an understudy for Karsavina, with whose parts she was alternated, with great success. Naturally she had more the spirit for these parts in the new creations than anybody else, and in *Faune,* Vaslav intended to give her an important rôle.

Artistically speaking, Bronia was satisfied, but of course the suggestion of her colleagues annoyed her. And several times she made peevish, girlish remarks to her brother about her disappointment at not living and travelling with him. Vaslav Fomitch tried to explain that it was a personal matter that made him share his life with Sergei Pavlovitch and not with her. He could not tell his own

sister of the relationship which made him stay with Diaghileff.

The reception in Prague was an exceptional outburst
of enthusiasm. The Russians were fêted as nowhere else
before. In this great popular success not only their tran-
scendent art, but the fact that they were Russians, played
an important part. Prague, the capital of the province of
Bohemia, belonged to the Austro-Hungarian monarchy,
and the greeting of the Ballet was in the nature of a
political demonstration from the populace—that as Czechs
they belonged to the Slav race and were a sister nation
to Russia. The applause was so wild that they even broke
the orchestra stalls and threw all kinds of objects on the
stage in their mad acknowledgment.

At last the Ballet arrived in Vienna. The quiet, distinguished routine of this Imperial capital, the ordinary
way of life of the common people, the streets crowded
with uniformed officers, booted and spurred, the hussars
with their dolmans, the Imperial equipages with whiskered
footmen on the box, the broad Khärtner Ring and the
beautiful buildings, all manifested the splendour of the
reigning house and the richness of the nation. Everything
and everybody seemed prosperous, gay, and light-hearted.
In many ways Vienna reminded Vaslav of St. Petersburg
and the broad Russian way of life, even to the big baroque
palaces and the atmosphere of regal ordered patronage.
Nijinsky loved the huge, majestic Opera, with its ideal
stage, the spacious rehearsal rooms where everything was
perfect for dancing. He felt quite at home here, for it
was very much like the Mariinsky in its surrounding atmosphere and the way in which it was run.

The Viennese ballet-master, as well as the *corps de
ballet,* received the Russian visitors with sympathetic
friendliness, which, after the first rehearsal they watched,
turned into incredible admiration. And the Ballet itself,
with its Italian *maestro,* who was a strict upholder of
the traditional Italian school, was the first to proclaim the
supremacy of the Russian dancers and the genius of
Nijinsky. He used to take his own artists to watch him
and show how hard and faultlessly, with what unbelievable

energy, he practised, never stopping, even after having
attained human perfection.

Cecchetti was radiant. At last he felt at home, and the
praise of his Viennese colleagues, who were in constant
attendance, delighted him. The rehearsals were of an easy
nature, as the stage and the orchestra were equally perfect, and Monteux, who was an ideal conductor for ballet,
clucking to the wood-winds as if they were horses, since
he spoke little German, made them understand exactly
what he wished to obtain. And, then, nearly all of the
Viennese spoke perfect French.

Sergei Pavlovitch chose the earlier novelties to show
Vienna for the first time: *Swan Lake, Armide, Cléopâtre,
Scheherazade, Les Sylphides, Carnaval,* and *Spectre* were
given. The press, as well as the public, were unanimously at their feet. The stage was laden with flowers,
and the applause tumultuous, in spite of the fact that the
Court, with its strict Spanish etiquette, and even the aged
Emperor, who broke eleven years of mourning for his
wife, appeared constantly. Archduke Raïner, the eighty-
year-old doyen of the House of Hapsburg, never missed
a performance. He was wheeled into his box, and followed
every step and every gesture like the keen *balletomane*
he was, and always led the applause. In the intermission
one could look up at the Imperial *loges* and see young
King Alfonso, on a visit to his cousins, trying to imitate
the *entre-chats* and pirouettes he had just seen. *Spectre
de la Rose,* with its Alt Wien *décor,* was such a success
that the audience applauded until Nijinsky and Karsavina
had to encore the whole ballet.

Diaghileff had many friends in Vienna, among them
E. Sachs, a cultured old gentleman who made occasional
trips to Russia, and spent a great deal of time in different
European capitals. He was a charming *viveur,* with the
same tastes as Diaghileff, and he lived in an old palace
in the Seilern Statte, which breathed an exquisite air of
art and a *mondain* life. One of the real "old school," he
was a perfect host, an enchanting *causeur* surrounded by
a highly intellectual group, and he was famous for his
collection of objects relating to old Vienna and had won-

derful prints and engravings. He also had an extremely
interesting dancer's library, with souvenirs of Camargo,
Vestris, and Elssler among his treasures. There were the
slippers of one, the Spanish comb of another, the manu-
scripts of Noverre. Nijinsky loved to pass his late afternoons in the quiet palace, among these mementos which
meant so much to him.

Baron Dmitri Gunsburg plunged readily into society, as
a branch of his family lived here and had a high
place in banking circles. Sergei Pavlovitch declared that
Gunsburg had really begun to develop into a *maître de
plaisir* of the Russian Ballet, and so he had, with his
gaiety, humour, and pleasantness. They fêted him like a
prima donna, and he thoroughly enjoyed it. He tried his
best to drag Diaghileff and Nijinsky with him, but he did
not succeed very often. He represented the Russian Ballet
in a marvellous way socially, and paid flying visits to
Diaghileff's suite to sign the cheques that backed their
enterprise, hardly glancing at the figures.

Diaghileff was guaranteed, even in the smallest city,
eight thousand gold francs a night, but he never made
less than fifteen or twenty thousand. The yearly income of
the Russian Ballet was about two million gold francs, as
the houses were invariably sold out weeks ahead of the
time they arrived, with the prices three times as high as
usual. In spite of this, if Sergei Pavlovitch made two million he always spent three, and Gunsburg, without a question, paid up the difference. It pleased him to do so. It
was a privilege, after all, to outplay Deutsch de la Meurth,
the Aga Khan, and Sir Basil Zaharov, who were also
helping Diaghileff. Sergei Pavlovitch often teased Gunsburg, saying: "Dmitri, you are like an aging cocotte, always on the go, always looking fit, and we, the Russian
Ballet, are your *amant de cœur.*"

Nijinsky liked Gunsburg. He was gay and amusing in
his whirlwind apparitions. He had always something entertaining to say and always knew the latest about everything that was worth while in the world of art and
politics, and he was a faithful reporter. He had a real
friendship for Nijinsky, whom he admired deeply, and

often wished he could take him along without Sergei
Pavlovitch's constant escort. But he was a man of the
world and tried to take things as they were.

Nijinsky spent hours in the Albertina, fascinated by the
drawings of Leonardo and Holbein. He visited the Lich-
tenstein, the Akademie, and the Kunsthistorisches, and
was really thankful that the orchestra made it possible
to have fewer rehearsals, to allow him more time than
was usual for himself. They stayed at the old Hôtel Bristol
and made occasional visits to Sacher's, where Frau Sacher,
the grand old lady of Vienna, the friend of Emperors, the
protector of the young aristocrats and artists, the wise
matchmaker and angel of peace in political intrigue as
well as in love-affairs, held her court. Frau Anna Sacher
was a great character, and her fame resounded even in
St. Petersburg, where she was known to be one of the
sights of Vienna. She was, of course, present at the performance, and welcomed Nijinsky and Diaghileff to her
world-famous restaurant. "Why, he is merely a boy,
this miracle," she would say in her charming Viennese
accent, *"Ja, wir haben auch einmahl eine Elssler gehabt,
unser Johann, ja, der hat mahl uns unter die Füsse
gespielt, wir lieben tanzen, aber so was wie Sie no das
ha'ma noch nie g'sehen."*

Karsavina had to return to St. Petersburg, and Kshessinskaya accompanied them to Budapest, where the next
appearance of the Ballet was scheduled in the first days
of March. Nijinsky contracted a very bad cold as soon as
he arrived in the Hungarian capital, and he had to stay
in bed, unable to appear at the first two performances,
as he was too feverish. Already, in Vienna, he had danced
with a high temperature. At the Hôtel Hungaria, in his
rooms overlooking the Danube, he was resting and thinking that soon his *Faune* would be produced. He hoped
people would understand it. It was a new path in choreography, extremely advanced, but it could not fail to
find a response. He was becoming tired of the eternal
success, and people staring at him as a prodigy, when
he was so much more than that. He was feeling and
thinking deeply. He wanted to show there was more in

life than the momentary satisfaction of a craving towards
beauty. His leaps, his lightness, his ease, his grace—could
not they see, could not they understand, that he had a
message for them, deeper than the pleasure he brought
to their lives? Dancing, as beautiful as it is, passes, dies
with the disappearance of the interpreter. Did Vestris or
Taglioni leave anything after them but a magical memory? A mere dancer only lives on in these ways. But he
wanted to show his public the meaning of life, the way
lasting happiness could be obtained. Success, wealth, were
passing. The real, the intangible good was helping and
loving unselfishly. He danced for these ideas, and in such
a manner to best express them, and this was the secret of
his miraculous performance.

Sergei Pavlovitch came back late to the Hungaria, after
the performance, and took his meals on a table near Nijinsky's bed. They heard the fascinating music of the
gypsy orchestra playing constantly in the restaurant below.
Vaguely it brought back to Vaslav Fomitch memories of
his childhood, his trips into the Caucasus and near the
flowing Volga.

Kshessinskaya was often with them and nursed Vaslav.
Her own golden samovar, with its accessories, was moved
near his bed, and she prepared tea in the Russian way.
"Foreign people don't know how to make it, anyhow,"
she declared. She had been received as a queen by the
public of Vienna and Budapest, the fame of her talent,
her beauty, and her close connection with the Russian
Court preceding her. Kshessinskaya surrounded Vaslav
with her exquisite feminine manner, and he, who was
always attentively cared for by Diaghileff, somehow felt
an inexpressibly soothing presence. Sergei Pavlovitch was
highly amused by Kshessinskaya's attentions, but he
knew it was merely a friendly gesture. She was so pleased
Vaslav had obtained success abroad, and wanted simply
to show her devotion. And she really intended to gain
some influence over Vaslav to balance that of Diaghileff,
if this was possible, as she was anxious to have Nijinsky
return to the Mariinsky, if only for a few months in the
year. She was a wise and diplomatic person, and Vaslav

passed the afternoons chatting happily with her, just as
any boy of twenty would do. Kshessinskaya travelled with
her own retinue and lived in the royal manner. Diaghileff
often teased her, and one evening at dinner he remarked:
"Oh, Matildoshka; yes. You are superb. You deserve all
your success, even to the two Grand Dukes at your feet."

"But, Sergei Pavlovitch," she answered quickly, "I have
two feet."

The troupe was enchanted with their stay in Budapest.
The whole city was wild about them, and the press could
not say enough. They were received with flowers, gifts,
and cheering, while the students at the University unhar-
nessed their carriage horses and pulled the artists home
themselves. Nijinsky flew from the demonstrations, but he
was glad they were so popular. At the rehearsals the
Russians could not rave enough over the Hungarian
hospitality, the beauty of their women, the wonderful
gypsy music, and the thousands and thousands of cafés
where the inhabitants of the city seemed to pass their
lives, discussing politics. Bolm was busily praising the
manners, the parties, the society, and of course Gunsburg
was so taken up that he swore to Diaghileff that unless
he took a rest after Vienna and Budapest he would col-
lapse. Luckily Monte Carlo seemed to promise some relaxation. But not for Diaghileff, who knew that Fokine
would arrive for the rehearsals of the novelties, and he
would have to be told about *Faune*, and not for Nijinsky,
who had to produce *Faune* in Monte Carlo. Even Vassily
disappeared from time to time and murmured on his return to Diaghileff that the Vengerkas deserved their
names, as no one could compete with them in making
love.

A few days after their arrival at Monte Carlo, Eleanora
Bereda Nijinskaya came. She was greatly excited at leaving Russia for the first time and by the wonderful luxury
of her journey all the way from St. Petersburg, on which
she had been escorted by one of Diaghileff's secretaries.
Vaslav and Bronia were waiting for her at the little
station near the Casino, and drove her to the hotel, where
she was to stay with them. The first time the family was

reunited she was so happy that she could only cry and cry. Diaghileff and Vaslav took her about, showed her Monte Carlo and the Grande Corniche. The performances began, and every evening she attended faithfully. Everybody tried to be of help and show her around, but she preferred Drobetsky's escort, as he was Polish, and therefore they could understand each other so well. Vaslav devised everything he possibly could to make his mother's stay happy, and never had Eleanora realised before in what triumph this company worked and how luxuriously they lived. But she had a profound respect for the Mariinsky as an institution, and, while she was pleased with their success abroad, in her heart she regretted that Vatza had left, and she did not believe that any good came out of this wandering gypsy life, which she had led when she had first married Thomas Nijinsky. She was sure everything would have been different if he had only had a permanent place as a member of the Imperial Theatre.

Diaghileff and his circle surrounded her with the utmost respect and attention, but she felt really at ease only when she could drive around with her Vatza and Bronia alone. She preferred this far more than all the stately dinners at the Hôtel de Paris. But soon Monte Carlo affected even Eleanora. After all, she was still a comparatively young woman, and one day she declared to Vaslav Fomitch that she had decided to go shopping. So they went over to Nice, and boxes and boxes of dresses and hats followed her back as if she had been a young bride. And she appeared every day in a different silk or taffeta dress, and with bonnets tumbling with ostrich feathers. Vaslav did not dare to venture to say anything about the newly chosen clothes, for fear of spoiling her pleasure.

Eleanora saw the novelties of the Russian Ballet and was at once won over. *Spectre* became her favourite, and, although she was distinctly of the old classical school, she had a quick, clear perception in artistic matters and felt the new era had come to stay and was right in itself. She was delighted to be with her old friend Enrico Cecchetti, whom she had practically always known, since he had

been *maître de ballet* for a time in Warsaw. They used
to sit on the terrace, almost like a loving couple, under
the palm-trees, and in the afternoons they could be found
at the Café de Paris, sipping their orangeade. There Eleanora sweetly tried to convince *Maestro* of the interest of
the new ballets, of *Petrouchka's* great qualities. But
Maestro defended the old style. So they had endless discussions on the subject, but *Maestro* held to his fortress
relentlessly, and would not concede an inch of his cherished tradition.

The rehearsals for *Faune* began, so as to be ready by
the time Fokine was expected, and also to give him ample
time to rehearse his own three ballets, *Dieu Bleu,
Daphnis,* and *Tamara.*

For *Faune,* seven girls were chosen, their heights playing a certain importance in the choice, as they had ap-
proximately to be the same, as it was composed on one
plane as in a bas-relief. The part of the chief Nymph was
given to Nelidova. She was the tallest of them all, and so
formed the centre of the frieze. Bronia was to be the
Nymph who confronts the *Faune* and runs away in a
panic, a small but very difficult part of which she gave an
extremely remarkable presentation.

From the very first rehearsal, Nijinsky explained to the
troupe that they would have to try to forget their technique of the five positions and to take utterly natural ones.
Almost as if they were children, he showed them the first
steps. In *Faune* there is no dancing in the old sense of
the word. It is a consecutive series of movements. All is
executed in profile; that is to say, the legs are in profile
as well as the head, and the hands show either the palms
or their flat backs. The torso is held opposite, hips turned
out toward the spectator, as one sees in archaic Greek or
Egyptian sculpture. This position seemed to cause the
artists extreme difficulty. They simply could not move. So
after two rehearsals, each of half a day, Nijinsky found
that he had first to teach them to walk, and thus slowly
build up his new technique. This took them almost three
months. *Faune* had one hundred and twenty rehearsals,
of which at least ninety were taken up training the danc-

ers in the method. *Faune* does not consist of any complicated form of steps or movements. The dancers always
walk backwards or forwards in profile, on the heel, with
very slightly, almost imperceptibly, bended knees. In the
beginning this presented an almost insurmountable ob-
stacle. The dancers would always fall back either into one
of the five positions, or into their ordinary way of walking,
and at this time Nijinsky found out that very few women
really know how to walk, that our civilisation has formed
an artificial way of walking which was influenced partly
by the *Grand Siècle*. Women have the tendency to put the
tip of the toe to the ground first, to give the impression
of grace and lightness, instead of first putting the heel
down, which gives firmness and natural rhythm to the
body. This is the way one should walk, and he taught his
artists to do this. This experiment of Nijinsky's actually
proved that the so-called "modern" or "natural" method
of dancing needs a training as long as, if not longer than,
the classical school requires.

Nijinsky spent his whole day rehearsing with the seven
dancers. The performances in Monte Carlo commenced in
the usual way, and he only went from the rehearsal-
room to his dressing-room for the evening's ballets, and
back to bed. Fortunately, they did not dance every day.
Eleanora had to return to St. Petersburg, and Vaslav hoped
to be able to go back to Russia after the London season
and spend the summer with her, as he was homesick.

Now at last Bakst and Diaghileff were admitted. Sergei
Pavlovitch was at once enthusiastic. At last the art of
choreography had achieved a new form. Both he and
Bakst immediately understood its tremendous importance.
The door was at last opened on a new vista and the
possibility of a new school, distinctly separated from the
classical; in fact, the dance of the twentieth century from
which the real modern form could develop.

For the other members of the troupe, the stay in Monte
Carlo passed agreeably. The performances did not follow
each other as rapidly as in the cities, and in the daytime,
when they were free, they could amuse themselves out of
doors enjoying the sunshine and gaiety of the Riviera.

Among the many persons who were seen a great deal with
the Ballet was the Aga Khan. He never failed to send
beautiful flowers and presents to the stars, as well as to
the other dancers of the *corps de ballet*. Once he presented
Karsavina with a string of pearls, and she, furious at what
she considered a proposal, stormed to Diaghileff. "Not at
all, Tamarochka," he said; "accept them as you would a
bouquet from anyone else. It is only his compliments to
your art."

The Aga Khan used to sit in the afternoon at Rumpel-
mayer's, before him a mountain of toast, easily resting
his feet on a table, and entertaining the members of the
Ballet, as well as for supper at the Café de Paris afterwards. Nijinsky liked him, and was greatly amused by his
suite and the two attendants, day and night, faithfully
before his door, seated cross-legged on the floor. The Aga
Khan extended an invitation to Diaghileff, Nijinsky, and
Karsavina to come to India. But how could they, as much
as Nijinsky would have liked it? They would never have
the time between seasons.

Finally their stay in Monte Carlo was over, and the
time approached to go on to Paris, where the rehearsals
with Fokine were supposed to take place for *Dieu Bleu,
Tamara,* and *Daphnis and Chloe.* There were two new
parts for Nijinsky. He told Sergei Pavlovitch that the rehearsals for *Faune* were well advanced, but in spite of this
he would have to keep them up until the very day of
the *première*.

The season was to take place at the Châtelet. Nijinsky
and Diaghileff stayed as usual at the Hôtel Crillon. Fokine was already there, and began to rehearse at once.
Diaghileff asked him over to the hotel, and told him in
a casual way that a new choreographic poem was going
to be introduced by Nijinsky, and the work was almost
finished. Fokine seemed to take the news fairly calmly.

Fokine's three ballets, including *Tamara,* were on a
grand scale, and needed the whole troupe. First *Dieu Bleu,*
and then *Tamara,* was rehearsed, with Adolf Bolm and
Karsavina creating the chief parts in the latter. The essentially Russian music of Borodin is well known, the

sinister choreography, as well as the tall, curious scenery, were suited to it, having all the cruelty and native colour that the mediæval Caucasian Queen's Court required.

The season began in the middle of May, and the first novelty was the *Blue God,* which received a lukewarm reception, except for the personal success of the performers. *Spectre, Fire Bird, Petrouchka, Prince Igor,* were also on the programme. *Tamara* was more enthusiastically received, but somehow Fokine felt that his constant faithful muse had deserted him. He began to complain about the lack of time he had for rehearsals, as *Daphnis and Chloe* was still in rehearsal. He asked Diaghileff for more rehearsals, but Diaghileff refused, saying that the troupe was already so much overstrained that they could not stand any more rehearsing. Three days before the *première* Sergei Pavlovitch suggested that they abandon *Daphnis* entirely. Fokine begged for the three days, although he knew six or eight rehearsals were imperative. The choreography was extremely complex. *Daphnis* had to be rehearsed even on the day of its first performance. Fokine was irritated and nervous. He had the feeling that his position as a *maître de ballet* was being undermined. He heard more news about *Faune.* Rumors were on foot that something utterly new was in formation. Nijinsky, as always, complied to all that Fokine requested of him, and gave an exquisite performance of a Greek youth in *Daphnis.* But, in spite of this, the ballet itself failed to obtain a permanent success in the repertoire. Not one of the three novelties choreographically attained the standard of *Carnaval* or *Spectre.*

Diaghileff saw that Fokine's mood was not all that could be desired, and also he was aware that part of his irritation was directed against Nijinsky. He could easily have tried to explain matters, and create a friendly atmosphere, with his great diplomacy, but Sergei Pavlovitch had more than one strange twist in his character. He never wanted his collaborators to get on well. On the contrary, if any ill will developed, he rather stimulated it. He wanted blind obedience and loyalty to himself and to no one else, and, if the others should hate each other, it fitted marvellously into his schemes. If the creative powers of the Russian Ballet could be friends one day, perhaps they would feel they no longer had need of Sergei Pavlovitch. Fokine had become too dominant. Diaghileff never liked this, and, in all his artistic career, as soon as an artist attained a supreme position, he tried to pull him down. Because there must be only one reigning power, and that should be Sergei Pavlovitch Diaghileff. Yes, certainly he was interested in bringing forward a new *maître de ballet* to further a new school of choreography, but the other motive was always there behind. He made Bakst, and dropped Roerich and Benois for him. He raised Stravinsky and played him off against Prokoviev. He launched Massine and changed him for Dolin, Lifar, and others. And thus Bakst was cast away for Larionov.

Diaghileff did not keep his artists with him, giving chances for all of them. Once they were discovered and really developed, he threw them away as a used glove. Again and again, during the twenty years of the reign of Diaghileff, there is in the troupe one dancer, one ballet-master, one composer, one painter, in a supreme position, and then out he goes. It was never the case that they had outlived themselves, or their art was *passé,* as Sergei Pavlovitch would always explain their disgrace to the public. Stravinsky, Benois, and Fokine are still great masters. Each of the artists who had been collaborators, or who were discovered by him, could have gone on for the glory and development of the Russian Ballet, but Diaghileff unfortunately, as he was a great constructor, so was he also a supreme destroyer. The Russian Ballet had had more and more of a success, and, since they had left the Mariinsky, Sergei Pavlovitch had begun to lose his head. He started to have *la manie de grandeur*. He liked to call the troupe the "Russian Ballet of Diaghileff." At first he played with the idea. Then he began to believe it himself, that he was its creator. He forgot that his dancers were members of the Mariinsky, that they were graduates of the Imperial School. He forgot that his guard of scenery painters, his composers, his choreographers, were the product of Russia and its art, with centuries of

tradition behind them. Diaghileff, the discoverer and organiser of genius, thought that he, like God, had created
in his image every single artist of this company. Few of
the artists sensed this at the time. Nijinsky began to notice
it, and Benois, who had known Sergei Pavlovitch so well,
must have. Later each one was to make this discovery of
Sergei Pavlovitch's character; and in many ways this
caused the downfall of the Russian Ballet in later years,
when it really became *Les Ballets Russes de Sergei de
Diaghileff*.

Fokine thought that a lack of time for the rehearsals of
Daphnis was caused on purpose by Nijinsky. Everything
that went wrong at this time he interpreted in this way.
Nijinsky, seeing Fokine's irritation against him, was inwardly hurt. He did not do anything to displease him. On
the contrary, he felt Fokine, who had been his *maître
de ballet,* should have welcomed and encouraged him, as
a younger artist, in his development. They were working
for the same ideal: the art of the dance. The atmosphere
was charged with electricity. This misunderstanding, the
expectations for *Faune,* keyed up the nerves of all the
artists. The final rehearsals arrived with the full orchestra,
and its members were dumbfounded. And they agreed
among themselves that the most outstanding creation they
had ever witnessed was *Faune.*

Chapter Ten

L'APRÈS-MIDI D'UN FAUNE

BAKST had his scenery hung, but Ni-
jinsky, who had only seen the models, was displeased.
They had rather lively discussions. Nijinsky said, "Bad

enough that the music is not the same as the movement. Now the scenery fails to form a harmonious part." But Bakst himself was enchanted with the scenery, and Diaghileff also thought it very good.

At last the day of the first performance arrived, the 29th of May, 1912. Perhaps for the first time in his life, Nijinsky was nervous. Would the public understand? Would they affirm that his ideas were right? This day was one of the most important in his life.

The dancers were instructed by Bakst in making themselves up. They had very whitish-pink eyes, like those of a pigeon. He painted them first himself. They wore no tights, and had nothing under their pleated gauze tunics, which were cream colour and painted by him with the motif of Greek keys, some in light blue, others in apple-green. They were barefoot, with their soles and their toe-nails pinked as well. They all wore tightly fitting wigs wound from cords painted in gold, their formal locks falling on to their breasts. The girls really gave the impression of Greek statues in a frieze. Bakst took infinite pains to make them so, and the effect was exquisite.

Nijinsky, as the Faun, wore closely fitting tights which came up to his neck and around the arms. They were painted by Bakst in a coffee colour with big brown spots, which were disposed in such a manner, continuing on to the bare arms and hands, as to give the impression of the skin of a Faun itself, and the difference between flesh and costume could not be discovered. Around his loins he wore a garland of small evergreens, which ended behind in a small tail. His head was covered with the same kind of a gold cord tight wig as the Nymphs', and he had, as well, two little flat curling horns. He was the very image of an adolescent Faun, a young being half animal, half human. In the costume, as in Nijinsky's expression, one could not define where the human ended and the animal began.

His facial make-up utterly changed the apparent structure of his face. He underlined the obliquity of his eyes, and this brought out and gave a slumberous expression. His mouth, chiselled by nature, he made heavier. Here also was an infinite languor and a bestial line. His face, with its high cheekbones, lent itself admirably to the transformation. His ears he elongated with flesh-coloured wax and made them pointed like a horse's. He did not imitate; he merely brought out the impression of a clever animal who might almost be human.

Even Diaghileff and Bakst had caught the nervous excitement of this evening. Sergei Pavlovitch was fidgeting backwards and forwards from the auditorium to the stage, where Bakst commanded the electricians, as he found lastminute improvements. The whole troupe was assembled in the overcrowded wings—Karsavina, Kyasht, Lopokova, Bolm, all of them.

A similar excitement reigned in the auditorium. Paris, all Paris, had gathered. They had heard of a new ballet —a new ballet by Nijinsky. The programme said music by Debussy, *L'Après-midi d'un Faune,* which was inspired by their own Mallarmé's exquisite Eclogue.[1] How would this young Russian interpret Greece in the creation of two eminent French artists? What would his conception be? Yes, they expected something utterly different from Fokine's ballets, but nobody supposed that a new form of art would be presented.

The audience sat motionless during the twelve minutes of this choreographic poem. They were so taken aback, so surprised, that they gave no sign whatsoever. But as soon as the curtain fell the most incredible uproar occurred. Like a storm, the approval and disapproval broke loose, giving out an incredible noise. Nobody could even hear the voice of his neighbour. Wild applause, shouting took place in one of the most exciting receptions in the history of the theatre. Rodin, sitting in a box close to the stage, stood up and cried, "Bravo! Bravo!" Others whistled. Calls of *"Bis! Bis!" "Épatant," "Ridicule," "Inouï," "Superbe,"* alternated, and the roar of applause

---

[1] During this season a French gentleman complimented Nijinsky on his expression of Mallarmé's *L'Après-midi d'un Faune* in movement. Surprised, he had to admit that he had never heard of the poem. So two artists' ideas met through the medium of Debussy's music.

grew and grew. The fight in the audience continued. They discussed loudly their impressions, and argued. One could clearly see how intellectual Paris was divided into two distinct camps, pro and contra *Faune*. But the approving part of the public won.

The curtain was raised and a second time *L'Après-midi d'un Faune* was performed. After this, the applause became frenetic.

Sergei Pavlovitch ran to Nijinsky's dressing-room, where already Bakst and the others were assembled. "It was a success." "No, they do not grasp it." *"Mais oui,* they feel that something stupendous has taken place." And each one reported their personal impressions of the public reaction. Friends of Diaghileff and Nijinsky, *balletomanes,* poured in. Vassily could not keep up his barricade, and Nijinsky was surrounded, praised, and consoled by those who thought the audience had not accorded *Faune* its merited acceptance. It was indescribable chaos. Nobody was certain what had happened, who had won; was it a success or not? Exactly as after a decisive if hard-fought battle, one does not at first know who has gained the victory.

Rodin came up, and with tears in his eyes took Nijinsky in his arms. "The fulfilment of my dreams. You brought it to life. Thanks." Certainly he was understood, Nijinsky felt now, at least by those who really mattered.

Sergei Pavlovitch, next morning, as usual after a *création,* read the criticism. He saw at once that *Faune* had received nearly unanimous notices in the Press, but that a real controversy over a new æsthetic form had sprung up. The whole press unanimously acknowledged that a revolution in choreography had taken place. And so the press went on in praising, discussing, this new form of art which so unexpectedly was presented to them.

The *Figaro,* one of the most important newspapers of France, did not include any criticism, but, instead, its editor, M. Gaston Calmette, well-known in political life, and as the owner of the paper, ran the following attack in an editorial on his front page on the 30th of May, 1912.

A FAUX PAS

Our readers will not find, in its accustomed place under "Theatre," the criticism of my worthy collaborator, Robert Brussel, upon the first performance of *L'Après-midi d'un Faune,* choreographic scene by Nijinsky, directed and danced by that astonishing artist.

I have eliminated that review.

There is no necessity for me to judge Debussy's music, which, besides, does not in itself constitute a novelty, as it is nearly ten years old, and my incompetence is too complete upon the transcriptions of these subtleties for me to be able to discuss with the eminent critics, or the younger amateurs who tax a masterpiece with the reading of "Prelude, Interlude, and Paraphrase Finale," transposed by a dancer upon the work of Mallarmé.

But I am persuaded that all the readers of *Figaro* who were at the Châtelet yesterday will not object if I protest against the most extraordinary exhibition with which they presumed to serve us as a profound production, perfumed with a precious art and a harmonious lyricism.

Those who speak of art and poetry apropos of this spectacle make fun of us. It is neither a gracious eclogue nor a profound production. We have had a faun, incontinent, with vile movements of erotic bestiality and gestures of heavy shamelessness. That is all. And the merited boos were accorded the too-expressive pantomime of the body of an ill-made beast, hideous, from the front, even more hideous in profile.

These animal realities the true public will never accept.

M. Nijinsky, little accustomed to such a reception, badly prepared likewise for such a rôle, took his revenge a quarter of an hour afterwards with the exquisite interpretation of the *Spectre de la Rose,* so prettily written by M. J. L. Vaudoyer.

Sergei Pavlovitch, reading the *Figaro,* for the first moment was greatly shocked. It was such an incredible action, such an unheard-of attack: Calmette of all people, to come out in defence of the morality of Paris! All of Diaghileff's fighting spirit was aroused; after all, important as Calmette was, he was no authority on art, but his opinions meant much to the public at large, and he thought, and then decided to challenge him. Diaghileff's friends, and the *balletomanes,* as well as the personal admirers of the Russian Ballet, came to the Crillon at once. They all had discussed what would be the right thing to do by the time Nijinsky, who had taken a well-deserved rest, awoke from his late sleep and came in to Sergei Pavlovitch's rooms. All sides of the question were considered. Followers and newspapermen called up, came to the hotel, and tried to talk to Diaghileff or to see Nijinsky, to know what they thought of the Calmette attack. Members of the Russian Embassy came in and explained that they were convinced that Calmette had made this attack, merely using *Faune* as a pretext, because in reality he wished to attack the policy of the French Foreign Office, Poincaré, and the Russian Ambassador, Isvolsky, who were trying to strengthen the Franco-Russian alliance and friendship. The *Figaro,* and the political group which the paper was representing, pursued a different attitude in politics, and, in attacking the Russian Ballet, the strongest propaganda for Russia in France, they attacked the *rapprochement* with the country itself.

News came that the prefect of police of the city of Paris had been requested to stop the next performance of *Faune* as an obscene spectacle. The news went through Paris like a hurricane, and threw the whole city into a great state of excitement; and in the *salons* and clubs, the newspaper offices, as in the corridors of the Chamber of Deputies, anyone and everyone was ready to jump at anything which was said for or against *Faune.* Just as the audience on the evening before, so now all Paris was divided into two camps. Of course, with Calmette and his party taking the side of the anti-*Faunists,* it made them extremely strong.

In an incredible agitation, rumours were repeated and grew. The *Gaulois* appeared with an article stating that an apology was due to the public. The anti-*Faunists* seemed to gain ground. What was to be done in this purely artistic matter which now rocked the whole public? Nothing was settled by Diaghileff as to what course the

Russians should take. Nothing was definite by evening, except that they learned that Calmette had obtained from the police an injunction to prevent the further performance of *Faune*. Inquiries were immediately made, and Diaghileff was informed that the last gesture of Nijinsky, the Faun lying on the veil, was the one to which the police objected. Sergei Pavlovitch and the others devised a subterfuge. They requested Nijinsky to change this last movement, but he refused, saying that he could not see any offence to the public morals in his conception. Nevertheless, for one or two performances the end of the ballet was slightly modified, but without any appreciable difference.

Next morning brought a great surprise to all the Russians as well as to the Paris public. An article, in answer to Calmette, appeared on the front editorial page of *Le Matin,* a paper as important as *Figaro,* signed by no less a person than Auguste Rodin. He said:

During the last twenty years, dancing seems to have set for itself its task of making us love the beauty of the body, movement, and gesture. First there came to us from the other side of the Atlantic the famous Loie Fuller, who has been justly called the rejuvenator of dancing. Then came Isadora Duncan, teacher of an old art in a new form, and to-day we see Nijinsky, who possesses at the same time talent and training. The intelligence of his art is so rich and so varied that it approaches genius.

In dancing, as well as in sculpture and painting, flight and progress had been smothered by routine laziness and inability to rejuvenate. We admire Loie Fuller, Isadora Duncan, and Nijinsky, because they have recovered once more the freedom of instinct and discovered again the soul of tradition, founded on respect and love of nature. This is the reason why they are able to express all the emotions of the human soul.

The last of them, Nijinsky, possesses the distinct advantage of physical perfection, harmony of proportions, and a most extraordinary power to bend his body so as to interpret the most diverse sentiments. The sad mime in *Petrouchka* seems, in the last bound of *Spectre de la Rose,* to fly into the infinite space, but in no part is Nijinsky as marvellous and admirable as in *L'Après-midi d'un Faune*. No jumps, no bounds, nothing but attitudes and gestures of a half-conscious animal creature. He stretches himself, bends, stoops, crouches, straightens himself up, goes forward and retreats, with movement now slow, now jerky, nervous, angular: his eyes spy, his arms extend, his hands open and close, his head turns away and turns back. The harmony between his mimicry and his plasticity is perfect. His whole body expresses what his mind dictates. He possesses the beauty of the antique frescoes and statues; he is the ideal model for whom every painter and sculptor has longed.

You would think Nijinsky were a statue when he lies full length on the rock, with one leg bent, and with the flute at his lips, as the curtain rises, and nothing could be more soul-stirring than his movement when, at the close of the act, he throws himself down and passionately kisses the discarded veil.

I wish that every artist who truly loves his art might see this perfect personification of the ideals of the beauty of the old Greeks.

This acknowledgment of Nijinsky's composition, coming as a public tribute from the greatest of modern sculptors, aroused one can imagine what feelings in Calmette and those critics who condemned *Faune*. To say anything further against *Faune* was impossible. But Calmette did not want to be ridiculed, and therefore immediately attacked Rodin.

I admire Rodin deeply as one of our most illustrious and able sculptors, but I must decline to accept his judgment on the question of theatrical morality. I have only to recall that, in defiance of common propriety, he exhibits in the former chapel of Sacré Cœur, and in the deserted chambers of the excellent nuns at the Hôtel Biron, a series of objectionable drawings and cynical sketches, which depict with greater brutality and in further detail the shameless attitudes of the *Faune,* who was justly hissed at the Châtelet. And, now that I am speaking my mind, I may say that the morbid mimicry represented by the dancer on the stage the other evening moves me to less indignation than the spectacle offered every day by Rodin in the ancient convent of Sacré Cœur to regiments of hysterical women admirers and self-satisfied snobs.

It is inconceivable that the State—in other words, the French tax-payer—should have purchased the Hôtel Biron for 5,000,000 francs simply to allow the richest of our sculptors to live there. Here is a real scandal, and it is the business of the Government to put a stop to it.

A world-wide controversy exploded. A storm of protest was hurled at Calmette. The admirers of Rodin were up in arms. M. Pierre Mortier, editor of *Gil Blas,* sprang to the defence of Rodin, pointed out that the *Faune* was the *leitmotiv* of his art, and declared that instead of expelling Rodin, as Calmette had suggested, the State should maintain him in the Hôtel Biron for life, and convert it into a Rodin Museum, providing he could leave his work to France; which was in fact done later.

A campaign to support Rodin was started, in which the names of the most eminent figures of France in the artistic, literary, and political world were enlisted: The ex-president Loubet, Raymond Poincaré, the Premier, Leon Bourgeois, Clemenceau, Aristide Briand, Barthou, Hanotaux, Anatole France, Mistral, Jules Lemaître, Monet, Besnard, Maurice Barrès, Octave Mirabeau, Paul Doumer, Jacques Émile Blanche, Rafaeli, Zuloaga, Catulle Mendès, Marie Cazin, Judith Claudel, and many others. Then the rest of the Paris public tried to get in to a performance of *Faune,* to judge for themselves what this question was that had stirred the intellectual world to its depths. It was a real *tour de force,* however, to get in, as all the tickets for the Russian season had been sold weeks before, and every conceivable influence and political pull was called into play to obtain places in the Châtelet.

Then *Figaro* published a huge Forain caricature showing Rodin, in his studio at the courtyard of the Hôtel Biron. A model enters with a dress over her arm:

"Oh, Master, where can I put my clothes when I pose?"
Rodin: "Just there, in the chapel."

This was carefully designed to arouse the clerical animosity of the Faubourgs, and a fresh list of adherents swarmed to Rodin's side. The new petition was signed by Isvolsky, the Russian Ambassador; the Senators Dubost, d'Estournelles, de Constant, Gaston Menier; Mm. Edmond Haraucourt, Pierre de Nolhac, and Mmes. Alphonse Daudet, Lucie Félix-Faure. Forain, the cartoonist, was attacked by the critic Louis Vauxcelles for his lack of æsthetic self-respect in demeaning himself to draw the caricature in the first place. A Government commission was asked to report, which was favoured both by the President of the Republic and the Prime Minister.

Rodin was asked to defend himself, but he merely said in a statement:

"I have no time to waste on answering M. Calmette's attack on me. I admire Nijinsky's work and consider him a marvel of harmony. He is a dancer of genius. I wish so noble an effort as *Faune* would be understood in its entirety, and that all artists could come for instruction and communion in this spectacle of beauty."

Le Figaro, Le Gaulois, La Liberté, the anti-*Faunist* papers, were silenced. The police appeared and witnessed the performance, but they inclined before the public opinion and *Faun* was not forbidden.

Finally there was a definite triumph for the pro-*Faunists*. Diaghileff was delighted. He realised that Calmette had rendered him a greater service than anybody else before. For from Paris to Constantinople, from London to St. Petersburg, from Berlin to New York, *Faune* was discussed. In later years Diaghileff found it convenient to create a furore of controversy by having his creations attacked, but there was never again the world-wide publicity that was spontaneously accorded *Faune*.

But Sergei Pavlovitch had not time even to gasp a breath, after this turmoil, before another arose. Fokine, through the extraordinary success and violence of *Faune*, seemed to drop into oblivion. Nijinsky was now hailed as the great modern choreographer, the innovator of a new school. *Daphnis and Chloe* was the last novelty of the season, and also a ballet with a Greek background. It was difficult for it to come after *Faune*. But, even in spite of *Faune,* the ballet would not have been a great success. The critics in the press, as well as the public, said of it: "Its composition is weak, and the choreography is confused and less characteristic than we are used to see at the Ballet Russe."

Of course, Fokine was greatly upset and blamed Diaghileff, and above all Nijinsky, for the failure of his novelties this season. So, by the time *Daphnis* was performed, the idea which for some time had been ripening in Fokine's mind became a determination. He would leave the Russian Ballet. He had been closely associated with it. He was one of the great monumental pillars on which the structure of it was built. The Ballet without Fokine, at that time, was inconceivable. Here in this troupe Fokine had had his first unchecked liberty. Here he had received the inspiration and collaboration to unfold his admirable talent. And here among them he had developed into one of the greatest choreographers of all time.

But nobody tried to displace the false ideas of Fokine, or to salve his hurt pride. In fact, those who should have done so only excited him the more against Nijinsky. And so, finally, after the performance of *Daphnis and Chloe,* Michel Fokine sent in his resignation to Diaghileff. He wished to sever all ties with the Ballet if other choreographers were with them. To this Diaghileff could not and would not accede.

Fokine, who, after Petipa's retirement, was attached to the Mariinsky, but could not obtain the position as an official *maître de ballet,* and was only able to compose on his own for charity performances, now, after his stupendous success abroad with the Russian Ballet, was at last nominated as first ballet-master of the Mariinsky Theatre.

The rumours that Fokine was about to leave quickly spread through the company. But they refused to believe it. Years ago, in the second Paris season, he had already threatened to do this. But that time it was for an infraction of one of his rules. It was understood that no part of the ballets or dances could be encored. Neither could any artist acknowledge applause during the performance.

One night, in *Cléopâtre,* somehow the Bacchanal was encored. Fokine was so upset that he immediately left the theatre with the intention of never returning. But Diaghileff, who agreed with him in this ruling, severely punished the stage manager who had made the mistake, and brought Fokine back next day.

This time they hoped it would be the same, but Fokine meant it seriously, and, as soon as they knew this, they decided to take formal leave of him. The company offered him a loving-cup, with flowers, and it was supposed that the principals of the company, Nijinsky and Karsavina, should present it. But Diaghileff told Nijinsky not to do this, as Fokine, according to Sergei Pavlovitch, did not even want to see him. So Nijinsky, hurt by this unjust animosity, kept to his dressing-room while the farewell took place on the stage.

Fokine was saddened deeply by his absence, and with tears in his eyes said good-bye to the other members of the Ballet. If Sergei Pavlovitch had permitted Nijinsky to appear, perhaps a reconciliation would have taken place, instead of this wilfully engineered misunderstanding, and the fate of the Russian Ballet would have been utterly different.

Chapter Eleven

JEUX AND SACRE DU PRINTEMPS

THE HECTIC season of 1912 in Paris was coming to an end. The novelties, the controversies, were hardly over, and the social obligations and prospective artistic plans filled the time and the mind of Sergei

Pavlovitch. Nijinsky could not very well free himself of
them either. There was a veritable onslaught upon him
from painters and sculptors. He had been painted,
sketched, sculpted, by innumerable artists all over the
world. In the past, Blanche, Bakst, Lepape, Serov,
Dethomas, and many others captured his traits and mo-
tions, but they had to steal the moments when Nijinsky
was free—a gesture, an attitude back stage, or in the
rehearsal-room. Now Rodin came forward, among many
others, to sculpt Nijinsky. And it was arranged that after
the morning practice he should go to Rodin's Meudon
atelier for the sitting.

The shopping tours also began. Nijinsky was extremely
neat and meticulous but simple in his dress. He possessed
a small wardrobe, and never had more than two suits
at one time. He spent most of his day in practice costume
at the theatre. This was the one luxury in which he indulged himself. Tremlett, the fashionable shirtmaker of
Paris and London, made his dancing shirts after a special
design, in delicate, lovely *crêpe de Chine* of pastel shades.
He had hundreds of pairs of dancing-shoes. During one
of his drives through Paris he discovered, at a small
boutique on the Rue Caumartin, some quaint braided
kid sandals which he bought and wore at rehearsals, when
not dancing, and this started the vogue for Deauville
sandals that became so fashionable.

After the *première* of *Dieu Bleu,* Cocteau, one of the
authors, offered Nijinsky a gold pencil with a sapphire
cabochon which Vaslav always wore. Nijinsky had a real
passion for sapphires, and Sergei Pavlovitch, knowing this,
offered him at each Parisian visit a sapphire ring from
Cartier. Vaslav was claimed to possess the finest sapphires,
and he was soon named "Le Roi du Saphir." Now the
advice of Gunsburg was needed, and he was delighted to
go on these errands accompanying Nijinsky as an arbiter
of fashion. Tremlett was given a large order for underwear, and dressing-gowns, in which Nijinsky looked very
well, as he did in pyjamas; but he looked very awkward
in street clothes, which did not suit his well-proportioned
body. He had broad shoulders and a slender waist—

sixty-three centimetres, not more than that of the Venus
de Milo. It was decided that the order for his suits would
be given to Davies, the famous London tailor who
worked for the Prince of Wales. At Thonet a beautiful
fitted case was ordered, and Nijinsky presented himself
with the flattest of watches from Benson. He was as happy
and proud as a child with it. Ever since the Tsar had
given him that watch many years ago, when as a pupil
he had danced for him at the Imperial School performances, the watch that ended at the pawnshop, he had
never possessed another one.

In the evenings Nijinsky loved to go for supper to the
Château de Madrid or the Pré Catelan. There, on the green
lawn, it was peaceful, and in the fragrant acacia-scented
air he felt restful. They were often accompanied by Debussy, who was delighted with the sensation that *Faune*
created. He was enthusiastic with the idea of collaborating
with Nijinsky on a new composition.

With Diaghileff as their interpreter, the proposition was
discussed, and one evening, dining on the terrace of the
Pré Catelan, under the arc-lights that cast rings of shadows through the fans of the horse-chestnut leaves on the
table-cloth, he noticed the flight of the moths attracted
by the lights circling round and round; and there he
conceived *Jeux*. He told Debussy that he imagined an
incident in modern life, athletics and the spirit of modern
youth, *"les jeux de sport, les jeux de l'amour."* The story
was supposed to be enacted near a tennis-lawn at dusk
after the game. It was to be the essence of flirtation,
the modern form of love. Half felt, half accomplished
gestures, emotions playing physically at the game of tennis, emotionally at flirtation—a love-affair between a young
boy and two girls both separately and simultaneously—
the eternal triangle under an utterly new aspect. This was
the basis of so many of the modern ballets conceived
years later by Massine, Nijinskaya, Balanchine, and
others.

Nijinsky was always interested in sport, and always
watched it enviously. He would have loved to take part,
but as a pupil of the Imperial School he was strictly

forbidden every sport except swimming, for sports developed muscles unsuitable for dancing. Even too much walking is not good for dancers.

Nijinsky began his sittings with Rodin. Usually Sergei Pavlovitch took him up to the studio, sometimes he motored to Meudon alone, and Diaghileff came to fetch him. The latter was much occupied, and Rodin wanted to be alone while sculpting. First he made many sketches, passionately interested in drawing all the muscles of his model. Nijinsky posed in the nude. Finally Rodin decided on a pose which was very similar to that of Michelangelo's *David,* the torso reposing on the right leg, while the left was slightly inclined, the head turned three-quarters to the right, the right arm raised, and the hand turned towards the head. Nijinsky patiently posed hours and hours for the master. When tired, Rodin would make him sit down and would show him all his sketches, and, as they could not speak together, drew what he wanted to explain, and Nijinsky indicated by movements. Their code might have been very complicated for others, but they understood each other perfectly. The sittings were divided by lunch, at which time both model and master rested. Rodin loved simple food but was a great lover and expert of wine. At his luncheons the most excellent wines of France, and especially the Bourgogne, which he preferred to all others, were served.

Sergei Pavlovitch was rather alarmed by the intimacy which developed so quickly between the aged sculptor and the young dancer. Rodin was an artist. There were so many things that they did not need even to say to each other, for they knew them instinctively. There was a unity between Rodin and Nijinsky from which, for this very reason, he was excluded. And he knew it. Sergei Pavlovitch became jealous, but he controlled himself.

Fêtes and entertainments succeeded one another; those of Mme. Euphrussy, of the Maharajah of Kapurthala, Mme. Edwards, the Embassies. And everywhere the presence of Karsavina, Nijinsky, and the Russians was demanded. Those receptions were of great splendour and elegance, each trying to outdo the other. But the Aga

Khan was the one who carried away the prize. During the London season that same year, at his garden party he had Nijinsky and Karsavina dance a Variation, in honour of Their Majesties and his other guests. Diaghileff asked, for Nijinsky alone, fifteen thousand gold francs for four minutes of dancing. At the last performance at the Châtelet, at which many foreign personalities were present, Richard Strauss, who for a long time had wished to collaborate with the Russian Ballet, was in the audience. He went back stage to see Nijinsky with his wife Paula, who was a very capable and energetic woman. She was very firm with Sergei Pavlovitch too and, entering Nijinsky's dressing-room, she clasped him in her arms, kissing him on both cheeks and patting heavily the shoulder of the *Spectre de la Rose,* almost crushing him as well as the petals of his costume. Rostand and the others, greatly amused, witnessed the scene. The enthusiasm of the public at this farewell performance was such that they had to encore the whole *Spectre.* Karsavina made a charming little speech to the public in the name of the whole company, and she who shared the success was literally bombarded with flowers.

The statue of Nijinsky was unfortunately never finished, for Diaghileff found continual excuses to prevent the sittings. His jealousy had now become uncontrollable. One day he arrived at the *atelier* sooner than expected. It was a heavy, storm-laden, suffocating afternoon, as only Paris can have in July. Sergei Pavlovitch went through the house and found both artists in Rodin's sanctuary, Nijinsky sleeping peacefully on the couch, covered by a shawl, and Rodin also asleep at his feet. The intense heat, the hours of posing, the heavy wine, had fatigued the aged sculptor as well as Nijinsky, who was not used to drinking. Diaghileff did not wake them. He left without being noticed, and only confided in Bakst. The incident was never mentioned, but he energetically hindered any further sittings, and because of this he undoubtedly robbed the world of a masterpiece.

Nijinsky had had practically no time since they left Monte Carlo to see his sister alone. Bronia was very successful this season. The part in *Faune* had increased her popularity. In the troupe she was greatly liked as a gay and good comrade. But her brother did not know that she had quite a lot of attention paid to her at this time by a young dancer of the troupe. Her fame grew; and being the sister of Nijinsky created some sort of halo about her. Some of the dancers secretly thought that a close relationship with the Nijinsky family might be helpful, and then Bronislava was kind, good-hearted, and charming. So many little flirtations began, from which the serious one was with the promising dancer Kotchetovsky. He asked Bronia in marriage, and she consented. The news greatly surprised Nijinsky. Somehow he had believed that she was as utterly wrapped up in her art as he himself, and the announcement, therefore, came as a disappointment. From now on Bronia would have some other interest in life besides dancing. He almost felt he was losing a comrade. He did not hide this feeling, but expressed it to Bronia, who bitterly reproached him with the fact that she could not be constantly with him, so she might as well get married. The marriage was celebrated very quietly in the Russian Church in London in the presence of Sergei Pavlovitch and Nijinsky, who gave her away.

The London season passed in its usual festive manner. Lady Ripon gave a garden party at Coombe Court, and in her theatre there Nijinsky and Karsavina danced. Queen Alexandra and the Empress Maria Feodorovna were present, both of whom expressed their admiration for the two artists. Queen Alexandra mentioned to Nijinsky that every time she attended a performance and *Spectre de la Rose* was on the programme, she changed from her box to an orchestra seat in the middle of the auditorium so that she could get a full view of his dancing and the final leap.

Sargent was a close friend of Lady Ripon's. She commissioned him to make portraits of her two favourites; Nijinsky in the costume of the *Pavillon d'Armide*.

Nijinsky came to many of these parties after the performances. He was silent, smiling, and extremely shy and boyish. Compliments coming from the public rather embarrassed him. He had wonderful manners, thanks to his innate charm and the strict training of the Imperial School, whose pupils were brought up in the spirit of the *Corps des Pages*. Then, also, Diaghileff had an excellent influence over him in this respect, as he was an *homme du monde jusqu' au bout des ongles*. Nijinsky wandered unnoticed through the *salons,* or sat eating quietly at a little table. His great favourites were Lady Morrell and her husband and the Bradley Martins, Americans who played an important part in London social life. Old Mrs. Bradley Martin was like a grandmother to him, spoiling, petting him, having him to private lunch, just the two of them. Nijinsky was presented with a gold and tortoiseshell manicure set by her, so that he would think of her daily. He spent many quiet hours at the town house of the Morrells. He was taken to tea on the terrace of the Houses of Parliament, and enjoyed immensely the atmosphere reigning there. One day, at a lunch at Lady Cunard's, where many were present, Nijinsky, who had already begun to pick up a few words in English, said, "Lady Morrell is so tall, so beautiful, like a giraffe." Diaghileff felt rather uncomfortable and tried to explain, but Nijinsky insisted, "No, no, giraffe is beautiful, long, gracious; she looks like it." And Lady Morrell understood the compliment.

The cosmopolitan society of the *grand monde* needed a fresh thrill, and M. Marquet, the owner of the Casino of Monte Carlo, launched a new resort. He wanted to do everything to make the place a success. Fabulous hotels were built, a racecourse as good as Longchamp was laid out. Smart shops, casinos, a lovely indoor swimming-pool near the beach, all in Pompeian style, and even grass was planted in place of the sand beach. Deauville had its opening. Marquet secured a few appearances of the Russian Ballet at the Casino. A very high price was guaranteed, and Diaghileff signed this contract. Nijinsky objected very much. He thought the Russian Ballet should stick to its tradition to perform only in operahouses.

Nijinsky again had to give up the idea of returning to

St. Petersburg that summer, for it would be nearly over by the time they could leave Deauville. Sergei Pavlovitch gave two months' vacation to the troupe. But he had many plans to decide and to settle with Nijinsky. Since they had left St. Petersburg in the early spring of 1911 they had never been separated for more than one or two days. Sergei Pavlovitch, who had a deep reverence for Vaslav Fomitch's genius as a dancer, and equally admired his developing qualities as a choreographic composer, held him under his influence in everything except choreographic art. Here Diaghileff recognised that he himself was the dilettante and Nijinsky the master. But he did not want to relinquish an inch of his influence in other matters. Until now he had had a comparatively easy task. At the beginning of their friendship Nijinsky was merely a boy, eager to learn, to listen, and to be guided. Diaghileff brought him in contact with artists, painters, musicians whom he valued, and whose influence on the development of his art was of the utmost importance. The atmosphere Sergei Pavlovitch created was the right one to bring his talents into bloom. In a way Sergei Pavlovitch was a barricade which separated him from real life and therefore gave him the freedom to live completely for his art. Sergei Pavlovitch, of course, continued to maintain the seclusion of Nijinsky when they left Russia. The continual travelling brought Nijinsky in contact with innumerable people who wanted to be his friends. He made friends, but in a few days' time he had to leave, and so any continuous relationship was made impossible. Whenever Nijinsky made an effort to learn a language, Sergei Pavlovitch discouraged him. "Why lose time on this? You have more important things to do." The more Nijinsky could be kept isolated from the world, and the longer, the more it pleased Diaghileff, who was desperately attached to him. His friends of the past had left him; some had married on account of social obligations. Never did he find in anybody the personification of his life dream as completely as he did in Nijinsky. This had to be a lifelong friendship that nothing could break. Of course, Diaghileff knew the rumours that went around in St.

Petersburg. It was inevitable that they should be repeated by "some good friend" to Eleanora. She was always the one who wished and prayed for Vaslav's return to the Mariinsky. Now the Dowager Empress declared openly that Nijinsky's return was required at the Imperial Theatre. If Vaslav Fomitch visited his mother's home, he would live there at her house. She would try to ask him to remain. Diaghileff knew Nijinsky would neither leave the Russian Ballet nor himself. He was too devoted to both, but perhaps he would appear a few times at the Mariinsky every season and form a tie outside of Diaghileff's sphere. No, this could not be permitted. As long as Eleanora could see her son only under his supervision she could not gain her point. Nijinsky himself felt that continuous travelling was too exhausting for all of them, and told Diaghileff that serious artistic work could only be accomplished if they had somewhere a permanent home where at least a few months could be spent. Bakst now maintained a home in Paris. Benois and Fokine were still in St. Petersburg. Karsavina was attached to the Mariinsky, and came to join them only for a few months. Stravinsky, on account of his wife and children, lived on the Lake of Geneva. But Diaghileff would not listen. He again arranged for a long German tour, including Berlin, Vienna, Budapest, a London season in February, then the annual season of Monte Carlo and Paris, and London again. An interminable succession of appearances. He was approached several times with very tempting offers from North and South America. But he said, "No, too far away. We have plenty to do in Europe."

The one deciding factor which Sergei Pavlovitch used to keep Nijinsky near him during the time of the vacation was that work had to be done on the intended new creation, *Sacre du Printemps*. Years ago young Stravinsky had, while composing *Fire Bird,* conceived a theme. It was too brutal and strong in its manner to be used in the more magical, delicate *Fire Bird*. This theme suggested to Stravinsky more than prehistoric Russia. The theme at that time was cast aside. Roerich, the great man on archaic Russia, always hoped Diaghileff would produce an

essentially Russian Ballet which would represent, not a
period or a mood of the Russian race, like *Igor, Fire
Bird,* or *Petrouchka,* but the very essence of the soul of
the Russians, a sort of national *épopée.* So Roerich
dreamed of the rituals of ancient times. After *Faune,* the
creative urge of Nijinsky became more pronounced, and,
now that Fokine had left the troupe, Diaghileff encouraged him in every way to compose. He needed Nijinsky
more than ever, but Nijinsky felt that creation should
come spontaneously. Luckily for Diaghileff and the Ballet,
he was now occupied with a new idea, which grew and
clarified itself in his mind from day to day, to create a
choreographic tableau where his ideas, his school of
dancing, could be developed in full. To do this he had to
take an archaic period, a primitive emotion. He wished
to return to the creative moment, and chose the primitive
period of Russia, the worshipping of nature and its rites.
He told his idea to Diaghileff, who exclaimed excitedly,
"How strange! Roerich's secret desire." So he brought the
three together, and Nijinsky's wish that a ballet should
not be composed on existing music, scenery, or story could
now be carried out. Here really the librettist, musician,
scenic artist, and the *maître de ballet* were obeying one
and the same inspiration, and so their composition was
started simultaneously. This complicated ballet needed
infinite time. Nijinsky warned Diaghileff that he would
require a great number of rehearsals as he developed the
technique, and that the steps would be extremely difficult
to execute.

With *Jeux* and *Sacre* in mind he had every moment
occupied, and he worked intensely during this whole
year, Stravinsky working in Clarens and making many
trips to meet them.

Diaghileff required a third novelty, and secured another
maître de ballet, Romanov of Moscow, to whom he gave
Florent Schmitt's *Tragédie la Salomé* as a ballet for
Karsavina. Soudeikine, the young Muscovite painter, was
commissioned to do the scenery. Monteux and Inglebrecht
were retained as conductor and assistant conductor re-
spectively. Nijinsky found that Monteux had developed

into an ideal conductor for ballet. He was musically very
well qualified, but during the last year he had improved
immensely his choreographic sense. Without changing the
tempi, which would have been unmusical, he had the
kind of sense to know how to conduct for dancing.
Petrouchka and *Faune* were played all over Germany during the tour of the winter of 1911-12. The Russian Ballet
again visited Leipzig, Berlin, Dresden, and Vienna, and
here the public without any reservation praised the new
school of dancing. Nijinsky had to be ready by the early
spring when they arrived in Monte Carlo for the rehearsals. Therefore in Berlin he made only one exception—to
visit Dr. Bode, who was a great admirer of his and who
wanted to present him with a wonderful copy of a frieze
of the fragments of the Parthenon at the Kaiser Friedrich
Museum. He arranged a reception where artistic and intellectual Berlin wished to pay tribute to *L'Aprés-midi
d'un Faune.*

This year Karsavina had great difficulty in obtaining
leave from the Mariinsky, for Teliakovsky did all in his
power to cross Diaghileff's plans. Kyasht, who was a
graduate of the same class as Karsavina, whose good
friend she was, danced her rôles after Vienna, as Karsavina had to return to St. Petersburg. Piltz, who developed
into an excellent dancer, received more important parts
than in the past. She was very lovely.

The tour of the Russian Ballet proceeded smoothly and
successfully, in comparative peace. Monteux and Inglebrecht, on account of the score of *Petrouchka,* which
presented difficulties, demanded that the orchestras be
reinforced. The number of rehearsals was insufficient
and the performance of this ballet for this very reason had
to be abandoned during the second Budapest season,
where the company arrived around Christmas of 1912.

Vienna also extended a most gracious reception to the
Ballet, which on its second visit there caused almost a
musical revolution. For Vienna undoubtedly is the most
music-loving city, and has so high a standard that its
orchestras at that time were the best in the world. The
symphonic orchestra, the Philharmonic, is that of the

Hofoper. With much ease and great artistry they had played until then, with few rehearsals, whatever score Diaghileff put before them. It was not the case now. As soon as Monteux gave them *Petrouchka,* they began to rehearse it with signs of disapproval, which augmented at each repetition. Monteux had great animosity to overcome. He tried to soothe them in the best way he could, but the orchestra, which was slightly influenced by the anti-Slavic propaganda in the press, on account of the Balkan War, was not so easily calmed. Diaghileff, who knew what was going on, resented that art and politics were being mixed up. So one day he made a remark about this which the orchestra ignored. Even at the last rehearsal they played *Petrouchka* with such mistakes that Diaghileff was annoyed. He thought it was done on purpose, and he remarked in French to one of his friends listening to the music, *"Quelle cochonnerie la façon dont-ils jouent?"* One can well imagine how shocked the orchestra was upon hearing this. They immediately put their instruments down and left the auditorium. A strike of the *Hofoper* orchestra was an unheard-of thing in Vienna. Each member was an eminent artist or teacher of the Conservatory of Music. The intendant as well as the director tried to quiet them, but not until late in the afternoon was the affair settled, when Diaghileff apologised.

This whole visit to Vienna did not seem lucky for Diaghileff. Karsavina wired that she was not quite sure if she could perform in Monte Carlo. And lately Nijinsky, who was now down with influenza, seemed irritable. He insisted on having his room to himself, saying that otherwise he could not sleep; that he was so absorbed in *Sacre* that everything and everybody disturbed him. It was unmistakable that he meant Sergei Pavlovitch, for nobody else gained admittance into their suite. He went so far as to keep to his rooms for three days, requesting Diaghileff not to come unless he was asked for, and for three days he was not asked for. Nijinsky was developing rapidly as a creative artist, as a real man. He felt he must be alone to think. There were so many things he wanted to under-

stand about himself. He was devoted to Diaghileff as much
as ever. He felt that their friendship and understanding
were perfect, but lately he had become annoyed whenever Sergei Pavlovitch wished for actual proofs of his
devotion. Diaghileff seemed in a way to humour him, and
tried to give him all possible attention, but he sensed that
there was something else behind this. One night, when
Vaslav Fomitch was feverish, he wanted to have some
oranges, but in Austria in early winter and at night it was
impossible to get any. When the Hôtel Bristol failed to
procure some and Vassily came home empty-handed, Diaghileff himself went out at three o'clock in the morning to
try all the restaurants and cafés. Finally, in desperation,
he awakened Sachs and, both joining forces, knocked at
the Sacher. The omnipotent *maître d'hôtel* was called, and
of course gave them the precious fruit, which both of them
triumphantly brought to Vaslav Fomitch at dawn.

The complete score of *Sacre* was now in their hands,
and Vaslav Fomitch worked at it note by note. He went
over it carefully with the pianist and visualised the dances
before him as he played. The groups of ancestors, those
different tribes and the adolescents, the young girls joining
hands, tramping down the ground to try to plant the seed
deeper and deeper in the earth, so that when spring came,
life-giving plants might bloom forth triumphantly. But how
annoying that amid those mental pictures the face of that
young dancer from Budapest should emerge. Vaslav Fomitch wondered, "Why do I remember her features?"
That silent figure dressed mostly in black velvet, who sat
modestly in the corner of the stage watching the dancing,
who appeared at every corner like a shadow, somebody
who loved dancing as much as he did.

Diaghileff took every pretext to talk to Vaslav Fomitch, who was more silent than ever these days, and in
Vienna one late afternoon he asked: "Vatza, there is a
young girl from the aristocracy of Hungary. She wants to
study dancing with Cecchetti. Shall I take her along? It
would be quite an interesting experiment, and would
enhance the prestige of the troupe. Later others might
join."

"No, I do not think it is right to take dilettanti with us."

"But she has an artistic background; her mother is the greatest dramatic artist in Hungary."

Nijinsky hesitated a moment, then said, "All right, give her a chance."

Neither Nijinsky nor Diaghileff ever suspected that at this time they were being constantly watched by my "associates"—at the Hofoper by Mr. Schweiner, the dresser. Usually if any foreign male celebrity came to the Viennese Opera House, Schweiner dressed him. And he knew everybody, from Reské to Caruso. He was an amusing Austrian with an intense sense of humour, who always identified himself with his charges. In the afternoon at the café he often used to say, "To-day we are singing *Tristan* or *Don José*," and he proudly departed. Schweiner felt like a king robbed of his throne, and looked upon Vassily with contempt. But he was useful in securing little bits of information. At the Hôtel Bristol my friend Dagmar Schmedes was invaluable. Not known either to Diaghileff or to Nijinsky, she bluntly followed them to the restaurant, everywhere in the hotel, and one day, as if she was making a mistake, even entered the room of Nijinsky, who was just dressing, and was rather surprised at this interruption.

It was in London, in February, that Bronia came up one afternoon to the Savoy to see her brother. She broke the news to him that she would not be able to dance the part he was composing in *Sacre*, as she would have to cease dancing shortly. She was expecting a child. Nijinsky could hardly believe it. Who could have expected this of Bronia, the ideal dancer, who had all the qualities he dreamed of in art? The terrifically difficult dances of this part, the chief girl's part, nobody could do but Bronia, who not only possessed the marvellous classical technique, but also to an amazing degree the new technique which Nijinsky created in *Faune*. It was a blow to the creator, and he could think of nothing else but that at the time. An ideal woman dancer should never marry, for having children was a terrific handicap for her. Ni-

jinsky was greatly upset, and told this to Bronia, who
burst into tears and left the hotel. They did not speak to
each other after this incident for several weeks. She was
also hurt that the promotion Kotchetovsky hoped to get to
assistant stage manager did not come, Kremenev being
nominated instead.

Back in Monte Carlo once again, the rehearsals took
place on the Casino stage, while *Maestro* held his classes
as usual at the Palais de Soleil. It contained a spacious
stage and a nice terrace where one could lie in the sun.
Diaghileff and Nijinsky did not live either at the Monte
Carlo Palace nor at the Hôtel de Paris, but at the Hôtel
Riviera Palace—a new hotel just opened on the top of
the hill. It took about thirty minutes to get there by
automobile. But the view was heavenly, and it gave absolute privacy, which was what Nijinsky was seeking at this
time. Karsavina, always attractive, smartly dressed, with
her interesting dark figure, used to take walks along the
terraces with the Aga Khan and the other friends of Paris,
London, and St. Petersburg. Everybody seemed to be on
the Riviera this year. All the other dancers, when they
had a moment free from *Sacre,* went to the Café de Paris
or rested under the palm-trees on the banks of the
Place du Casino. It was a free, open, out-of-door life.
Sometimes one could see Nijinsky arriving in the autobus
from the "Olympus," as we called the place where the
Riviera Palace was built.

Often in the evening I used to walk around the Place
du Casino and watch Nijinsky sitting with Chaliapine or
Diaghileff at the Hôtel de Paris, having supper on the
terrace. I lay down on the bench under those blooming
magnolia-trees and watched them for hours and hours.

Jeux is perhaps of all Nijinsky's ballets the least known
and understood. Unjustly so, for it is another cornerstone
in the evolution of the modern school of dancing which
Nijinsky started. From all remote traditional surroundings,
from tales of poetical content, with one leap Nijinsky
carried the ballet into the midst of modern life. The
musician expresses his epoch. The author writes about the
very century in which he lives. Only the choreographer

took refuge always in past ages. In *Jeux* three young moderns live, feel, and play, through the absolute medium of dancing, the very essence and emotions of the twentieth century. This contemporary tennis ballet challenged to its deepest root the until now accepted traditions of choreography. The dances were of plastic lyricism, athletic and youthful, for Nijinsky was an adept of youth. In *Jeux* the individuals are young, in *Sacre* the society, and in *Faune* the earth itself. The scores as well as the dances are interludes; all wonder, hesitation, and with no knowledge of the end. The dances presented a parallel to emotional experiences, yet without imitating the actions of real life. For Nijinsky said, "Art is not an imitation of nature, but it is the image of nature obtained through artificial means." The choreographic movements in *Jeux* were stylised, and were on the same principle as *Faune*, only in this new work the frieze was alive and moved in space, the gestures were split up so that it would give the impression of many small movements consecutively following each other as they logically developed, and through this it gave the impression, as some called it, of a *ballet cinematographique*. Each limb made a different movement and followed a different rhythm. Here Nijinsky gave a clear demonstration of the ideas that Dalcroze advocated and which could not be carried out to the full in his school. Again a new idea was lost, for the pupils were not professionals and did not have adequate training, as in the case of Duncan. *Jeux*, according to many, was a triumph of angularity, and introduced post-impressionism to the Russian Ballet. Nijinsky wished to give the expression of lightness, and for this reason he wanted to do all his dances on the point. This had never been done by a male dancer. *Maestro* was greatly amazed, therefore, when Nijinsky asked him to coach him. He thought it would be impossible, but within three months Nijinsky mastered this difficulty. However, it was not applied to *Jeux*, because, after consideration, Nijinsky decided that it would be contrary to the ballet's athletic conception.

In *Jeux* the scene is in a garden near a tennis lawn,

the game just concluded, and dusk falling. Electric lan-
terns shine among the summer foliage, and a lost ball
rolls across the stage. A young man appears, searching
for the ball. He is joined by two young girls. At once the
search is forgotten and they flirt, first the youth with one
girl, and then a change of partners, but this does not suit
the other. While the young man hesitates, the two girls
console each other and begin a flirtation between themselves. The young man decides, rather than lose either,
to take them both. From somewhere another tennis ball
is thrown across the garden, and with a sudden scared
glance they look around and run off merrily. In emotional feeling Nijinsky made a step forward. In *Faune* it was
the awakening of love in a youthful being. Here in
Jeux the feeling is modern too. Love becomes, not the
fundamental driving force of life, but merely a game, as
it is in the twentieth century. The object (here the excuse
of finding the ball) is easily abandoned and flirtation begins, but this is also quite as easily given up when the
idea of the former activity is recalled. He sees here love
as nothing more than an emotion, a pastime, which doesn't
even require consummation, which can be found among
three as well as among the same sex.

Bakst created a charming setting of vivid greens and
blues and purples. The music of Debussy was youthful
and fresh, but with a number of passages of a more ro-
bust nature than he had previously used.

The costumes this time were not designed by a scenic
painter but by the fashionable leading couturier of Paris,
Paquin. Nijinsky wore a white tennis shirt and flannel
tennis trousers, buttoned tight below the knee. The two
girls, danced by Karsavina and Schollar, wore white flannel
skirts and pullovers.

Nijinsky was supple, athletic, and acrobatic in his part.
The critics said: "We admire Nijinsky and the faith of this
young artist, who in the very moment of his greatest
triumphs abandons those prodigious dances in which he
is unique in the world, and which bring him a safe success,
for his conscientious and tenacious research, for strict
charm of the sculptural lines and the beauty of attitudes.

It seems that very intimate and sensitive bonds exist between the intelligent efforts of this dancer-genius and the art moderns, whose aim is not to reproduce with servility the aspects of nature, but to find an idealistic and personal transposition."

Jeux had a fairly warm reception, but no doubt the meaning escaped the great public. It was a great mistake of Diaghileff, and perhaps the first proof of coming short-sightedness in artistic matters, that he did not produce *Jeux* at another time. It was too refined, too delicate to be followed by the primitive, dynamic *Sacre*, which was awaited with great excitement. It was the first collaboration of the two moderns, Stravinsky and Nijinsky. The one with *Petrouchka*, the other with *Faune*, had convinced Paris that they were the epoch-making geniuses of their respective arts. And much was expected of their joint collaboration, when it was known that for the first time music and choreography were created simultaneously.

On the 29th of May, 1913, at the Champs Élysées Theatre, the *Sacre du Printemps* was performed for the first time, on the very anniversary of the *première* of *Faune*, for Diaghileff was superstitious. I wondered what the reaction of the brilliant, excited audience would be. I knew the music of *Sacre*, and had seen bits of the dancing from back stage during the last rehearsals, where I hid behind Karsavina and Schollar, and had been escorted by Dmitri Gunsburg, and Grigoriev threw furious looks at me, but I just looked through him as if he were of air. With Gunsburg beside me he could do nothing. I thought the public might fidget, but none of us in the company expected what followed. The first bars of the overture were listened to amid murmurs, and very soon the audience began to behave itself, not as the dignified audience of Paris, but as a bunch of naughty, ill-mannered children.

One of the witnesses, Carl Van Vechten, wrote about this memorable evening: "A certain part of the audience was thrilled by what it considered to be a blasphemous attempt to destroy music as an art, and, swept away with wrath, began, very soon after the rise of the curtain, to make cat-calls and to offer audible suggestions as to how

the performance should proceed. The orchestra played
unheard except occasionally, when a slight lull occurred.
The young man seated behind me in the box stood up
during the course of the ballet to enable himself to see
more clearly. The intense excitement under which he was
labouring betrayed itself presently when he began to beat
rhythmically on the top of my head with his fists. My
emotion was so great that I did not feel the blows for
some time."

Yes, indeed, the excitement, the shouting, was extreme.
People whistled, insulted the performers and the composer,
shouted, laughed. Monteux threw desperate glances towards Diaghileff, who sat in Astruc's box and made signs
to him to keep on playing. Astruc in this indescribable
noise ordered the lights turned on, and the fights and
controversy did not remain in the domain of sound, but
actually culminated in bodily conflict. One beautifully
dressed lady in an orchestra box stood up and slapped
the face of a young man who was hissing in the next box.
Her escort rose, and cards were exchanged between the
men. A duel followed next day. Another society lady spat
in the face of one of the demonstrators. La Princesse de
P. left her box, saying "I am sixty years old, but this is
the first time anyone has dared to make a fool of me."
At this moment Diaghileff, who was standing livid in his
box, shouted, *"Je vous en prie, laissez achever le spectacle."* And a temporary quieting-down followed, but only
temporary. As soon as the first tableau was finished the
fight was resumed. I was deafened by this indescribable
noise, and rushed back stage as fast as I could. There
it was as bad as in the auditorium. The dancers were
trembling, almost crying; they did not even return to their
dressing-rooms.

The second tableau began, but it was still impossible to
hear the music. I could not return to my stall, and as the
excitement was so great among the artists watching in
the wings I could not reach the stage door. I was pushed
more and more forward in the left wing. Grigoriev,
Kremenev, were powerless to clear this part of the stage.
Opposite me there was a similar mob in the back of the

scenery, and Vassily had to fight a way through for Nijinsky. He was in his practice costume. His face was as white as his *crêpe de Chine* dancing shirt. He was beating the rhythm with both fists shouting, *"Ras, dwa, tri"*. to the artists. The music could not be heard even on the stage, and the only thing which guided the dancers was Nijinsky's conducting from the wings. His face was quivering with emotion. I felt sorry for him, for he knew that this ballet was a great creation. The only moment of relaxation came when the dance of the Chosen Maiden began. It was of such indescribable force, had such beauty, that in its conviction of sacrifice it disarmed even the chaotic audience. They forgot to fight. This dance, which is perhaps the most strenuous one in the whole literature of choreography, was superbly executed by Mlle. Piltz.

The story of the *Sacre du Printemps* is already contained in its title. It is the adoration of nature in its most primitive and powerful form. Winter death reigns. Vegetation is in decay. It is the weakening of nature's impulse to fertility. But the everlasting, omnipotent, inherent power of growth breaks through, and spring comes.

Choreographically this ballet is the highest and purest composition of modern dance which has been created up to now. The movements express fear, joy, and religious ecstasy. They are first purely ritual movements of a primitive kind. The dancers shiver, tremble, and vibrate at the entrance of the seer. Later come emotional values in the movements of the dance of the Chosen Maiden. Her leaps, her jerks, are the ultra-modern descendant of the pirouettes and *entre-chats* of the classical school, and their choreographic value is the same. Nijinsky contradicts the classical position by making all steps and gestures turn inward. The choreography was the most amazing and correct visualisation of the score. Each rhythm was danced, the counterpoints were built up choreographically in the groups. It is through rhythm, and rhythm only, that the dance identifies itself with the music. The rhythmical counterpoint is employed in the choral movements. When the orchestra plays a trill on the flutes, movements thin out, and so do the dancers. Then the tune begins on wood-winds two octaves apart, and on the stage two groups of three dancers each detach themselves from the lines and dance, corresponding to the tune. The mouse-like shuffling of the sorceress, the rapid steps of the young men, correspond to the musical expression of the movement as the intricate rhythms of the joyful dance of the Chosen Maiden. At the end of the first tableau great circles (women dressed in scarlet) run wildly, while shifting masses within are ceaselessly splitting up into tiny groups revolving on eccentric axes. It is in this direction that the development of ballet is infinite. Even the costume colours were reflected in the music. With *Faune,* Nijinsky led us near to nature in the archaic, mythological period. In *Sacre* he took us far back to the awakening of nature itself and to the instinctively found rituals of the primitive man. No doubt in *Sacre* Nijinsky most clearly expressed his creed. Both choreographically and musically it was far ahead of its time. The dancers as well as the orchestra, and especially Monteux and Mlle. Piltz, accomplished a gigantic task. Even to-day, to dance or conduct *Sacre* is difficult, but in those days it was almost a superhuman effort.

Everybody at the end of the performance was exhausted. The month's long work on the composition, the endless rehearsals, and finally this riot——. Once more Vassily's guard broke down and Nijinsky's dressing-room was stormed, Diaghileff, surrounded by his friends and the *balletomanes,* explaining, discussing. Nijinsky took the whole affair more quietly now that it was over, and, nobody needing his energy and encouragement, he could let himself go. Stravinsky was in a frenzy. But they all agreed and knew that their creation was good, and that it would be one day accepted. They were so excited that they could not go and have supper right away, so somebody suggested a drive *au tour du lac.* And Diaghileff, with Nijinsky, Stravinsky, and Cocteau, drove around in the Bois to quiet down, and only toward the morning did they return home.

Chapter Twelve

NIJINSKY'S MARRIAGE

WHENEVER we moved from one city to the other *Maestro* gave me two or three days' vacation. I always travelled alone with Anna and not with the company, as we used better and faster trains. We always tried to get the train on which Nijinsky and Diaghileff were travelling, but until now we had failed. Anna, as usual, had to do the intelligence service to find all details about Nijinsky's trip to London. I did not quite trust her information, so that my joy was so much greater, boarding the midday express train at the Gare du Nord, when I saw Vassily ordering Michel around with the luggage, buying illustrated papers, and handing them through the open window of the train's corridor to Nouvel. Nijinsky was on the platform talking to Drobetsky. Anna had done well; our places were reserved in the compartment next to that of Nijinsky's. I quickly hid myself so that Diaghileff should not notice me. Finally the train pulled out and everybody settled down. I was desperately trying to read the illustrated paper, but could not understand anything, as my thoughts were constantly in the other compartment. I sent Anna out, who came back with the report that "le Petit," as we called Nijinsky between us, was reading quietly. She also went over to the dining-car to find out when they were going to have their lunch, at the first or second *série,* and to try to obtain accommodation if possible at the same table. But she failed. We could not even get to the same service. I was furious. Finally I could not resist, Diaghileff or no Diaghileff. What was the good of travelling by the same train if I could not see him? So out I went. Cautiously smoking a cigarette in the corridor, I passed the window of Nijinsky's compartment. He was with Nouvel, reading and talking. I wondered where Diaghileff was, but, throwing all caution aside, I remained. Nijinsky looked exceedingly smart in a greyish-green travelling-suit, with light grey cap, suède gloves, unbuttoned, on his hands. He did not notice me; at least, I thought he did not. After a while he stood up, came out, bowed, and passed before me. I did not know what to do from gladness, and ran breathlessly into my *coupé*. "*Anna, Anna, 'le Petit' vient de passer et de me saluer!*" I was triumphant. Again for two months I could live on the memory of this incident. What I did not suspect was what all this journey held in store for me. Five minutes later I was again in the corridor, seemingly smoking and admiring the landscape we passed by. I sat on a *strapontin* and gazed out, turning my back to Nijinsky's *coupé*. I don't know how long I was looking out, but suddenly I felt the same peculiar electric shock as when I saw him entering the stage, and turned slowly round and looked into Nijinsky's fascinating, Oriental face. He smiled, looking curiously like my pet Siamese cat that had given me the first impulse to follow him all around the world. His eyes were more oblique than ever, but I noticed they were not green, as they had seemed on the stage, but soft brown, like velvet. He stood near me, overtowering me as I sat there. He took hold with one hand of the copper railing of the window and put one foot on the radiator. I could not help looking down. His foot looked so elegant in his yellow shoes; there was something so fascinating about it that I could not take my eyes off it. Nijinsky smiled, followed my gaze. Then, trying to divert my attention, in his broken French he said: "*Mademoiselle, vous connaissez Londres. Content voyager?*" I answered with a torrent of French all about London—my school years there, England, its charm. He did not understand a word, but listened indulgently. Then I realised that I was delivering a monologue, and stopped abruptly, so embarrassed that I could not move, and my eyes followed each movement he made—how he arranged his glove; it was so enchanting. I must have seemed impossibly stupid to him. He gazed silently out. I followed his eyes, how long I do not know. I was spellbound. Then suddenly Nouvel called him—and I became frightened, but Nijinsky not in the least; softly, naturally, he opened the door, talked to him without any nervousness, as I had expected, and went in. I fell into my compartment half fainting. I was so excited that on arrival in Calais I could not say a word to Anna. Nijinsky, followed by Nouvel, without bothering about anything, went on the boat. I could not see Diaghileff anywhere. We left Paris in glorious weather; by the time we arrived in Calais it seemed clouded and grey and a high wind was blowing. Anxiously the passengers asked the porters and sailors what kind of crossing we could expect, and they reassured us. Within five minutes after we sailed the boat seemed to leap to the sky and fall into a bottomless precipice. The passengers who had proudly sat and arranged themselves on their deck-chairs, with covers, pipes, candies, and books, hurriedly disappeared below. Within half an hour all state-rooms were engaged and the deck deserted. I too felt deadly sick. The whole boat seemed to go round with me. I did not know what to do, it was so suffocating. So courageously I tried the advice of one of the sailors to go on the deck. As soon as I arrived, the wind almost blew me down the stairway. I fought against it and made the round of the deck. Not a soul; everything deserted. I wondered what had happened to "le Petit." There he was, leaning against the railing with his back to the sea, laughing and chatting with Nouvel, who lay flat, opposite him, in a deck-chair, all rolled up in covers like a mummy, with a greenish-blue complexion, so hidden by shawls that only the tip of his nose could be seen. I immediately decided that though I die I would stay. With all my will-power I stood there smiling, in the howling wind which blew my veil, my skirt. A sailor pulled up a chair in the sheltered side near Nouvel, tucked me in covers, and I bravely smiled at Nijinsky. He seemed to be greatly amused. Nouvel crawled more and more under the covers, closed his eyes and became mute. Nijinsky began to talk to me in Russian, with a few French words. Now it was my turn to listen and not to understand, but his expression, his mimicry, were so expressive that I hardly noticed that our conversation was merely pantomime. I forgot the stormy sea. It seemed like a minute and we were already in Dover.

Poor Anna had been terribly sick. "Never again." "But, Anna, I found a marvellous cure against sea-sickness; to flirt." And she actually doubted my word when I told her I flirted *"avec 'le Petit.'"* But where was Diaghileff, where was Vassily? I don't know. I suppose too sick to come on deck to keep their vigil. For once I had succeeded. As we pulled up at the station in London I saw Diaghileff, smartly dressed as always, standing there with a group of distinguished-looking men waving their straw hats to Nijinsky. He jumped alertly off the train and was immediately surrounded and whirled away to a motor-car. As I passed by, to my great amazement he took off his hat and waved good-bye. Diaghileff turned around and looked at me. I was surprised at Nijinsky's courage.

Back at work again, Cecchetti was very pleased with me. I practised even at home, until he forbade me to overwork myself. I lived in a very smart but small hotel in Mayfair behind St. James's Palace. I knew London well, and had a wonderful time with my English relatives, who took me around, visited the picture galleries, and took me for beautiful drives in the park. As often as I could I asked them to take me to lunch and dinner at the Savoy. Nijinsky and Diaghileff, as usual, were staying there; their headquarters were at the grill-room around three o'clock. There, near the open fireplace. Diaghileff had his reserved table, where he held his court.

The London programme was practically the same as in Paris. The favourite ballets, *Sylphides, Spectre, Igor,* of course, were repeated, as well as the same novelties. *Dieu Bleu, Salomé, Jeux,* and *Sacre* were given. The *Dieu Bleu* and *Salomé* had a polite but not over-enthusiastic reception. In the first Nijinsky, in the latter Karsavina, achieved great personal success. *Jeux* puzzled the audience immensely. They were greatly interested to see for the first

NIJINSKY

Elliott and Fry

Vaslav Nijinsky at 22, at the height of his career.

Courtesy of the Dance Collection. The New York Public Library

Serge Diaghileff "He was a genius, the greatest organizer, discoverer, and developer of talents, with the soul of an artist and a grand seigneur...."

Brown Brothers

Petrouchka   "Nijinsky at once grasped the possibilities of the marionette with the living soul...."

Petrouchka Perhaps Fokine's greatest masterpiece and Nijinsky's favorite role.

Brown Brothers

Brown Brothers

Le Spectre de la Rose "Nijinsky's famous last leap in *Le Spectre,* in which he crossed the whole stage from front to back in a single bound, was an astonishing tour de force...."

Festin Presented at the premiere of the Imperial Russian Ballet in Paris, Nijinsky's performance created a furor of enthusiasm.

(Below) Nijinsky in the Siamese dance from *Les Orientales.*

Brown Brothers

Culver Pictures, Inc.

Culver Pictures, Inc.

Scheherazade "The slave, danced by Nijinsky, brought out the animal side of human nature—physical love...."

Courtesy of the Dance Collection, The New York Public Library

Igor Stravinsky and Nijinsky at
the premiere of *Petrouchka*.

Culver Pictures, Inc.

Narcisse Dissatisfied with Fokine's idea of Ancient Greece, Nijinsky began to work out the concepts that resulted in *L'Après-midi d'un Faune.*

L'Après-midi d'un Faune "He was the very image of an adolescent faun, a young being half animal, half human...."

Wicked Paris Shocked At Last!

How the Ballet of the Faun (More Stupid Than Wicked) Has Set the French Capital by the Ears, and Threatens to Cost the Great Sculptor Rodin His Palace for Approving It

EVEN Paris has been shocked, and now all Paris is talking in a most voluble manner about the shocking performance that has shocked it. It is the sort of discussion that delights Paris inexpressibly.

It might have been supposed that Paris was beyond shocking, but the miracle has been accomplished and everybody marvels in it.

With the shocking of Paris many elements are involved, including the great sculptor Rodin ... chapel with ...

and to enable the fauns to enjoy themselves more thoroughly. They added: were the handmaidens of nature. Pan, the god of nature, was particularly fond of them, and never appeared anywhere without an attendant train of nymphs and fauns.

Nijinski made himself look as much like a Faun as possible, but he had to omit the goat's feet. He wore almost nothing; but the nympha wore costumes.

The performance was certainly audacious but not very clever. It demonstrated chiefly the unsuitability of the subject for the mod... ... were curio...

ballet in the ordinary form. He "Any one who imagines that such an exhibition is poetic or artistic is sadly mistaken. Realism of this character will never be tolerated by the representative French public."

On the following day a host of defenders of the ballet began to arise and assail its critics as prudes and Puritans. "You would put frock coats on the fauns and paniers on the nymphs," cried the defenders. One of them coined a new phrase to describe Nijinski's characterization of the faun. He ...

confined wit... imposed b... tionality."

Then the ously. Rod... that let loo... had a roo... sculptor...

To und... took it French quired a cost...

Courtesy of the Dance Collection, The New York Public Library

Nijinsky shocks Paris with his first original ballet, *L'Après-midi d'un Faune.* "Parisian audiences are very broadminded, but this piece appeared too gross and animal for the majority of those present.... M. Nijinsky, who has been a great favorite with the Paris theatre-going public, was roundly hissed."

Courtesy of the Dance Collection, The New York Public Library.

Signification des principales indications éventuelles pouvant figurer en tête de l'adresse.

D...... = Urgent.
AR..... = Remettre contre reçu.
PC..... = Accusé de réception.
RP..... = Réponse payée.
TC..... = Télégramme collationné.
MP..... = Remettre en mains propres.

XPx..... = Exprès payé.
NUIT.... = Remettre même pendant la nuit.
JOUR... = Remettre seulement pendant le jour.
OUVERT= Remettre ouvert.

Dans les télégrammes imprimés en caractères romains par l'appareil télégraphique, le premier nombre qui figure après le nom du lieu d'origine est un numéro d'ordre, le second indique le nombre de mots taxés, les suites désignent la date et l'heure de dépôt.

Dans le service intérieur et dans les relations avec certains pays étrangers, l'heure de dépôt est indiquée au moyen des chiffres de 0 à 24.

L'État n'est soumis à aucune responsabilité à raison du service de la correspondance privée par la voie télégraphique. (Loi du 29 novembre 1850, art. 6.)

ORIGINE.	NUMÉRO.	NOMBRE DE MOTS.	DATE.	HEURE DE DÉPÔT.	MENTIONS DE SERVICE.

Indications de service.

Timbre à date.

N°

+ BUDAPEST 42.-7739 20 4 10/30.-

PRIERE COMMUNIQUEZ AUX JOURNEAUX QUE JE NE TRAVAILLERAI PLUS

AVEC DIAGHILEW ADRESSE 51· HIDEGKUTI UT BUDAPEST AMITIES = NIJINSKY +

RECU LE
5 FEC. 1913
N° 4.66/.

Nijinsky's telegram of resignation, breaking his relationship with Diaghileff and the Ballet Russe, 1913.

Nijinsky and his family. "From the first day the child was shown to him, the adoration which he always had for his daughter began...."

Culver Pictures, Inc.

Studying a ballet score at his piano. "He was attempting to find a system through which dances and all human movement could be written down...."

Underwood and Underwood

Courtesy of the Dance Collection, The New York Public Library

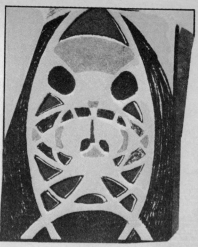

Nijinsky's watercolors and drawings at the time of his approaching madness.

Courtesy of the Dance Collection, The New York Public Library

Nijinsky and his wife, Romola, in Vienna after
World War II.

time sports done on the stage, it was so novel. But somehow the extreme *finesse* of the underlying subject and
the stylisation of the movement escaped their understanding. They expected a real game of tennis played by Nijinsky, Karsavina, and Schollar. The critics complained the
tennis-ball was too big. But they never realised that the
tennis was merely a suggestion to bring to choreographic
art the atmosphere of sport and the modern athletic spirit,
and poor Bakst had to make the ball bigger to make it
visible. He was dealing with art and theatrical effect.

There were also lengthy comments in the papers about
Nijinsky's tennis trousers, because they were not made
according to the classical pattern. The *première* of *Sacre*
was of course the chief event of the season. Many of the
public had already seen it in Paris. The critics were discussing *Sacre* in the foyers during the *entr'actes* of the
other performances. One could feel they were greatly impressed, and finally tremendous applause broke out. Part
of the audience did not take part in it. But everyone felt
that they had heard and seen something quite unusual
and far-reaching, only they could not quite comprehend
it yet, and their reaction was expectation of what this
new creation would lead to. They responded intellectual-
ly and not emotionally, as had Paris.

As often as I could I went on the stage before the
start of the performance. Sometimes I was lucky to find
"le Petit" practising. He did not turn his head quite so
abruptly away when I looked at him. Sometimes I noticed a shadow of a smile. During the *entr'actes* he always
disappeared in his dressing-room. And after the performance, as usual, he was surrounded by his friends and
the adoring audience. Outside the theatre big crowds always waited, not gesticulating, shouting, as in Paris, trying to touch or to kiss Nijinsky or Karsavina, but politely
murmuring, "Bravo! Bravo!" Nijinsky and Diaghileff, with
their friends, had a late supper at the Savoy restaurant.
Nijinsky sat there like a prince. He had something so
refined about his appearance, and a dinner jacket suited
him. He so often had a distant observing look in his half-
closed oblique eyes which I adored, and which was fas-

cinating beyond all else. He seemed now almost to take it
for granted that I was here, there, and everywhere where
he appeared in public. He must have wondered how I
managed it. I was really glad now that I had spent so
much on my clothes in Paris. As I always went with some
friends, it must have seemed natural to Diaghileff that I
was present. He realised that I moved in the same society
as he himself.

Nijinsky was simply adored by his English friends. They
loved his simplicity, his naturalness, his enjoyment of all
the fun, and he tried to take part in their sports.

Maestro also liked London. He had so many friends,
Italians, artists, and *ballerinas* of the old school. When he
was free he made his usual rounds of the different ballet
schools to see Adeline Genée dancing at the Coliseum,
Astafieva in her school, Pavlova and her troupe at the
Palace. Then also the nice Italian restaurants were to his
taste. The only rather upsetting moment was when
Madame Cecchetti announced her arrival from St. Petersburg. She was carrying on *Maestro's* school in St. Petersburg during his absence. She was a splendid teacher, an
energetic, kind, but self-willed woman. She knew what she
wanted, and *Maestro* was rather henpecked. The nice
flirtations with the young dancers had to have an end; no
more taking them out for supper. But *Maestro,* being
a great pedagogue, and believing in discipline, never took
out his own pupils or members of the Russian Ballet.

He was overjoyed, and showed us proudly, on his
birthday, the presents he received, and especially his cane
with its heavy gold knob, given him by Nijinsky. He used
it always now, correcting us with it, and we wished there
were less gold on it. I was luckily told in time about the
approaching birthday, and gave *Maestro* a golden purse
filled with sovereigns. This present pleased him immensely, and it proved later on to be a diplomatic move on
my part. One morning, while I was practising, Nijinsky
and Karsavina arrived for their lesson. This had been
advanced for some engagement they had later on, so we
were dismissed. I took a long time to change my dress.
As there was no other exit, I knew I would have a chance

to see them. As I passed, Nijinsky and Karsavina were
doing their *grand battement* already in the centre of the
hall. *Maestro,* who had no corrections to make, watched
with the eyes of a hawk to detect at least some little
mistake. "Tamaroschka, please, just a little bit higher
your arms" (they were perfect). "Vaslav Fomitch,
*glissade, entrechats cinq, pas de basque-double, cabriole
en arabesque, pirouettes, quatre tours en l'air,"* and invented the most unbelievably difficult combination of
steps, yet with the precision of a clock immediately the
obedient pupil executed them. It was a real joy to watch
this lesson. The exercises *à la barre* then in the centre
were executed without stops, in perfect unison. The following adagios, allegros, whatever step came to the mind
of *Maestro,* were promptly done. Both at the same time.
Or he took Nijinsky separately. While he was making
pirouettes, or *tours en l'air,* Karsavina practised her
points quietly in a corner. *Maestro* made a point of making them do all exercises and steps strictly according to
the classical tradition. And invariably before each lesson
he started his little speech. "Tamara Platonova, Vaslav
Fomitch, you may be celebrated, great artists, but here in
my class you are my pupils, nothing but my pupils. Please
forget here all your crazy modern movements, all
that Fokine, Nijinsky nonsense. Please, *ras, daw, tri,
chetiri . . ."* I was speechless. The two obeyed him far
more than we ever did.

Karsavina wore some worn pink or white *tutus* with a
deep décolleté blouse of the same colour. She brought
her own darned ballet-shoes in her hand, shoes which had
seen many days. She became rather disarrayed at the end
of the lesson. Nijinsky, as usual, wore his black, close-
fitting dancing trousers, blue, green or white beautifully
made *crêpe de Chine* shirt (like the one in *Sylphides*),
and white or cream *chevreau* ballet-slippers. Often he
himself took the watering can from *Maestro* and sprinkled
the floor, while *Maestro,* with devilish joy, criticised the
ballets of the evening before, showing that this or that
step was made with a millimetre of error; that in spite of
all the success their dancing was all rubbish, and the good

old days of Petipa were the real ones. He could hardly even forgive the existence of *Spectre* or *Sylphides*. His love stopped at *Swan Lake* and *Giselle*.

He never got tired of complaining of the music. "Very soon, Gaspada, I will not be able to go on the stage, to listen to that sick-cat music of Stravinsky and those crazy French composers."

Vassily was not admitted to these lessons, to my great joy. *Maestro* was omnipotent at his classes. All Vassily could do was to wait in the dressing-room. Diaghileff only appeared sometimes at the end to fetch Nijinsky.

I learned that a new ballet, *Joseph and Potiphar,* was contemplated by Nijinsky, and the principal part was for him. Diaghileff commissioned Richard Strauss to compose the music for it. Ever since the Russian Ballet appeared in Berlin and Vienna, Strauss had expressed his wish to compose a ballet for them. This plan was discussed several times among them. Strauss wanted very much that his customary collaborators, Count Kessler, and the Austrian poet, Hugo von Hofmansthal, should write the story. So they finally agreed. The story of Madame de Potiphar was chosen with the help of Diaghileff; Bakst, who was consulted, conceived the idea of transposing the whole period for the scenery and settings in the time of Paolo Veronese. With its luxurious possibilities, it was more appealing to him, and he saw much more variety in this style to be developed than in the biblical period. The part of the innocent, shy, but religious youth, Joseph, suited Nijinsky's appearance and temperament. Diaghileff signed a contract with Strauss for a hundred thousand gold marks for the musical rights of this ballet. An unheard-of price, and an unheard-of thing for Diaghileff to sign a contract. The artists worked merely on a verbal agreement. The lowest salary, a thousand francs a month and second-class travelling assured, was paid to the *corps de ballet.* They used to get their salaries every month from the stage manager, Grigoriev, or the secretary, Mr. Drobetsky, or, as it happened quite often, they gave the troupe something on account, with the apologies of Sergei Pavlovitch. He had had to pay out so much for scenery, musical rights, etc. Next month the default amount would be replaced, and so on. Only Karsavina got her sixty thousand francs for two months paid punctually, for she was still a member of the Mariinsky, and Diaghileff did not wish her to tell at home that he was not prompt in payment. As for Nijinsky, his salary only existed in theory, for Sergei Pavlovitch, very soon after Nijinsky had left the Mariinsky Theatre, had asked him to lend the money he earned for the enterprise. *"Vatza, j'ai besoin, je dois travailler sans être payé tout de suite. Ce qu'il est payer les nouveaux décors, ou Stravinsky ne veut pas mercenaire. Je prends ton salaire pour les prochains mois."* And so Nijinsky's salary, during those years of enormous financial success, wandered into the *caisse* of the Russian Ballet and was spent for its upkeep. That Nijinsky worked harder than any of them, that the whole structure of the organisation rested upon him, never entered the head of Diaghileff. Neither that, if Stravinsky insisted on being paid, it was not only for mercenary reasons, but because he had a delicate wife and small children. Nijinsky never reminded Diaghileff, who, except for the modest sum Nijinsky sent for his mother and brother, never gave him any money.

There were rumours of a South American tour. I could not believe it. After all this effort, now to be separated from the Ballet! What could be done? I interviewed *Maestro*. "Is there any truth in these rumours?" *Maestro* confirmed them. They were supposed to leave on the 15th of August, after a brief vacation of two weeks, for the Argentine and Brazil. These countries had often invited the Russian Ballet, but they never could fit this trip in with their plans. This year, finally, Diaghileff was able to accept a most profitable contract, and the troupe had to sacrifice its annual vacation.

The soloists were not very enthusiastic, especially Karsavina, and it needed a lot of pleading on Diaghileff's part to induce them. All of them were deadly afraid of the long ocean trip of twenty-one days. The crossing on the Channel was bad enough. So many of them declared that for nothing in the world would they go in that *pays du nègre*. Diaghileff was worried. Monteux refused also to go, so he engaged René Baton, the capable conductor of the Pasdeloup Orchestra in Paris, to replace him. I too was worried. How could I go? I still had a part of the money left which had been advanced to me by Mr. K., the banker, but how to induce the Ballet to take me, my family to let me go? My chance came through the refusal of many of the dancers to go. Drobetsky was commissioned to go to Warsaw and to bring back from there a few talented young dancers. *Maestro* was also requested to find some. And there I reaped what I had sown with my birthday present to *Maestro*. He declared to Sergei Pavlovitch that it would be quite a gain to engage me, and that also Hilda Munnings and Hilde Bewicke were sufficiently advanced to enter the troupe. So we were engaged. Honestly I was not yet entitled to be a member of the troupe. I wired home. A few days later my mother and stepfather arrived in London. They were pleased at last that after all the studies I had achieved something constructive. My mother must have already seen me as a *prima ballerina*. They attended my lessons, which *Maestro* gave in private. He became purple in his efforts to make me dance properly. My parents, in ecstasy, rushed up to the Savoy to make an appointment with Diaghileff. Diaghileff did not appear next day, but instead Drobetsky came and excused Diaghileff, who was too busy to see us. We waited for more than an hour in the lovely yellow reading-room of the Savoy near the lobby, and I was alternately gazing in the fireplace and watching the lobby to see if I could get a glimpse of Nijinsky passing by. How many times I had been watching there for him!

Everything was settled. I was to be taken on a trial tour. If I proved that I could dance they would engage me in the autumn as a regular member, with a salary. At present they would only pay my fare—second class, as for all the other members. My parents consented. I was to buy a first-class ticket for myself, and Anna would use my ticket, for I had to have a *garde de dame* on this journey. Drobetsky promised to look after me with his wife; so later did Baron Gunsburg, who had met my mother through mutual friends.

At one of the last performances in London I was in the balcony, from where I had an excellent view of the stage. *Sylphides* was being danced. By this time I had become not only familiar with the music, which was comparatively easy for me, but I knew practically all the steps of most of the ballets. Nijinsky in *Sylphides* was a dream. I could see it again and again and discover new beauties. This evening he danced the mazurka; suddenly a prayer came to my mind which repeated itself silently: "Thank you, my Lord, that you have permitted me to live in this century, to see Nijinsky dance." As a child I had always regretted not having lived in the Cinquecento, not to know the great artists of the Renaissance, and now my wish in a different way was granted.

At the end of the season Anna and I, after completing all preparations for the South American tour, finally went to an enchanting little village in Sussex. I used to lie in the green grass and gaze at the sky and the majestic old oak-trees, and dream about the ballet and my impressions of Nijinsky. That feeling of apprehension about him I had lost. On the contrary, now he fascinated me. I could not resist the desire to be near him. It is true he was only absorbed in one thing—his art. Society, success, wealth, fame, and flirtations did not seem to mean anything to him. He was surrounded by an impenetrable wall built around him by Diaghileff and by his own reserve. But hadn't I pierced this wall just an infinitesimal bit? It is true we all heard that he had no interest in us women. I knew it. But didn't I catch, in spite of this, here and there a smile, a glance which he threw to me? Where others failed, why shouldn't I succeed? We were both of a different race, nation, could not speak each other's language—a world of difference separated us. He was a world-famous artist, I merely one of the millions of society girls. Every logical argument was against me, but I had in me something more, the invincible desire to awaken Nijinsky's interest. And if ever his genius should be perpetuated, I wanted to be the medium of this transmission.

I passed these two weeks determinedly concentrating upon my wish.

On the 15th of August we left for Southampton. Not speaking Russian, I was lonely. I had never been in daily contact with the troupe and they had already formed little groups on the train. On arrival at Southampton the immensity of the boat impressed me. I had never been on an ocean liner before. The Royal Mail Steamship Company's *Avon* was quite the latest novelty in ocean service.

We were soon on the high seas. I went down to lunch, and found my place at Drobetsky's table. So he kept his word, which he had given to my parents. His wife and Bolm were seated there, and a charming young French Argentinian, M. Chavez, who had some great dressmaking establishment in Buenos Aires. Some of the artists were sitting at other tables. Baron Gunsburg, with his friend Mme. Oblokova, a charming divorcée of St. Petersburg society, was occupying a table with Piltz and Kovalevska.

René Baton and his wife were at the captain's table. Mr. Baton was a great stout man, like a kind, big bear, with a long beard. His wife was typically French, talked with great volubility, and, as I heard, was a capable singer.

After lunch I rushed to see the passenger-list, which was posted on a board. I could not see Nijinsky and Diaghileff anywhere. My God, if they had not come! Was it possible? And I already under way to South America. I heard that Karsavina would join us in Buenos Aires, that she was travelling with her husband on an Italian boat, which was faster. I trembled. If Nijinsky were to go also on that boat! I spent two solid hours trying to find out, and faced the possibility of disembarking at Cherbourg, where we were due at five in the afternoon. But on reading the passenger-list my heart gave one great jump. "Deck A, Cabin No. 60, Mr. Sergei de Diaghileff. Cabin No. 61, Mr. Vaslav Nijinsky."

At once I became gay and happy and raced all through the ship, looking at the passengers, making friends with the stewards and stewardesses, with the sailors, barmen,

and began to flirt with the officers. Quite exhausted
by all this, I went to my cabin to rest. Anna had already
arranged it, and it looked almost like home; photos, flowers in silver vases, cushions, and silk covers, all over the
place. And near my bed a picture of the "Miraculous
Jesus of Prague." I fell asleep, and only awoke around
tea-time. On my way to the dining-room I met Drobetsky,
who was rushing with Grigoriev and Kremenev, Michel,
his wife, and a few of the dancers towards the lower
decks. "What is the hurry? Aren't you coming to tea?"
"Sorry, I can't; we are going to receive Nijinsky who is
boarding the ship here in Cherbourg." What a relief! I
could have kissed Drobetsky for it. I joined the group.
We went on Deck D, where the staircase had been
lowered to take up the passengers. As we looked down
on the approaching tug, we saw, among a group of French
passengers, some dancers of the troupe standing with Nijinsky, and close behind him the gloomy Vassily. "Le Petit"
was in a very elegant travelling-suit and coat and a
smart round travelling-hat which became quite the
fashion. He was looking up to us, saying in Russian,
"Kak bolsh'oi parahod." As he came up the gang-plank,
everybody rushed to him and asked questions. *"Vaslav
Fomitch slava Bogou sh'to wie zdes. Kak pojivaete."* He
smiled, took off his hat—*"Spasiba gaspada ochen hara-
show"*—and disappeared with quick steps into the lift.
I pirouetted away in my happiness. At last Nijinsky was
safe on board. All was well, and I had twenty-one days
before me. Fate was kind. My cabin was also on A Deck,
on the very same corridor as Nijinsky's, some distance
away, but I could quite well supervise his door. In my
great satisfaction and joy I had completely forgotten Diaghileff. Where was he? But I had no chance to find out
until dinner, when Drobetsky told us that he was not coming to South America. It was said officially that he was
kept back in Europe by unexpected business, but he told
us in confidence that Diaghileff could not overcome his
terrible fear of an ocean trip and went for a rest to the
Lido. Baron Gunsburg was officially in charge of the com-

pany. He also was co-director, but only in name until then.

We all soon settled down to the agreeable routine of deck life. My deck-chair was on the north side, near those of the Gunsburgs and Drobetskys. I spent a great part of my days with Oblokova, Kovalevska, and Piltz. Oblokova was already in the forties but extremely well preserved and smartly dressed. She had beautiful jewels, and her greatest pleasure was match-making or arranging little love-affairs. In the morning I used to pace around the deck for one or two hours either in Gunsburg's or Bolm's company. I soon noticed that a sudden friendship had sprung up between Nijinsky and the Batons. They took hold of him the very first morning on deck. I overheard the conversation. With deep respect Baton was praising Nijinsky's art, and Mme. Baton joined him in an unending flow of words. But Nijinsky shook his head.

"No, no, moi pas comprend, moi parle petit nègre."

At this Baton flung his arms around Nijinsky, kissed him on both cheeks, so it could be heard on the whole boat, and declared, shouting, *"Quel enfant adorable, quel simplicité, c'est moi qui serai votre nana pendant le voyage."* And Baton was true to his word. No real nurse could have looked after a child with more attention and devotion than he and his wife had for Nijinsky on the trip. The day after we left Cherbourg the members of the company who were travelling second class got permission to visit us. Thereafter they came over quite often.

Lisbon was the last European port where we called, the last chance where Diaghileff could still join us, as I heard that he might. I dreaded this, and prayed steadily that he should not. By this time I was on friendly terms with most of the passengers and seemed to be quite a favourite.

We formed a little group to visit the Royal Castle at Cintra, the Gunsburgs, my old flirt Kovalevska, Piltz, and Bolm, all attired for the *escale* loaded with photographic cameras, binoculars, and hats as if we were already in the tropics. We got into small boats and were taken to the shore. We had the whole day before us. I could not see Nijinsky. One day lost for me. We took carriages and drove all around this quaint old southern city. It was frightfully dusty—even the palm trees looked grey—but it had some beautiful palaces and cathedrals. We had a queer, spicy lunch with a lot of Portuguese red wine, and departed to Cintra in high spirits.

This palace and its gardens were really enchanting. We enjoyed it, and after spending a small fortune on postcards and small souvenirs, returned to the port. The launches were waiting for us, and we were rapidly transported. I could have cried with disappointment, seeing Nijinsky in the next boat with Chavez and the Batons. Next time I resolved to be with him.

After breakfast I usually came on deck and found Nijinsky in his deck-chair reading or studying some designs. He seldom looked up and never greeted me. I was furious. Why, what had happened? After all, in London he melted just a tiny bit. Now he ignored my existence again. My God, how hopeless! The day Nijinsky came on board I said to Anna, "Now here is my chance. Twenty-one days of ocean and sky—no Diaghileff. He can't escape. By the time we arrive I will have a flirtation with 'le Petit.' *Ce que femme veut Dieu le veut.*"

Anna smiled unbelievingly, and every evening, without a word, she tore off one day from the calendar, looking at me. I was quite annoyed by this, but never said anything to her. We were all on deck until lunch, after which many read or went to sleep.

I soon discovered that Nijinsky spent his time differently. On Deck C, in a small hall where the staircase led to the dining-room, was a piano. Here, around three, René Baton played Bach preludes, fugues, and Nijinsky was composing. At first I sat very timidly on the top of the staircase, and was requested to leave by the chief steward. A day later I came back. This time René Baton politely asked me to go. Nijinsky seemed sunk in the notes. I could have boxed his ears. Always indifferent! It was exasperating. Suddenly he looked up and pantomimed to Baton that I could stay. So I was officially installed on

the step. Every afternoon I was the first to be there, and
I appeared unfailingly. It was remarkable to watch him
compose.

Baton played on the piano and Nijinsky stood beside
him. Sometimes he closed his eyes and gave the impression
that he did it to concentrate more on a whole choreographic theme. Or with his fingers he danced a full variation, which he composed while Baton played the piece; or
he stopped him suddenly, made him play the same bar
several times. All the time, as he stood there, one could
feel that he was dancing constantly the steps he invented.
And so a whole ballet was created before my wondering
eyes. Occasionally he searched with Baton for hours for
a suitable chaconne, or prelude. He stopped Baton often,
saying, *"Crois, plus vite";* and Baton laughed. "How true.
I made a mistake. It is supposed to be faster." Nijinsky,
as I was told later on by musicians, was extraordinarily
musical, and he felt the very essence of the music. Baton
told me Nijinsky was composing a new ballet on the music
of Bach, to be as pure dancing as his music is pure sound.
He wanted to lay down the harmony and the fundamental
truth of the movement. It was supposed to be put in the
period of Louis XIV, but without a story, as it should be
purely choreographic. Always when Baton failed to make
himself understood, Gunsburg was summoned as interpreter. Very soon I tried to make myself liked by them.
As I had been educated in Paris, and spoke French like a
native, I won Mme. Baton's heart easily. But I liked them
both. They were kind, good-hearted people. Among all
these Russians we formed the little Western European
colony. Of course, nobody knew that I was admitted to
observe these hours of composition. I often wondered why
I was permitted.

The days passed very quickly in this gay, peaceful atmosphere. Nijinsky used to come on deck every morning
around eleven. He was always very smartly dressed in a
light-coloured suit or white flannel trousers and dark blue
coat. I often wondered what he was doing so late; sleeping
probably. One morning, as I could not sleep, I walked
around the upper deck. It was a clear breezy day, about

eight o'clock. On the north side of the boat I saw a crowd watching attentively. What could it be? Nobody plays tennis or deck games at such an unearthly hour. The crowd was around a space which was kept apart by ropes tied from the railing and the life-boats up to the wall of the funnel-house. In the middle of this space, in the sunshine and the refreshing breeze, Nijinsky practised. So that was the way he spent his mornings? It had never occurred to me. The passengers who loved a brisk walk in the morning, and the sporty Englishmen who had seen and admired the Ballet in London, were looking on, with exclamations of approval and admiration.

It was interesting to watch how much those sports-loving men could understand and appreciate the tremendous work which was needed to make a perfect dancer. To watch Nijinsky practise was a special pleasure. All movements were perfect, without hesitation, with an assurance that gave one the feeling that the dance for him was like breathing for any other human being. Each attitude so like sculpture, that I could well understand why Rodin had said that "each pose was a living Michelangelo, Donatello, Giovanni da Bologna." Vassily "the inevitable" stood near the watering-can and rosin-box with a bath-towel. The audience seemed to annoy him, but Nijinsky did not mind. He was smiling. He seemed to be so much gayer and rested than I had ever seen him before. Once or twice he even gave explanations about his steps to the Englishmen, who discussed each motion from their athletic point of view. Mr. Williams, Nijinsky's private *masseur,* stood in their midst. The sailors hidden near the life-boat, the officer in the crowd, and even those on duty on the bridge, peeped from time to time. I wondered if the boat would not stop soon if they went on in this way. For an hour and a half every morning he practised under the same conditions. Of course, I was present; I even sacrificed my morning sleep. When he finished he slipped his dark green silk dressing-gown over his practice costume and disappeared, accompanied by Mr. Williams and Vassily, in the lift. It did not take me long to make the acquaintance of Mr. Williams.

I had suddenly developed an interest in athletics. For hours I listened about the boxers and their matches, the Henley regattas, the training for them, about the athletic club where he was chief *masseur;* the difference between the Swedish school and the medical massage—I became almost an expert—also about the family of Mr. Williams, his four sisters who were nursery governesses on the Continent, his parents, and his native village. But in return for my enthusiastic listening I learned to know the whole musculature of Nijinsky, which Williams knew and loved, each muscle separately. Because Nijinsky was so perfectly built, he gave up his steady position in London to travel with him all around the world, only to give him an hour's massage each day. He could talk for hours about dancing—only anatomically, of course. After one hour of this soothing massage he was exhausted, he who could massage the strongest boxer for several hours easily, but Nijinsky's muscles were of iron.

I walked around the deck from eleven to seven, always when Nijinsky was in his deck-chair. My *beaux* alternately had to escort me. Every time I passed "le Petit" I either greeted him or talked louder or laughed so that he should look up and see me. I was determined not to give him any peace until he noticed me. I got tired of being introduced all over again, always to be forgotten and ignored the next second. What miles I walked around that deck, I who hated so much this kind of exercise! Every evening Anna slowly, silently, triumphantly, tore off another slip of the calendar.

Bolm by this time knew everybody worth while on the boat. He was amusing and sociable, perhaps too quickly familiar, but well liked, and he shared the position of *maître de plaisir* with Gunsburg. We used to take long walks around the deck after dinner. Often Kovalevska, with whom I became very friendly, joined us.

Nijinsky sometimes passed near us with Baton or Chavez, but never was aware of us; was it only pretence? One morning Kovalevska came with a flushed face and talked to Piltz like a torrent. Finally they told me what had happened. Grigoriev had ordered all members of

the troupe to practise every morning on deck. We had to
have a class. It was, as we found out, Nijinsky's idea.
He thought twenty-one days would be too long for the
troupe to be without training if they had to dance afterwards. I was panic-stricken. I was used to *Maestro,* and
was shy and afraid of the others; he knew my shortcom-
ings and could help me out. Somehow I always hoped
that a miracle would happen and I would be a good
dancer by the time we arrived in South America. I confessed my fright to Kovalevska, and she proposed to show
me all the parts I was supposed to have, so that I should
know the steps before rehearsals. Often she came to my
cabin or I went to hers, and we had breakfast together.
We looked at each other's wardrobe and clothes, her
beautiful jewellery, the photos; we discussed lengthily
all gossip and happenings.

She was perfectly beautiful, with the face of a Ma-
donna, and had great success as a woman in Paris and
London, yet she remained unspoiled. We started to practise next morning. It was not as easy as it looked. The
boat seemed to glide on the water, which was like ultra-
marine oil, but the moment we began our *pliés* or *battements* we lost our balance. How could Nijinsky do it?
It was ten times as difficult as usual. I wished for a storm
so that he could feel how difficult it was for us to practise
on the boat. But next morning, when a terrific sirocco
blew up, he was dancing with as perfect ease as ever.
The days passed in practise, enjoyment, flirtation and
laziness. Anna went on tearing the calendar's slips.
Nijinsky was keeping his daily routine: practise in the
morning, study, reading in his deck-chair until lunch, then
composition with Baton, which I faithfully attended. Now
I knew from Baton that the Bach ballet was to be
transposed for organ and big orchestra, and the clavichord
would not be used. He chose Benois to design the scenery
as the most familiar with this period. Nijinsky had visited
Richard Strauss previously with Diaghileff at Baden-
Baden, and later in Garmisch, where he had a villa.
Strauss played a part of the score of *Potiphar* for them.
Nijinsky was greatly disappointed by the music, as it was

not at all what he had expected from Strauss after *Salomé* and *Elektra*. He thought it a very feeble composition, and told Diaghileff he did not want to compose the choreography. Diaghileff tried to persuade him, but Nijinsky could not be influenced, not even by Diaghileff, if he felt a thing was wrong from an artistic point of view.

Baron Gunsburg flew on deck after lunch one day saying they had just decided there would be a costume ball that evening. Of course, the members of the Ballet must have the most amusing costumes. The hairdresser of the ship had costumes for hire, but we decided they were unworthy of our company. Also they were quickly taken by the other passengers. Oblokova suggested everybody should make up his own costume. A mad rush began. Every one of us raced from one another's cabin backwards and forwards. Everyone made his costume in secret. They advised me to have a Hungarian gypsy costume. The second class was invited. After running around for hours to get together all I needed, with Anna's help I tried it on, but did not like it. I immediately went over to Oblokova. She was pleased with it. Maria Stepanovna and our hairdresser were as busy as on the day of a dress rehearsal. Gunsburg came after me, advising: "Romola Carlovna, I have thought it over, I have a brilliant idea for a costume for you. It would be so original. You are so slim, you look almost like a boy. Hide your hair and put on these pyjamas of mine." And he passed a pair of lovely tailored apple-green pyjamas to me. "Great! But don't tell anybody," he said.

When I was all dressed—or, that is to say, undressed—I showed myself to Gunsburg, who approved it. As the time came to go to dinner, somehow I felt something was wrong. I looked at myself in the mirror. It looked all right. But an inexplicable feeling kept me back. I changed and put on a lovely evening dress from Callot Sœurs, dressed my hair, and half an hour later I descended to dinner. They all shouted at me, "Where have you been? Where is your costume? What happened?" I only shook my head and, going down the staircase, I met Nijinsky's eyes. He looked up at me, and I noticed a sigh of relief. The two of us, and of course the officers, were the only ones not in costume: Oblokova as an odalisque, Gunsburg as a marquis, Bolm as Nebuchadnezzar, and so on. Of course, all the prizes went to the members of the Ballet.

The ball was gay, and lasted until late in the morning. Most of us had breakfast in costume. Nijinsky disappeared around one o'clock, after having watched the merry-making.

The following day we were all sleepy, but had to be at Gunsburg's "Equator Party" at 12:30 p.m. As we passed "the line" we were baptised with champagne by those who had already crossed this latitude.

One evening as we paced around the deck, Chavez turned to me saying: "That is all very well, Mlle. de Pulszky. I understand your admiration for the ballet, for Nijinsky's art; for all of us on the stage he is the *Dieu de la danse;* but in life he is a human being, a charming young man in fact. Why are you afraid of him?"

"I am not," I replied furiously.

"Then come on. I will present you to him."

"I don't want to."

"Now, come on, don't be silly. You admire him. He is captivating. He won't harm you. We are great pals, in spite of the fact that we can't speak to each other very much."

"I refuse. I won't go. I am sick of it. I have been presented to him over and over again, and he does not even know I exist. Let me alone." By this time Chavez had dragged me to the other side of the deck.

It was a beautiful moonlit night; the ocean looked superb. In the main lobby they were dancing some tango, and the lights of the hall threw their shadows on the dimly lighted deck. It was practically empty. A few men smoked in their deck-chairs, and couples were in the dark corners, flirting, whispering.

Nijinsky was half leaning against the railing, in "smoking," holding a small black fan which was ornamented with one gold painted rose. He was rapidly fanning himself. He looked so strange. His eyes were half closed and oh! so slanted. He conversed in a soft, melodious voice with Kovalevska in Polish. I was trembling as Chavez said, *"Monsieur Nijinsky, permettez moi de vous présenter Mlle. de Pulszky."* He did not move; his eyes just closed with an imperceptible *nuance* and he slightly inclined his head. Kovalevska at once began to explain to him who I was and all about my love of dancing. Nijinsky listened without saying a word. Chavez insisted, *"N'avez pas peur,"* and repeated to Nijinsky what he told me before about him. I felt that both Kovalevska and Chavez were expecting me to say something. But suddenly every thought deserted me. I felt a chaos of emotion, saw nothing and nobody any more except the dark, graceful silhouette of Nijinsky and his fascinating eyes. I suddenly heard myself speaking. *"Je veux vous remercier que vous avez élevé la danse à la hauteur des autres arts."* Kovalevska translated. He did not move. Suddenly he looked at the small ring I wore. I followed his gaze, and, pulling it off my finger, I passed it to him, explaining: "My father brought it from Egypt; it is a talisman supposed to bring luck. My mother gave it to me as I left with the Russian Ballet." It was a green-gold serpent whose head was crushed by a scarab. It had a strange design. Nijinsky held it for one moment and then put it on my finger, saying in Polish, "It will bring you happiness, surely." We all four of us began to walk around the deck. Suddenly Nijinsky stopped, looked into the phosphorescent waves. They were more luminous tonight than I had ever seen them before. I saw he was fascinated by the motion of the sea. He looked and looked. For a long time we watched in silence. Then I began to talk in French, choosing the easiest words about dance, music, and Wagner, whose work I idolised: *Lohengrin, Valkyrie, Tristan,* Bayreuth, and my childhood days, which I had spent with my sister and brother-in-law at the Wahnfried at the rehearsals in the Festspielhaus. I don't know if he understood a word of what I said, but he seemed to listen attentively. I had to talk to hide my nervousness, my confusion. Then Chavez called us.

They were pacing up and down the deck. "Come, come

and look at the new constellations, the stars which cannot be seen on the northern hemisphere." We looked up and saw in all its brilliant splendour the Southern Cross.

The great part of this night, as usual, I spent in kneeling before the picture of the Petit Jesus de Prague, praying for His miraculous intervention. Hours and hours, with a fanatic concentration, I implored, almost forcing the "divine child" to grant my wish. At first my request was personal—to make Nijinsky interested in me. Now that for the first time I began to feel, to see, the super-human intelligence working for me, now it was, "Make Nijinsky happy some way, somehow; save him from the way of life he is leading with Diaghileff." Unacknowledged even to myself, I wanted to reform him for myself, but cunningly I thought I might deceive God with my un-selfish prayer, taking it for granted that the Almighty Himself had an orthodox attitude towards sexual relation-ship, and would condemn a form of it which He Himself created.

We were nearing the South American continent. The next day we saw from the distance a brown line; it was the coast of Brazil. We were all happy and almost wish-ing that this trip should never end. I was in high spirits, of course, but great was my amazement when Nijinsky the following day, except for a polite bow, ignored me as much as before. Once I managed to get in the lift in the morning in which he was also going to practise. I thought that perhaps he would now look at me, as my coral silk dancing costume and ballet-shoes suited me well, and were quite becoming, but not even a glance. I walked and walked around the deck almost to exhaustion. Ni-jinsky was taking lessons from an Englishman on how to light and smoke a pipe. It must have been fun, for they were all laughing a lot. As I knew, he never even smoked a cigarette. But I was more furious than ever. I passed the days with my usual set and never even referred to "le Petit's" existence. I was peeved, and decided to ig-nore him.

Kovalevska proved a patient, kind teacher. I had al-ready learned from her the parts from *Igor, Scheherazade,*

Cléopâtre, that I was supposed to dance. We were learning *Sylphides,* but she was not quite sure, neither was Grigoriev, if I would be cast in it. It depended upon what Nijinsky would think. I felt that I would rather die than dance before him. That whole appearance on the stage seemed to be a hazy nightmare, and I put even the idea itself away from me. If only *Maestro* would come along! But instead of that he was eating spaghetti in Milan.

During the trip we had many balls, as did the second class. This night after dinner, as we were chatting on deck, we heard weird, enchanting Spanish music. One of the dancers came over from the second class and called us. "Come on, they have a ball in the steerage. They are dancing boleros and fandangos, tarantellas and real tango." We all went. The steerage was full of Italian and Spanish peasants called "swallows," going over to the Argentine for the harvest. On the deck they danced, they played their music on cisharmonicas, singing among them. All around, the curious spectators looked on. Their dances were enchanting. "Le Petit" was there with the Batons. The latter explained with words and hands the rhythm, the eight pitches of a single note of the Spanish Tsigane music. Nijinsky seemed to have extreme pleasure watching these genuine dancers of folk-lore, and he applauded. Gunsburg found that they had a decidedly far better time in the third class than we had.

Returning, I managed to come close to Nijinsky. Exasperated by his last days' indifference, and encouraged by the champagne we had at dinner, I pulled myself together, and taking Kovalevska by her hand, I asked her to translate with infinite excitement and determination. I said, "Vaslav Fomitch, you have forgotten last year at the Monte Carlo Palace Hotel, the little pillow your mother sent to you, on which you always slept and which I heard you cherished so much. I have it. May I send it back to you?"

Nijinsky gave me one long look and, mounting up the stairs, said to Kovalevska, "Tell her please to keep it."

I could have choked him.

Only a day more and we were due in Rio de Janeiro,

the dream city with the most beautiful harbour in the world. Our friends and fellow passengers could not praise its site sufficiently. And then five more days—and Buenos Aires, the end of our trip, and of all our delightful intimacy and the possibility for me to be so informally near Nijinsky. I had failed; I was beaten. I could not even reply to Anna when, the previous evening, tearing the calender slip off, she said calmly, "The sixteenth day. Really, Miss Romola, I wouldn't run after a hay-cart which refuses to give a lift," quoting an old Hungarian proverb.

As we were sitting in the bar before lunch, the Batons, Kovalevska, Piltz, and the others, Gunsburg came up. "Romola, please come. I have to talk to you." I became quite upset. My God, what had I done? Did I dance too badly? Did Kremenev or Grigoriev report me? I could not think. The others teased me. I followed Gunsburg silently on deck. There he stopped, and with a terribly formal face he said, "Romola Carlovna, as Nijinsky cannot speak to you himself, he has requested me to ask you in marriage." We looked at each other, and then I burst out: "No, really, Dmitri Nikolaivitch, it's awful. How can you?"; and, blushing, half crying, I ran as fast as I could down to my cabin, where I locked myself up for the rest of the day.

So they all made fun of me. This terrible joke. They had noticed what I was up to. I felt like a fool. I could never face them again. But what was I to do? To stay in the cabin until Buenos Aires and then to return home to Budapest directly? Yes, that was the only possibility, without even seeing them again. But Nijinsky I could not leave. Never to see him dance! Certainly he would be greatly angered if he knew about Gunsburg's incredible joke.

I stayed in my cabin. They knocked at my door, the page-boy saying, "Please won't you come up for tea?" Kovalevska asked admittance, inquiring if I was sick. I did not even let Anna in, saying I had a terrible headache, didn't want to be disturbed and was trying to sleep. How much did they know?

After dinner a nice note came from Gunsburg: "Dear Romola Carlovna,—I am so sorry you are not feeling quite well. Why did you run away? If you are unable to come on deck, please let me know your answer. I must say something to Nijinsky. I can't keep him waiting like this." I wondered. The note fell out of my hand, and it seemed to me that on the face of my miraculous Jesus of Prague a smile lingered.

Quickly I put on an evening dress and summoned Anna. She fixed my hair, and I sent her up to find out where they all were. She reported: The Batons were with some French people in the drawing-room; Gunsburg, Bolm, and my set were all in the bar, where pools were held. Nijinsky she could not see anywhere. I was relieved. Probably he had retired already. It was past eleven o'clock, so I went on deck and walked around. Unexpectedly, from nowhere Nijinsky emerged and said: *"Mademoiselle, voulez-vous, vous et moi?"* and pantomimed, indicating on the fourth finger of the left hand a ring. I nodded and, waving with both hands, said, *"Oui, oui, oui."*

Very gently taking my hand, without a word he led me up to the upper deck. This was deserted. He pulled two deck-chairs under the captain's bridge, and there we sat in silence, hearing the rhythmically recurring steps of the officers on duty, the sound of the waves, following the line of the smoke which rose from the funnels, a dark ribbon against the clear night sky, which was covered by milliards of stars. I could feel the soothing, unceasing throb of the boat, and my own wildly beating heart. Everything was so peaceful in this tepid tropic night. I knew Nijinsky felt as I did. And as this white boat sailed placidly, with an inward, hidden tremor, in the vastness of the infinite ocean, towards its destination, so did we towards our fate.

Next morning as I woke I lay motionless. Was this all only a dream, or was it really true? Could it be possible that I was engaged to be married to Nijinsky? The stewardess, followed by Anna, brought in my breakfast tray. Soon somebody knocked, and Kovalevska, fully dressed, whirled into the cabin, flung her arms around me, kissed me in the Russian fashion. "Ah, Romola Carlovna, I am so happy, so happy! This is indeed wonderful news. I congratulate you with all my heart. Unbelievable. But somehow I always knew Vaslav Fomitch is not as people say." And suddenly, as if she would have caught herself on something, she stopped. "I mean, I am glad for both of you."

"How did you know it?"

"Well, I just received a note from Vaslav Fomitch asking me to tell you that he wishes to take us both on land to see Rio, and to get the engagement-ring. He invited me to escort you both as chaperone and in the capacity of an official interpreter." And so she pirouetted around. "I am as glad as if it were my own day of betrothal. Oh, to see the faces of the others when they hear! Now hurry up. Take your bath. Dress quickly. We are supposed to meet Vaslav Fomitch on the quay at eleven. And we must not miss the view of the entrance to the port."

As we arrived on deck, everybody was there viewing the panorama which was unfolding itself before our enchanted eyes. We steamed slowly up the bay. The bay of Rio. Against the deep azure sky in blinding sunshine, all enveloped in a golden glamour, stands out the circular range of palm-covered mountains like a cascade, following an inexhaustible torrent of plants, trees, flowers; in the middle of the bay the mighty Peak of the Pão de Asucar, the mountain directly and proudly rising from the sea in the shape of a loaf of sugar, with the blue-white waves splashing all around, playing, caressing. The houses became more distinct, white, lovely marble buildings, graceful against the deep green background. A huge, beautiful, natural amphitheatre encircled us. We could only look and look, and we ran from one side of the boat to the other, exclaiming at each turn: *"C'est presque mieux que du Bakst."*

Here we drew alongside the well-constructed quay, and very quickly we could disembark. Everybody was so occupied with the beauty of the spot that I could escape with Kovalevska without being noticed and meet Nijinsky at the quay. We jumped into a car and drove through the lovely broad streets, through a wide avenue full of shops, bordered with slender palm-trees which stood hundreds of metres high, like a long line of soldiers. At the end stood the lovely theatre. Kovalevska and Nijinsky spoke all the time I sat between them, and I felt like a schoolgirl out on a Sunday treat.

We stopped before a jewellery shop, and they both asked for rings. Heavy wide golden marriage-rings were shown. Probably they were after the taste of the fat Spanish and Portuguese women. Nijinsky did not like them. I was glad, because their weight had inspired me with awe. Finally he selected two rather flat, dull gold bands, and wrote on a piece of paper the names and dates which he wished to have engraved.

We changed our horse-car for an automobile, and drove up to one of the mountains called Sylvestre, the most heavenly place on earth. Here, in the middle of the virgin forest on the top, was a hotel, the smart place of the town in the early spring. The first people we saw at the place were the Drobetskys and our friends the Anglo-Argentine couple. They were just finishing lunch and were ready to go for a drive in the jungle which surrounded the hotel. They were rather surprised to see our trio.

We were very gay during our lunch. It was the first time I ever sat with Nijinsky at a table. We decided to drive through the dense forests, with their towering, orchid-laden trees, amidst flowers, millions and millions, quaint, unwholesome-looking, but sensual blooms, in all kinds of shades—violent reds, greens, blues. The mountain-tops rose above here and there. We were lost, plunged into this ocean of foliage. The air was tepid and caressing, and suddenly, by certain turns of the narrow road, a stream of icy-cold current hit us for a second. It was all like a dream, this drive, all the time sitting between Kovalevska and Nijinsky. Until dusk we drove, and then, on our way back to the steamer, Nijinsky called for the marriage-rings. As he jumped into the carriage, I noticed the engraving on the ring: "Vaslav-Romola 1/9/

1913." He put it on my finger. Kovalevska congratulated us again and kissed us both.

Later in the evening, as the boat steamed out slowly from the bay of Rio, I went on deck. It was almost deserted. Everybody was dressing for dinner when Chavez came up excitedly. "Ah, is it true what I have just heard? What a day! This marvellous city, and the two great bits of news: The *Imperator* on fire, and Nijinsky engaged. I do not know whom I should congratulate, myself or you. You see, I was right. He is the *Dieu de la danse,* but off the stage he is a human being. I am so glad, but so glad."

Coming down to dinner, I went straight to my table as usual, to the Drobetskys' but, as I wanted to sit down, the Batons waved frantically, Vaslav smiled, and Gunsburg came over to fetch me, and they made me sit from then on by Nijinsky. The whole dining-room noticed the change, and the members of the Ballet who were present whispered to each other nervously.

As we went on deck, Bolm met me on the stairs and pulled me aside. "Romola Carlovna, I have heard—I can't believe it—what is this talk about you and Nijinsky? I never imagined. Why, you did not seem to be interested in him. What happened?"

"Well, well, I don't always say what I think and feel."

"But, after all, to get married—to a man you don't know—a perfect stranger—a person you can't even talk to."

"But I know Nijinsky. I have seen him dancing many, many times. I know his genius, his nature, everything."

"You are a child. You know him as an artist, not as a man. He is a very kind young man, a charming colleague, but I have to warn you he is utterly heartless."

"Why do you think that?"

And then Bolm told me that two years before, during a rehearsal, the news came of the death of Thomas Nijinsky. Bolm apparently went up to Nijinsky and expressed his condolences. Nijinsky only replied with a smile and a

low "Thank you." Imagine anybody smiling at this kind
of news—must be a heartless person.

"Not necessarily," I replied. "No, no, I am sure he
has a kind heart. Anybody who dances as he does must
be so. And I don't care."

"Romola, I have to warn you. I know your parents. I
have received the hospitality of your family. It is my duty.
Nijinsky's friendship with Diaghileff, you may not understand, is more than merely a friendship, you see. He can't
possibly be interested in you, and it will ruin your life."

I faced him now and very determinedly said: "I thank
you. I know you mean well, but I am going to marry
him in spite of everything, even if you are right. I'd rather
be unhappy serving Nijinsky's genius than be happy without him." Bolm bowed very low and left me.

Finally I joined the others, the captain coming towards us, regretting not having known the news sooner
so he could get loads of flowers in Rio, begging to have
a wedding on board where he could officiate. Gunsburg
was all for the idea. A marriage on a steamer. Oblokova was just like a mother, worried how we could get a
decent trousseau in South America. "My God, if we were
only in Paris."

Mme. Baton rushed up complaining, *"Pour l'amour de
Dieu,* some of you come on and rescue René. One of
the girls is having hysterics because Nijinsky is to marry
somebody else, and with all the men on board she had to
faint in my husband's arms."

The control between the first and second class was
broken through and the whole troupe rushed across to
verify the news. I was surrounded and asked questions
and questions, everybody glad and excited. They almost
crushed Nijinsky.

So the evening passed. We were all exhausted by the
excitement of the last days. On my way down to my cabin,
Nijinsky accompanied me. At the door he stopped. I was
rather surprised. I was nervous, as I was not sure, and
confused about what might happen. I knew so much
about love theoretically, ever since I was nine years old,
from the world of literature; from Boccaccio to Shake-

speare, from Sappho to Casanova; but I was a stupid
girl. Our education in Hungary was peculiar. We were
brought up in the idea of polygamy for men always and
in all circumstances, and liberty for a girl as soon as she
had an engagement-ring. But I did not know Russian
men, and especially the type of Nijinsky, who had a
profound respect for womanhood and admitted the sensuality only of consecrated deep affection. He smiled and
kissed my hand—I could not help admiring his movements—and he left me. I pressed my hands against my
madly beating heart and felt faint, and was not quite sure
if I should be flattered or offended. Perhaps, after all,
Bolm was right.

Next morning, as Anna came in, I just said very casually, "Anna, I am glad to say you will have less to do
from now on. You need not count the days, tearing off
your calendar slip. *The hay-cart is willing to give me a
lift.* I am going to marry Nijinsky."

The whole day passed in wild preparations for the
engagement dinner which the captain was offering us
that evening. Before lunch Nijinsky and Gunsburg
emerged from the radio-room. After obtaining the captain's permission, they were able to dispatch a radio to
Budapest to my mother. That time the radio was only for
emergency and official messages—S.O.S. The cable was a
beautifully worded *demande en mariage* inspired by Nijinsky and set into literary French by Gunsburg, who was
very proud of it. Gunsburg was so busy he felt his importance. Now he not only had to represent Diaghileff,
but also to arrange everything for the wedding.

Our engagement, and the fact that we were nearing
the end of the journey, upset the daily routine of the
boat. Everybody began to make preparations. We passed
Santos and Montevideo and entered the La Plata River.
My radio officer congratulated me with a pained smile.
Grigoriev, who regally accepted my greetings before, almost went to the floor, curtseying to me. I never saw
anyone in my life transformed so suddenly from a slave
to an autocrat. Since Diaghileff was no longer with us, he
had become haughty and made himself dreadfully impor-

tant. The three strange-looking men dressed in white,
who according to Chavez were *des marchands de femme,*
never approached me now as before. And the nuns and
monks due for the Argentine gave me a beatific smile.
Late in the evening we saw a range of brilliant lights on
the horizon. It was Buenos Aires. Waiting to arrive, Nijinsky stood with me at the railing and said: *"Ya ne
hatchou mariage parahode, hatchou véritable terre église."*
("I don't want a marriage on ship-board. I want a real
church wedding.")

We went to stay at the Majestic Hotel, the Batons,
Gunsburg, Kovalevska, Nijinsky, and myself. He had a
big suite on the first floor. I had my room on the third
The next few days passed in a frantic way. The usual
work of the troupe was supposed to start on Monday.
We arrived on Saturday night. Sunday we went sightseeing
with the Batons. The city was very interesting, the lovely
park called Palermo, with its rare plants and trees, and
the Penguins Aigrettes walking on the grass. Mme. Baton
and I were chasing them, as we wanted badly to pull a
few feathers out of them. Chavez was our guide. Buenos
Aires was a mixture of Paris, Madrid, and Brussels, lovely,
luxurious palaces, buildings, trees, and vegetation. We met
Nijinsky later on. He had already investigated the Teatro
Colon, the operahouse, and its stage. Karsavina, whom
we met at dinner, and to whom I was introduced, was
quite excited about the news of our engagement. She
was charming, lovely, a real *grande dame.*

Gunsburg was running around to the Embassy, church,
and city hall, to arrange for the marriage.

I was called to the first rehearsal on Monday, and
cast in a number of ballets by Grigoriev. The theatre
was enormous, the largest operahouse in the world—a
wonderfully built stage, and the dressing-rooms, with their
bathrooms, were the last word in comfort.

Nijinsky was practising, and sent over a message that
he wished me to keep on my dancing costume as he
intended to give me a lesson. I was petrified. I tried to
escape but could not. Trembling, I went up, almost crying, and began my exercises *à la barre.* I looked at him.

A strange person stood before me. There was no recognition in his face: the impersonal look of a master towards his pupil, I ceased to be his *fiancée*. I was just a dancer. I expected shouts and cursing, *"à la Maestro,"* but instead found infinite patience. And as I made a wrong step or position he showed me the way to do it, and I found it easy and succeeded in executing the required steps. He always stopped me when I wanted to force any movement.

Rehearsals, practising, drives in Palermo. Every afternoon Nijinsky came up to my room at the time of the siesta. It was full of flowers, and it seemed so strange to see him there; and the little Jesus of Prague on the table was mocking.

Gunsburg arrived every hour with some fresh news and new complications. I was an Austrian subject; Nijinsky, a Russian. We had no papers. I was under age. Cables to Hungary, to Russia, were dispatched. I think this was the first time that the Embassies in Argentina had anything to do. Oblokova ran around for dresses and presents. Finally, the following Tuesday, Gunsburg whirled us off to church. He declared that we had to go to confession, as Nijinsky and myself were both Roman Catholics and we could not be married in church unless we did so.

The Iglesia St. Miguel was the church in Buenos Aires where all smart marriages took place, so of course our *mondaine* Baron made the arrangements there. We were taken to that place for confession. Nijinsky disappeared with the priest and very soon he was released from the confessional. No wonder, as the priest could not speak a word of Russian or Polish.

I followed. I always disliked confessions, as I could barely regret my sins and never liked to promise things which I was pretty sure not to keep. But I went through with it and it was not so bad after all. The priest made a point of it that I should promise him to prevent Nijinsky from dancing *Scheherazade,* so that the performance of this "immoral ballet" should be made impossible. I told him I would do my best. Then we were dragged into a nice cool parlour, where three priests were

waiting for us, to make us sign a document that all our
children would be brought up as Catholics. The priest to
whom I had confessed was very good-looking and I liked
his black eyes, so I asked Gunsburg to arrange that he
should marry us. But this was impossible, as he was too
young, and the bishop wanted to hold the ceremony himself; but they promised me that he would assist.

Four days after our arrival Gunsburg finally completed all the necessary arrangements. The marriage ceremony was set for Wednesday, the 10th of September. As
everybody was excited and nervous, running from one
room to the other, racing out to hairdressers and shops,
I got hold of Mme. Baton and we had a lovely walk and
talk in the city. At one o'clock I was taken down to the
city hall by Oblokova and Gunsburg. There were assembled already a few intimates, the Drobetskys, Kovalevska,
Chavez, the Batons, with Nijinsky and the Russian and
Austro-Hungarian ministers, the staff of the legations,
and the representatives of the Press.

A squat Spaniard came out with a huge ribbon across
his chest in the Argentine colours. He looked terribly
formal, and stood before us. On the desk full of flowers
stood a crucifix on a dark green blotter, which was covered with a huge parchment document on which a lady
was floating, holding a band on which our names and the
date were printed in huge red letters. It was the smartest certificate of marriage, in full accordance with Argentine taste. Then this kind old gentleman asked questions
in Spanish. Baton pulled out a notebook and gave dates
and names in French, which were immediately translated to the Mayor by the official interpreter. The two
ministers confirmed it in Spanish. Then Vaslav was questioned and answered in Russian. I talked in Hungarian
and French. Finally the Mayor made a speech in Spanish,
to which we listened very attentively. We were made to
sign the document which was to make us man and wife.

During the whole wedding breakfast toasts were proposed and we were congratulated. They all seemed happy
and Karsavina was constantly smiling at us.

I hoped to spend the afternoon quietly, but failed. Anna, who was very superstitious, could not agree to my plan of wearing a pale blue dress at the marriage ceremony. She considered it unlucky, and went to complain to Mme. Oblokova. Mme. Baton and she dragged me to all the dressmakers of Buenos Aires in search of a white dress. Finally, after hours of seeking, we succeeded in buying a lovely pale cream-coloured wedding-dress. But our difficulties were not at an end; white shoes, orange blossoms, and a veil had to be found. With the help of Maria Stepanovna, late in the afternoon finally everything was ready. Everything except the orange blossoms, which could not be obtained and were unknown at all the flower shops. By the time I arrived at the hotel to dress, Anna was frantic and Baron Gunsburg almost in tears. It was nearly seven o'clock, the time fixed for the ceremony, and the others were already waiting for us at the church. I was flung into my dress and whirled away by the Baron.

At the entrance of the Iglesia St. Miguel, M. and Mme. Baton, Nijinsky, and the others of the wedding party were waiting for us. I was taken up the aisle to the strains of the wedding march from *Lohengrin*. I felt guilty at being late, and noticed a disappointed look on Nijinsky's face, who seemed to be anxiously waiting, so I did not look around. The ceremony was long. The clergy, greatly ornate, officiated. The flowers were lovely; everything seemed to be so hazy and strange: the priests, the escort, the guests, even the bridegroom. Was it true or only a dream? Could it be really possible that in a few moments, before God and men, I was to be given in marriage to the *Spectre de la Rose?* I glanced at him. He was very serious and solemn. To him it seemed a sacred moment. The ceremony, which was said in Latin and Spanish, was of course incomprehensible to me. I was rather nervous. Would I know when to say "Yes"? I was strangely fascinated by the heavily gilded wings of the baroque angels. The altar was the most atrocious sculpture one could imagine, and I could not take my eyes off it. But everything went well. The questions were asked of us in French, and

we both answered clearly and audibly. Nijinsky produced
the wedding-rings at the right moment. The good-looking
black-eyed priest smiled at me encouragingly. During the
whole long, fatiguing ceremony the only sentence which I
could understand, and always later remember, was when
the priest asked me in Spanish: *"Will you always stay
by him in happiness as well as in misfortune, in health
and sickness, forever?"* And I promised.

So he blessed us, and as we turned we faced the
others. Some of those present were laughing happily;
others were in tears and rushed up to us. We were kissed,
congratulated, by the clergy, the artists, and the society of
Buenos Aires who were present at this unusual wedding.
I was almost crushed in the embrace of fat, old, but
charming fashionable Argentine ladies. They were beam-
ing with smiles and all wished us happiness.

As we drove back to the hotel, Nijinsky and I were
very silent. A few moments before the carriage drove up
to the entrance, Nijinsky took my hand and, kissing it,
placed a beautiful yellow-pink pearl engagement-ring on
my finger.

On the very evening of my wedding, which had taken
place in accordance with the Argentine customs, we held
our dress rehearsal at the Teatro Colon. I had been extremely upset the whole day, more on account of the
rehearsal than my wedding. I was supposed to dance in
Scheherazade and had stage fright.

As I arrived on the stage, the girls all rushed up to
me, congratulated me again, and admired my beautiful
ring. Somebody remarked that pearls were unlucky, but
I had always wanted one. The ballet began, and everything
seemed to go fairly well until the moment when we
had to make our entrance. We had a *pas de trois* to dance
before Zobeide (the Sultana) and her golden slave
(Nijinsky). The idea that he would see me dance froze my
blood, and I do not know how I made my entrance. I
danced and danced, and when the others stopped I went
on dancing, and in their abrupt pause fell headlong on
the stage, but I remained on the floor and the audience
did not notice anything.

The dress rehearsal was apparently successful, but this did not lessen my nervousness. The ordeals of the day were not over. I had to go home to face Nijinsky—my husband.

Ever since the evening, a year and a half ago, when I had seen this marvellous vision for the first time I was drawn to him with an irresistible feeling. I hoped, prayed, willed for this miracle to share his life, and now that it had become true I was frightened, desperately frightened.

What was going to happen? What was marriage, anyhow? I had nobody to turn to or to ask; I was alone in a strange land.

Anna very thoughtfully ordered a cold supper for us, in my little drawing-room, which awaited us upon our return to the hotel. Nijinsky came upstairs with me. We ate in silence. Anna retired as soon as she saw that everything was in order. I was getting more and more nervous, being left alone with Nijinsky. But he only smiled, and served me attentively. We were both so embarrassed that we could not even express ourselves in pantomime. And when, after supper, Nijinsky kissed my hand and left me, I was so relieved that I almost cried from thankfulness.

My début was better than I had dared to hope, and I was relieved when I was cast in the *Swan Lake* with Bolm. He made it easy for me, as during our dances he spoke to me on the stage and made me forget my stage fright. One evening in *Swan Lake* Nijinsky danced the part of the Prince. I was cast in the part of the Princess, his *fiancée*. I arrived gaily at the wings and gave him my hand, so that he could lead me on to the stage. As soon as we were seated on our throne and Karsavina began to dance her Variations I turned to Nijinsky, wanting to chat with him as I always did with Bolm in the same ballet. But, to my utter amazement, he gave me a strange look of complete lack of recognition. He was no longer my husband, but the Prince himself. The stage, his work, his art, were sacred to him; this understanding flashed to me. He lived his part, and everything else for him ceased to exist.

Many times at Buenos Aires this was proved to me. Of
course, I thought that now that we were married I could
come and go to his dressing-room; but to my great amazement, when I went in he very gently caressed my hand
and asked me to leave. Sometimes I met him back stage
before he made his entrance, and more and more I saw
that he had become his part. Once he passed me before
the performance of *Faune,* and already, going from his
dressing-room on to the stage, he walked in the same way
as in the ballet. This was not a pose; he already had
placed himself in the very mood of his part. His greatness,
his genius, revealed themselves to me. I felt that there
was an indescribable distance between us.

My amazement grew, for at home he was gay, laughing,
mischievous, like a boy always trying to play some prank.
We could not speak to each other yet—only a few sentences—and the Baron had to translate. The morning
after my wedding we went to practise at the theatre as
usual. Everybody smiled in a way which rather annoyed
me. I also resented their inquisitive questions. I wondered
what they would have said if they knew that Nijinsky had
not returned to my apartment the previous evening, and
that there had been no necessity for my placing all the
movable furniture in front of my door, which I had so
carefully locked.

Every morning I received a large bouquet of white
roses from him. This was handed to Anna by Vassily
with a furious look. Then we went to the theatre to practise separately, and finally I received my lessons. How
happy I was to have them. I myself felt the immense
improvement I made under Nijinsky's tutoring. The most
difficult steps became easy if I carefully imitated his movements. The sense of harmony in the movement was the
chief factor. He insisted on this more than on acrobatics.
But when I did the exercises he made me do them correctly, according to the rules. We repeated not only those
of the classical school, but also the ones established by
Nijinsky himself, which are of infinite variety. Exercises
for the arms, hands, even fingers, shoulders, and the head.
In the afternoons we used to take long drives in the park.

Especially we enjoyed the Zoological Gardens, which are extremely interesting, with all the tropical birds and animals. Nijinsky would watch their movements for a long time, and made me notice everything lovely around us. It seemed to me that life began to have a new meaning. Suddenly I realised that so much beauty surrounds us which, before, I had failed to observe.

The whole day seemed to me like a holiday; I could be constantly with Nijinsky; at his meals, out driving, at home. I often watched him as we walked along the path near the lake at Palermo. He seemed to float. Every movement of his was soft and powerful, like those of a tiger, with an indescribable elasticity.

By this time I had moved down on to the first floor to Nijinsky's apartment, at his own request, which was made to me through Baron Gunsburg. This "suite" was composed of five rooms. The centre of the apartment was a large drawing-room, where we used to take our meals. On both sides the adjoining chambers were turned into living-rooms, and each of us had a bedroom at the opposite end of the apartment.

On our return from the performances Nijinsky used to write to his mother; he never forgot to do so. He seemed to be gay and happy and very proud when he spoke of me, and said, *"Maia Jena"* (which means "my wife"). I felt myself quite important. My fear of Nijinsky began to vanish. The charm of his personality, the tenderness of his whole being, radiated so much goodness, such beauty, that the evening he chose to remain I felt I was making an offering on the altar of happiness.

Part Two

Part Two

Chapter Thirteen

THE BREAK WITH
SERGEI DE DIAGHILEFF

THE FOLLOWING weeks passed in infinite happiness. Nijinsky danced more wonderfully than ever, and the serious meditative look which he always used to have off stage gave place very often now to one of mischievous gaiety. Sometimes he seemed to me like a child who has received his first grown-up suit. To Nijinsky, marriage meant tremendously much, as I found out later. He became himself at last. His genius had always bloomed irresistibly, but now Nijinsky himself grew up and became a man. Always, since his childhood, he had been seeking the truth in art and life—the meaning of it. Now he found that love in marriage was the way. His profound affection for Diaghileff did not change but he was sure now that Diaghileff was mistaken in his ideas of love and in thinking he could turn him, Nijinsky, into a puppet.

Nijinsky was honesty itself. He came one day and told me, after having learned the words for hours from the Baron, his past relationship with Sergei Pavlovitch. He wrote a long letter to Diaghileff, explaining the reason which had made him marry, and assuring him that unalterably he would remain his true friend and serve the cause of the Russian Ballet.

Vaslav, as I now called him, told me that Diaghileff would understand; he was such a wonderful person that, even if he was unable to love in this way, he would approve. Vaslav had unlimited faith in Sergei Pavlovitch. I wondered. But surely he must know better than I!

Late one evening, when we were alone, Vaslav came and sat on my bed and handed me a note translated by the Baron:

"I have a brother, Stanislav. He is insane. You have to know it."

For a second I was numbed and frightened. As I looked up, Vaslav had an impassible drawn expression. I threw my arms around him.

Vaslav wrote to his mother about our happiness.

At this time I was cast in the part of a nymph in *Faune,* and was intensely proud, especially as Vaslav was very pleased. I learned in eight rehearsals what had taken other dancers one hundred and twenty. And it was really difficult; we could not follow the music by the measure of the dance as in the other ballets—we had to count uninterruptedly, otherwise we would have been unable to keep the right rhythm.

I had requested Vaslav not to come to watch at *Prince Igor* as he intended. This was the first ballet in which I danced and he did not take part. I saw an expression of extreme amazement in his face; but, "I have to watch, to see that everything goes well. I am not watching you alone, but all the artists," was translated to me. And, as I saw him in the wings, I ran off the stage panic-stricken! As punishment I was suspended for a week. At first I could not comprehend why Vaslav had punished me, but always and always I could see that he separated the artist and the person, and treated each as they deserved.

For two days I was disagreeable. He failed to understand my reason. Finally, one afternoon, in my broken Russian, I asked him what he thought of my dancing. He told me frankly I had great dispositions for it, but, as I began late, I lacked the technique and could never become a perfect dancer. "But you could dance very beautifully certain dances which I will compose for you." So then I understood that anybody who is not trained as a child can only obtain a limited way of expression in the art of dancing. "Will I never be able to dance like Pavlova, like Karsavina?" I cried. "No, never," he told me. Then and there I decided that I would give up my

career as a dancer. Vaslav tried to persuade me not to
do it, but I decided I would study with him but never
appear in public. To serve his genius was far more important than my own ambition.

The first impulse which made me follow the Russian
Ballet, or, in reality, Nijinsky, was the wish that his genius should be perpetuated through me. This intense desire never left me since a spring morning in 1912, when I
awoke, and on the wall opposite my bed the sunrays
through the shadows of the leaves of the acacias danced
so beautifully and gracefully, and I saw before me Nijinsky. But now that we were married, which fact I never
dared to hope or dream of before, I became so enraptured
in him that I did not wish to have a child. First of all
I consulted Mme. Oblokova, but she only shook her head
and laughed. Mme. Baton read me a strict sermon, and
said how marvellous it must be to become a mother.
Then I went to the Baron, who faithfully translated my
request, and Vaslav said: "For five years we shall live
for art and our love, but the supreme happiness and the
fulfilment of life and marriage is to have a child, and,
after that time, when we will be in our permanent home,
we shall have one." I agreed.

We continued our tour. In Rio we stopped at the beautiful hill-top hotel in Sylvestre. Vaslav and I were never
tired of driving in those glorious forests to admire the
flowers and butterflies, which were huge and in all imaginable lovely colours, deep turquoise blue, emerald green,
orange. Even the sparrows in this country were beautiful.
The woods were full of small but inoffensive monkeys,
which gaily jumped around—to Vaslav's intense pleasure.
One morning he found one in our bathroom.

I was very much afraid of the snakes; they were abundant in the forests, and I was told by the servants at the
hotel that they frequently glided into the rooms. Anna
lived in constant terror of them, and also in a constant
state of war with Vassily. The latter performed his duties
near Vaslav as faithfully as ever, but completely ignored
both myself and Anna. I did not pay any attention to this
impertinence, but Anna deeply mistrusted him. She

claimed that only for the sake of Vaslav Fomitch our lives were spared. She was sure that otherwise it would be the greatest joy for Vassily to poison us. Sometimes, when I caught Vassily's glance, I myself was not sure whether Anna was not right. He certainly hated us. I learned also that he was the only one who did not come to our marriage service.

Already, in Montevideo, I sometimes felt faint; here I took an intense dislike to food, especially to coffee; I could not even bear the smell of it; and in Brazil everything seemed to smell of coffee. Vaslav became worried about my paleness, the artists smiled, Drobetsky extended his congratulations, and the doctor on whom I called confirmed that I was going to have a child.

Vaslav seemed to be pleased and proud.

Early in November the tour ended in Rio. The homeward journey seemed ghastly to me. I was laid up in my cabin, constantly sea-sick. I used to cry to the English doctor, who tried everything in his power to help me. Vaslav became a little nervous, seeing that I felt depressed. But to have a child was such a blow to me now that I wanted to live only for him. Vaslav consoled me, and said the baby was going to be a wonderful dancer, and called him, in memory of South America, "Le Petit Nègre."

His days were passed in composing, Baton playing for him. I noticed only once a weariness come over him.

Now we could speak pidgin French and Russian, and used to carry on quite a conversation. I began to rave about all the Callot dresses, Reboux hats and Cartier jewels, and of all the *mondain* life I was going to lead in the future. I was brought up to believe that this was what marriage meant, and Vaslav, to whom all this was strange, perhaps, for a second, felt a little tired of it all; he had yet to teach me. But he smiled and said: "I am only an artist, not a prince, but anything I can have is yours. If these things make you happy, I will give them to you." But I sensed that he did not approve of my point of view, and this irritated me. Vaslav's idea was to spend a few days in Paris, where we were supposed to

meet Sergei Pavlovitch. Then to go to St. Petersburg, where
he wanted me to meet his mother and sister and to know
my new home. We decided on the way we would stop a
few days in Budapest, where Vaslav wanted to pay his
respects to my mother. This did not overjoy me, as I was
anxious to get to Russia. We left the troupe at Cadiz,
where we took the Sud-Express for Paris. While we passed
the frontier, at Hendaye, we were sitting in the dining
saloon having dinner when Vaslav suddenly became livid,
jumped up, and left. I went after him, and found him in
our compartment—having fainted. I tried to summon a
doctor immediately, but there was not one on the train.
The *chef du train* brought some ice and smelling-salts;
and as Vaslav came to himself he complained of intense
headache, which he had often when on a long train
journey. From that time I gave up smoking, as he could
not stand even the smell of cigarettes. At the Imperial
Schools they were not allowed to smoke.

Our stay in Paris, which we had intended to spend
quietly, became a series of entertainments. The papers
announced our arrival, and the Russian nobility present
gave one reception after the other in our honour. They all
wanted to show me the hospitality of my newly adopted
country. I was spoiled and entertained. Lovely presents
and exquisite jewellery were showered upon us. The newly built Trianon Palace Hotel in Versailles was turned into
a *féerique décor* for the reception which Prince H. gave
for us.

On our way to Budapest, my sister met us in Vienna.
At last Vaslav hoped to arrive in a peaceful family circle,
but he was painfully surprised. On our arrival in Budapest, instead of the loving embrace of a mother, a crowd
of reporters, camera-men, and photographers awaited us.
My mother entertained largely, and we were dragged
from one reception to the other, stared at like strange
animals from the jungle, and questioned. I knew Vaslav
was disappointed, but he never said anything, and politely
went wherever my mother wished us to go.

All this time, I had made up my mind not to have a
child. I spoke to my mother about it, and she agreed with

me. She was still a very young and lovely woman, married a second time, and, as a leading actress, she knew that the fact of becoming a grandmother would be widely advertised to her own disadvantage by her women colleagues. Our house physician was called in, and he explained to me that, as I used to be rather a delicate child myself, it would endanger my life to become a mother. An intervention, therefore, was imperative, and every arrangement was speedily made for this.

Vaslav was rather sad, but only ventured to say he would like to consult another authority. The night before I was supposed to enter the sanatorium I became suddenly terrified, and explained to Vaslav that I would rather risk dying than allow an operation to take place. An immense relief and pleasure was expressed in his face. He kissed me gently, and whispered: "Thank God. What He has given, nobody has the right to destroy." Later, when we could speak to each other, he told me that every human being has the right to decide in these questions of life and death, and he did not feel the right to interfere or prevent me as long as I was firmly decided not to become a mother, but he was infinitely thankful to God that he made me understand in time.

We decided to spend Christmas in St. Petersburg. Vaslav was immensely happy to return to his mother and country. He tried to explain how good she was, and also told me what a devoted sister and friend I was going to find in Bronia, for whom his attachment was deep. Two days before our departure, in the evening, a telegram was handed to Vaslav. As he read it, he gazed for a long time, and seemed not to comprehend it. After a long while, he gave it to me. It was in French, and ran as follows: "Your services with the Russian Ballet are no more required. Don't join us. Sergei de Diaghileff."

I was petrified. Vaslav, the glory, the greatest dancer, the pillar of the Ballet, outcast, dismissed, as a servant, from the creation of art for which he was responsible, because of his marriage. This was Diaghileff's revenge.

Now, for the first time, it dawned on me that perhaps I had made a mistake; I had destroyed, where I had wanted

to be helpful. But as I burst out crying, Vaslav smiled
with great gentleness, and said: *"Pas triste, c'est erreur et
si c'est vrai! moi artiste peut travailler seul."*

The news of Vaslav's dismissal was known in a few
days throughout the world. Offers were showered upon
him, from impresarios, theatres, with incredibly high salaries. But Vaslav refused. The agents came personally
to Budapest to win him over. The fee rose higher and
higher, but Vaslav shook his head, and asked the secretary of the Russian Consulate, who was constantly with
us: "Please tell them I cannot do anything inartistic. I
must first have the right ballets, artists to appear with me.
I must think, create, and, under no circumstances will I
appear in a vaudeville house. I cannot be unfaithful to
my art."

No money could tempt him.

Monsieur Rouché, the director of the Paris Opéra, offered him one hundred thousand gold francs a year if he
would consent to become *maître de ballet* and *premier
danseur*, appearing twenty times a year. But when Vaslav
saw the material that the Opéra offered, he was obliged
to refuse.

He had always done everything to heighten the art of
dancing, and this he was determined still to do in the
future. The impresarios became discouraged, my family
was furious; my stepfather, who had an excellent business head, was distracted to see such a fortune cast quietly
away. I understood Vaslav and agreed with him, feeling
unhappy that he had to go through this trial for my sake.
But whenever I brought up the subject he immediately
stopped me. My stepfather tried to explain to him that
he would have to earn money for me, and for his future
child, which I thought very tactless of him, as Vaslav
married me without any dowry. Vaslav calmly smiled,
and, with a pitying look, told him: "I know. I have also
a mother and an insane brother to look after, but I have
some little savings, they will not be in need. I will dance,
but in the right way." He was so harassed by everybody
that we left for Vienna.

But we did not find peace there either. The son of a

famous London impresario personally followed us everywhere, with an exceedingly high offer from Alfred Butt,
the owner of the Palace Theatre in London. Vaslav believed that this place was not a variety theatre, but one
of the most distinguished houses in London, equal to
Covent Garden or Drury Lane, where he had appeared
before; and Alfred Butt gave him full liberty to form his
own company and programme. So Vaslav signed a contract for eight weeks for the following spring. Everybody
seemed at peace except Vaslav and myself. Bronia wrote
him that she as well as her husband Kotchetovsky had
resigned from the Ballet, and were at Vaslav's disposal.
Vaslav asked them to come to Paris and talk everything
over.

Vaslav planned to form a company of thirty-two dancers, and to compose ballets. From the old repertoire he
was requested to give the *Spectre de la Rose,* and two
classical ballets, *The Princess Enchantée* and possibly *Les
Sylphides.*

He had to have scenery and costumes designed, and
new music composed, and all this meant tremendous work
and time. But Vaslav undertook this courageously. His
first visit was to Bakst, to whom he wanted to entrust the
scenery. We drove up to the Boulevard Malesherbes,
where he had his studio. I remained in the carriage, as I
did not wish to disturb their meeting. After a very long
time, perhaps two hours, Vaslav came down. I saw tears
in his eyes, which he tried to hide, but he had to tell me
the result of his conversation with Bakst. He flatly refused to work for Vaslav. He told him that he personally
could understand Vaslav's feelings, but had to withdraw
from all artistic associations with him in the future, as
Diaghileff insisted on this. He also felt it his duty to tell
Vaslav the truth, that his dismissal from the Ballet was
not the end, it was the beginning, of a state of war which
Diaghileff had declared against Nijinsky. And he repeated
Sergei Pavlovitch's own words: *"As high as Nijinsky stands
now, as low am I going to thrust him."*

After long debates with Bronia and Kotchetovsky, it
was decided that they would go back to Russia to choose

and engage the dancers, and bring them back to Paris. Anisfeld the painter was summoned; he accepted the offer, and began to design the *maquettes* for scenery and costumes which were of extreme beauty. Vaslav personally supervised everything; even the execution of the costumes at Mme. Muelle's, who always worked for the Russian Ballet. Among the musicians, he invited Ravel, who proved to be of great loyalty and kindness. He was a charming young man, always a little extravagantly dressed, but full of gaiety. Untiringly he played for Vaslav, helped him in the choice of music, went to the music publishers to obtain the rights, and orchestrated the new ballets in an exquisite manner. The superhuman effort on Vaslav's part seemed to promise a programme of great artistic value.

But I knew that this was not the work Vaslav wished to do. He wanted to create a ballet of pure abstract dancing more on the line of *Sacre* or the Bach ballet. To compose something similar to the pre-*Faune* time was against his conviction. But now he was forced to create a frame in which he could appear, a new medium through which he could express and further new ideas. I knew he suffered from this forced task, but he never complained or referred to it.

Vaslav tested dancers in Vienna and Paris, but, as much as he wished, he could not engage any of them, as they lacked either the artistic understanding or could only dance with their legs. Bronia returned with a well-chosen company, mostly graduates from the Imperial Schools, who were dissatisfied with things in Russia and revolted at the news of Diaghileff's scheme. They were engaged for the period of one year.

The rehearsals began. Vaslav worked practically day and night. Now all administrative and organising tasks rested on his shoulders. He had hardly any time to eat or sleep. I became worried. Bronia was untiring too. She spoke only Russian and Polish, but I soon noticed that she did not like me; she seemed to resent everything that happened and blame it on me. I was the intruder in the Russian Ballet, in the family. She isolated herself behind a screen of ice which I could never penetrate. At Larue's, or at Viel's, I used to await them for lunch sometimes until four or five o'clock in the afternoon. But they worked and danced all the time.

Finally the day came when we had to leave for London. The Press received Vaslav with enthusiasm. Lady Morrell was standing at the door of our suite at the Savoy, her arms full of spring flowers, to welcome us. Lady Ripon came in the afternoon, and assured us how happy she was about our marriage, and that we could count upon her in every way. She told me that it was always her wish that Vaslav should marry, and that she had tried in the past to introduce him to suitable young ladies! But as long as he himself had chosen, she could only approve, and offered to become the godmother of our future child.

The next two weeks passed in feverish preparation. Zenon offered his services to Vaslav and was accepted; he proved to be of real service. The theatre was sold out. But we seemed to be pursued by bad luck, or, more truly, by Diaghileff. First a police injunction was brought forbidding Bronia to appear, as Diaghileff claimed in the court that he had not accepted her resignation. Endless proceedings were taken to allow Bronia to dance, and to prove that she had not broken her contract.

Vaslav was greatly upset several times, which did not improve matters. The first day, he was requested to come personally to Alfred Butt's office and pay him his respects. Vaslav could not make out what they wanted of him. Brought up at the Imperial School, a member of the Mariinsky Theatre, he was taught to pay respect to only one person in the world, the Tsar. Everybody else, even the grand dukes, came to bow before the artists. Alfred Butt, whom he had never met before, was, for him, the owner of several theatres, a business man, and, as much as he was ready to call on him as a private person, he refused on principle to call as an artist on a theatrical manager.

Of course, this gesture of his was misunderstood, and caused a lot of trouble. Then a very regrettable incident occurred. Vaslav was practising quietly alone on the empty stage of the Palace Theatre, when a stage hand passed, and, not noticing him and seeing me, before I realised it, patted my cheeks with an impertinent suggestion. Vaslav jumped at him and knocked him down. Of course the man screamed, and a fight began. I was dumbfounded, I had never seen Vaslav like that.

All these incidents put him in an extremely nervous condition. Once, at a rehearsal, Bronia was not feeling very well, and, although she did not say anything to Vaslav about it, she did not dance quite so well as usual. Vaslav criticised her and she burst out crying and left the stage. As soon as Vaslav had entered his dressing-room, he was followed by Kotchetovsky, who insulted him, and spat, like a Russian *moujik,* at the floor before him. Vaslav did not answer, he only became a shade paler.

His sensitive soul was hurt; he was attacked from every side, and why? Now I understood why Diaghileff had isolated him from the world. Perhaps he was right after all. At the dress rehearsal, Vaslav realised that he had been misled, that the Palace Theatre was a variety theatre, a very smart one, but nevertheless it was a vaudeville house. He could not break his word given to the public, or let down the thirty-two artists who had faith in him; but to lower the artistic standard of the Ballet was equally impossible. He had to go through the ordeal which the appearance at the Palace meant to him. What no money could make him do, he accepted for the sake of loyalty to his fellow artists and respect for his public.

The day of the opening, Mr. Williams told me that Vaslav seemed to be very feverish, but he went to the theatre. The public received him with enthusiasm, but I was blinded with tears to see Vaslav dance, in his exquisite programme, after a clown's number, and before a popular cabaret singer's act.

The second day brought a fresh attack; now Fokine, who had returned to the Russian Ballet, was persuaded by Diaghileff to bring an injunction to prevent the *Spectre de la Rose* from being given. Again he was used as a tool in Diaghileff's powerful hand, who convinced him that he had had to leave the Ballet before on account of Nijin-sky.

By now Vaslav was unable to stand on his feet, and, alarmed, I 'phoned to Lady Ripon, who called in Sir Alfred Fripp and Sir Bruce Porter. I had given Vaslav some aspirin, as I knew, from home, it was good for fever. But Sir Alfred told me that I almost killed him, as he had an athlete's heart and was in an extremely dangerous condition. He was very, very sick. He tried to go and dance, but could not. Sir Alfred went personally to the management of the Palace Theatre and explained. They said, of course, that they understood, and we assumed, no doubt without warrant, that the clause in the contract, which stated that in the case of his not appearing for three consecutive nights he broke the contract, would not be enforced. But we were mistaken and, after three days, they declared that Vaslav had broken his contract. This was a very serious matter. Vaslav had spent about two thousand pounds on scenery, costumes, authors' rights, orchestration, and transport of the artists from Russia; and, in addition, guaranteed to pay thirty-two artists during the year. All this was based on the contract with the Palace Theatre, which now was suddenly ended. On the advice of our friends I called in Sir George Lewis, and requested him to make an arrangement with the Theatre so that no loss should occur to either party. Vaslav was willing to go through with the agreement, but the negotiations broke down. It is possible that the management of the Palace realised that Nijinsky did not make the concessions to the taste of the variety theatre's public as Pavlova did—and, after all, they paid him five times as much.

Vaslav was ill for two months. Sir Alfred Fripp assured me that, as strong as he looked, he was not the type of man who could stand so much excitement and worry. "Let him dance and rest, but no organising—no administrative work." Vaslav had realised this always—that an artist should live only for his art—but now we had a new problem. Sir George Lewis made an arrangement with the company; the artists themselves went to him, and said they were satisfied with the salary they had received during the rehearsal period and the week which had been paid to them for the three days they had danced, and they asked only their fares back to Russia, releasing Nijinsky from their one year's contract. It seemed fair to us all, but Vaslav refused. He said: "They trusted me. It is not their fault that I became sick, that my contract was broken. I signed to pay them for a year, and I will do it." So his savings from the Paris bank were withdrawn, and Vaslav paid all the thirty-two artists in full.

I now insisted that Vaslav should rest, and live only to restore his health. I could induce him to do this as I was approaching the time of the birth of my baby, and Vaslav was willing to stay with me constantly. We took long walks in Richmond Park, and used to picnic in the beautiful Surrey country-side.

Vaslav said that the last weeks before a child is born the mother should spend in privacy—"To me it is lovely, and sacred to all men who love their wives, but no stranger should witness this transformation." So we went to the Semmering.

At this time, Vaslav received an invitation from Madrid to dance for the King and Queen of Spain at the wedding reception of Kermit Roosevelt, which was to be given at the American Embassy. He did not want to leave me, but a Command Performance was hard to refuse. The salary offered was three thousand dollars for one dance. We needed the money now that the savings were gone. My stepfather was willing to accompany Vaslav on the trip, and they left for Madrid. I received every day a short note, written in Russian, of which I was proud, as I knew Vaslav never wrote to anybody. He addressed me as "Femmka," or "Roma."

In Madrid, Vaslav was received with the warmth and appreciation to which he was accustomed. King Alfonso as well as the Queen led the others to make him feel at home. I heard from witnesses that the dance on the stage, which was placed in the beautiful gardens, was unforgettable.

On the return journey, Vaslav decided to stop in Paris,

and to be present at the first performance of the Russian Ballet, and the *première* of *Joseph and Potiphar*. Vaslav wanted to show the world that he was not afraid of Diaghileff, that he did not regret his marriage, even if his former friends tried to ruin him for it. The intimates of Sergei Pavlovitch, of course, knew the reason of the break. What they did not know was that Diaghileff dismissed Nijinsky of his own accord, and without consulting anybody. He gave vague excuses to his friends: "Nijinsky is greatly changed, under the influence of his wife. She wishes to be the leading *ballerina. Sacre* was too modern, we ought to have more of the Fokine ballets, and he won't return unless Nijinsky is out of the troupe." Nobody knew exactly what had happened. The Comtesse de Greffuhle, Lady Cunard, and others were too tactful to ask Diaghileff. Many rumours were in circulation. The suite of the Russian Ballet backed Diaghileff, as well as all the men who led lives like Sergei Pavlovitch; and they proved to be extremely powerful, strong, unforgiving enemies. In all classes and positions they were everywhere against those whom they considered unfaithful to their ideal; like a steel wall they stretched across the world. But could Vaslav help it that he had found himself, and changed?

We learned that Richard Strauss was extremely disappointed that Nijinsky would not dance in his ballet. The *première* of *Joseph and Potiphar,* then called the *Legend of Joseph,* was a world-wide artistic event. A German composer's work would be performed at the Opéra, where that year the performances were scheduled. The French Government also decided to accord the Cross of the Légion d'Honneur to Richard Strauss. It was almost a political event.

But Diaghileff tried to console Strauss and his co-authors, Count Kessler and Hofmansthal, and to convince them that the ballet would have the same artistic standard as all former productions. Bakst was replaced by José Maria Sert. The idea to place the scenery at the time of Paolo Veronese was kept, and proved a success. The whole ballet was produced with old Venetian splendour, and Diaghileff lavished all the money he could obtain from his backers upon this season. It was the most expensive the Russian Ballet had ever given. The part of Potiphar's wife was given to Kusnitzova the singer, who was a beautiful woman. Joseph's part caused Diaghileff a lot of worry. He went personally to Russia the preceding winter, to invite Fokine, and to find a dancer whom he could star. Some of his old collaborators had the courage to tell him that he was mistaken in letting his private emotions interfere with artistic creations and matters, but it was of no avail.

Diaghileff was dominated by only one idea, to ruin Nijinsky, nothing else mattered.

Diaghileff engaged a young dancer, from one of the Moscovite private dancing schools, by the name of Leonide Miassine, later changed to Massine. He was a good-looking boy with dark eyes.

At their arrival he gave him over to *Maestro's* care, with the request: "Teach him all you can, and make him dance like Nijinsky."

But in spite of all the expense, luxurious scenery lavished on this season, of all the exciting novelties offered by Diaghileff, the season proved to be a disappointment. Never were the bill-boards more carefully designed, never had Diaghileff appeared so faithfully at all social occasions, never before had he entertained the Press. He did all this now. Yet *Joseph and Potiphar* failed. It represented an enormous effort, but it lacked the spontaneous impulse of true artistic creation. *Midas* did not receive a good reception either. *Papillon,* a weak copy of *Carnaval,* failed. The only success of the season was Rimsky-Korsakov's opera, *Coq d'Or,* which was produced as a ballet. At the rehearsals, when Diaghileff saw the old-fashioned movements of the singers, he suddenly got a genial idea, which was to place them as a chorus all round the stage from where they sang, and their parts were played by the dancers. It proved to be of extreme artistic interest, and had the great success it deserved. The triumphant success of the two, until now, unknown young Russian painters, Larionov, and, especially, Goncharova, the de-

signer of the scenery and costumes for the *Coq d'Or,*
saved the season. Both were from the Moscow School.
Larionov was a Russian futurist, Goncharova was already
well known through her original and beautiful illustrations
of fairy-tales for children's books. Her work had a fresh-
ness of design, a new range of colour, so much virility and
imagination that with one stroke she was placed equal to
Bakst.

Vaslav was enchanted by her talent and work. Also the
Rossignol, an early opera of Stravinsky, was completed
especially for this year, and produced exquisitely. Benois
designed the scenery as a *chinoiserie.* Diaghileff tried
everything with which to tempt the public; all kinds of
rarities to make them forget the absence of Nijinsky, but
he failed. Everywhere, everybody was asking, complaining, missing him.

At the *première* of *Joseph and Potiphar,* Vaslav attended in an orchestra stall, and very few of those present
knew that the deeply regretted favourite was sitting in the
audience. In the intermission, Vaslav went to Mme. Edward's box, which was full of the Diaghileff suite. A frozen
silence greeted him. Mme. Edwards tried to keep up the
conversation. Then Cocteau, and some other young men
present, laughingly turned to Vaslav and remarked: "This
year, your creation is a child. The *Spectre de la Rose*
chooses the part of a father. How utterly disgusting is,
birth." Vaslav was hurt, and stood up and answered:
"The entrance of the *Spectre de la Rose's* child will be
quite as beautiful as his own entrance, which you always
admired." He bowed and left them.

Now he realised that he, as a man, had never really
been understood in this fashionable, cosmopolitan society.

Upon Vaslav's return to Vienna, we made all the necessary preparations to receive our baby. We had engaged
a suite in the sanatorium, a wet nurse was chosen for the
child as well as a nurse for me. The professor awaited
our telephone call and we were breaking our heads for a
name for *Le Petit Nègre.* There was never any doubt
that we would have a son. We both intensely wished for
it, and it simply could not be otherwise. I wanted to call

him Boris or Loris. Vaslav suggested Wladislav, and we decided on this.

The days passed, we visited all the lovely places of the Wiener Wald, but there was no sign of Wladislav. Finally we got tired of waiting. Even my brother-in-law Erik Schmedes, who liked Vaslav immensely, and was with us all the time, declared that this was an unheard-of breach of etiquette! Everybody in Vienna was waiting for the event.

Richard Strauss's new opera *Elektra* was having its *première* at the Opera House, and the intendant of the Hoftheater, Prince Montenuovo, knowing that Vaslav was in the city, sent us an invitation to attend, and had offered us a box, with the remark: "If this modern music won't hasten the baby's arrival, then nothing will!"

The opera was extremely interesting, and Vaslav liked it. Afterwards we dined gaily at the famous Opera Restaurant. Prince Montenuovo's prophetic words proved true. *Elektra* was too much for the baby, and next day, the 19th of June, our child was born.

Kyra Vaslavovna Nijinsky was a girl, and I was very unhappy about it. Vaslav did not show his disappointment. He waited with my sister next door to the operating-room, and, as the nurse announced to him, "It is only a girl, but a nice one," for one second he lost his self-control, and threw his gloves to the floor. But he never said anything about this to me. On the contrary, he tried to console me and praise the loveliness of the baby. Her hair was curled and black, like a *petit nègre*, but she had beautiful green eyes, as strangely fascinating, as oblique as Vaslav's very own. At least one of my wishes had been granted. She was extremely muscular and the more she grew the more she resembled Vaslav.

From the very first second the child was shown to Vaslav the adoration which he always had for his daughter began. I think that, after his art, she was the most precious thing to him. Vaslav had always a great reverence and understanding of children.

Vaslav superintended the trousseau of the baby. He could not admire enough every movement and gesture of the child. She was placed in a lovely white basket which he had near to him in the garden, where I was carried.

Vaslav's happiness in the baby seemed so limitless that I forgot every difficulty of the past month. My mother, at my own request, was not called in time, as I did not want her to be present. She blamed Vaslav for this, and as soon as she arrived attempted to get hold of the child. I was extremely upset, especially as I remembered that a few months back she was the one who endeavoured to persuade me not to have it. Vaslav defended my mother when I complained but asked her not to interfere. My stepfather raised his hands against Vaslav. I jumped out of my bed, which brought on serious complications. My mother was requested not to visit us any more. This painful incident proved to me that my family and ourselves could never get along.

Congratulations poured in from all over the world. Then an official invitation from the Production Committee of the Russian Ballet Performances in London arrived, with a special request from Lady Ripon. For the Marchioness proved to be the most loyal friend Nijinsky ever had. She had used her tremendous influence, and declared to Diaghileff that unless Nijinsky danced with them there would be no season of the Russian Ballet in London.

So Diaghileff had to consent.

Lady Ripon insisted in her letter that Vaslav should travel to London at once, whatever his decision. We all wished Vaslav to go and dance, and he was willing to forget Sergei Pavlovitch's unjust behaviour. So Nijinsky left to join the Ballet, and take part in the London performances.

I was still laid up, and he went alone. Lady Ripon and Baron Gunsburg were awaiting him, and told him he was to dance *Faune,* and *Spectre,* and some other parts. Three performances in all. They hoped that with Vaslav once back everything would be arranged satisfactorily. He was overjoyed. He wanted to be a part of his beloved Ballet. He wanted to be a true friend to Sergei Pavlovitch. But the latter avoided him. Vaslav did not meet him, and as he went to the theatre accompanied by Drobetsky, who always remained loyal to him, he realised at once that the kind scheme of the Marchioness could not succeed. The company completely ignored Nijinsky. They did not speak to him; they did not even bow. Of course this was all done under the instructions of Sergei Pavlovitch. He was forced to call and tolerate Nijinsky, but he wished to show that he had not forgiven.

Vaslav went through the rehearsal and returned to the Savoy. He wrote a letter to Lady Ripon thanking her for the great effort she had made, but explained to her that as long as Diaghileff kept to his present attitude an artistic collaboration between them was impossible.

He left on the next train for Vienna, as he was afraid that if he saw the Marchioness again he would have to give in to her entreaties.

Chapter Fourteen

PRISONERS OF WAR

ON SUNDAY, the 28th of June, 1914, I was resting in my bed in the Loew Sanatorium in Vienna. Through the open windows came the scent of the acacia-trees and roses in bloom. I could see Kyra in the garden in her little snow-white basket, guarded by the nurses. Everything seemed to be peaceful, and I thought fate had been very kind to me. The little *Jesus of Prague* had granted my wish. I was the wife of Nijinsky, and the baby might have inherited his wonderful gifts. So, after all, I had served him. Vaslav was on his way to London. He would dance again with the Ballet. Diaghileff would be a friend. Great ballets would be composed, and we would all be so happy.

Suddenly a loud, ceaseless ringing of the church bells broke out. For a long time I listened, then later Kyra was brought up, supper served, and everything made ready for the night's rest. The church bells still tolled on. Nobody knew why. The assistant doctor came to make his round. As usual, he sat down to chat with me and to smoke a cigarette. I knew that he was off duty in the afternoon and had intended to go to the races. He trembled as he lit my cigarette. "Well, doctor, did you win? What is new in town?"

The face of the light-hearted, flirtatious Viennese assistant quivered, as he said: "His Imperial Highness, the Archduke Franz Ferdinand, and his wife, the Duchess of Hohenberg, were shot this afternoon at Sarajevo, by a Serbian subject."

Among the many visitors I received, my godfather, His Excellency Thallocy, came often. Thanks to his intimate connection with the Imperial Family, he was well informed. He said it was a blessing for the monarchy that Franz Ferdinand was out of the way, but that Serbia must receive an exemplary punishment—not only the murderer, but the whole nation, as it was a political crime and they were all responsible. In a few days Vaslav returned, and I had forgotten all about this incident.

We decided to return to St. Petersburg as soon as I was allowed to travel. We constantly received letters and wires from the Marchioness of Ripon requesting us to return immediately to London, all three of us. We thought, of course, it was to allow Vaslav to take part in the season of the Ballet.

But as she insisted that we should come, Vaslav asked Professor Halban, who declared that he could take no responsibility for me if I undertook so long a journey. So we made up our minds to take his advice and stay in Vienna until the end of July, and then, with a week's stop in Budapest, to allow a rest for Kyra and myself, to proceed to Russia.

We arrived in Budapest on a hot summer day—the 23rd of July. A dreadful storm broke out—almost a hurricane—that broke all the windows at my mother's villa, and the big bell of the St. Stephan Basilica fell.

"Some misfortune is going to happen," one of my mother's peasant maids declared.

Next day I saw in the papers that an ultimatum had been sent to Serbia.

The following evening Vaslav and my mother decided to go to the circus; Vaslav had loved clowns ever since his childhood. I felt tired and stayed at home. Late in the afternoon great crowds formed in the streets, all covered with garlands of flowers, singing and dancing. Strangers kissed each other; it was like a national fête. My family returned, also in a great state of excitement. I could hardly get the news out of them. Vaslav could not insist enough how amusing the clowns were, how lovely the dancing of the peasants was in the streets. The reason of this hysterical rejoicing, which I finally learned from my stepfather—it had escaped Vaslav, who did not understand the language—was that at last war was declared.

We spent the following days quietly with Kyra in my mother's garden, but, even so, we could feel the intense excitement of the city. Ceaselessly regiments of soldiers marched by, covered with flowers, singing, accompanied on the roadside by their laughing and frantically waving women relatives.

Vaslav was always a pacifist, and condemned war and all recourse to force. Politics had no interest for him. He claimed that all misunderstandings and quarrels could be settled if we only had the strong wish for it and would grant others the same right to happiness as we claim for ourselves.

We went to the city to make our reservation on the Nord Express, but, to our utter amazement, we learned that the frontier towards the east was closed. We immediately proceeded to the Russian Consulate. It seemed deserted. We rang the bell, and after a very long time it was answered by a footman, who showed us through a long range of rooms. The carpets having been taken up, the marvellously polished floors were now visible; the furniture, covered with white linen, made the place look uninhabited.

Nowhere was there a sound. In the Consul's drawing-room everything was tidied and covered with paper. Only the two great portraits hanging opposite each other on the wall and smiling—that of the Tsar and the Tsarina—seemed unaltered. Somehow I had the feeling that no harm could happen to Vaslav as long as they seemed so quiet.

Excellency Priklonsky, the Consul-General, rushed in with outstretched hands and began to talk excitedly in torrents of Russian, of which I understood very little. It seemed that he had packed everything, as he could not get any sensible instructions from the Embassy in Vienna. There they did not know, either, what was happening. They had orders apparently to prevent war. "It is true that the frontiers are closed. The Embassy will probably leave in case of an ultimatum." But he himself did not know if he could go with the diplomatic train, for he had to stay as long as he was not officially recalled. He advised us to stay quietly where we were for the next few days, as everywhere trains were full of troops and it would not be possible to travel with the baby. But we could count upon him to let us know in time, and he would do everything in his power to take us with the diplomatic train to Sweden, from where we could easily reach Russia in case of war, which of course was unthinkable.

But the unthinkable happened, and, before we could realise it, the whole world was aflame. And the marching of the troops went ceaselessly, endlessly on.

Vaslav stood sighing before the window, "All these young men marching to their deaths, and for what?"

I was amazed. Why did he think of those utter strangers? What did it matter? Why didn't he think of all the worries and complications this new state of affairs might bring to him? Every day I made a new discovery. Vaslav was thoughtful, modest, not in the least conceited, and so embarrassed if anybody complimented him. All his thoughts were for the happiness and welfare of other people, not only his family, his friends, but perfect strangers. I have never known anybody like him.

From morning till evening I tried to find a way whereby we could leave Hungary, but there was no escape; all railway lines were in the hands of the military authorities. Finally my uncle, Garibaldi de Pulszky, president of an important private railway company, came to my rescue and promised to smuggle us out through the south to Italy. Our great difficulty was Kyra, only six weeks old. She had a wet nurse, as I could not nurse her. Anybody would recognise us with her. Then there was the danger of travelling with such a small baby in the terrific heat, in countries at war. Vaslav was worried, but I felt I had to find a way to bring him to his friends and country.

The following morning a shy-looking man came to the house. He was in civilian clothes and almost apologetic. One could see at once that he was carrying out an order to which he was not used, and it seemed to embarrass him. He spoke to me in Hungarian and asked us to follow him to the Prefecture of Police. My heart stood still. What did they want from us? Why? He refused to answer. Vaslav smiled wearily and tried to quiet me. "It's nothing; don't worry; let us go."

In half an hour we stood before the chief of the detective bureau. In fluent French he said: "Mr. and Mrs. Nijinsky, in the name of the military authorities I am obliged to arrest you and your daughter Kyra as enemy subjects. All three of you have to remain wherever you will be allotted on our territory until the termination of the hostilities, as prisoners of war."

Prisoners of war! Impossible! I spoke to the chief in Hungarian. "But certainly you must be mistaken. What has my husband to do with the war? He is not in the army; he never has been. He was exempt from military service as soloist to the Tsar. He is the greatest artist of the dance. Surely this must be a mistake? A cultured nation like Hungary cannot treat Nijinsky this way."

But he repeated, "I am sorry; it seems unjust, but war is war. You are Russians. We are at war with your country."

"But do not be silly; there must be a way. The relatives of people in high positions all stay at home, they do not go to the front. So there must be a possibility for me, with relatives near the Emperor at Court, to have my husband released. My uncle is Minister of the Foreign Office."

"Try it; perhaps you will succeed, but I must carry out my instructions."

We were shown into the next office, where three red slips were handed to us. Each had a number on it and bore our names: Vaslav Nijinsky, Romola Nijinsky, Kyra Nijinsky. In French we were told that we were to stay at my mother's house, confined until further orders. We must report every week to the police and avoid passing barracks, fortifications, or any buildings of a military nature. All correspondence must cease, of course. We were supposed to pay all expenses.

Silently we returned home. Vaslav's face was expressionless. I was deeply depressed and revolted. So not only had he to leave the Russian Ballet, now he had lost even his freedom on account of our marriage.

But Vaslav had faith, and turned all his attention to Kyra. The world seemed to cease to exist for him. From morning till late evening he accompanied the baby everywhere, and watched over her sleep. At our arrival we found the rooms in the tower of my mother's villa arranged as a nursery, and here he made his refuge.

I had not given up my attempts, and went to my aunt, Polixena de Pulszky. She was an extremely influential person politically, with a brilliant mind, and had the leading political and artistic *salon* in the country at that time. We thought and plotted together in every way, and she insisted, and succeeded in making my Uncle Garibaldi send us the necessary authorisations for the railways for the Italian frontier. But, on the day we were supposed to leave, my old governess, Miss Hegedus, who had chaperoned me the first time I saw the Ballet, came with the message from my uncle to warn us that it was too late; the authorities had learned of our intention; we would be arrested and punished; it was safer to stay. So we had to abandon all idea of escape.

Every day the papers announced a new victory of the German and Austro-Hungarian Army. It seemed that by

Christmas everything would be all over and we would be free. Kyra developed beautifully, and we spent all our time with her or walking in the woods near my mother's house.

All this time Vaslav had great difficulties in practising. He could not obtain permission to exercise in a theatre or school. The rooms in my mother's house were not big enough. During the summer months he exercised on the big terrace, but this was paved with stone and was too hard for dancing.

One day we were again summoned to the police for some kind of registration. A young bureaucrat, feeling extremely important in his new uniform, questioned us. When I gave him my maiden name, he looked up. "What! Romola de Pulszky, the grand-daughter of the great Francis de Pulszky, the first founder of Hungarian democracy, the friend of Kossuth? But you are Hungarian."

"No," I answered, "I am the grand-daughter of Francis de Pulszky, but I am the wife of Nijinsky and a Russian now."

"You should divorce," he said.

"I thought you were here to fill in the slips for the prisoners, not to give advice." And I turned my back on him.

Next day the papers were full of the incident. They called me a "traitor." According to them, I had denied my country and claimed to be Russian. Many of my acquaintances did not greet me any more. One very patriotic young poet, who used to rave about Vaslav, spat on the ground before us as we passed in the street. I could have choked him. But Vaslav impassibly walked on and said, "Don't take it to heart; be sorry for them that they do not understand better. They are not bad, only misled." But I could not take Vaslav's attitude.

My mother was furious. She made me understand how disagreeable, in fact, it was to have Russians in her house; how impossible it was for her, the first actress of Hungary to have a son-in-law who was Russian. It was harmful to her career, as well as to my stepfather's, who was

at that time in the Press department of the Prime Minister
Count Tisza, and of course anxious to advance.

So intrigues began to make me divorce Vaslav, naturally without success, but the constant nagging was painful.
I now knew not only how unwelcome Vaslav was in
my mother's house, but that he was despised, and he, with
his fine instincts, began to feel it too. We were not allowed to leave the house and more and more we withdrew from everybody into Kyra's room. But soon my
mother penetrated even there, and began to give orders
concerning the upbringing of the child which were in
opposition to Vaslav's ideas and mine. We wanted the
child to be at peace, to have meals at regular hours. My
mother ordered her to be fed any moment she cried and to
have her carried in the nurse's arms day and night. This
naturally gave cause for new scenes.

My mother changed her tactics. One day an official of
the city came, to whom she had promised that Vaslav
would dance for the Hungarian soldiers at a benefit concert. Vaslav refused to do it. "I am a prisoner. I cannot
dance for those who are killing my countrymen, even
though I consider all mankind my brothers. If I danced
for the wounded, it could only be if half the proceeds were
given for the Russians." With this the proposition was
dropped.

The servants, seeing my mother's attitude, refused to
serve us. Soon we had to do most of the things ourselves,
but this we did not mind. We received our food very
irregularly, sometimes lunch at four or five in the afternoon, and I saw that Vaslav felt faint.

My stepfather never failed to tell us the contents of the
bulletins, and with great triumph declared: "To-day we
have taken twenty thousand Russians," or "To-day the
whole Preobrajensky regiment and seventy thousand men
perished in the Lakes of Mazuri." Vaslav became livid
and left the house. I went in search of him. He came
back after hours of walking in the woods alone. He suffered intensely through the knowledge that thousands of
people were daily killing each other, and he could not
help, he could not prevent it. He was unable even to

exercise his art and to give joy through this. He was
beaten in his ideals of humanity, of charity, and of
friendship. Then Diaghileff had failed him. Everything
sacred seemed to tumble.

Sometimes in the evening we went to my Aunt Poly's
house. We had to use the servants' staircase going up to
her apartment, to prevent difficulties for her, but, once
there, we felt at home. She treated Vaslav as the artist,
not the enemy. They all made cigarettes for the Red
Cross, and we helped. Their broad-minded intellectual
conversation was the only distraction Vaslav had during
those long and weary months.

The year 1915 began, and the victories of the Central
Powers became rarer. My stepfather had little occasion
now to boast, but this did not ease our position. We were
completely isolated from the outside world. Vaslav and
myself had to suffice for each other. I knew that he was
happy in his marriage, and that he never blamed me for
anything that had happened to him since. And in this
winter, when we were completely left to each other, in
spite of the circumstances we were perfectly happy.

Kyra's nurse became gloomier and gloomier. Her
fiancé was sent to the front. She had expected to marry
him and to take her own baby to herself in the spring,
but the war frustrated her plans.

As the spring began we prolonged our walks, and
through Vaslav I learned to love nature. Each flower, each
tree, had a meaning for him; he could find an expression
of beauty in them, which he made me understand. Our
funds at this time diminished rapidly, our letter of credit
on a Paris bank, of course, no longer being honoured. We
had to use our ready cash, which at this time was low.

One day the Chief of Police noticed that we arrived
rather exhausted when we had to report to him. We told
him we had no more money for carfare and were worried
about the nurse's wages. He advised us to go to the
American Consul, who had taken over the interest of the
civil Russian prisoners. Our sole income was an allowance
of 30s. a month for the three of us.

Then a sudden stroke of luck happened. My chief oc-

.cupation was to pack and unpack our trunks. Somehow
it seemed to me we would soon be able to leave. In
brushing Vaslav's dinner-jacket, I found in the inner
pocket several hundred francs in gold. This meant a fortune to us, as we got a high rate of exchange.

During the winter we read together the works of Tolstoi,
Chekhov, Pushkin, and the marvellous treasures of the
Russian literature unfolded before me. Not only its style,
but the deep meaning of its contents, were revealed by
Vaslav. How well he could explain in *The Resurrection*
the feeling of Prince Nekloudov, the altruistic love of
Maslova. And these were Vaslav's people, who felt and
thought and loved unselfishly like he did. I understood
him. But I could not help feeling, as we read Dostoievsky's *La Maison des Morts*, that I had brought a similar
fate on Nijinsky. His days passed in complete isolation
from the world and of all artistic manifestation. When I
spoke about it, he bravely replied, "Others are dying,
suffering far more. I have my art in my soul; nothing
and nobody can take it away. Happiness is in us; we take
it with us wherever we go."

Naturally, in a way Vaslav was glad of the Russian
victories, but we knew that German troops were called
to the help of the Austrians. We knew also that, in case
Budapest was attacked, German and Austrian officers
would be lodged in my mother's house, and how could
Vaslav alone, as a prisoner, defend me from the attentions
of the officers, which were unavoidable?

Lately Kyra had been very restless. We could not find
out why, then suddenly one morning I discovered the reason. The nurse gave her almost no milk. I asked her why.
She impertinently declared, "I found out that your child
is a Russian, so she had better starve. My *fiancé* is fighting the Russians. I am not going to nourish her any more."
I burst out crying. What should I do to find another wet
nurse, who would perhaps be bad for the baby? Where,
how could I do this? I began to plead with her. Vaslav
came in and found out the cause of my sorrow. Quietly
he told the nurse to go, and said to me, "Don't worry; I
will take care of her."

And he kept his word. He went to the city to a children's physician and returned with him, carrying under his arm a book about the upbringing and care of babies and a sterilising apparatus. With infinite care he sterilised and prepared the bottles, and from that noon on he fed Kyra himself.

Vaslav carved small wooden toys for her and painted them. They were in brilliant colours, but he was always careful to use inoffensive paint; he seemed to think of everything. He repainted the whole nursery and its furniture. Instead of a white hospital room, it became an enchanted habitation of a Russian fairy-tale.

My cousin Lily de Markus, a virtuoso, a pupil of the famous Sauer, played the piano brilliantly. She had a good heart and realised what it must mean to Vaslav to live this life without art. So she offered to play for him every day. And immediately the ideas regarding a new composition took form in his mind. He had for quite a while thought of creating a ballet of the mediæval age. The angularity of the movements and dances of this period lent themselves admirably to express Vaslav's ideas. He danced before me a few parts of his new ballet, and they reminded me of the attitude of statues on the purest Gothic cathedral. Naturally he would have loved to have the music composed for the ballet, but this was impossible at the time. So German music was the kind to be considered, as the Gothic composition of the ballet required it. So my cousin Lily played all the modern Germans. As she played Strauss's tone-poem, *Tyl Eulenspiegel,* Vaslav became enthusiastic. He saw the ballet at once. It was the very thing that he wanted.

Again he wished to use masses, not altogether as in *Sacre,* but in groups and by making twenty people do the same movement as if they were one. Where and when this ballet could be produced was a mystery, but we did not think of it. Vaslav was a changed person. He became mischievous again, and I saw his face light up with joy.

Sometimes he danced for us the gypsy dances of Russia. He would suddenly be transformed into a wild, fierce, savage girl, trembling all over from the tips of his fingers to his toes, shaking his shoulders as if they were independent of the rest of his body. And then he would imitate the different *ballerinas* of the Mariinsky. We often begged him to show us how Kshessinskaya danced. But we loved it most when he showed us how the peasant women flirt whilst dancing. He had an inimitable way of throwing inviting glances, and undulating in such a lascivious manner as to stir up the senses of the spectator almost to frenzy.

For many months I watched him designing and counting, drawing with infinite care; sometimes very late at night, I awoke from my sleep and Vaslav was still bowed over his writing-desk. My mother complained he used too much electricity.

I became interested in this work, which seemed like geometry, like mathematics, and which was neither. Vaslav was pleased by my sudden manifested interest, and explained to me that he was attempting to find a system through which dances and all human movements could be written down. He said that for centuries noted *maîtres de ballet* and dancers had tried to find a solution to this problem, but had never succeeded in a satisfactory way. "Music can be noted; so can words; but unfortunately dancing cannot. And so the most precious compositions get lost and are forgotten."

Also he explained to me that the music and the art of movement were very similar, and obeyed the same laws. The difference was that they came to our mind in different ways, the one orally, the other visually, but in fact their theory of harmony was founded on the same principles. He developed the theory of the dance. Every day, as a test, to see if it would be practical for general use, he taught me the system of notation.

The Russian Army retreated and the war seemed endless. My mother became more irritable with Vaslav, and for everything that went wrong in or round the house, he was blamed, first secretly, then openly. The automatic boiler of the hot-water system broke. "Mr. Nijinsky must have spoiled it," said the valet. My mother forbade him to take a bath or use hot water.

In the ante-chambers the walls became mouldy; small mushrooms grew there, which ruined the velvet wall-covers and the parquet floor. "Mr. Nijinsky brought the mould in with the child's plaid from the garden and infected the place," they declared.

And then one day my mother's pet cat disappeared. It was a fat, old, ordinary cat. My cousin, who lived at the next villa, was a great hunter; he had excellently trained dogs, and those dogs took a great dislike to my mother's cat and chased her whenever they could. My mother, as she returned from the city, received the news that the cat could not be found. She flew into a rage. "It is Vaslav; he must have killed the cat." Vaslav's eyes closed; his face was immobile. He looked very much like a Tibetan lama. Everybody was in an uproar; they all searched for the cat. "There she is, darling Mima," said the valet, and pointed to a linden-tree, in which the cat blissfully browsed, and my cousin's dog was lying in wait at the bottom of the tree watching her.

But this did not make any difference to my mother. She turned to Vaslav, convulsed with rage, and screamed:

"You hateful man, you damned Russian, you! You are the one who did it. I wish you were out of my house forever, you silly acrobat, you circus dancer!"

Already, at the start of her cursing, Vaslav turned round, and in a second mounted the two storeys up to Kyra's room—to peace, to his child, away out of all this hatred.

But my mother's powerful voice followed him: "You cursed one, you hateful one!"

I could not comprehend my mother. Why was she so unjust? Why did she hate Vaslav so? He was always kind, respectful to her, and came, at first, with the reverence and love of a son.

When I complained, he said, "It is your mother; you have no right to judge."

But I could not stand this any longer. Next day I went to our Chief of Police and begged him to send us to a concentration camp.

"I will see what can be done," he said. "But Nijinsky is

a civil prisoner; he can't be sent to a concentration camp. It is against the international regulations, which cannot be offended."

I asked Vaslav to let me go to Vienna. I wanted to consult Professor Halban. He was rather anxious on account of the risk I was taking. Should I be discovered, they would arrest and punish me. But I was born a Hungarian. It was my native country and language. There was no reason why they should discover me. Vienna was four hours away by train. I could easily make the journey in a day and return the same night. Vaslav could spend the day at my Aunt Poly's, who did not like my mother and had ceased all relationship with her at the death of my father years ago. So at home they would not notice that I was away.

I carried out my plan successfully. I boarded the train and at noon I arrived in Vienna. So far so good. But the difficult task now began. I had to see my godfather, His Excellency Thallocy, who at that time was one of the five members of the War Council residing at the War Office. How to get in without being noticed? But I had to take the risk. At the entrance, a soldier with bayonet questioned me. I said, "I am the god-daughter of Excellency Thallocy, and have to see him urgently." I was shown into an inner office. An officer looked me over, and I asked him to take in a note to my godfather asking him to receive me.

Within a few minutes he came out himself. He pulled a serious, strict face, but as soon as we were left alone he said, "You Russian subject, I am going to arrest you and send you to gaol. The idea of penetrating to the War Office, when our respective troops are fighting at Przemyšl!" Then he kissed me and patted me on my shoulders and said, "In spite of it all, I like your bravery and your loyalty to your husband. That is how it should be; that is the way Hungarian women have been through all ages.

"No, to send you to the concentration camp is impossible, but we might transfer you to a place in Bohemia, where Russians are liked. These Czechs were always for the Allies. Or we can exchange you to Russia against some other prisoners. I will see what I can do.

"Of course, I know your mother; she is a great woman, lovely; I was very much in love with her in my youth. A very, very great actress, but as a mother-in-law—brrrrrr! I can just imagine. But, you stupid child, can't you understand? Don't you know human psychology? Your mother, the great artist, was chained to Hungary all her life. Her success never passed the frontiers, because she played in Hungarian. Your husband's art is universal. He is known and admired everywhere. Your mother is jealous, perhaps unconsciously. But she could control herself. In fact, I am going to reprimand her personally on my next visit to Budapest. She has no right to mistreat our prisoner, and one of our most precious ones." He smiled mischievously. "You do not know how many crowned heads and representatives of neutral countries have approached us. But as long as he is so valuable to them and to Russia, we are going to ask a great price for him."

Then I learned that they were bargaining with Russia, through the International Red Cross Offices, for the exchange of Vaslav against five high officers of the Austrian Army—generals, colonels, and a major. He told me to return to Budapest and wait quietly, and gave me a pass, so that I should not get into trouble on my return journey.

The few hours I still had left I spent at my brother-in-law's. He knew from his own experience my mother's temperament and the family situation, and was very, very sad about out life. Erik Schmedes was a Dane, and through his legation he promised to send news of us to my mother-in-law in St. Petersburg, and try to get some answer. Which promises he kept.

I did not bring any change to our situation, but I brought hope.

Now Kyra began to take her first steps, and Vaslav was enchanted. Also she began to utter *"Tataka,"* which meant, in her special Russian, "Father." Vaslav worshipped her, and Kyra seemed also to reciprocate this feeling; nobody else interested the child except him. So his constant, unfailing care day and night, his patience, were rewarded. Vaslav could play with Kyra for hours. He threw her in the air, to Kyra's delight, rolled with her in the grass, and they pulled the carved coloured duck together.

She used to jump in her bed, arching her body. "You see, she will be a dancer; she is dancing already." But Vaslav's great joy came one morning when Kyra, sitting in his arms, began to move her arms and head in perfect rhythm to the tune of the street-organ. "She is my little Camargo."

The weeks passed, and then a new ray of hope came, in the form of a letter from the Marchioness of Ripon, which was smuggled through by a Spanish friend who came on a special mission to Austria-Hungary.

She wrote with great affection: how she tried to warn us, when she thought there was danger of war, how unhappy she was that her dear Vatza had to go through this trying experience. But she was working for our release; we would be liberated; all her friends were trying to help. She asked news of "my little *ballerina*," as she called Kyra, and told us all about her hospital, and the sadness the war brought to all of us. "Never will I be able to laugh again after seeing all this human misery, and in these hopeless days the memory of your dancing is the only beautiful thing. It was worth while living to have seen it," wrote Lady Ripon.

Vaslav avoided my mother, and they hardly spoke to each other. Now she came with a new proposition. She advised Vaslav to change his citizenship, to become Hungarian, Polish, or anything. But Vaslav refused. "I was born a Russian; I can give thanks to my country, which made me an artist, and I will remain Russian."

One day, when we had to report, we were reproached with teaching Kyra only Russian, and forbidding her to learn Hungarian. But I said, "She is only sixteen months old. Of course she will be learning Russian, but she is too small to speak any language yet." But I wondered who had denounced us.

During this winter my mother was supposed to play the part of Zaza in Victorien Sardou's drama. She came to

Vaslav and asked him to show her how to make up for
this particular part. Vaslav asked her to describe the
character. He then made her up as a very refined woman
would look in middle age—still beautiful, but faded. The
make-up was extremely suitable and artistic. But my
mother thought Vaslav intended to be unkind. "Well, you
don't make me look like a young woman," she said. "But
you are supposed to be a *demi-mondaine* round the fifties,
you told me; that is what I tried to portray," he replied.

This incident again aroused her antagonism, which I
hoped had quieted down, but I was mistaken.

My Aunt Poly, to whom I had spoken about the attempt
to exchange us for some Austro-Hungarian officers,
thought of her own son, who was a physician in the Army
and a prisoner now at one of the concentration camps
at the Lake Baikal. She decided to see my uncle, Baron
Burrian, Minister of Foreign Affairs in Vienna, to obtain
his help so that this exchange should be made.

Vaslav must have missed very much the possibility of
dancing. Practising alone could not be satisfactory to him.
Often he took hold of me and we waltzed together, humming the tunes of the lovely waltz in Tchaikovsky's
Eugène Onegin. Vaslav did not waltz the same way as
we did, but very smoothly and with the correct beating
of the three steps, as it was danced in the time of the real
Viennese waltz, 1830.

During those long months of our internment, when
we were thrown utterly on each other's company, we
gained a knowledge of each other's character which under
different circumstances would have hardly been possible.
Vaslav inspired and influenced me, in my feelings and
outlook on life and art. He opened to me an unlimited
vista of humanity, and gave me constantly new ideas from
the undrainable richness of his thoughts.

In our great isolation we talked over many subjects. I
asked Vaslav about his parents, his childhood, and the
years in the Imperial School. He told me all about it—
this school where he was so happy. Then he recounted
to me those years with Sergei Pavlovitch, their friendship,
and the great love he had for him. "I will never regret

anything I have done, for I believe that all experience in life, if made with the aim to find the truth, is uplifting. No, I do not regret my relations with Sergei Pavlovitch, even if ethics condemn it." Then he related how, on the boat going to South America, he first felt he was after all mistaken in love, and the overwhelming desire took hold of him to go to Siberia, and to live the life of a preaching monk. But dancing—dancing—to give that up was so difficult. "And then I saw you; in fact, I noticed you on that wintry day in Budapest when you were sitting in your black velvet dress in a corner, watching with such adoration the exercises of the artist at the rehearsal. I saw you worshipped my art. This struck me—'A spoilt girl of Society and she possesses a soul.' Later, when Sergei Pavlovitch told me he intended to take you with the troupe, I advised him to do so. Then I began to watch you, and on the boat the day you spoke to me about my little pillow from my mother—of Wagner and his music—I decided to marry."

"But how dangerous. I might have been a flirt, a coquette, anything; you did not even know my name."

"Yes, I knew everything. I knew, in that first moment, we were meant for each other."

He explained to me, "You are so very young. At present you feel I am the whole world for you. We married; this is a sacred bond, but only if we make it sacred. This is only possible if we are always frank with each other. Every human being has the right over himself at any time. You promised to love me, to be truthful. But how can anybody promise to keep up an emotion? If you meet somebody you love more, you must come and tell me. I will do everything, if the person is worthy, to obtain your happiness. Do not think that you are not free because you married."

Our marriage was so completely happy that I often had a feeling of anxiety that something would happen. Vaslav was a playmate for Kyra, a child when he was with her. For me he was a real companion, a friend, a brother, a husband, a lover. He could understand all my moods, my thoughts and desires, and he took an interest in everything with which I was occupied. I found that no friends of mine could share my feelings as he did. He was able to place himself in the soul of a woman. He treated me with great reverence and natural gaiety. I had unconsciously the feeling that I lived with an extraordinary being, a genius, but he never made this felt. He was the simple and natural young man. One could almost forget that he was Nijinsky. In love as in art, Vaslav was a master.

One morning, while I was still in bed, a detective came to fetch us. We reported to the police. Vaslav and I were immediately separated at the entrance, led into different rooms, and questioned. For hours I was put under cross-examination; so was Vaslav. I could not make out at what they were driving.

The chief told me. "I understand that for months your husband was working on some kind of a plan. It is a military one. Do you know of it? It must be some code. Our attention was called to it by patriotic people."

"Ridiculous! My husband is working on the system of notation of the human movements. Ever since the time of Louis XIV dancers have been searching for it. It is true that he spends the greater part of his day, till late in the night, on this work. But it has no more to do with war or military schemes than the canals of Mars."

"This matter is very serious," he replied. "There is evidence against you that you try to make a Russian of your daughter. A manuscript was found in Nijinsky's desk which looks like mathematics, but it is not geometry and it is not music, so what can it be?"

"The system of notation of the dance."

"Well, unless Mr. Nijinsky is able to prove this, you will be separated from each other; he will be sent to some fortress and come before a court martial. We are at war."

I began to tremble. I knew that Vaslav was the most pacific creature, that he was the most honest being, that he could never, never do anything of this sort. But everybody seemed to be in an abnormal state of mind; a real war-psychosis was raging.

Experts of music and mathematics were called in, and

Vaslav explained to them his system. It took several days of investigation, and then those men congratulated him on his epoch-making creation.

The next time we reported, I insisted on knowing from our chief who had denounced us. "I cannot say; it is an official secret. But it was really a ridiculous thing to do. It also put us in a rather awkward position, but we had to investigate the matter once it was brought to our notice. Of course, we were told Nijinsky was working on a military plan."

"But who—who could have insinuated anything of the sort?"

"Well, well, over-anxious, blinded persons, who are perhaps rather nervous about their own position. Family misunderstandings often cause remarkable events."

I understood he referred to my parents. "Did it come from home? Please, please say."

He bowed his head and said, "Don't ask me, but I wish you could be sent to some other place of internment."

Years later, when the terrible tragedy happened and I came back with my sick husband, I met this chief, and he said, "I wonder if that regrettable incident during the war is not greatly responsible for this horrible drama."

One autumn day a Hungarian theatrical impresario came up to see us, telling us that he had just returned from Switzerland, where he had received word that Diaghileff was trying to communicate with Vaslav. He intended to go with the Ballet to America, and Vaslav must come. To America! It seemed so fantastic, and a message from Diaghileff did not seem genuine to us either.

I received a postcard from my godfather quoting an old proverb: "Now as long as you have hoisted the bell in the church tower, go and ring it." I could not make out what it meant until an order came from the police that as we were to be transferred to Karlsbad, in Bohemia, we should get ready. Never have I packed everything so quickly before in readiness for a departure. We reported to the police. As the prefect bade us farewell, he said, "I do hope we have not been too hard. I tried to do my best.

Sometimes we are obliged to carry out instructions which we do not approve ourselves. You have my full sympathy." And then, turning to Vaslav, he said, "You should interrupt your journey in Vienna and see her doctor." He looked me in the eyes and almost suggested, "You feel very sick, don't you?" I replied, "Yes." "All right, I will report this to the authorities." We understood he showed us the way to liberty.

Chapter Fifteen

"LENT" TO AMERICA

WE ARRIVED in Vienna early in January 1916, without money and still war prisoners—and for how long? But in spite of all this we felt relieved. In Karlsbad, even if we were going to be interned, we would be among Slavs.

At the station, we looked at each other; we had to go to the police, but we must leave Kyra somewhere. She was tired out from the railway trip. So we called on my brother-in-law, Schmedes. He was very popular in Vienna —he was their very own Tristan and Lohengrin—and now he was treated doubly with respect; not only was he *"Kammersanger* of the Hofoper," but also a neutral subject. He came with us to the police.

"Here, Excellency, I am introducing to you a prisoner, my brother-in-law, Nijinsky."

"I am so pleased, but enchanted. What luck! Would you give me your autograph? Oh, the *Spectre de la Rose,* how divine; and the *Princesse Enchantée*—I really do not know which I prefer. What a joy it has been to see you dance! If only this unfortunate war would be over! What

a handicap for art, which can only develop in a monarchy, in peace and prosperity! Oh, I see—your papers.
Of course, of course—interned. Well, well, we here in
Vienna know how to differentiate, we can make distinction. The law is all right, but we have to know how to
apply it; a great artist is at home everywhere." He
was humming to himself the *Gralserzahlung*. "By the by,
dear Schmedes, do you take the breath just before '*bin
Lohengrin genannt*,' or before '*Mein Vater Parsifal tragt
seine Krone*'?" And he rang one of the numerous bells
on his desk. A very elegant young man appeared in a
cut-away.

"Mr. Nijinsky, allow me to introduce to you my secretary, Count Ludwig X. Count, we have the honour to
have as a guest in our city the world's greatest dancer;
he will remain here some time, as Madame Nijinsky is
not feeling well. You can always let me know, Mr. Nijinsky, when you want to go to Karlsbad—perhaps next
summer; that is the best season there; don't bother to come
here to report, and do go and see the revival of *Die
Meistersinger*. I really think it is an excellent performance. I love your Walter Stolzing, Schmedes.

"Any time you wish to communicate with your family,
just ring up the Count, he will take care of it, we can
send the letter through the International Section of the
Red Cross. Sorry to inconvenience you in this way."

Indeed this was a most unexpected reception. But
where and how were we going to live? At the American
Consulate in Budapest, before we left for Vienna, we were
given some American identification papers, specially is-
sued for Russian prisoners, which allowed us to travel.
The Consul told us that in Austria the Spanish Embassy
looked after the Russian prisoners, so we knew we had
to report there.

Vaslav went up to Mr. Wolff, the proprietor of the
Hôtel Bristol, and asked him if we could have a room
for a few days, and told him that we had no money to
pay. Mr. Wolff laughed, "But Mr. Nijinsky, you honoured
my hotel in the past, of course you are welcome. I will
give instructions that one of the suites be prepared—

a bedroom, a room for the baby, a living-room, and bath. You are to make yourself at home, order anything you wish, stay a year—two—as long as the damn war lasts! You pay me when the war is over."

As we reported next day at the Spanish Embassy, the first secretary of the Ambassador received us, and told us how pleased they were that we arrived in Vienna.

"In fact, you know, we have transmitted several demands to His Majesty the Emperor Francis Joseph for your release. His very Apostolic Majesty, King Alfonso of Spain, intervened just a few days ago on your behalf, after the attempt of the Danish and the *pourparlers* for an exchange from the Russian side failed. Believe me, Mr. Nijinsky, we did our best, but the Austrian conditions were ridiculous. Five high officers of the *Generalstab*, among them General Kuzmanek, the defender of the fallen fortress Prezemyšl, for a civil prisoner, were unacceptable. As much as Russia wanted to have you, on military principle, they could not consent.

"His Holiness the Pope asked for your liberation also —you are a Catholic and an artist. Of course, after this, it will be impossible for them to refuse."

Later we found out that the Marchioness of Ripon and the Comtesse de Greffuhle tried every way for our release, and called the attention of Queen Alexandra and the Dowager Empress Maria Feodorovna to Nijinsky's fate.

When Vaslav told him about our financial distress, he laughed. "But we shall give you money, on your letter of credit on Paris, or the amount you wish without it, naturally."

It seemed we were dreaming. Vaslav just caught me as we arrived home, and we waltzed until I fell breathlessly into the chair.

M. Gregor, director of the Hofoper, told us we could go any day to the Opera, and gave us a pass.

"Where are you going to practise?"

"At home, in my room," said Vaslav.

"Oh, no, we cannot allow that." Next morning he wrote to us that unfortunately he could not let Vaslav practise, on account of the war, at the Hofoper, but that the stage

at the Theatre an der Wien was, at any time during the
day, at Vaslav's disposal—the lovely old-fashioned theatre, with an ideal stage for dancing, where once Fanny
Elssler celebrated her greatest triumph.

At this time, Vaslav was composing the *Mephisto Valse*.
It caught the romantic, the languorous Slavic chord of
his soul, and showed how romanticism could be expressed
with strength, virility, exuberance. Vaslav took an imaginary episode of Dr. Faust's life: Faust, accompanied by
Mephisto, in search of love, enters a roadside tavern, attracted by the sound of music. Dusk is falling. A group
of villagers are gambling round a table; the landlord is following the game with interest and is flattering an elderly, fat, rich merchant, who is eyeing the greedy landlord's
beautiful golden-haired daughter. The village bag-pipers
are playing. A servant unceasingly replenishes the foam-
ing tankards.

A young peasant, suitor of the landlord's daughter,
clumsily begins to dance with her, but the father stops
them at once. Faust and Mephisto enter. The landlord
rushes up to the distinguished, richly dressed cavaliers.

Mephisto, with a quick glance, sums everybody up, and
takes his stand behind the rich merchant. Immediately
the calm and jovial atmosphere changes. They become
frantic with desire . . . to win . . . to win. . . .

The proprietor's daughter comes in with drinks, and
stands spellbound before Faust. Her suitor has began to
gamble with money lent him by Mephisto. Mephisto suddenly seizes the violin and begins to play. The village men
and maidens openly abandon themselves to love-making,
the girls no longer repel but seek the lecherous advances
of the men, and the landord's daughter until now resisting,
begins to dance for Faust. As the frenzy reaches its climax
the singing of a lark is heard in the starlit woods—through
the open door. Mephisto, still playing, approaches the
door, and pair after pair disappear. Finally, with complete consent, the landlord's daughter throws herself into
Faust's arms, and he triumphantly dances with her out
into the woods—towards love.

The whole story was told as a choreographic poem, in

gestures of the period, which Vaslav translated in a brilliant series of classical dances—as he understood the classical school and could make use of it. It was a living Dürer—full of fire, brilliant, flaming, from the moment Mephisto appeared. The "variation" of the maiden was a sequence of *entre-chats, tours en l'air,* jumps, all toe dancing, but in an exquisitely mediæval way. In spite of its languid romanticism, of its amorous feeling, it was strong and plastic, with clearly defined gestures, and it had the neatness and sparkling of a beautifully cut glittering diamond—and it was in complete harmony with Liszt's music.

Vaslav danced for me the parts of the forty-five dancers in his simple practice costume. He rendered the characters of the old fat landlord, the lecherous rich merchant, the awkward heavy *fiancé,* the servant, Mephisto, Faust, the guests, the girls. I forgot that it was one person dancing and not a whole troupe. And he danced, with infinite lightness and brilliancy, the part of the maiden. Never, never, have I seen among all the great *prima ballerinas* anybody so tender, so maidenly, so light, so harmonious, so perfect in their attitudes, and so matchlessly equal on their toes.

Vaslav just laughed. He thought it was a success if I had so utterly forgotten the absence of the troupe.

He visited the private collections, escorted by friends. The Hofmuseums and the Albertina were a source of joy to him. So were the concerts at which we assisted, and the performances at the Opera.

My brother-in-law, brought up in the strictest traditions of Bayreuth, where he sang at the festivals—taught by the great Cosima herself—listened to Vaslav's conception of how Tristan, Lohengrin, and Tannhäuser should be acted.

Vaslav played these parts for us, and Erik agreed that they were in the spirit of Wagner. After those discussions, he changed in many ways. His performance gained in beauty and originality, and especially in correctness of style and gesture.

For Vaslav, Wagner was not only a great musician but

also a great *maître de ballet.* His operas were full of
choreographic composition, as Vaslav pointed out to us.
The arrival of the guests at Wartburg, in the second act of
Tannhäuser, that of the pilgrims in the third, the Grals-
ritter scene in *Parsifal,* the march of Elsa, before her wedding, from her Kemenate to the Cathedral, are purely
choreographic and of great beauty.

Vaslav liked the idea of composing the dances for
Parsifal, Tannhäuser, and *Die Meistersinger,* and hoped
that after the war he would be able to do this for the
festival at Bayreuth.

At this time Kokoscha, the Viennese painter, made a
drawing of Vaslav. Vaslav often assisted the ballet rehearsals, and when they were practising.

Vaslav was requested by my sister to watch the dancing
of the daughter of a friend of hers, Mme. L., who was
herself interested in art and did a lot for artists. She had
put one of her villas at Schonberg's disposal. Her daughter wanted to become a dancer, and we went to see her.
Vaslav believed in an early training, not later than twelve
or thirteen years if possible—after that age, the muscles,
the tendons, are too far developed to get the necessary
flexibility. The daughter was sixteen already, and danced,
but did not know how. This in itself would not have
mattered; all Vaslav was looking for was disposition, but
I could see from his face that she did not have any.

Vaslav was gentle and kind-hearted. He always tried
to encourage and help, but on the question of dancing he
was adamant, was just, but told the truth.

"My advice is: you should not waste your energy, your
time, your money on studying, you have no talent whatsoever for the dance." I felt sorry for the girl. She looked
crushed and hopeless.

Going home, I reproached Vaslav: "But how could
you be so cruel, why did you not leave some hope?"

"Because there isn't any; that girl will never dance,
and it would be far more cruel to let her live with an
unattainable desire, when she would only waste her life.
We must show, for the sake of the art of dancing, that
dilettantism is a great danger. Those who love dancing,

but have neither the ability nor early nor adequate training, why can they not just learn for themselves enough to appreciate fully the ballets? So many music-loving people play their instruments at home; but why do they show before the public their pitiful performances? I wonder if any audience would stand for a piano recital, full of mistakes or improvisations, glorifying the 'modern school,' saying Beethoven is old-fashioned and impossible. That is what all these so-called 'modern schools' of dancing and its representatives are doing to our art, which needs, more than any other, the public's true understanding. Then began the fashion so prevalent to-day for any untrained person to set up as a teacher of dancing."

So many have taken a few lessons of rhythmic gymnastics or have been on a cruise in the Orient in search of a few native movements, and on the strength of this have declared that the "classic school" was old-fashioned. "Mushroom dancers" was the term Vaslav used for them.

Rumour reached us that Richard Strauss had heard we were interned in Austria-Hungary, and had requested the German Ambassador in Vienna to try to release us.

A few weeks later, when he came to Vienna, we met him. Vaslav was keen on asking his consent to produce *Tyl Eulenspiegel* as a ballet. Strauss was overjoyed when he heard that Vaslav had already adapted it. He wholeheartedly accorded his permission, and even offered to make changes, if necessary, in the musical score. But Vaslav replied that he would not want a bar to be altered, he found the symphony so perfect and so suitable.

Mephisto Valse was ready. Vaslav began to work on an idea he had had for a long time—to create a Japanese ballet. He was interested in the Orient and knew all their dances, though how he did was a mystery to me. He loved Hokusai and the ancient periods of the Far East. But how different was his idea of all those dances from the ones we had witnessed in the different recitals and opera houses! Vaslav's Japanese dances, monumental in the extreme, were a series of poses, few movements and distorted like a Laocoön group; pauses, then a slight inclination of the head, a lowering of the eyelids, an unbelievable turn of the wrist, the fluttering fingers. The Japan of Nijinsky was that of the Samurai—powerful, grim, tragic, and full of tradition.

Unfortunately this ballet was never completed.

Mme. L. took us to visit Schonberg. It was a wet and dreary afternoon when we went to the villa in Hietzing where he lived. Vaslav felt great sympathy for him, and was interested to hear some of his new compositions. He had heard *Pierrot Lunaire* two years previously, whilst in Berlin, and wondered how Schonberg would develop.

Schonberg and his wife received us very warmly. Schonberg and Vaslav soon forgot our presence and exchanged their ideas.

Schonberg painted at the time "curious and mystic pictures," which certainly had a strange appeal.

A very heated discussion broke out between Schonberg and Vaslav. The first claimed that in music no training is needed, as anybody who has talent could compose or play the piano without certain study. Vaslav tried to apply the question to dancing, and finally they decided they were mistaken and training in both arts was essential.

My godfather told us, at lunch one day, whilst he served us *borscht* and *koulibiaka* (as good as can be made at St. Petersburg), that we were quite often discussed at the sittings of the *Kreigsuberwachungs-Amt*.

"Then, my dear Vaslav, you seem to be a very rare and precious person to the 'Holy Russian Empire,' and to our distinguished enemies the Allies. We have received more requests for your release than history has ever known for a war prisoner. I must say that, in spite of the fact that you are a Moscovite, I like you, and, though I am no judge of dancing, I do feel that you not only dance with your feet but with your brains and soul. This is the reason that I defend your interests at those sittings —not because my very charming and foolish god-child ran after you to the Antipodes and made you marry her. After all, to be a bachelor is the only sensible way of living. Anyhow, to those very eminent colleagues of mine the name of Nijinsky is like the red cloth to a bull. I am sure we will have a new demand for your release at the

next sitting, but who will make it? It is a puzzle to me
since all the crowned heads and neutrals have already
intervened on your behalf!"

His prophecy, in fact, became true, and from a most
unexpected corner.

Early one morning the telephone rang. I did not answer
it quickly or over-enthusiastically, as I thought it was very
stupid of my sister to ring us at such an unearthly hour.
But as I listened to the call I became mute and could
hardly answer.

"Vaslav, we have to dress and go at once to the American Ambassador, Mr. Painfield; he has some very urgent
news for you."

We went; it was the Ambassador who received us.
"Dear Mr. Nijinsky, I am so glad your release has been
sanctioned. On instructions from home, I have requested
your release, and I received, yesterday, a favourable answer from the Foreign Office. You are free, and can at
once proceed to America."

He then told us that the Russian Ballet was going to
New York, that, in fact, they were already there; that Mr.
Otto H. Kahn, the chairman of the board of directors of
the Metropolitan Opera House, had requested Mr. Lansing,
head of the State Department, to arrange that the Austrians should release Nijinsky. After great difficulties, the
Austrians had agreed to lend Nijinsky to the United
States for an indefinite period, with the understanding that
he should go "on parole."

First they wanted an official guarantee that Nijinsky
would be prevented from returning to Russia, but they
had trusted the faith of the Ambassador, who promised
that Nijinsky would obey the conditions.

Our great joy was short-lived. The secretary reported to
the Ambassador, in our presence, that the Foreign Office
had made one reservation: that Kyra and I should be
retained as hostages. Mr. Painfield thought this a very
strict measure, and Vaslav refused to go to America while
that condition remained.

"I will not leave my wife and child, as happy as I

would be to go and dance in America. That would be impossible."

Mr. Painfield became very anxious that Vaslav should go, and promised to interview Baron Burrian, the Minister of Foreign Affairs, at once.

My well-informed Aunt Poly went to see Baron Burrian, to make a desperate effort that Vaslav should only be exchanged against my cousin Feri; but though she failed, the American Ambassador, being more influential of course, soon advised Vaslav that all three of us were free.

We received instructions to leave next evening for Berne, Switzerland, where a representative of the Metropolitan Opera House would await and conduct us to New York as quickly as possible—Vaslav being anxiously expected there.

Our journey to Berne passed in comparative comfort. We were given a first-class compartment, and the two detectives who accompanied us to the frontier were occupying the next one. The train was full of officers returning to the front. Some windows were broken, and the steam heating left much to be desired. The velvet upholstering of the seats was ragged and stained, as were the carpets. It was evident that the railway carriages had seen better days and were in great need of repair.

On one side of the carriage I made a bed for Kyra, and arranged her as comfortably as I could, and the other side I prepared for Vaslav. Travelling was always hard for him. He could not stand being locked up in such a small place for many hours, and the motion of the train seemed to affect him, also he suffered from violent pains in his head.

I could not sleep; the change from our past mode of living to liberty was so tremendous, and the painful incident, which we had had on the last day, troubled me. My mother came to Vienna, as soon as she heard we were released, with flowers to congratulate us. After all it seemed that we were not entirely forgotten by the world. Nijinsky once more became to my family a celebrity. I could not forgive, and Vaslav, for the first time since I have known him, showed that he could be hard. When my mother approached him, he turned away, and with a strange look, said to the person standing near him, "Who is this lady who wishes to talk to me?"

Ceaselessly through the night, trains passed us, full of soldiers going to the Italian front. I was sorry for those exhausted, haggard, and pale-looking men who were crowded into the baggage-cars and were taken to death. They looked dirty and hungry, and did not sing now like they did in those August days of 1914 when they were covered with flowers.

At the small mountain station of Feldkirch, the frontier, we descended, and, having reported with our papers at the military office, we were instructed to go to the village and stay there until we were notified that we could leave. I was inquisitive to know how long it would be before we received this notification, on account of the child, but the authorities were unable to enlighten me.

Our luggage was taken from us by the authorities, to be inspected, and we were told that no papers or books, in any form, could be taken with us. The snow-covered Alps glittering in the brilliant sunshine surrounded Feldkirch with its neat Tyrolean houses, nestled among the dark pine trees on the flank of the mountain. We were shown to a hostelry called Posthotel. Our lovely big room was so cosy, with the window where the bright sunshine poured in; the big porcelain stove was fully loaded, and threw out a great heat; the furniture was made of light wood, and the clean beds, with their enormous old-fashioned eider-downs, delightful.

"How much like Russia," exclaimed Vaslav. He became a real child; the whole day he was pulling Kyra on a sleigh, or sliding down with her from the mountain-side —to their mutual joy.

At last we were free again! Once a day we used to go down to the station and inquire when we would be allowed to leave Feldkirch, but always the officer on duty shook his head and said, "I do not know."

One day, as we were lunching, a middle-aged woman, in deep mourning, was seated at our table. She began to speak to me, but I hardly answered. We seemed to meet her wherever we went, and one evening, while we were having tea, she joined us without invitation, bursting out crying, telling me that her husband was killed in the war, and venomously declared that the Austrians had willingly provoked the war; that it was an injustice to humanity to slaughter people. She tried to see our reaction, by engaging me in conversation, for she knew she could not succeed in interesting Vaslav. He slightly closed his eyes, and I understood he wanted to let me know something was amiss. I excused myself, without answering the widow's question, and said good night.

We found out next day from our chambermaid that the widow was employed by the military authorities; she was an *agent provocateur*.

One day, at noon, one of the detectives burst into the room: "Within fifteen minutes you have to be at the station!" I threw everything into the suit-cases. Vaslav put Kyra on the sleigh, and pulled her, galloping, to the station. Upon arrival, we were shown into different rooms; Kyra and myself were completely undressed, and our skin tested to see if there was any secret writing on it. I had to undergo a medical examination to prove that nothing was hidden on me. I was livid with rage, but did not dare to say anything. Finally we were put on the train. I cannot describe the emotion we felt as we passed the little bridge dividing the Austrian Empire from Switzerland— and freedom.

In Berne, where we were received by the Russian Legation our hotel windows faced the Eiger, the Monch, the Jungfrau, the glorious panorama of the Berner Oberland. It appeared to us like heaven; wanting to fête it, we ordered a big lunch. Cream, butter, chocolate, sugar, all in profusion, we did not dare to touch. It first seemed unreal—then we fell on it. Vaslav stopped us very wisely; even so, Kyra and myself were upset for days by these unusual delicacies. Next morning, the Russian Minister, Baccharat, presented us with a diplomatic passport, according to instructions received from St. Petersburg. It was a very imposing-looking document, with big seals and a coat of arms, which said, in French and in Russian: *"Au nom de Sa Majesté Nicolas II, Empereur et Autocrate de tous les Russes, je vous prie de laisser passer, accorder protection et tous les facilités à mon sujet Vaslav Fomitch Nijinsky, sa femme, et son enfant."*

In the evening there was a dinner in our honour at the Legation. Already, when we had visited the Legation in the morning, several members of the Embassy had been introduced to us, among them General X, the military attaché. Everybody received me with every kindness, and treated me as their countrywoman. Not for a second could I feel that they considered me an enemy; I was the wife of Nijinsky.

Vaslav said to me, "Do not speak of our past experiences, and of what is going on in Austria-Hungary; we must be fair to everyone." But I could not forget the way some people treated him in Budapest; I could not forget those past hopeless months, the unjust accusations against Vaslav.

At dinner the military attaché was seated next to me. He very cleverly turned the conversation on conditions in Hungary, the food, the clothing, what the people said and thought, and the journey near the Italian front. I was tempted almost to tell the truth; after all I had not promised not to do so, and they certainly had made Vaslav suffer; but again Vaslav imperceptibly closed his eyes. I bowed my head, and replied, "I am sorry, we were so isolated I do not know anything," and thought of the piece of uneatable bread, hard as stone, I still had in my suit-case. The attaché would have loved to see it, and to be able to judge the food conditions in Austria-Hungary, but I obeyed Vaslav, who was always just and correct, even to his enemies.

Here for the first time we heard what was going on in the world and in Russia. Vaslav became pensive and said that this unfortunate war in which so many millions were losing their lives was the beginning of a new phase of social order. They would all lose, victorious and vanquished. Human nature was alone to blame for the war. Never would we have peace unless it was understood

that we are all equal, all entitled to live under human
conditions, all here to help to better mankind. The system
itself should not matter so much as the aim: Love, Kindness, Charity and Understanding. Nobody should know
need. This war would not end at the cessation of hostilities.
I listened intently to Vaslav's prophetic words.

Two days later, in Lausanne, we met Mr. Russell, the
representative of the Metropolitan Opera House. He came
to escort us to New York. We were a little surprised, as
Vaslav had not received any direct invitation from America, and we did not completely understand all that was
going on, but Mr. Russell explained.

The Metropolitan Opera House wished to present the
Russian Ballet to the American public in its original
splendour. Diaghileff signed a contract, which, financially,
was extremely satisfactory, and the Opera House requested
him to bring the original Ballet, with all its stars, Karsavina, Nijinsky, Fokine, and Bolm, to the States. When
Diaghileff signed the contract, he knew that if he could
succeed to reassemble the troupe, whose members were
largely dispersed in the Allied countries, the stars, with
the exception of Bolm, he would not be able to bring
along. He trusted that, once in New York, the management of the Metropolitan Opera House would accept
whomever he brought over.

As Diaghileff knew, Fokine was in military service in
Russia, Karsavina was expecting a baby, and Vaslav was a
prisoner of war. He went to New York, and simply told
the Metropolitan that he was sorry, but this was *force
majeure* and he could not help it. The Metropolitan was
naturally surprised, and explained to Diaghileff that it was
impossible to perform under the conditions; they had
promised the American public the original cast, and it
was impossible to cheat them.

Diaghileff told his intimate friends that, after all, he
had come to America to make money, and even if the
performance was not as perfect as that rendered in London and Paris it would be still far better than anything
ever seen in America. This indeed, coming from Diaghileff, was an amazing statement.

Vaslav told Russell that in the ordinary course he did not think he would have been able to dance in the Russian Ballet after all that had happened between them before the declaration of the war, but, as long as the United States had worked for his liberation, he was at their disposal, and was ready to dance before the American public.

In Lausanne, we received word from Sir George Lewis that the lawsuit he had opened against the Russian Ballet to recover the half-million gold francs, which the Ballet owed to Vaslav as unpaid salary, had been won in the English courts, but, as Diaghileff was not a resident in any country, there would probably be great difficulty in collecting it.

At this time, Stravinsky lived at Morges, near the Lac Leman, with his family—a short distance from Lausanne. As soon as he heard of our arrival, he came over and took possession of Vaslav. I only knew him by sight—now I made his acquaintance. He was dressed like a dandy, with the most indescribable taste. He thought it was very chic, and there was something touching in his *naïveté* and conceit. He seemed extremely sure of himself, and was fully convinced of his genius, which he undoubtedly had, but the way he spoke of it seemed rather childish, and, at the same time, charming. One would have thought a man as great as he would have been more dignified. When he came to see Vaslav he was extremely courteous to me. He spoke to Vaslav for hours of his plans, his compositions, the ideas of Diaghileff, his injustices; the torrent of his words never seemed to stop. He tried to assure himself he was independent of him: "I am a composer, and sooner or later people will realise the value of my music. Of course, Sergei Pavlovitch is a great help, and especially now that the war is on. In Russia, anyhow, it is impossible to be played, when one has modern ideas. He can't crush me. His enmity against you I fully disapprove, but we must be just; he suffered terribly when he heard that you had married—he never imagined this possible. He received a cable, I understand, from Vassily Ivanovitch, at the time you had your wedding ceremony. Sergei Pavlovitch received it in London

at the Savoy Hotel, where he was staying at the time,
and we learned that he became livid and fainted. It must
have been terribly hard on him. We could all understand
this, but what was one to do? It was one of these insoluble
conflicts. All these personal feelings have no right to
hinder the development of art." After all, Nijinsky, Stravinsky represented the modern art in Russia. Diaghileff
was an equally important factor in a different way. Why
should small matters like money and love-affairs stand in
the way? I felt so crushed. What did I have to do among
those men—those gifted initiates of God? After all, Stravinsky, Vaslav were young and we were all full of hopes.

Stravinsky immediately made friends with Kyra. He
was a father, and rather an expert on handling children.
We went around Lausanne to the different cafés with
Stravinsky as our guide. Vaslav was like a boy of seven;
at last he was with a friend, a fellow artist, somebody to
whom he could speak the same language, somebody who
understood him fully and completely.

Stravinsky asked us to come and see him at his home
at Morges. We went to his house, which was near the
lake and faced the Mont Blanc, but in spite of this it was
Russia. The arrangement of the rooms, the furniture—a
simply furnished villa, but somehow Stravinsky and his
wife had transformed it into a place near Moscva; the
walls were hung with drawings by his eldest son, who
had already proved himself a possessor of talent. The
wife was a real Russian woman, a devoted wife and
mother; in her great simplicity there was the strength
of one who devoted herself—her life and personality—
to the genius of another. She was the ideal wife for a
great artist.

We enjoyed the home life, and the peaceful atmosphere
of the Stravinsky family.

Madame Stravinsky was a real artist in handicraft. She
embroidered, knitted, and painted beautifully. I always
tried to please Vaslav by emulating these Russian women,
but with little success.

Igor began to tell us about the new quintet he was

composing for wind instruments only, and also of *Mavra*
and the contemplated ballet *Noces*.

A very heated discussion developed between him and
Vaslav. Stravinsky was bitterly attacking Beethoven, Bach,
and all those composers who some years before he so
respected and now were just "the Boches." It seemed almost incredible. The Russian School, ever since the "big
five," declared war on the German School of music and
its traditions. Since Moussorgsky, they had wanted to
affirm their native conception, and had allowed themselves
to be influenced by the French point of view.

It seemed terrible that Stravinsky should let himself be
blinded by the fact that Russia was at war with Germany
—that the war should make any difference to his opinion.
I was sure he could not feel as he spoke, deep down in
his heart. It was—it must have been—just a protest. Vaslav could perhaps understand him when he raged against
Richard Strauss and Wagner, but Bach—to drag him off
his pedestal was too much.

"Why should we take any regards towards those Boches,
when my own publishers in Germany are not publishing
me at present? God knows if they will go on distributing
the compositions of Tchaikovsky and Rubinstein."

"Of course, I do not agree with you concerning *Faune*,
the music is spiral and the choreography is angular."

"You are right—absolutely—but Sergei Pavlovitch and
I could not find anything else at the moment," replied
Vaslav. "It is inartistic from the musical point of view, as
much as I admire *Faune*, which in itself is a masterpiece."

One evening he came to us in a frightful temper. This
time, Diaghileff had played him a really dirty trick. It
was arranged that as soon as Sergei Pavlovitch arrived in
New York, he should arrange that an official invitation
should be extended to Stravinsky, who was to go and conduct his own ballets at the Metropolitan. This would be
an appropriate occasion to present himself to the American
public. But, as soon as in New York, Sergei Pavlovitch
forgot his promise. Naturally Stravinsky was hurt at this
lack of attention. He insisted that if Vaslav was a real
friend, he would make it a condition to go to America

only if Stravinsky was asked also. I thought this was
rather stretching the bounds of friendship. Stravinsky
talked, raged, and cried; he paced up and down the room
cursing Diaghileff.

"He thinks he is the Russian Ballet himself. Our success
went to his head. What would he be without us, without
Bakst, Benois, you and myself? Vaslav, I count upon you."
The two departed to the post office, filled with the decision to counteract this new outrage. Luckily they could
not write in English, and I was summoned to help them
out; the rather violently worded cable to Otto H. Kahn
I was able to translate into a politely worded request.
The hoped-for invitation for Stravinsky did not arrive, and
we had to leave for Paris.

As we pulled in at the station of Pontarlier, Russell
asked me not to say that I was Hungarian born. I had
the Russian diplomatic passport, which did not show my
original nationality—the Russians had given this, as a
courtesy to Vaslav.

Russell and I passed a most disagreeable quarter of an
hour. Vaslav was not aware of this; an official interpreter
was present, a Frenchman, who spoke fluent Russian, but
he was so busy talking to Vaslav, and so interested to see
somebody who had escaped the Austrians, that he did not
pay any attention to me.

Russell gave the necessary explanations, after which
we were shown into a wooden waiting-room. On the
French side, near a small iron stove, were soldiers, covered
with big shawls, trying to keep warm. They gave us the
best seats and covers for Kyra and myself. As soon as
they learned we were released prisoners of war, they began to serve us with boiling red wine, which they prepared
on their stove, and which went down excellently in the
bitter cold February night.

When in Paris at last, we could stay only one day, as
our boat was due to leave next evening from Bordeaux.
The Préfet de Police had to countersign our French visa.
Everything had been attended to. The Comtesse de
Greffuhle very kindly made all necessary arrangements
in advance, so that after the official visit we were able to

make a tour of the leading dressmakers and millinery establishments.

Nobody would have recognised us twenty-four hours later as we went to the Quai d'Orsay to catch the train. We were elegantly dressed, and followed by sixteen trunks, loaded with flowers, and accompanied by our maid and nurse and escort, Mr. Russell. Many old friends and admirers of Vaslav turned out to say good-bye to us.

On the luxurious train, we met the future wife of Bolm —a charming woman whom I had met several years before in Vienna. She was to join Bolm in America. Bolm had cabled to us, and we had promised to bring her safely over. We had to pull down the curtains to ward off the spying eyes of the German aviators. All trains leaving the capital had to obey this regulation; it gave us a rather creepy feeling.

On reaching Bordeaux, we boarded the *Rochambeau,* a French liner, which even at that time, well deserved overhauling. Our crossing lasted almost two weeks, and was very stormy the whole time. Vaslav was constantly with the doctor of the steamer, Louis Moret, who was the celebrated etcher, and, on account of the war, was in the service of the shipping line.

They discussed, at length, Vaslav's theory of notation, and he corrected the few anatomical errors that existed. We both wondered what awaited us in that distant land. Would it bring at last, peace and understanding with Diaghileff? Would it mean artistic and personal liberty for Vaslav?

One morning, while walking on the deck, we saw the first seagulls circling over the mast, and we were told we had passed the nearest point to the American mainland, that of the Nantucket Lightship.

Chapter Sixteen

THE NEW YORK SEASON

GREAT excitement reigned over the whole boat as we steamed slowly towards "quarantine." Some magic place, it seemed to us, as everybody on board for the last twenty-four hours spoke of it with awe. The captain, proud to have brought us safely all over the Atlantic to American waters, gave his last orders on the bridge. The few Americans on board had proudly told us about all the marvels we might expect; that immense fortunes could be made overnight in the land of unlimited possibilities, where everybody had liberty and could make a living if they only wanted to work, where no class distinctions hampered advancement, where idealism and humanitarianism were still guiding forces.

A small boat appeared and the pilot came on board. A few minutes later a larger steam launch came alongside. Officials in uniform boarded, the first being the doctor, who immediately was taken by the arm by Dr. Louis Moret and they disappeared behind an immense sheaf of papers. He was followed by rather stout-looking officials, the immigration officials, who had a very serene look. Right after them came an agitated, gesticulating group of men carrying cameras. Mr. Russell hurriedly pulled Vaslav into his cabin. "Those are the reporters and cameramen. Wait here until I take you along to the immigration authorities first; we can see them later."

In a very short time they had searched through the whole boat, from the bridge to the hold, and had found out everything that had happened since we had left the French shores. I have never seen such wizardry as the

work of those reporters. Vaslav was discovered within a
second, in spite of Russell's scheming. And they made
friends then and there. Vaslav liked their natural good-
humour and *naïveté*. They were here to report about him;
they were all earning a living; each one wanted something
exclusive—and Vaslav tried to satisfy them. They patted
his shoulders, grasped Kyra, spoke a few words in Russian
to her, got hold of Vaslav's legs to feel his muscles, and
chewed gum. Vaslav became extremely interested in this,
and one of them right away volunteered to show him how
to do it. Then they took us all up to the upper deck and
photographed us from every angle. Vaslav only smiled
and said a few words. Russell looked crushed under the
torrent of questions he tried to answer. "Mr. Nijinsky,
what do you think about the war, and will it last long?"
"Who is greater, Karsavina or Pavlova?" "Have you heard
about Rasputin?" "Is he really the power behind the
throne?" "How many teeth has little Kyra?" "How do you
spell it?" "Do you prefer American women to French?"
"Your opinion about the submarine warfare?" "Is Picasso
a cubist or futurist?" "What is your favourite sport, and
rôle?"—and so on, until the chief steward came up to tell
us that the immigration officers were ready for us.

Once past the authorities, the reporters took hold of us
again, but this time to reward us for our docile submission to their former interviews, and we were taken to the
upper deck to witness one of the most enchanting and
stupendous sights of the world—the skyline of New York.

Vaslav lost his head completely as, from the heavy
yellow, grey mist, suddenly slender, tall buildings rose to
the sky like a city of minarets and campaniles.

To the great pleasure of the reporters, Vaslav in his
enthusiasm began to jump, and we had to laugh as those
newspapermen called out, "Hallo, Mr. Nijinsky, you just
stay here. Do not fly away, for God's sake."

As we walked down the gang-plank we saw a group
waiting for us with flowers: the representatives of the
Metropolitan, some former school-friends of mine, members of the Russian Ballet, and, in the front, Diaghileff.
I walked down first, and he bowed very low and, kissing

my hand, offered me a beautiful bouquet of American Beauties. Vaslav, carrying Kyra, followed me closely. Sergei Pavlovitch kissed him on both cheeks, according to the Russian custom, and Vaslav, with a quick gesture, placed Kyra in his arms. He looked embarrassed, and handed the child to the next person standing near to him. Drobetsky was smiling like a full moon. Massine was introduced, then Sergei Pavlovitch walked away with Vaslav, and I prayed that this might prove a real pact of friendship.

Vaslav seemed to like the stimulating rush of New York and the quickness of the elevators, especially those called "express." I think, if he had had time, he would have ridden in them the whole day long. He immediately saw how much easier and more practical the arrangements were here than in Europe.

As soon as we entered our apartment the telephone bell rang uninterruptedly. Maria Stepanovna arrived for fittings—ballet-shoes were brought—photographers came —flowers in profusion arrived from well-known people, then unknown to us. Then the secretary of Mr. Otto H. Kahn came to take us to his office.

After polite phrases were exchanged, Mr. Kahn recommended the sights we must see. Vaslav thanked him for the American intervention on our behalf. I thought the moment had come for me to explain the situation: that Vaslav would readily dance at the Opera, but not with Diaghileff, as long as he did not pay the amount he owed Vaslav for his past salary. And I explained that Sir George Lewis was unable to collect the money, as Diaghileff always very cleverly evaded payment. Kahn, being a business man, was understanding, and asked me to send him over the judgment, so that they could see what could be arranged, and also said that they were willing to make a private contract with Vaslav.

We tried to forget the disagreeable fact that Diaghileff owed Vaslav half a million francs, for which he would be obliged to fight. Vaslav would have preferred to drop the matter altogether, but, thinking of his family, he felt he could not do it, and left the whole case in my hands.

I could not deal with the situation alone. Years before I had met a young girl, Madeleine, in Karlsbad, and we had become very friendly. She welcomed me now at the docks, and said her uncle's office would take care of our legal matters. He was one of the most eminent lawyers of the United States, and had a charming wife with whom I used to go to Bayreuth as a girl, Mrs. Minnie Untermeyer. Madeleine took us down to the office in the Equitable building, which was quite an experience for Vaslav: a subway station in the building, hairdresser, soda fountain, drug store, where we could eat. With Madeleine he went all over the building, whilst her brother, Mr. Untermeyer's young nephew, Laurence Steinhardt, and myself, discussed the matter.

Laurence was to represent Vaslav in business. This was the first important case which was entrusted to him by his uncle's office. He was a very agreeable, good-looking young man, with a brilliant mind, and was extremely quick to grasp a difficult situation. In a short time he was quite at home in the complicated mediæval intrigues of the Russian Ballet, and within three days he settled the case in which many eminent lawyers in Europe had failed during three years. The fight was not easy, as Diaghileff, King's Bench Division's judgment or not, did not want to recognise that he was indebted, and, when he finally did, he refused to pay.

Vaslav was ready to dance for nothing for the New York public. The Metropolitan was ready to boycott him if he did. Some kind of black-listing and theatrical trust arrangement was explained to us—that if Vaslav did not dance at the Opera, he would be forbidden to appear anywhere in America. After three days, during which we had ample time to visit all the marvels of New York, Steinhardt arrived with a contract with the Metropolitan for eleven performances, and the arrangement that every week Diaghileff had to pay a part of his debt to Vaslav through the Metropolitan, from the amount he was supposed to receive after the troupe's expenses and salaries had been paid.

Vaslav's first impression and sympathy for America

strengthened with every day. He always believed in youth, and here, in this country, youth was given the opportunity which it lacked in Europe. "Here one need not be a long-bearded professor to be in an important position and to achieve something," remarked Vaslav.

The Russian Ballet arrived in January and had performed at the Century Theatre, leased by the Metropolitan for this purpose, as in their own building the regular opera company was performing its annual season. The arrival of the Ballet was greatly heralded. It was not such a triumphal success as in Europe because Diaghileff failed to bring the stars. Now the opera season was at an end, and the Ballet was to perform at the Opera House itself for three weeks. The Director of the Opera, Mr. Gatti-Casazza, and his nearest associates were displeased with Mr. Kahn's newest importation, the Russian Ballet.

The golden days of the Metropolitan when Caruso, Tetrazzini, Reské sang were followed by a very important phase of German influence under the dictatorship of Conried, who introduced German music and world-famous German singers to the States. Then Gatti was engaged, and everything became Italian. He reigned over the Metropolitan for years without any interference, and, thanks to the glorious voice of Caruso, who made every season a success, he could get away with mediocre performances. Gatti settled down for a lifetime, and the arrival of the Russian Ballet meant new influence—Russian operas, singers, and the much-feared Diaghileff. The same dreaded idea came to their minds as to Teliakovsky's; would not Diaghileff, with his great knowledge and culture, make a very suitable director for the Metropolitan?

So the Italian clique got busy to prevent this, and the first step was to see that the Ballet should not become an undisputed success.

Vaslav did not have the attitude towards the public in general that many other European artists had: "Anyhow, they will not know the difference." "On the contrary," he said, "maybe this public has not yet the artistic understanding and clear perception that ours has after centuries of long training."

We lived at Claridge's, where, thanks to Laurence and Madeleine Steinhardt, everything was arranged for us in a perfect way. She looked after Kyra and the nurse, and helped me to sort out the numerous invitations to open exhibitions, charity bazaars, receptions, meals, football and boxing matches, church meetings, and heaven knows what else. Thanks to their help, we accepted the right things; and I appeared in Vaslav's place when it was necessary, and the reporters received ready typewritten interviews. Everything was American and businesslike.

Rehearsals began, and the company behaved very politely to Vaslav; also great courtesy was shown to me, more even than in the old days. Diaghileff must have given his orders. Bolm arrived, and we were truly delighted to have him with us. He was one of the few who kept aloof from petty intrigue and who regretted Diaghileff's attitude towards Vaslav, just as he had regretted Fokine's leaving previously. Bolm was ever a good friend and a loyal colleague.

Vaslav's American début took place at the Metropolitan Opera House at a matinée on the 12th of April. The Diamond Horseshoe was present in full force, and the audience was as brilliant as in the great Paris galas. The programme consisted of *Prince Igor, Spectre de la Rose, Scheherazade* and *Petrouchka.* When Vaslav made his *entrée* in *Spectre,* the entire public rose and for a second he was embarrassed by this royal reception, but they had reserved a still further surprise in the form of a shower of American Beauty rose-petals, and in a few seconds the whole stage was inches deep in scented leaves. Vaslav, standing in the midst of them, seemed to be the very spirit of the rose.

A few days after our arrival Diaghileff invited us very formally to lunch at Sherry's. He was alone, Massine having been left at the Ritz, where they were staying. Over our first cocktails he adopted a very *mondain* tone, but soon he dropped into Russian, and I could see that he was reproaching Vaslav and that his anger was rising. Vaslav answered him calmly, and turned the conversation into French: "Seroja, all matters of business are attended to by my wife, and must be discussed with her. I now have a family to support, but I am willing to do now, as in the past, my utmost for the Russian Ballet. I am the same; I have not changed towards you. I am grateful for our past friendship, and it only depends upon you for us to be united again in our common aim. My wife is a part of me, and she understands this, and wants, as much as I do, to further the cause of the Russian Ballet. Please, please understand me."

But Sergei Pavlovitch was beyond forgiveness. I could see that he still loved Vaslav and deeply resented my existence. He began to reproach him for the lawsuit. "We never had a contract; there was never any question of money between us. What has happened to you, Vaslav?"

"But, Sergei Pavlovitch, you take money from the theatres, and make them pay in advance too. Be just," I told him.

"No, it will become impossible for me to run the Russian Ballet. Fokina wants to manage Fokine and dance all the leading rôles. You, madame, are mercenary. How do you expect the Russian Ballet to exist under such conditions?"

Then Vaslav began to speak to him about his new compositions, *Tyl* and *Mephisto*, but Diaghileff showed no interest. "It can't be worth much if it's German music." "But it's Richard Strauss, whose music you yourself produced a year and a half ago," I ventured. "Well, times have changed; the war is on and in any case Strauss, *c'est du cabotinage.*"

During the three weeks of the season, when I had to represent Vaslav at various functions we could not refuse, my time was one mad rush. There were not only the endless social obligations, but Kyra's daily routine, and it was essential always to be ready for some new complication with Sergei Pavlovitch, who worked with subtle determination on his scheme "to ruin Nijinsky." Every day some fresh surprise awaited us. First he circulated the rumour that Vaslav was a deserter. It so happened one evening that the Russian Ambassador, Bakhmetev, was in my box, and, as Diaghileff came up to greet him, I at once brought up the subject. "Excellency, I don't know if you are aware that Vaslav, through our lawyer, has made inquiries about his military position, and that he has decided to return to Russia at once unless he is fully authorised to stay here, as we understand that Sergei Pavlovitch says that things are not in order." Diaghileff excused himself and pleaded a misunderstanding, but the Ambassador made it clear that Vaslav was released on parole and "lent to the United States." Mr. Kahn joined us and tried to quiet me, then Diaghileff said, "I give you my word of honour that it is all right." "That does not suffice, Sergei Pavlovitch." "But my word will, I hope," said Kahn. My affirmative reply made Diaghileff pale with anger, but the episode was closed.

Diaghileff's next move was to spread the rumours that Vaslav had gained weight, that he had the manners of a *prima donna,* that he was the Caruso of the Dance, old-fashioned. This hurt Vaslav, all the more as it came from Diaghileff.

At that time in Venice a great flood had taken place, rendering many homeless, and it was decided by the members of society, who knew and loved the Lido, to organise a benefit performance of *tableaux vivants* after Italian Masters. Mrs. William K. Vanderbilt, Sr., a gracious, regal woman, who by her manner and understanding reminded us of Lady Ripon, lent her house for the occasion. I did not understand at the time that this exclusive mansion, usually closed to all save the four hundred, was on this occasion open to all those who would pay two hundred and fifty dollars or more for charity. Diaghileff passed me, and as usual complimented me on my dress, a *chef d'œuvre* by Callot Sœurs; but he was not fêted, and seemed bored. When Vaslav came to change from his chosen costume, a Gondolier of Carpaccio, it was discovered that most of his underwear had disappeared, taken by some of the society women as souvenirs!

When we arrived in New York we heard that the *Faune* was being danced in a very changed manner. Massine excused himself by saying that it was taught to him that way, and that it was not possible to remember it movement by movement. Vaslav offered to rehearse it, but Sergei Pavlovitch would not hear of it, so that finally Vaslav said that he preferred that under the circumstances it should not be produced at all. Diaghileff made a scene, but I reminded him that, as he did not own the rights of this ballet, the least he could do was to respect the author's wishes. All the time Vaslav still hoped that Diaghileff would change and that they could be friends once again. It could not be said, now almost three years after Vaslav's marriage, that Diaghileff was still reacting from shock and anger, yet his hatred was ferocious and his pursuit of Vaslav relentless.

One afternoon I noticed smoke coming out of the closet in our bedroom. Vaslav promptly gave the alarm, quietly took Kyra in his arms and made for the fire-escape, taking me by the hand. I hesitated, thinking that I might save the money, jewels, furs, and passports. Vaslav only laughed and pulled me away. "Leave those material things. You give them far more importance than they really have." Luckily it proved to be nothing. We were not so fortunate on a second occasion. On our return from the theatre one night, Vaslav noticed that Kyra was restless, and that her hands were bandaged. The nurse had to confess that she had spilled boiling soup on the child's hands. She was very badly hurt, and, though we summoned a doctor there and then, could only get real relief the next day when Miss Cottenet took us to Dr. Robert Abbé, the famous surgeon, who attended her for three months, and who became our very dear friend.

On his free evenings Vaslav loved to walk up and down Broadway. The brilliant lights, the stream of traffic, and the sky-signs interested him. He never tired of watching the procession of "types." The "movies," too, were always a great attraction for him, and he had implicit faith in their future. He believed that in time it would be possible to photograph dancing; but he also believed that special dances must be composed for motion-pictures. He said that even the acting must differ from that of the theatre. He and Diaghileff had often discussed the possibilities of motion-pictures, which Vaslav claimed as the future form of entertainment, which could eventually be developed into a fine art.

Sergei Pavlovitch saw in them merely a technical invention that was a cheap form of entertainment, and always refused to have the Ballet filmed. He was also upset that gramophone records had been made of some of the ballet music. All mechanical invention was distasteful to him. Once we went with friends to the Ziegfeld roofgarden. The programme was excellent; the girls beautiful and well disciplined. The noise of the new form of music was infernal, but Vaslav loved jazz. Ever since he had heard it for the first time in a night-club he realised that it was typical of our time, and would influence the future of music. He loved the rhythm, the saxophone and brass combined with the percussion, so unusual at the time.

We met the so-called Stanislavsky of America, David Belasco, who called Vaslav *l'homme oiseau,* and his son-in-law, Morris Gest, the impresario. Gest undoubtedly knew the ways of American production; he was very enthusiastic, but artistically left much to be desired. He came with the most incredible propositions, that Vaslav should dance *Spectre* sixteen times a week—whether in a booth or a circus I cannot remember.

The Metropolitan was contemplating a new season of Russian Ballet for the following year. Mr. Kahn asked us to come and see h'm about it. He explained that he would like to arrange a coast-to-coast tour, and that even if a deficit were involved he did not mind, as he wished to educate the American public. He realised how disturbing was Diaghileff's presence, and asked Vaslav to become artistic director and to supervise the entire tour. The proposition surprised Vaslav, who did not wish to offend Diaghileff, who was anxious for a Metropolitan contract, vital to the very existence of the Russian Ballet. It was only when Kahn declared that the return of Diaghileff was not to be considered that Vaslav agreed. In fact, the Metropolitan rented the Russian Ballet from Diaghileff under the specific clause that during this time he was not to return to the United States. They hoped that in this way

peace would reign on the tour, but how little they knew
Diaghileff, and his ability to make his presence felt even
at a distance.

As the heat-wave began in New York we moved up to
the Majestic Hotel, on Caruso's advice. He had already
initiated us into several of the mysteries of American life.
Week-ends we spent with friends at Long Island, in houses
whose luxury could only compete with Grand Ducal palaces. Vaslav loved especially the bathrooms attached to
each bedroom, with their towels and bath-mats in the same
vivid colours as the salts and scents. *"Très ballet russe!"*

A friend, M. Pali Strauss, took us one day to the Bilt-
more to see Maurice and Florence Walton. As soon as
Maurice heard Vaslav had arrived he had a spot-light
thrown on our table, and made a little speech, while
Vaslav hid himself behind the table-cloth.

Strauss gave a luncheon in his apartment at Sherry's in
honour of Duncan and Vaslav. The Kreislers were present,
and the art critics of New York. During lunch, Duncan
said to Vaslav, "You remember, Nijinsky, years ago in
Venice I proposed to you that we should have a child
together. What a dancer we could have created! The
idea did not seem to appeal to you then; I see you are
changed now; you are less intolerant towards us women."
A frozen, embarrassed silence followed her words. Vaslav
smilingly replied to her challenge: "I did not change. I
love everybody, as Christ did." Later Duncan wanted to
dance with Vaslav, but he was against improvisation and
only accompanied her with a few gestures.

One Sunday, on one of our various excursions, dining
at a little country inn where coloured people served, one
of the waiters danced a cake-walk for us. He danced it
wonderfully, and proudly declared that he could dance
Spectre like the great Nijinsky. He was amazingly light
and graceful. He was as pleased as a child when he heard
that Vaslav was "the great Nijinsky."

The difficulties of the coming season were beginning. It
was agreed that two novelties should be given, and *Tyl*
and the *Mephisto Valse* were chosen. The Metropolitan
wanted a star as *prima ballerina,* and representatives were

sent to St. Petersburg, but it was doubtful who could come. We were in constant touch by cable with Benois and Soudeikine, as Vaslav wished for one of them to design the scenery, but neither would come on account of the war. Finally, Mr. Cottenet, a director of the Metropolitan and a patron of artists, came to Vaslav's rescue, taking him to Greenwich Village to see a young American painter, "Bobby" Jones, who might be able to undertake the work. He was a tall, shy man, but he inspired confidence in Vaslav, who agreed to give him a trial. He explained to Jones his ideas for choreography and design, and made him familiarise himself with the music.

By way of relaxation, Vaslav decided to buy a motor-car, and our choice fell on a Peerless. He learned to drive and in the mornings used to take Kyra out. At the time a terrible epidemic of infantile paralysis broke out, and our one idea was to get Kyra out of danger, so we left for Newport, where we had been invited. There again it was one long round of invitations, till we felt we could stand it no more, and then, when a few cases of the illness were reported on Rhode Island, even our hosts did not try to detain us any longer. We left by car for Boston. Next morning, to my great amazement, the chauffeur waved good-bye and jumped off the car. "What does this mean?" "I am going to drive," said Vaslav. I was aghast, because, while he could drive straight ahead quite well, he would back the car round with a fearful swing, and he knew nothing about the engine, which was essential then. I saw ourselves stranded in the open country. The first day passed comparatively calmly, though in a few small towns Vaslav drove on the wrong side, and was shouted at by the passers-by. He almost ran into a tramcar, but at the last moment pirouetted aside. I was so angry that I sat silent, but Kyra, alone in the back seat with all her dolls, was enjoying herself immensely. Once we entered Maine the scenery became so lovely that I almost forgot to be angry. We passed the seashore, with its large beaches, the pine-woods with century-old sweet-smelling trees. It was not easy to travel with Kyra. The food was uneatable; coffee, ham and eggs the whole time.

The ham was sugared, and we could not swallow it. We were offered a dreadful drink—ice cream soda—and once Vaslav was so brave that he even tried a drink called coca-cola, but this was his first and last venture. We had to change tires at least half a dozen times; we had trouble with the carburetor. Vaslav in an important and knowing manner opened the bonnet and disappeared from view. Then he lay under the car and made some mysterious repairs. He loved all mechanical inventions, and had an undoubted talent that way, but in this case I suspected he was better able to take the car to pieces than to put it together again. He had many little tricks of driving that I disliked intensely. He was never quite sure with which gear to take a hill, so he tried them all in turn and then, when the car refused to pull, he just let it slide backwards, to Kyra's immense joy. Our trip took us six days instead of three. Finally we arrived at Bar Harbour, one of the most beautiful places in the world, and, as the Cottenets and Dr. Abbé had houses there, we met with a great reception. In fact, we were very seldom at home. Vaslav would leave in the car early in the morning with Kyra, the nurse, and the painted duck. There was a beautiful marble theatre on the top of the hill among the pine-woods, with sliding doors. On the lawn was an open Greek amphitheatre, where performances would be given during the season by the world's greatest artists. Here Vaslav put Kyra on the lawn with her toys, slid the doors back, and practised for hours alone. Sometimes I came to watch unnoticed. Kyra often forgot her toys and watched "Tatakaboy, how he leaped and flied." The higher he jumped, the more she shouted for joy. It was wonderful to see these two beings, who adored one another and forgot everything else as he danced for her and she tried to imitate. Then suddenly Vaslav jumped off the stage, got hold of Kyra in his arms, dancing across the lawn, till finally he threw himself on the grass and they rolled down the hill together.

Later in the day we would go to the swimming-pool, where Vaslav tried to teach me. He was such a wonderful swimmer that crowds used to watch him when he dived or swam under water so long that they thought he would never come up again. He pirouetted in the water and leaped like a fish. He also began to play tennis and was a constant winner, jumping high so quickly, with such a sense of speed and distance, that he was able to hit each ball, and make its return impossible. It was incredible to think that he had never played before.

Every Thursday afternoon there was a concert in the theatre, and as, owing to the war, most of the artists did not return to Europe, we outdid New York. Kreisler, Hofmann, Zimbalist, Godowsky, Bauer, and others performed. Each gave a recital, and sometimes they combined. Vaslav created special dances, one the cake-walk of Debussy, which he called *Le Nègre Blanc*. We often went over to see the other artists at North Seal Harbour. Harold Bauer played Scriabine a lot for Vaslav, who also, at the Schellings', took lessons in flirting from the "debs." Carlos Salzedo, the young French harpist, came over from Camden to visit us. He and Vaslav were great friends and planned future recitals, which, unfortunately, never materialised.

The Hofmanns also came to us, and he and Vaslav shared a taste in mechanics and would tinker with their cars. Hofmann would sometimes play for us and accompany Vaslav. He told us that since seeing Vaslav in *Sylphides* he played Chopin differently.

In Bar Harbour we had our first and last domestic fight. I had to visit the dentist, and, as he wanted to give me an injection, I slipped out of his chair and flew out of the house, leaving the surprised dentist and Vaslav alone. I was so scared that I took a car and went some sixty miles away, only returning at dawn. By that time all Bar Harbour was aroused and armed, looking for me in the woods and at the bottom of the lake. Vaslav was angry and scolded me, but I threw some pillows at him and we both laughed and made up.

Then Jones arrived, escorted by Laurence Steinhardt. Vaslav found the designs for the costumes to his liking. They were different in colouring from the Russians', although equally brilliant, but it was obvious that Jones had

felt their influence. The scenery designs were interesting,
but not what Vaslav wanted, and they spent days together working at it. Vaslav suggested a drop curtain
which would represent an open book and on its page an
awkwardly designed owl, sitting with its claws on a
mediæval hand-mirror. Tyl's *Eulenspiegel*. He conceived
of a market-place with city hall and cathedral, exagger-
ated in their slant leaning towards one another, distorted
as the life of those ages.

Meanwhile, with Steinhardt I went over the Metropolitan contract, which called for forty weeks, a transcontinental tour, and three weeks in New York. I was
worried, as they wanted Vaslav to dance five times a
week, which seemed too strenuous. We finally arrived at
the solution that three times he should dance two ballets
and on the other two evenings just one. Even then I was
afraid that he would be overworked, with the travelling
and all the artistic direction.

We had to leave for New York, as the company was
due to arrive at the end of September, and the season
was to open in two weeks' time. Vaslav had only this time
at his disposal to teach two ballets as complicated as
Petrouchka. How he would be able to do it I could not
understand, but Diaghileff would not send the company
over sooner, in order to economise rehearsal salaries. We
were sad to leave this enchanting island, where for the
first time in years Vaslav found relaxation and recreation.

Chapter Seventeen

THE AMERICAN TOUR

In the old Grand Central Palace, one autumn morning, the troupe of the Russian Ballet assembled in practice costume, waiting for Vaslav.

Grigoriev, the general stage manager nominated by Diaghileff, assisted by Kremeniev, Barocchi, Lopokova's husband, and Drobetsky, as secretaries, formed the general staff. They received Vaslav in polite silence. He spoke a few words asking them to give of their very best, as he was determined to do, to make the Ballet a success in the new countries, in order to assure the very existence of the Russian Ballet itself, which, Vaslav pointed out, must survive the war. The rehearsals began. There were quite a number of new members sent over by Diaghileff instead of sixteen of the best dancers, whom he retained in Italy, and some of the new ones were of mediocre talent and capacity. The two *ballerinas* brought from Russia did not yet deserve this title, as they had just graduated and were still inexperienced. In one of the new dancers, Mlle. Spessivsteva, he thought he had found very fine material. Her dancing was very light and ethereal. She would be excellent in *Sylphides* and in all classical ballets.

Vaslav had also to superintend the painting of the scenery in Jones's studio and explain to him how the paint must be poured on the canvas according to the Russian style and not put on by brush.

By this time *Tyl Eulenspiegel* was cast, and Vaslav was doing the same for *Mephisto*. He had always dreamed of a dancer who would look and act like Chaliapine, but, as such an artist did not exist, he asked Bolm for this very

important rôle. Bolm resented the fact that Vaslav was
chosen as artistic director—at least we were told so—and
did not show much enthusiasm to dance in this ballet.

The very first disagreeable surprise we had was that
one morning, arriving at the rehearsal, there was only
one dancer present as a strike delegate. They had discovered that in America "the strike" existed, and had
promptly begun one. They said they were Russian citizens
and refused to dance to German music. Mr. Herndon,
representing the Metropolitan Opera, at once took the
matter up and explained to them that, although strikes
existed, there were also laws to prevent them. They were
artists and not organised factory labour; that they had had
no injustice done them and their contract required them
to dance to all kinds of music, and they would be de-
ported if they did not fulfil their obligations.

What they really wanted we did not know, but two
valuable days were lost. Vaslav was saddened to see that
the troupe was trying to cause trouble, but he plunged
himself all the harder into work, so that the two new
ballets should be produced in time. There were only twelve
days before the opening at the Manhattan Opera House.
Tyl is a ballet on a grand scale. The dances were technically difficult. Only two members showed great zeal, H.
and a new member, Kostrovsky. The latter was a very
able dancer, a silent man with calm manners, rather
strange eyes looking very much like a Kalmuk. His wife
was also a dancer, and if possible still quieter, and with a
crushed, hunted look. This man, Kostrovsky, used to hold
court during the intervals at the rehearsals; the greater
part of the troupe sat around him at his feet, listening attentively whilst he made speeches. I asked Mme. Spessivsteva, the old mother of our new *ballerina,* what all this
meant. She explained that Kostrovsky was preaching; he
was a disciple of Tolstoi; lived according to his ideas, tried
to save the world, and in the meantime reform the Russian Ballet. "A harmless dreamer," said Drobetsky. "A
nut," declared the American administrative staff.

Kostrovsky took to Vaslav from the first moment, and
showed an adoration which was not only for his art but

for his nature. He followed Vaslav everywhere like a dog, eagerly looking for a smile. To the troupe he began to preach Nijinsky as a saint. "He is working for us, for our children; he is unselfish. Do not strike; you are harming yourselves. He can exist without us, but we cannot successfully without him." His words seemed to create a quieter atmosphere.

The dances of *Tyl* had fascinated the artists, and, in spite of the fact that they had made up their minds to be disagreeable, they could not resist its merits. Vaslav, who rehearsed them, had to supervise the costumes, the make-up, and he did each artist's himself, for in this ballet he not only wanted to bring the make-up in harmony with the costume, but also to be symbolic. Each character was supposed to be a personage from a mediæval tale. The candy merchant had to look like a "lollipop," and a very thin, tall dancer was chosen for the part. The baker's costume was designed like a *Baumkuchen,* one of the national sweets of old Germany, and so on.

But Vaslav had to be everything, *maître de ballet,* scenic artist, *régisseur.* He had to supervise all the work usually done by the composer, Diaghileff, Bakst, and Benois, to arrange the lighting, to instruct the administrative staff, and to arrange the programmes.

At the costume rehearsal, Vaslav, who had to be one moment on the stage, the other in the auditorium, kept on his rehearsal shoes with heels. One of the dancers constantly made mistakes, so Vaslav jumped on the stage and corrected him, but his shoes were slippery and he twisted his foot, with one painful gesture falling back and fainting. For one second we were all nailed to the floor. Had he broken his foot? If so, we did not want to know. Nobody dared to lift him.

One of the American stage hands picked him up and carried him to his dressing-room. A terrible rush began. Dispatches were sent out; messages, telephone calls. The artists stood silently in front of the door crying: "Nijinsky has broken his foot! How dreadful!" Bolm rushed up. In one moment, as from nowhere, everybody was there. As soon as he regained consciousness, he was taken by ambulance to Dr. Abbé's clinic to have an X-ray taken. Many of the artists came along in their practise kit and waited, until they heard Nijinsky had sprained his ankle, but would be unable to dance for at least six weeks.

The management was in despair, with so much money involved, the whole tour organised, theatres engaged all over the country. The cancelling of these dates would mean a tremendous financial loss to the Metropolitan, and one hundred and fifty people's salaries were at stake. "I must dance. I have to," said Vaslav. It was arranged that the rehearsals should go on, now that the troupe knew *Tyl,* but its opening should be postponed to the last week of the three weeks' season in New York. Dr. Abbé could not make any statement as to whether Vaslav would appear, but promised to let him dance on the tour. So they had to open without Vaslav. He worked in bed. Conferences were held about the programme, and all other questions settled. Vaslav was usually a very good patient; now, when he injured his foot, he was extremely difficult. Dr. Abbé insisted on having day and night nurses, so that his orders should be carried out, but Vaslav would not tolerate anybody near him except me and his *masseur.* Kostrovsky and H., who seemed to be the latter's disciple, came, and begged to be allowed to stay, and tried to keep him company. I was not convinced of H.'s religious and ascetic tendencies, as I remembered his past.

Among the many flowers which were sent to Vaslav, perhaps the loveliest basket was that of Anna Pavlova, who was dancing in New York. One morning she asked me personally to the telephone. As she inquired after Vaslav, she asked me: "Please tell me the truth; Vaslav Fomitch has broken his leg, hasn't he?"

"No, fortunately, though we thought so at first."

"Oh, really not?" And her voice dropped, as though she were disappointed. I did not say anything about it to Vaslav.

Then Vaslav was allowed to stand and make a few steps, but still bandaged. He was practically carried to the theatre to conduct the rehearsals of *Tyl.* The season opened, but the box office receipts proved that Vaslav's absence was keeping the public away. Dr. Abbé showed me the X-ray picture and explained the amazing fact that Vaslav's foot anatomically was not constructed like that of other human beings, but was a mixture of the construction of man and bird. "How do you explain this?" "Oh, it is atavism—fifth generation of dancers. The result not only of his training and constant practising, but of those of the ancestors. This is the secret of his amazing elevation; no wonder he can fly; he is a human bird." He asked me to give him the X-ray, which he wished to present to some medical museum.

Vaslav's foot was in fact remarkable. It was sturdy and very muscular; he could use his foot and toes as he could his hand. He could even grasp a bar or rope with his toes, like a bird on a perch. But his ankle was extremely thin, the bones very apparent, and the muscles seemed to quiver even when the foot itself was at rest. His legs, so muscular, but especially his ankles, looked like those of a fine, full-blooded racehorse. When he flexed his foot upwards, the distance was exactly the same from the ankle to the heel as from the toes to the ankle. Vaslav claimed that owing to this he was able to rise so easily.

Finally, Dr. Abbé consented that Vaslav should dance a few times in New York, but with a bandaged foot, and that all the steps which made his bodily weight rest on the right foot (which was the injured one) should be shifted over to the left. How extremely difficult this was only a dancer can realise.

A few days before the opening, Monteux suddenly discovered that he was French. Now he came out with the amazing statement that as the Allies were at war with Germany, he could not and would not conduct a work of Richard Strauss. He would rather break his contract. Again Mr. Herndon was patience itself, and the good-humoured Alfred Seligsberg, who had withstood many storms with tenors and conductors as adviser of the Metropolitan, tried to smooth the matter over, but with no avail. Monteux steadily refused.

"But you conduct *Carnaval*. Schumann was Austrian. Wasn't he an enemy?" ventured Dr. Seligsberg.

"But he is dead. Strauss is alive. A living Boche. No, never will I conduct his music."

This was extraordinary conduct, seeing that it had been on Vaslav's special request that Kahn had intervened with the authorities in France and obtained Monteux's exemption from military service. Kahn was furious, and ordered that another conductor should be summoned. This meant that during the entire coast-to-coast tour they had to engage a second conductor for the sake of one ballet.

Mephisto Valse had to be given up, anyhow, as Vaslav was unable to rehearse it, and Dr. Abbé simply forbade him this extra strain.

Tyl Eulenspiegel took the public by storm. The artists, the dancers themselves, raved about it. They declared that it was Nijinsky's finest piece of work. It was his first ballet since the break with Diaghileff, who was always anxious to make the world believe that the ballets "by" Nijinsky, Massine, and the other choreographers were really his own creations. But *Tyl Eulenspiegel* showed the world how little Sergei Pavlovitch had to do with the creation of a ballet. Vaslav was particularly pleased with the ungrudging approval of the musicians present for his greatest work. Hofmann, Zimbalist, Godowsky, and Bauer all congratulated him on a perfect interpretation of Strauss.

Tyl, the hero of mediæval Flemish folk-lore, was danced by Vaslav. He embodied what Tyl was—the spirit of humour of his race. Tyl is the prankish youth who encourages and helps the poor and torments the tyrant. Always gay, always elusive, nothing can subdue him. His love for the people is victorious, for, though he is put to death for helping his townsfolk, his spirit triumphantly lives on in the heart and mind of the Flemish race.

Tyl was indeed the most perfect of Nijinsky's choreography. It was sheer dancing from beginning to end. Critics who asserted that Nijinsky's methods were too sculptural, and could not therefore be applied to flowing movements, were silenced. *Tyl* was as much "dancing" as *Carnaval*. Only each gesture, each dance, expressed a thought ac-

cording to Nijinsky's fundamental idea. He did not share
the theory that movement should be for its own sake,
later laid down and followed by Bronislava Nijinsky when
she became *maître de ballet,* or that it should merely
express a mood or a feeling or simply the music, as Fokine
and the others maintained.

On the 30th of October we began the transcontinental
tour. The troupe consisted of about one hundred and
twenty people: fifty-five dancers, fifty-two musicians, and
the technical and general staff. The press agents went
ahead. The train was run in two sections. The baggage-
cars, with the scenery and lighting apparatus, went on with
the technical staff, to give them time to unload and set up
in the theatre before our arrival, as in many of the forty
cities we visited the artists only arrived an hour or so
before the show was due to begin. Everything had to be
ready. There was the difficulty of setting up scenery on
stages of different sizes. Often the orchestra pit was so
small that we had to sacrifice the first few rows of
stalls.

On the Russian Ballet Special everything was arranged
as pleasantly as possible for everybody. Sleepers, diners,
observation cars, on which we lived for five months. The
chef made whatever we asked for, even Russian dishes.
Our drawing-room had been very nicely fitted up, and
we soon made ourselves at home. Only the nights proved
disagreeable, for the beds in American sleepers are
along the windows, so that there is always a draught.
Also they were much too narrow and short for Vaslav, who
was used to sleeping in a large bed, where he could
stretch himself. He usually slept in every angle of the bed,
and mostly across it. If the bed was not a double one, he
often fell on the floor. He needed space, in sleeping as
much as dancing. When the stay in a city was very short,
the company could remain on the train. But we always
tried to go to a hotel, even if only for a few hours, so that
Vaslav could be able to rest in a real bed and get some
fresh air.

Vaslav and I went to Mr. Herndon's compartment
every morning to discuss whatever needed attention. Dif-

ferent towns asked for different ballets. Interviews for the
Press had to be prepared. They were made out on the
train and handed to the reporters on arrival. Alterations
had frequently to be made in the cast, owing to illness.

When we arrived in Boston, Vaslav was upset from the
very first day of our arrival. The reporters told him
that again the rumour was around about his being a deserter, and it was also printed in one of the papers. We
tried to find out who had done this mischief. We had
many friends in Boston, and were much entertained, but
Vaslav enjoyed most the evenings in the company of
Sargent, who at the time was painting the library in the
city, and George Copeland, the pianist, who played Debussy for him.

About the end of November we arrived in Washington,
where we gave three performances. President Wilson
and the whole Diplomatic Corps were present, and Vaslav
went up to render thanks officially for their help in securing his release from Austria. Also we were magnificently
entertained by the different Embassies. Our days passed
in a social whirl which we could not very well avoid. We
tried during the whole trip to keep away from social obligations as much as we could, but this was difficult, for in
each town the Mayor, the leading clubs, the Elks and
other prominent people, all wanted to entertain us. But
the travelling was so hard on everybody that we were glad
to rest as often as possible.

On our arrival in Atlanta, Vaslav received an official
summons to appear within ten days at St. Petersburg before the military authorities. Vaslav could not understand
it, as he was exempt for good, but thought it might be
some new regulation. Of course, he wanted to leave at
once for Russia, but to be in St. Petersburg within ten
days would have been impossible. Laurence explained to
us over the telephone that the Metropolitan would not let
Vaslav go until his contract was fulfilled. The other difficulty was that he was still a war prisoner to Austria,
only lent to the States on the understanding that he
would stay in neutral countries during the war and not
take arms against the Central Powers. He was really in a

dilemma. It was arranged with Mr. Herndon that Vaslav
should return immediately to Washington escorted by one
of the secretaries, and take up the matter with the Russian Embassy. So he did. Before he left he rehearsed the
Spectre with his understudy, Gavrilov. Vaslav was supposed to rejoin us in New Orleans.

I stayed with the troupe, and as usual went to the
theatre. I was amazed to see on the programme that
Vaslav's name was still on as dancing the *Spectre de la
Rose*. I went to the management and asked them why it
was not changed. They told me that so many people
would have returned their seats if they had known that
Vaslav was not dancing, that to avoid the loss they did
not make this change, and as Vaslav was obliged to leave
they were sure he would not object. I did not feel that
under the circumstances I had the right to interfere. The
lady next to whom I was sitting was in ecstasy over the
Spectre. "Oh, the great Nijinsky! How marvellous!" Such
is the power of suggestion. But later she remarked: "I
can't see that he leaps so very high."

By this time many friendships had been made in the
company. The musicians and the great part of the technical staff played cards and dominoes. The dancers read
a lot. Vaslav bought them a very large library. Kostrovsky
was the chief librarian, and he continued his lectures on
Tolstoi. We were very often with the Herndons. Mrs.
Herndon was a very lovely woman and a very agreeable
companion. The Fradkins were newly married and he
was very gay. Vaslav was amused by him, and we became
very friendly. Fred Fradkin was a first prize winner from
the Paris conservatoire, and had been chosen as concert
master for our orchestra. He was a very promising
virtuoso.

Old Mme. Spessivsteva, who was teaching me Russian,
was a character straight out of a Chekhov play. We
laughed ourselves sick when she began to show us what
she was like when she was a young member of the ballet
and flirted with the officers at Moscow. She baptised our
troupe the "Circus of Sergei de Diaghileff." She was the
first to know of everything that happened, and under

the seal of great secrecy she went around and told it to
everybody. But she was a kind-hearted old woman, and
used to serve tea to all the troupe in her compartment.
She carried her own samovar, but, as she almost set the
train on fire, she was requested to get the boiling water
from the dining-car. Of course, she found, and we agreed,
that the tea was not the same as when she boiled the
water herself.

New Orleans proved to have a great charm. With its
quaint old streets and buildings, it impressed us as a
Southern French town. The lovely Opera House in which
we performed was beautiful, very old and in exquisite
taste. Here we first saw palm-trees and all the surprising
Southern vegetation. We visited Antoine's, the famous
French restaurant, and we did not regret it. The lunch he
served us, the wine and his famous *omelette surprise,*
were as good as those of Larue. We were told that the
"high spots" of this town were the brothels, so we decided with the Fradkins that we would go and see them.
But Vaslav refused. He thought it very much against his
principles, and his respect for womanhood, but I insisted;
I had never been to such a place and was curious to go.
I told Vaslav I would go anyhow. He warned me I would
be very much disgusted. I told him he could not know,
as he never had been in any. So we went. What amazed
us most was to see all the mixtures of different races.
Vaslav had no racial prejudices, and was always kind and
considerate to people, whatever race they were. He talked
with them and offered them drinks. They were all amazed
to see that otherwise he had no interest. As we left we
met a number of our dancers, and, to my amazement, one
of the preachers among them.

During the trip some differences arose between Monteux
and Fradkin. We heard it was chiefly due to the difference
in the exchange of the French francs as, owing to the
exchange, he received less than his own concert master.
Frequently Fradkin was unjustly rebuked during rehearsals. Vaslav always tried to make peace, but did not
succeed. As he could not very well interfere between the
conductor and the concert master, he showed his respect

for Fradkin by taking his violin out of his hand and carrying it himself after Fradkin to the restaurant where Monteux and others were already seated.

We had a lot of trouble in the South, as we were requested not to make up as negroes, and to perform *Scheherazade* as it was composed was unthinkable in any of these cities. So we left it out of the programme. Then in some cities the women's clubs objected to the bare legs and wanted tights on. Of course, we did not give in on this point. We were usually met at the station by a committee of the most prominent people, the Chamber of Commerce, then the reporters. Vaslav, who never cared for publicity, was usually exhausted by meeting strangers.

To escape the usual reception, Vaslav and Fradkin decided one day on the train to change parts, and at Tulsa, Oklahoma, they carried out the plan. We were received by a Committee of Freemasons. As the hotels were very primitive, they kindly invited the company to stay in their houses instead of the train. Vaslav got off the train after Fradkin and carried his violin. Fradkin answered the advancing reporters as they were sent on to our group by Herndon. "This is Mr. Fradkin, the concert master," Fradkin introduced Vaslav to them. "Where is Nijinsky?" "I am," replied Fradkin. As he was rather stout, there was a wondering expression on the faces of the newspapermen. It was a great surprise when Fradkin's kind, fat face smiled at the reader in the evening papers. The dancers were aghast until we explained what happened. But this was not the only joke Vaslav and Fradkin played. Before our arrival in one city we gave the management, as usual, the name of the hotel where we wanted to stay. We went there, but did not like it, and as we were to stay only the day we decided to return to the train and spend the day driving in a motorcar. Great was the consternation of the staff when they looked for Vaslav in the afternoon and were told that he had left.

But they were not the only ones who made trouble. Revalles was presented by a Boston admirer with an alligator, and she took it along with her; she used to keep it in her washstand at night, and on her neck during the

day. Mme. Spessivsteva senior and myself were frankly
afraid, but so were the negro porters and one day they
refused to serve her in the diner unless she took the
alligator back to her compartment. Finally all the porters
decided to go on strike, as they said it was unlucky to
have it on the train, and in the end she was asked by the
management to give it away, which she did to some zoo.

One day real trouble broke out. Mr. Herndon used to
arrive at the station about twenty minutes to two (our
departure from each city was set at 2 a.m.) so that he
could see that everybody was there and all in order. When
he arrived he saw the musicians collected in the waiting-
room. They refused to leave. Their spokesman, Fradkin, explained to him that as the orchestra were entitled
to a first-class Pullman berth according to their contract,
they would not accept a second-class car. One of their
Pullmans had had to go to the repair shop and a new
second-class car was switched on for the time being. But
they were all union men and would not hear of it. Herndon told them it was impossible to get a first-class car that
night, and that he was going to leave on schedule. He
went to the engineer and told him to start at two, but
slowly. The whistle blew, the train started, and the musicians with a mad dash scrambled on board.

During the trip very often different members came to
our drawing-room to talk, or we met them at the observation car. Kostrovsky and H. came up to Vaslav first with
questions to ask regarding the new books to be bought,
then for some other instructions. Then Kostrovsky remained always longer and longer in our compartment, first
reading to Vaslav, then talking for hours and hours. I
knew, of course, that it was a pleasure for Vaslav to be
amongst his countrymen and speak Russian. But I would
rather have seen him with Bolm, or others of the Imperial
School graduates, than with those *moujiks*—not on account of their origin, but because of an instinctive distrust
I had of them.

As we boarded the train at Kansas City we saw some
Indians sitting in a great central lobby. The Fradkins
were with us, and we went up and talked to them. They

had clear-cut features; some of them were very beautiful but all had a distinguished look. They spoke nicely and showed us their babies on their backs; then they asked where we came from, and Vaslav explained, adding a few words about his dancing; they immediately praised their own dances; and then they noticed Fradkin's Stradivarius, which he always carried in his hand. "Is that your baby?" "No, I haven't a baby." "Are you married?" The old Indian shook his head, then he turned to Vaslav. "And you?" Vaslav began to tell him all about Kyra's perfection. "Where is she?" "In New York." "No good; child should be with her parents," said the old man. And Vaslav agreed with him.

From there we went to Des Moines and then to Omaha. By this time we were so tired that we decided to take rooms in a hotel just for a few hours. We left the luggage on the train. Fradkin did the booking, as always. We went in and immediately ran a bath. While Vaslav was in the bath, somebody energetically knocked on the door. I opened, and a man told me he was a sheriff and wanted to arrest us, as he declared we were renting rooms for an immoral purpose. I ran to the Fradkins, who violently explained that we were married. But this did not help. They wanted proof—certificates and what not. I went to fetch Drobetsky who was at hand, and finally, I think, Herndon came and we were allowed to proceed with our baths.

The evenings when Vaslav did not dance he used to watch the performance from the wings or the auditorium. *Scheherazade* was played, and I, who had seen it so many times, was surprised to see the outstanding miming of the old Eunuch. I had never noticed it before. Since Cecchetti was not with the troupe, one of the other soloists danced it. I was so intrigued that I went back stage and found that the unknown artist who played the Eunuch that night was Vaslav. He had jumped in in the place of the usual dancer, who was suddenly taken ill.

Vaslav decided that every part should be understudied, and the understudies should once in a while dance their parts in a small town. Until now only Vaslav and Karsa-

vina were "rested" in cases when the programme called
for three ballets in which they were supposed to dance,
but never did except on special occasions, in Paris or in
London, when Bolm had replaced Vaslav; Nijinskaya or
Kyasht, Karsavina. No regular system had ever been applied to understudying. But Vaslav thought that through
such a system it might be possible to develop a new
generation of dancers. So he cast each starring part;
Gavrilov, H., Kremeniev, all received instructions among
the men, and, among the women, Hilda Munnings,
Nemchinova, and others. Directly Diaghileff heard about
it he protested, but later he must have been glad enough
that Vaslav had given those members of the *corps de
ballet* a chance. How else could he have starred
Nemchinova or Sokolova in the years to come? Some of
the soloists immediately complained to Kahn.

By the time we arrived in Denver trouble was definitely
brewing on this account, and a part of the troupe again
went on strike. Vaslav told them that his mind was made
up and that he would cast the one he thought most suitable for the part. The ones who were thus passed over
again sent a threatening letter to Vaslav that they would
treat him "as the choir served Chaliapine in London."
That meant a fight to a finish. Vaslav was quite unmoved,
and as we passed those hostile dancers at the end of the
performance he just raised his hat and said, *"Das vedania,
Gaspada,"* and they gave way like sheep and let us go by.

One day we went to Pike's Peak by car. Vaslav had
invited Kostrovsky and his wife and H. Kostrovsky
preached all the way, while H. maintained a slightly
hostile attitude towards me. I wondered how he dared;
it wasn't till later that I understood.

We left Denver after the performance and headed for
Salt Lake City. The country we had to cross was lovely,
and everything lay in a deep snow. The whole country,
especially the mountains, seemed to be asleep.

At our first performance in Salt Lake City the prominent people were introduced to me, as was usual wherever we went. Among them was the head of the Mormons,
a very strict and distinguished-looking elderly gentleman.

I returned his call in the next interval. To my confusion, four ladies in his box were introduced to me as "the prophet's many wives"—Mrs. X. the first, Mrs. X. the second, and so on. The first invited us to visit their place the following day. As soon as the interval was over I rushed back stage and told the dancers about the incident. They all thought I was joking. The next morning we actually did go over, and were guided by the prophet's second wife all through their museum, library, and schools, finishing with their great hall, which has remarkable acoustics. She explained to us how the work is divided between the wives. One acts as secretary to the husband, another looks after the children of all, the third does all the housekeeping. I ventured to ask if they were not jealous of each other. "No," she said. "Why should we be? We all have our interests, and we share in the affection of our husband." I thought it was quite a sensible institution, and most suitable for artists, since their wives have a real job. If they only aim at helping their husbands and protecting their interests, there is little enough time left for household duties or children.

We left as usual at two in the morning. Next day was Christmas Eve, which we had to spend on the train, as we were going on to Los Angeles. Mr. Herndon showed us very nice attention in arranging an empty baggage-car for an informal dance. Some of the orchestra played and a buffet supper was served, with hot grog and punch. After dinner I had a Christmas-tree in our compartment, hung with the presents for the company. They were all invited to come in, but they had to do so in turns, as the drawing-room, of course, was too small to hold so many people at once.

Great was our amazement the next morning at breakfast when we looked out of the dining-room car window. Instead of the snow-capped mountains, a sea of orange-groves was all around us, deep green studded with golden fruit. Vaslav was so tired of hotels that we decided to split an apartment with the Fradkins and "keep house." Fred immediately wired for one while we were still some way from the city, and at our arrival it was ready! Inside another half hour a Japanese cook was engaged, and he cooked a wonderful dinner for us. Vaslav played all the time with the bedsteads, which he found he could pull out from the wall and swing up vertically out of the way. The Japanese cook taught us how to make tea, and we applauded him for his artful way of cooking rice. Vaslav had never been in the kitchen since his childhood, but he found his way there to watch the Japanese. The cook's movements amused him. Vaslav danced a Japanese dance for him, and the cook said, "Gentleman lived long time in Japan!" which was complimentary but untrue.

To amuse the Fradkins, Vaslav did all kinds of acrobatic tricks; he rolled, threw himself about, and jumped in the most incredible way. Fradkin asked why he did not use all this in a ballet, but Vaslav said he just did it to show that for a dancer to be an absolute master of his body he must be an acrobat, but that acrobatics was not an art in itself and that was why he did not apply it.

We visited the Spanish missions, and of course were invited to see the studios in Hollywood. To the latter place we had to cross about twelve miles of waste land by motor. Hollywood itself was then a few wooden shacks, and one or two studios among the pepper-trees. Chaplin was very enthusiastic about the ballet. He never missed a performance, and tried hard to get the ballet to stay another week, but this was impossible, as our tour was settled. The first night when we heard that he was in the audience all our company was excited. We all admired him. He came back stage in the interval and was taken to Vaslav's dressing-room. Vaslav always thought Chaplin was the genius of the cinema, a wonderful mime. They immediately became friends. Chaplin then went on to the stage and was introduced to the troupe. They all applauded, and Chaplin returned the compliment by walking up and down in his own special way and doing a few tricks. The company enjoyed it so much that they did not want to let him go, and the interval lasted twice as long as usual. The public became impatient, but, when they heard what the reason of the delay was, took it good-humouredly. On Chaplin's invitation we went to visit his studio. He was making *Easy Street* at that time, and we were all photographed on the set. He said how much he would like to make a film with Vaslav, but at that time he did not feel he could stay in California.

Vaslav was approached to buy land in Hollywood, but I unfortunately dissuaded him. Wherever we performed he received offers to buy all kinds of things—oil well shares, cattle, mines, and so on.

I was very glad that during the last week Vaslav was constantly with us. The Fradkins and Herndons had a good influence on him. I noticed that he was gay and natural with them. But as soon as Kostrovsky and H. got hold of him, he reacted like a sensitive plant and folded himself up. He became silent, meditative, almost gloomy, more so than I had ever seen him before, even in our most difficult days of the break with Diaghileff or during our internment in Hungary. I could not follow their conversation in Russian, as it became very abstract philosophy, but I could make out enough to see that Kostrovsky was like a parrot repeating Tolstoi and the teaching of Christ. Vaslav was impressionable and was open to any ideal of charity or love of mankind. When it came from him spontaneously I welcomed it, for I knew it was a part of the unselfish nature of his genius. But now that I noticed they were trying to accentuate it and provoke it, I was rather resentful. We all saw it: the Fradkins, the Herndons, myself. But the reason it was done was not clear. "To be with Nijinsky makes them feel important," said some of the dancers. "H. always runs after Diaghileff, Massine, and now Nijinsky for personal advancement," said the others. I thought myself the reason was that Kostrovsky was a fanatic; one could see it at once. He was genuine; he lived according to his ideas and made his family miserable while he was trying to make the world happy. Kostrovsky and H. stayed in our compartment sometimes the whole night through. Vaslav was exhausted, and needed rest after the performance, but they went on preaching to him. With the stubbornness of mules and the slow understanding of *moujiks* they pretended not to understand my hints and requests to leave

him in peace. Then I openly tried to keep them away
from Vaslav, but they were like leeches; it was impossible
to get rid of them.

Barocchi, Lopokova's Italian husband and for that reason Diaghileff's new secretary, a strange-looking man
with a long, heavy beard, of which he was very proud,
was nicknamed by the troupe "Bluebeard." We did not
see him after Denver, as he was hiding on account of the
"misfortune," as he called the incident that happened to
him in that city. He went to a barber's shop and dozed
off in the chair. The barber shaved off his precious beard,
and when he awoke and found his beard gone he fainted
and for days did not want to show himself to anybody.
He was a very strange person, somnambulist, and some
claimed he had clairvoyant powers.

In San Francisco, Vaslav discovered a second-hand
flying machine which looked more like an abandoned
sewing-machine than anything else. For $2.50 a ride was
promised. Vaslav was at once all for a trip. We tried to
keep him back, but he had set his heart on it, and, before we had time to realise it, was circling above us. Even
with an expert pilot and in a first-class machine, at that
time flying was a great risk, but there in these conditions
it was tempting the gods. I prayed all the time until the
machine was sighted and Vaslav stood by me again. I was
really angry with him this time. He was enthusiastic and
pleased, and explained that it was one of the most glorious, exhilarating feelings one could imagine, and that from
the air the world was extremely beautiful.

The day of our arrival was New Year's Eve, and we
spent the evening together in the hotel, and, as New
Year's Eve celebrations always have a touch of the mystic,
we asked Barocchi to tell us our fortunes. He could read
palms very well, and did so; when he arrived at me, he
promised a long life and good health, but said, "Within
five years you will be separated from Vaslav Fomitch. I
see a divorce, but not exactly." I laughed—"Ridiculous
and impossible"—but felt rather uneasy. Then he looked
at Vaslav's palm and, as though he had received a blow,

staggered back and covered Vaslav's hands with his own. "I don't know, I can't say . . . sorry, it is strange . . ."

"Am I going to die? Come on, say it."

"No, no, certainly not, but . . . but this is worse . . . worse."

"He is hedging," we thought, and turned away from him, little thinking that Barocchi saw correctly.

We stayed two weeks in San Francisco, but for the second week we lived in Oakland, where we discovered a nice quiet hotel. We were much entertained by society here, and visited all the surroundings. Also we were invited to Berkeley University. The grounds were lovely, but very different from Yale. It was a great pleasure ten years later when I revisited the University, to see an exhibition of paintings and to hear from the teachers that Vaslav's visit and dancing had made a lasting impression and had deeply influenced the art students.

Never since we married had there been the slightest misunderstanding between us. Vaslav's ever-present genius was overwhelming, but he was so natural, so kind, that whatever question came up, whatever complication arose, I knew and felt that I could always come to him and find understanding, comfort, and affection, even if it was a matter to his personal disadvantage. Lately I had begun to feel a change in Vaslav, so subtle that one could only sense it. He was the same and yet I felt that there was a new nuance in his attitude towards everything, even to his art. What had happened? I felt alarmed. I could not confide in anyone. So I sat down and wrote a letter to Bronia in Russia: that Vaslav, who could not be influenced by anybody, not even by Sergei Pavlovitch, seemed strangely hypnotised by the sermons of Kostrovsky and H. It seemed not only to affect his mental attitude towards life, but also his health, which began to worry me. Unfortunately, Bronia never received this letter. Kostrovsky, following Tolstoi, was of course a vegetarian, and very soon induced Vaslav to become one. This was most inadvisable. Vaslav, with his constant strenuous work, was told by his doctors to eat light but very nourishing foods, and especially those which gave strength to his

muscles in a concentrated form. Meat was a chief part of
his diet. Now that he did not even eat eggs, of course
he was greatly weakened.

In Vancouver I received a letter from my Uncle Gari,
who asked me to extend some financial help to my kinsman, who had been sent to the Argentine some time
before and whom on account of the war he could not
now reach. Vaslav gladly instructed his bank to pay him an
allowance regularly. After Vancouver, during the whole
of January, we performed in the Western States, Seattle,
Tacoma, Spokane, St. Paul, Minneapolis, Milwaukee, and
the whole trip seemed to us a nightmare. I hardly saw
Vaslav. When he was not dancing he was closeted day
and night with Kostrovsky and H.; he hardly slept or ate,
and they went on with their reformatory ideas. To have
chosen Vaslav for this I thought outrageous. The salva-
tion of the troupe was entirely forgotten by these self-
constituted prophets. His rest, his nourishment, taken
away, Vaslav became strangely irritated and weak. I felt
that something had to be done.

I spoke to Vaslav very frankly, and told him that with
all my love and admiration for him I could not agree to
his new idea that he should give up dancing and become
a peasant farmer or live the life of a *moujik* in Russia.
I could understand that he was exhausted by the caravan
life which the Russian Ballet had led since his separation
from the Mariinsky. That he was right that art needed
peace, and that creative work could only be achieved in a
quiet atmosphere; that he was not a being who could exercise his art for commercial purposes. I was ready to go
to Russia, to any place with him, but I could not believe
that he wanted to throw away what he loved most—
dancing; that it could not be his own conviction, that he
was under some spell. Vaslav became thoughtful.

At the time of our arrival in Chicago I declared that
on account of this interference with our life I would return to New York and stay with Kyra, and if he had
really decided to live the life of Tolstoi I would return
alone to Europe. He could keep Kyra if he wanted, as I
could never adjust myself to that life. Vaslav took me to

the station, and he looked so sad and so humble that I could not help telling him that whenever he needed me he had only to call and I would always come.

For another six weeks the company went on touring Michigan, Ohio, Indiana, Tennessee. Vaslav used to send wires all the time and call me up. I felt he was rather lonely, but I wanted to make him see that he had to choose between the gloomy pair and me.

Laurence agreed that I had made the right move in frightening him thus. Nijinsky was far too sensitive to be left the prey of such adventurers, whatever their aim was. The company was tired out by the time they arrived in Chicago, and Vaslav was disappointed because everywhere the audience had raved about his leaps and his pirouettes but had no real understanding.

In New York my time was passed with Kyra, who had improved greatly and was now very lovely. She resembled Vaslav more and more. I was also very busy with all my social obligations.

At that time we heard the first rumours of the possibility of the U.S.A. entering the war on the side of the Allies. I wondered what our status would be in case of war. I was informed that Vaslav could stay in America or perform in a neutral country during the hostilities.

On the 24th of February the transcontinental tour ended in Albany. I went to the station to meet Vaslav.

Vaslav called me up long distance from Cleveland to ask my advice, as he had received a cable from Diaghileff asking him to come to Spain as soon as the American tour was finished and to take part in the Russian Ballet's performances there and in South America later in the autumn. I told Vaslav not to promise anything until he had consulted Laurence. I was surprised to hear of Sergei Pavlovitch's invitation. During the whole winter he was in Italy with Massine and the sixteen dancers whom he had retained. With them he formed a second company, and told his intimates that it was the "modern one" with which in the future he would create artistic ballets. The other one was going to be the money-making organisation. I noticed a change in Vaslav. He began to wear his silk

shirts again, his rings, which under Kostrovsky's influence
he had discarded. At lunch he ate the same dishes as we
did.

The season was over; the troupe was returning very
soon to Europe. We also had to make our plans. Vaslav,
much as he liked the States, declared that it was not the
atmosphere in which to create, and travelling constantly
annihilated all artistic inspiration. He wanted to settle
down and do some creative work. But where? To Russia
we could not return. He took it for granted that I would
go with him. I knew that in everyday life he was rather
lost. His upbringing in the Imperial School isolated him
from the routine of ordinary existence as much as the
years spent in Diaghileff's company, where everything was
done for him. I often noticed that to buy a ticket or to
rent a room seemed a task for him. How would he be
able to manage to obtain a visa while travelling? I felt as
though I were abandoning a child. I said to him, "Vaslav,
until the war is over, I will stay with you whatever happens." The hope in Vaslav flared up again that an understanding could be after all reached with Sergei
Pavlovitch. Undoubtedly he missed his friendship and the
Sergei Pavlovitch of the days gone by.

Laurence and Vaslav discussed future plans, and decided that Vaslav should go to Europe, either to take a
rest in Spain or Switzerland or, if a suitable contract could
be arranged, to go with the Ballet to South America. A
tentative contract was drawn up. Vaslav told us that on
Kostrovsky's and H.'s request he wired to Diaghileff:
"*En principe j'accepte discuterons projets en Espagne.*"
Neither of us three knew at that time that Spain is the
only country in the world where, according to law, a
cable is a binding contract. But Diaghileff, who was in
Spain, knew. He could not send the troupe to America
without Vaslav, as the Teatro Colon in Buenos Aires,
after the happenings in New York, insisted that a signed
contract from Nijinsky should be shown to them before
they concluded their agreement with Diaghileff.

Vaslav made me presents of most exquisite jewellery and
furs. During the last few days, when we had completed

all our arrangements for a departure, we went up to Laurence's office to make our wills. The submarine warfare was raging, and we were told that this would be advisable under the circumstances. Then and there I learned that Vaslav had given me everything he earned in America and disposed only of the things he owned in Europe. I refused, but Vaslav was determined. "You have to; you cannot work; anything might happen to me, then you will be left with Kyra. I can always take care of myself; I can dance."

The day of our departure arrived; we left on the same ship as the company. A great crowd of our friends accompanied us to the steamer. We felt rather depressed. We had found a hospitable country which became a second home, and now we had to leave it. We stood together waving, and as the skyline of New York slowly faded in the mist I began to cry hysterically. Vaslav turned toward the open sea, trying to hide his tears. We felt that safety and liberty were vanishing together with the last faint outline of the North American coast.

Chapter Eighteen

SPAIN AND SOUTH AMERICA

THE STEAMER on which we sailed for Spain was in *"perfecto estado hygienico"* according to a shiny brass plate on the upper deck, but whoever made this bold statement must have been blessed with an extremely vivid imagination. It was a veritable museum piece, known to have been abandoned under water for at least sixteen years, and as insecure as a shell on the waves. The whole place was infested by well-nourished rats, and it was quite impossible to put one's feet on the floor. After one night, I simply refused to go to the cabin, and installed myself on deck, in a chair, for the thirteen days of the trip. It was bitterly cold and stormy during the whole voyage. Vaslav stoically accepted the situation and slept a few hours in the cabin, but mostly he kept vigil over Kyra.

We intended to spend our two months' holiday in Spain, so that Vaslav could talk his new offer over with Diaghileff, and work in peace on the system of notation, but, at the time of our arrival, Diaghileff was in Paris.

Vaslav had danced in Madrid before, and the friends he had made then constantly invited us out. We became very friendly with the Duc and Duquesa de Durcal, who were related to the King. Within a few days, Vaslav received an invitation to visit the Royal Palaces when he pleased. The Royal Theatre was put at his disposal, and he at once began to practise there.

We thought Madrid would be a real southern city, warm and brilliant with sunshine, but it proved at this time of the year extremely cold, with biting wind. Our first few weeks passed very pleasantly with new friends, work, and visits to cathedrals and museums. Vaslav loved Goya. He never tired of looking at his work, especially of *Los Caprichos,* and we went over to Toledo to visit the places where he lived and worked. In the evenings, we were usually taken to the theatres and cafés to see real gypsy dancers. The austere movements of the men dancers appealed forcibly to Vaslav, and very soon he used these movements himself in dancing.

Spring came, everything was bathed in sunshine. We used to sit and read together in the Prado while Kyra played among the irises. Our reading was mostly Oscar Wilde's poetry and the work of Selma Lagerlöff and Sir Rabindranath Tagore. The latter had got hold of Vaslav's imagination, and I was glad, because this philosophical poetry counter-balanced the fanatical teachings of Tolstoi which seemed to have had such a destructive effect on

Vaslav's peace of mind during the past winter. We had entirely forgotten the inconveniences of our recent trip, until one afternoon when I opened one of the closets and found it full of mice. I began to cry, seeing the damage they had done to my dresses.

"I give you furs, jewellery," said Vaslav gently, "and anything you wish, but can't you see how silly it is to attach importance to them? And have you ever thought how cruel it is to kill those animals? And how dangerous for the pearl-divers and for the miners who provide your jewellery—they also have children, and yet they must endanger themselves daily for the adornment of women."

So, after all, Tolstoi was still preying on his mind.

One morning, I picked up the paper, and saw: "The abdication of the Tsar in Mohilew." The Russian Ambassador could tell us no more than was in the papers. To us, in Spain, the revolution gave the impression that it was going to be an extremely peaceful one.

Soothed by the beautiful surroundings, Vaslav worked very hard on perfecting his system of notation. Undoubtedly he now hoped that at last the reconciliation with Sergei Pavlovitch would really take place. He also discussed with me the possibility of a return to his own country.

"I am sure the revolution is not going to make any changes in the artistic life of Russia. We love art and we will always work for its sake, and of course they must ask Sergei Pavlovitch to be Director of the Mariinsky now."

He wanted to discuss his own plans with Diaghileff. Vaslav intended to dance until he was thirty-five years of age, and then to devote himself to composition. Also he wished to found a school where he would teach his own ideas, and, attached to this, an artistic laboratory, where composers, *maîtres de ballet* and artists, regardless of nationalities, could work out their ideas. Another of his plans was to arrange a yearly festival where some of the performances would be entirely free. The festival theatre was to be built in the Russian style, carved in wood and painted, like some of the private theatres that have already been designed by great artists for wealthy people in Russia. Vaslav hoped to earn sufficient money during his dancing career to realise this project.

The day of his return from Paris, Sergei Pavlovitch burst into the lobby of the Ritz and embraced Vaslav passionately. *"Vatza, daragoi moi, kak tui pajivayesh."* The greeting was as affectionate as if they had parted only a few hours ago, and no misunderstanding had ever occurred. It was the Sergei Pavlovitch of the old days. They sat down in a corner and began to talk. Hours and hours passed, and it seemed that the old friendship was restored. From that day on we were practically all the time with Diaghileff. The contract for South America was just brushed aside, and Sergei Pavlovitch simply said: "We open in Madrid at the Theatre Royal, and then we will give some performances in Barcelona. Massine has composed new ballets. I want you, Vatza, to look at them and give me your opinion. Have you composed anything new? I want you to do so."

Recent events in Russia were also discussed at great length, and Vaslav explained to Diaghileff his plans for the school and festival theatre. But Diaghileff objected: "Why think of the future of ballet? That is not our task. Dance and compose for our company, and leave the future generation to look after itself. I do not wish to return to Russia; I have worked too long abroad—the artists at home would ask what I wanted there. They would say that I wanted to take advantage of the newly acquired possibilities of the liberty for which they had had to fight. They would say, *'Je suis vieux jeux, vieux régime.'* I could not survive in the new Russia. I prefer to stay in Europe."

But Vaslav did not yet give up the idea of gaining Diaghileff for his plan. "We can't go travelling about the world forever like a caravan of gypsies; we shall never be able to create real artistic work that way. We belong to Russia; we must go home and work there and make a trip to the West once in a while."

Diaghileff's little circle, here as elsewhere, was formed of the *élite* of the advanced guard. He brought Picasso, who was very little known at that time, to us one day.

He was reticent and very Spanish looking, and when he began to explain anything, he became full of excitement, and used to draw on the table-cloth, the menu cards, and on the top of Sergei Pavlovitch's ivory walking-stick. Diaghileff was to me as a fatherly friend, protective and kind, at this time. Vaslav triumphantly said, *"Tu vois femmka je t'ai toujours dit qu'il sera notre ami."* And Vaslav told me again how Diaghileff had helped a former great friend when he got into difficulties, years after his marriage, and his wife sought Sergei Pavlovitch's aid.

Vaslav was so happy that he would have done anything to please Diaghileff, and the matter of the contract was not brought up. "Sergei Pavlovitch is the same as ever; there is no need of discussion; he will be fair to me—let us give him a chance to prove it."

Every day, Diaghileff thought of some place of interest to take us to. He was very friendly to me during those days in Madrid. His amazing hypnotic power did not seem to have lessened with the years; while listening to him at dinner once, when we were watching the ladies dancing at the Palace Hotel, I could understand how he subtly suggested his ideas about women to his youthful followers. For as he criticised the lines of the women's bodies, I myself, too, could see only the ugliness of them.

One evening we went to a theatre where Pastora Imperio was giving a recital. To us the name did not mean anything. We were told that she was a gypsy singer from Cadiz, that her fame extended to the Latin-American countries. She was the idol of Spain. As she appeared on the stage, behind the simple curtain, she did not make a great impression. We saw only a rather faded, stout southern woman, but the moment she began to sing, accompanying herself with movement and castanets, we forgot that she had no voice, that she was middle-aged and fat. With a few gestures she offered the history and the soul of Spain. Vaslav and Stravinsky, as well as Diaghileff, could not keep quiet on their seats, and, like three school-children, applauded, laughed, and cried, according to the mood this ageless marvel dictated.

The performances in Madrid began. Vaslav danced

his usual parts. With great interest, he watched the new ballets of Massine. Vaslav always welcomed with enthusiasm the advent of a new artist if he brought something to art. Feelings of jealousy or envy were quite foreign to him. For him, Massine was a young artist with ambition, and his only wish was to help and applaud him, when he deserved it. The fact that Diaghileff used Massine as a tool to ruin him, did not in the least alter Vaslav's attitude towards Massine. Just the contrary. He said, "I do hope that Massine will fulfil all that Sergei Pavlovitch hopes from him as a dancer and as a choreographer. I only wish there were many more choreographers." Unlike the other *maîtres de ballet*, he was solely interested in the advancement of dancing; the personal question never entered his mind.

His enthusiasm for *Les Femmes de Bonne Humeur* was very great. He was glad to find that Massine had undoubted talent for composition. He discussed this ballet with Diaghileff, making a few remarks about certain things he would have done otherwise. Sergei Pavlovitch immediately said, "Of course, *tu sais,* Vatza, I found him as a private pupil in Moscow, when I had to have a youth for the part of Joseph. He has had very little experience as a dancer. He never thought of composition until I guided him. Naturally, it was a tremendous task for me to put this ballet on, as I had to explain to him all the steps and gestures, which he then showed the troupe." In one word, Sergei Pavlovitch claimed to have composed all the ballets instead of Massine—as in the past he had tried to do with Vaslav. We already knew, of course, this weakness of Diaghileff, which in later years developed tremendously, but, just as Vaslav had done, Massine also composed ballets after he separated from the Diaghileff company.

Parade did not please Vaslav. "Sergei, this production is an essay, not fit to be shown to the public yet. You were trying to do something here which was not even clear to Massine himself. It comes out of a desire to be modern, but it is not felt, it is an artificially constructed choreography."

"But, *mon cher,* we must do something new for Paris every year. We can't be less modern than Marinetti. Futurism, cubism, is the last word. I do not want to let the position of an artistic leader slip away from me."

Vaslav simply could not see this strained point of view. There were many other questions now on which they could not agree. Vaslav was no more a pupil, he had become sure of his own views; he strongly urged that motion pictures should be taken of the ballets as documentary evidence for future productions, though of course not for public show. But Diaghileff brushed this suggestion aside in the same easy way as the plans of the school and the system of notation. "Vatza, why think of the future generation, of the future of the dance? Let them take care of themselves, just let us occupy ourselves with the present."

Now that the performances had begun, we had less time to go out with our friends, but I insisted that we should not give them up entirely, for I did not want Vaslav to isolate himself from the rest of the world and live only with Diaghileff and the Russian Ballet. I could not trust them after all that had happened in the past. As soon as they returned from their holiday, Kostrovsky and H. practically installed themselves in our apartment, day and night. They hung around Vaslav after rehearsals. H. seemed to forget his courting and Kostrovsky his wife. The latter stood, with his shining, fanatical eyes, in the middle of the drawing-room, talking, talking, while H. pretended to listen with awe. Every second sentence was a quotation from Tolstoi, and Vaslav listened attentively. Either purposely or because he was unfortunately not only fanatical but also unintelligent, Kostrovsky mixed up the teachings of Tolstoi. He preached that art is not justifiable for its own sake, but must have as its end the spiritual development of the individual. He wanted to convince Vaslav that he should work for the Russian Ballet as long as it needed him, and then retire to the land, like Tolstoi.

I began to resent the growing influence of these two self-appointed "teachers." They not only tried to influence

Vaslav in his attitude towards Diaghileff and religion, but
in his private life, his diet, his choice of friends, and
lately his relationship with me. This indeed seemed to fill
the cup. One evening, in a dark corner near the stage, I
saw Diaghileff conversing very excitedly with H., not as
an officer with his subordinate, but like two accomplices.
The truth flashed through my brain; what I feared, what I
had not dared to admit until then, was suddenly clear. It
was all a carefully laid plot to estrange Vaslav from me
and restore him to Sergei Pavlovitch's clutches.

I had to use my influence to counteract this scheme,
and tried to surround Vaslav with people who meant well
for him. I accepted invitations, and even encouraged the
Duchess of X.'s advances to Vaslav. I almost threw them
together, because, unconsciously, I felt that two loving
women could achieve more than one in holding back
an idealist from falling into the abyss of utter day-dreaming to which these fanatics were dragging him. Sergei Pavlovitch knew Vaslav's character; he realised that only
through altruism could he estrange him from marriage,
normal life, and art, and make Vaslav give up dancing
forever in order to cultivate the earth, like a peasant.

The idea of becoming a preaching monk which he
had in his youth, the wish to retreat from the world to
the isolation of a Siberian monastery which he had had on
the boat going to South America before our marriage,
haunted him. On that voyage he was in conflict with himself. He understood that Diaghileff was an invaluable adviser in art, that Diaghileff's very being was necessary for
his own existence, but he also fully realised that their
relationship was a mistake, that love for him must come
through a woman.

But now that Vaslav was fully aware of himself, not
only as an artist but as a man, why, why did he want
to renounce all that love, life, and art could offer, and
return to the soil? I sensed now that Sergei Pavlovitch
would rather annihilate Vaslav completely if he could not
own him both as an artist and as a man.

We discussed what was to be done with Kyra in case
Vaslav went to South America. To send her to my moth-

er-in-law in Russia, in the middle of the revolution, was quite out of the question. We had decided to send her, with a trustworthy nurse, to a well-known children's sanatorium in Switzerland, but, at Kostrovsky's and H.'s instigation, Vaslav now said: "The child has the first claim on a mother's care." But I firmly put my foot down: "The child that needs my care is you, Vaslav, and I go with you."

I tried to provide as many distractions as possible for Vaslav, and we often passed the day with the Duchess of X., who was so obviously madly in love with Vaslav that he objected to going out alone with her, as I suggested. One day, we motored out to the Escorial; a dreary trip through barren desert, but at the last turn of the road we could not restrain an exclamation, for suddenly the grand austere building arose out of nothing, like a mirage, and dominated the whole horizon. The strict, imposing lines of the structure were overwhelming. Vaslav, rooted in admiration, said, "Spain. Religious fanaticism expressed in granite."

As he stood there, so small, so confident in the dazzling sunlight, before entering the gloomy pitiless home of the Inquisition, I wondered how it was that he did not see how the "teachers" were trying, through religious fanaticism, to seize his soul and destroy him.

The Duchess of X., being related to the King, was able to show us everything. After the rooms of Charles V, the crypt seemed almost cheerful.

At lunch, on the terrace, Vaslav seemed to have regained his mischievous ways. He said to me, "Please, *femmka,* do not leave me so much alone with her." He was too discreet to give her away, but too honest not to put me on my guard.

The King with his court attended almost every performance and was expressive in his admiration. He often came to the rehearsals, and the Duchess of X. told us that in private he attempted to imitate Vaslav's leaps. One evening, he came so late that we could not keep the public waiting any longer. Alfonso said to his aide-de-camp, "Please ask Nijinsky to excuse us for the delay, and tell him: *Je viens d'accoucher d'un nouveau gouvernement.*"

Our intimate life was ideally happy. Sometimes the strangest feeling would come over me, and I felt that the women of mythology may have felt as I did when a God came to love them. There was the exhilarating and inexpressible feeling that Vaslav was more than a human being. The ecstasy that he could create in love as in art had a purifying quality, and yet there was something intangible in his being that one could never reach.

Now Vaslav began to wonder if cohabitation were only justified in case a child is born as the result. Before he had considered the state of my delicate health and the responsibilities of parentage, but now he suggested that either an ascetic life or a child every year was the right way. I immediately understood that this must be Kostrovsky's idea, in order to get me out of the way. One night, when they were discussing this subject, I declared open war.

It was three in the morning. I had listened for hours, seeing how cunningly they were trying to destroy our happiness, and at last, on the verge of tears, I exclaimed, "Why don't you leave my husband alone? You don't dare to talk about his art, because you know that on that subject you cannot influence him. You are not his friends, but his enemies. If you want to create happiness, do so first in your own homes. Your wife, Kostrovsky, is miserable, your children without shoes, because you give your money away to strangers; and you, H., if you want advancement, why not ask for it frankly? Vaslav Fomitch would help you. I forbid you both to interfere in our married life. Leave us, this place belongs to Vaslav and me."

Vaslav had never seen me like this before, and for a moment he was taken aback, but then said, "Please *femmka,* they are my friends; do not try to withhold our hospitality."

Kostrovsky and H. sat waiting, with impertinent provoking faces, to see how things would develop, but I turned round; "Vaslav, you have to choose between the

diabolical influence of these people and me. If within half
an hour these people are still here, I shall leave you."

I waited in the other room, and Vaslav came in to try
and persuade me that they were both of good faith, but
my determination was unshaken, and, as they were still
there when the time was up, I went out into the night.

Next morning, Vaslav found me in the Prado and begged
me to return, saying, "It shall be as you wish." From that
day on, Kostrovsky and H. never entered our home any
more; but in the theatre they still seized opportunities to
get at Vaslav.

We now left for Barcelona, where the Russian Ballet
was to perform for the first time, and lodged in the same
hotel as Sergei Pavlovitch. The Duchess of X. followed
us, and I was rather glad, for I felt she was an ally.
Drobetsky, who was ever our staunch friend, informed
me that my suspicions that Diaghileff was working through
Kostrovsky and H. were not unfounded, and that some
trouble was looming. So I thought it was time to ask if
Vaslav's salary was to be paid, or did they expect him
to dance for nothing as in the past?

One morning we did a lovely motor trip to Montserrat,
accompanied by the Kostrovskys and H. Four thousand
feet high, Montserrat has a very architectural effect, and
the oddest granite cliffs, which take on the forms of curious
human figures. Rising suddenly from a plateau, abundant
with vineyards and luxurious southern vegetation, it is
almost unapproachable, only a narrow path, flanked by
perpendicular rocks and bottomless precipices, leads up
to the summit. This mountain is supposed to be Parsifal's
"Montesalvate." The higher one gets, the lovelier the view
is, and on the summit there is a monastery, which Vaslav
visited with Kostrovsky and H. alone, we women not
being admitted. At lunch at the little inn, Kostrovsky,
having ordered a vegetarian lunch, reproved Vaslav for
ordering meat, but Vaslav said, "I approve of the idea
of vegetarianism, but I cannot, unfortunately, carry it out;
as long as I dance, I need solid nourishment." Kostrovsky
said, "Then give up dancing."

The evenings we spent with the Duchess of X., who by

this time wanted desperately to become Vaslav's mistress. Jealousy never entered into my head, and I was even rather pleased when Vaslav returned later than usual one night, but this escapade had quite a different effect upon him than I had expected. He was mournful, and told me frankly:

"Femmka, I am sorry for what I did. It was unfair to her, as I am not in love, and the added experience, that perhaps you wanted me to have, is unworthy of us."

Lunching one day with Diaghileff, the latter began to talk about our South American trip, but Vaslav said, "I am not sure I will go, Sergei Pavlovitch. I need a rest, and do not like the idea of being separated from my child in war-time. South America will not be a creative trip artistically."

Diaghileff, with a freezing smile, returned, "But you have to go, you are under contract."

"Have to?" said Vaslav. "I have no contract."

"You cabled me from America agreeing in principle. That is a contract."

"But I also cabled that we would discuss the matter in Spain."

"That is beside the point. In this country, a cable is a binding contract"—and S. P. laughed—"I will force you to go."

In the afternoon, Vaslav notified Sergei Pavlovitch that, as no contract existed, he would take no further part in the Russian Ballet, and we left for the station. But as we boarded the Madrid express, two men touched Vaslav's arm: "M. and Mme. Nijinsky, will you please follow us, you are under arrest." We were aghast.

"On whose authority?" I ventured.

"On that of His Excellency the Marquess of Z., Governor of Catalonia, in the name of the King."

We were escorted to the police station, where, with the aid of several interpreters, they explained that we had been arrested at the behest of Diaghileff—as Vaslav was breaking his contract. If he did not dance that night, he would be put in gaol. Vaslav was pale, but determined:

"Very well, put me there! I have no contract. In any case, I can't dance now; I'm too upset." He sat down.

"M. Nijinsky, please promise to dance, then I will not have to imprison you."

"No, I won't; I can't."

"Show us the contract which Diaghileff pretends to have, and then Nijinsky will dance," I said. "Anyhow, you have no right to arrest me; I am a Russian citizen, and not a member of the Russian Ballet. I will complain at the Embassy at once if you do not let me go immediately."

The prefect became rather uneasy, but, very much against his wish, released me. Followed by a detective, I dashed to the telephone, called up the Duc de Durcal in Madrid, who informed the authorities there of what was going on. Within an hour an order arrived from Madrid for our immediate release, and Señor Cambo, the eminent Spanish lawyer, arrived to take up our case with Diaghileff.

The Barcelona authorities now realised that they had made a dreadful blunder, and were full of excuses. It was too late to catch the train, so we returned to the hotel, where Drobetsky and the Spanish director were awaiting us. The director cried out at once: "The public are disappointed, they are returning their tickets by the hundreds. It's you they want to see dance. I am ruined, because I have to pay Diaghileff whatever happens, and now I have not made a peso. My last season was a failure, too."

Vaslav was sorry for him. "For your sake, I will dance to-night. Tell the public, please, why I am late."

Next day, Cambo discussed the situation with us. Spain was the only country in which a cable was a binding contract. So Vaslav was bound to go to South America. He regretted now that he had not listened more carefully to Laurence Steinhardt's shrewd advice, and that he had not shown him the cable drafted, word for word, by Kostrovsky and H. But Cambo assured us that Diaghileff would have to grant Vaslav the terms he asked. So he drew up a contract, that Vaslav was willing to go to South America, and that his salary was to be the same as in the U.S.A., payable, in gold dollars, one hour before the curtain rose at every performance. I insisted on such a clause. I did not want any lawsuits later on. If this clause was not fulfilled, the contract became void. It was originated by Fanny Elssler after she had been cheated many times by dishonest impresarios. Vaslav agreed to appear in all parts first danced by himself. The penalty for breaking the contract was twenty thousand dollars. Cambo and I went to Diaghileff with the contract. He received us in his drawing-room, with his usual tactics, sitting with his back to the window, and letting others talk while he listened. The contract was so cleverly drawn up that, while it fulfilled all his stipulations, there was no possibility of any trick being played on Vaslav. While Diaghileff's signature was being affixed, my mind went back to that meeting at the Bristol Hotel, years ago—how very different, and yet how very alike, the situation was.

Shortly afterwards, the Governor called on us, in gala uniform, with white gloves, and a huge bouquet. He came to apologise for the arrest, over which he seemed to be extremely worried, and asked Vaslav to put in a good word for him at Court by saying that he was not to blame for the incident.

We now returned to Madrid for a few days, and from there Kyra was sent to Lausanne.

Diaghileff and Massine and sixteen dancers departed for Italy, and we left with the troupe in the middle of July for South America. This time the troupe was in the hands of Grigoriev. Vaslav seemed worn out by the excitement of the last few days, especially by the blow that had clearly unmasked Diaghileff's attitude; now he knew that an understanding was forever impossible.

On the journey, Michel said how sorry he was that Sergei Pavlovitch and Vaslav could not agree. "I wanted to, I did everything, I am heartbroken about it," replied Vaslav.

In Cadiz, we seemed to be shadowed all the time; perhaps they were afraid that we would not embark.

We sailed on the *Reina Victoria Eugenia*. This boat was the last word in luxury, but it did not have the home-like feel of the *Avon*. However, we soon settled down, and

Vaslav became very busy teaching his system of notation to Kostrovsky and H., and discussing it with Cecchetti.

Maestro was rather depressed on this voyage. He did not like the atmosphere of strife that had reigned lately in the Russian Ballet, and disapproved of Diaghileff's action. He shook his head, and asked me, referring to his warning in Budapest long ago, "Well, is the sun giving you any warmth?"

"*Maestro,* I am perfectly happy, so is Vaslav too, in our marriage; our only sorrow is Sergei Pavlovitch's attitude."

"Yes, yes, I know. I was in London when the news of your marriage arrived. The cable was delivered to Diaghileff at the Savoy. He went livid in the face and fainted. It must have been a cruel blow. These Russians are a strange lot. For thirty-five years I have taught and studied them. They are my friends, I love them, but there is something about them that we Europeans can never, never penetrate. I do hope unhappiness won't come to you through your marriage. I warned you at the beginning. Sergei Pavlovitch should not mix up love and art; it's a very great mistake. And you, Bambina, should have stuck to your lessons; I worked so hard with you, and you were a very promising pupil. But I am tired now, and I won't travel any more. This is my last trip."

Instead of Monteux, we had a new conductor, Ansermet, whom Diaghileff had discovered some time before in Lausanne. He did not seem to us nearly so good as Monteux. Once more the troupe seemed to be split in two camps, for and against Vaslav. The new conductor seemed to side with the last, who were led by G., and Kremeniev. We paid as little attention to them as possible, and kept away from the troupe as much as we could, spending a lot of our time with Andre, Brulé, and Regina Badet. Brulé called Vaslav, *"Le Dieu de la danse"*—which was what he was always known as in France.

Among the many passengers who tried to approach us was a young Chilean, a typical gigolo, extremely well bred and dressed. He was a nephew of some Spanish marquess, from whom he eventually inherited the title

and fortune. At that time, however, he was completely
broke, and, we all thought, on the look-out for an heiress.
There was a slight cut of the adventurer in him, but he
was amusing, played bridge excellently, and danced the
tango divinely. Vaslav never allowed me to dance modern
ball-room dances; he greatly disliked the then fashionable
fox-trot, grizzly bear, etc.—"It is not like a waltz or even
Boston; *c'est frotter le plancher"*—but he liked the tango,
and was interested to learn it from the Chilean Georges
C. Vaslav danced it with indescribable elegance and
smoothness. The lessons, of course, made us quite friendly with C. He tried to make love to me, and Vaslav seemed
quite amused. He appeared absolutely devoted to Vaslav,
and followed him about like a dog. "I wish I could be of
service to him, as a friend or as a secretary. Do let me
help you with your correspondence." But I did not; there
was something about him which made me cautious—he
was too eager.

Madame Kostrovsky seemed more distressed than ever,
and one day she called Vaslav for help, and Vaslav then
confided to me that Kostrovsky often had bad fits, falling
unconscious to the floor. Vaslav was worried about him,
and decided to consult a specialist on our arrival.

In Rio we were greeted by a group of friends and the
staff of the Russian Embassy. We immediately went up
to Sylvestre, to the hotel where we had stayed four
years previously. Our little circle was composed of the
Diplomatic coterie and some of the Brazilian families. We
saw a lot of Edwin Morgan, the U.S.A. Ambassador, and
Napoleo G., the music publisher, who introduced us to
the native music, with which Vaslav was pleased to make
some acquaintance.

The pleasantness of our life among these Brazilian
friends was reversed the moment we entered the theatre.
With the exception of Drobetsky, the management of the
troupe did everything to make life difficult for Vaslav
and to antagonise him. Vaslav, who adored his art, now
almost dreaded the hour he had to go to the theatre. He
went through his exercises, and through performances,
more silently than ever. *Maestro* spent a lot of time with

him, and one could see that with the golden heart of a
real artist and colleague, he was trying to counteract the
painful atmosphere created by the others.

One night, Vaslav woke me up, *"Femmka,* do you
know that *Faune* is on the programme the day after to-
morrow, and they did not even ask me?"

"It can't be possible."

"I told them it wasn't fair, as they don't own the rights,
but they just shrugged their shoulders. But, *femmka,* I
just won't allow them to do it."

"But, how can you prevent it, Vaslav?"

"Just wait," and he laughed in his mischievous, irresistible way.

Early next morning, Vaslav departed, with Napoleo and
his other friends, on a mysterious errand, and at lunch-
time they all came back triumphantly smiling at me. I
could not make out what they were up to.

At this time Vaslav had a lot of trouble with the
conductor. Vaslav was very strict about not changing
tempi. He had a very orthodox conception of the interpretation of the classics. He always held that, in drama,
music, and the dance, the author's idea must be adhered
to absolutely. With Beecham, Monteux, Baton, and the
others there never was any trouble. It was different now.
Discipline in the ballet had greatly slackened, and if a
dancer had some difficulty with a certain step, he or she
just asked the conductor to change the *tempi.* Of this,
Vaslav frankly expressed his disapproval. That evening the
performance seemed to go very smoothly. The *entr'acte,*
during which I admired the colourful audience, seemed to
me unusually long. *Faune* was the next ballet on the
programme. The public became restless; I wondered what
could have happened. Vaslav's friends were smiling like
conspirators. I went back stage; everything was ready,
the scene lit, Vaslav in position waiting for the curtain to
rise. But at one side of the stage there was a gesticulating
group. The impresario, Grigoriev, Kremeniev, pacing up
and down in a frenzy, Drobetsky trying to hide a smile.
The impressario was talking to two police officials. What
had happened? They told me: "Nijinsky, the author of

Faune, has brought an injunction to prevent the presentation of *Faune,* as it does not legally belong to the Russian Ballet."

Nijinsky, the dancer, however, stood waiting to begin his part in the *Faune* according to the terms of his contract. "But, Nijinsky the author, and Nijinsky the dancer, are the same person," said one of the ballet. "Sorry; have you anything in writing to prove that you have the author's permission to perform it—yes or no?" And *Faune* had to be cancelled. Vaslav admitted that it was a trick on his part, but he thought it rather an innocent one after what he had had to endure the previous year from Sergei Pavlovitch and his sycophantic staff.

Our most pleasant recollection was meeting the great poet Paul Claudel, at that time French Ambassador in Brazil. He invited us to the Embassy to lunch, and introduced Vaslav to the promising young musician Darius Milhaud; one of the "group of six." Milhaud and Claudel were then composing a ballet, *L'homme et son désir,* and they wanted Vaslav to do the choreography. Vaslav was pleased with the idea.

Often Claudel took us motoring; he knew the most enchanting places. It was a great change and relief to be with persons like him, and to get away from the stifling atmosphere of the ballet. Claudel, who had lived in the Far East, made Vaslav intimately acquainted with Oriental art.

The heat was overwhelming. The only thing that made the performances tolerable for the artists was the refrigerator system, with which the theatre was equipped. We accepted with alacrity the Russian Ambassador Tscherbatckoi's invitation to visit him at his summer residence in Petropolis, in the hills behind Rio, where we were welcomed with real Russian hospitality.

On our return to Rio, we had disturbing news by the mail from Europe. Kyra was well, but the head doctor of the sanatorium in Lausanne complained that he was in great difficulty because my mother had arrived from Hungary and, with the support of the Austro-Hungarian Consul, had claimed the child. We immediately cabled instructions, through the Russian Consulate, to keep Kyra in Lausanne until our arrival.

Our next city on the schedule was São Paulo. We went on one of the Royal Mail Company's boats. Painted grey, even to the port-holes, it looked gloomy, but this was the necessity of the submarine war. We were told that after sunset we were not allowed on deck, or to light lamps or cigarettes. At the stern of the boat there was a cannon. We laughed at the sight of it, but not for long. One day a ship was sighted on the horizon, and we all rushed to see it, for it was a rarity to meet ships on the high seas in those days of the war. The ship came rapidly towards us. An officer explained to Vaslav that, according to the international regulations of war, ships have to approach each other close enough to prove that they are friendly. This one suddenly turned round, put up a smoke-screen, and became invisible. The officers rushed to the gun, and the women shrieked. I ran up to the radio officer. Vaslav came after and tried to quiet me. I cried, "I have had enough of all this; please Vaslav, let us go to Switzerland and have peace."

"Yes, yes, we will."

Calmette, the head of the Research Institute in São Paulo, brother of Calmette of the *Figaro,* who had caused so much fracas at the first performance of *Faune,* showed us round his extremely interesting place, where serums against snake-bites and insects are prepared.

Claudel was at São Paulo, and we spent most of our time with him.

Already in Rio, I had received a letter from my kinsman B., who was then living in Buenos Aires, to welcome us to South America. He requested me to send him a photograph of Vaslav, which I did.

Montevideo was our next stop. This time it proved full of great social activities. The Embassies entertained us, and we became very friendly with Jules Lefaivre, the French Minister. Mitchell Innes, the English Minister, invited us to a lunch, where we met several members of the Pavlova Company, who were then dancing in Montevideo.

On this tour, I used to sit in Vaslav's dressing-room, with a watch in my hand, waiting for Vaslav's salary— one hour before the beginning of the performance; and poor Drobetsky had to explore all the banks to find enough gold *à la Elssler*. In Montevideo he was unable to find it, and Vaslav again danced for nothing.

My kinsman B. now arrived from Buenos Aires. He had been sent by the family to the Argentine, in disgrace, a few years before the war. He was a brilliant lawyer, and had a real genius for politics, an incredible memory and knowledge; but unfortunately he lavished his talents on unworthy objects. His passion was to expose people's private lives. He knew the law so well that he could always get away with his attacks, on leading politicians, officers of the general staff, and society women, in a paper he edited himself. Even his own family was not exempt from his attacks. However, he got into real trouble when he exposed a high Hungarian general, and was then exiled to the Argentine. At the request of my Uncle Gari, Vaslav had given him some financial help. He failed to make a good impression on Vaslav, who, however, gave him the several thousand pesos he asked for. Later in the night, he came back, saying that the money had been stolen from him, and asked for some more!

Vaslav and I took Kostrovsky to a specialist here, who told me, as I was the only one to speak Spanish, that Kostrovsky had epilepsy, was incurable, dangerously insane, and should be repatriated to Russia.

Four years had elapsed since we were in Buenos Aires. It was almost like coming home—this city where we had first known happiness. Great improvements had been made in the city. We were met at the docks by old friends, among them Señor Quintana, the son of the ex-President, and, in the group that welcomed us, we also found the Chilean C. who had taught us the tango on the boat.

Our apartment was in the New Plaza Hotel. Mr. Gavuzzi received us, saying, "Your secretary is in your drawing-room, with the gentlemen of the Press."

"But there must be a mistake," answered Vaslav. "I have no secretary."

When we were shown in, we saw the reporters drinking cocktails and holding printed sheets in their hands.

"What is this?"

"It is Mr. Nijinsky's interview."

Vaslav and I looked at each other speechless. Don de B., as my kinsman liked to call himself, had prepared and distributed this "interview" himself. The reporters also showed us some photographs, apparently autographed by Vaslav, and we recognised these as copies of the one I had sent privately to my kinsman!

Quintana took us all round, to the Races, and to the Jockey Club, where we met Sir Reginald Tower, the British Ambassador, with whom we became very friendly.

C. and my kinsman became very friendly. The latter asked me to come and see his home, and there he showed me his beautifully arranged dossiers of all the important people of the Argentine; every peccadillo, every love-affair, was recorded. "But what is the idea? Why do you waste your time in this way?" He replied, "You do not understand. To become a great politician, one has to know all the weaknesses of the leaders of society."

I now began to receive curious letters from acquaintances in Europe, asking me if any of their letters to me had been stolen, and repeating rumours that were being spread about liaisons that Vaslav and I were supposed to have had with various people. I could not make it out. One day, my kinsman came in rather excitedly, saying that he needed a considerable amount of money at once to prevent a newspaper attack that was being organised against Vaslav by one of the Russian Ballet. I did not mention it to Vaslav, but gave B. the money. One morning later, to my amazement, I saw an article of political content in one of the papers, with my name as author. The article calmly divided up the Austro-Hungarian Empire! I rang up Quintana, and he undertook at once to deny my authorship of it.

Lately, too, B. had insinuated that there was an *affaire*

between Vaslav and C. I laughed in his face. I knew Vaslav
too well—he would have been the first to tell me. B. also
wanted to take us to indecent motion-pictures, but Vaslav
refused to go, and said: *"Femmka,* I would rather not see
B. in our home. We can help him financially of course."

So we were not "at home" any more when he called.
But he was too cunning, and, by making love to my
elderly Spanish maid, and promising her a position with
an arch-duchess in Vienna, he not only got her to allow
him into our apartments during our absence, but also to
give him our correspondence. All this, however, we only
found out later.

The anniversary of our wedding arrived. The priest who
married us gave a lunch in our honour, and Vaslav surprised me with a beautiful bag of heavy gold, and a
vanity-case set with sapphires.

Pavlova was dancing at this time in Buenos Aires. We
met her in the grill-room one day, when she came over to
our table, and talked to Vaslav very sweetly in Russian. I
looked at her curiously, remembering her telephone call
at the time of Vaslav's accident in the U.S.A.

Things with the Russian Ballet did not go smoothly.
But Vaslav went on with his work, seemingly not noticing
their attitude. Curious things began to happen in the theatre—Vaslav stepped on a rusty nail. "How did it happen
to be on the stage?" I asked. "By accident." Then, one
evening while Vaslav was practising, a heavy iron counter-
weight fell down from the grid. Vaslav instinctively jumped
away, and only his quickness saved his life. An investigation was ordered: "An accident." I began to wonder
about these happenings, and mentioned them to Quintana.
He shared my opinion. In Vaslav's contract, there was a
clause that he had to pay twenty thousand dollars if he
did not fulfil the terms. Some people may have wanted to
assist the hand of fate. So Quintana, who was a prominent lawyer, arranged with the authorities for detectives
to keep watch on Vaslav—they used to come back stage.

One day, a menacing mob surrounded our hotel owing
to strong anti-German feeling and Gavuzzi, the manager,
came complaining to me that my kinsman had attacked

him in the papers, saying that he was an illegitimate son of the Kaiser, and a spy. He thought this was probably because he had given orders that B. was not to be admitted to the hotel, after a scene which had almost cost my kinsman his life and myself my freedom.

One day, when Vaslav entered his room, he found B. waiting. He insisted on speaking to him, and rapidly began to tell Vaslav that I was his mistress, and had also been C.'s mistress. When I first heard B.'s voice, I went to enter the room, to stop him tiring Vaslav with his talk, but, when I heard the atrocious lies about myself, I was nailed to the floor. Suddenly I remembered how, one day, my kinsman had complained of the heat, and undressed and put on Vaslav's dressing-gown. He then lay down on the couch, and invited me to come and sit by him. But I refused, and asked him to dress and leave. I never thought then that he had any hidden motive for his behaviour, but now I understood the whole frame-up. As he could not get all the money he wanted out of me by loans, he was now resorting to other methods. I seized a revolver, and opened the door slowly. Vaslav was standing there motionless, pale, but very quiet. "Please leave this place at once; my wife is above all your calumnies, and whatever she pleases to do is right"; and, luckily for B., as Vaslav spoke I was surrounded by the manager and staff of the hotel, who put my kinsman into the street.

But B. was relentless. The next thing he did was to attack Vaslav, by accusing him of spying for Austria-Hungary, in the very paper which he had told me was going to print an attack on Vaslav by some member of the Russian Ballet. Quintana immediately brought a libel action, and B. was ordered to admit that the whole thing was a lie. It turned out that he already had a very bad record with the police, as he was known to have gone to the English, French, and German Embassies and offered his services to them all simultaneously. Someone at one of the Embassies told us how he had outlined to them his plan for starting a revolution in Hungary, and undermining the Army, if the Allies would supply him with

funds. He was told however that revolutions are made on
the spot, not thousands of miles away.

All this time Vaslav behaved with extraordinary calm.
But in his strained, pale face, I noticed the same expression as at the time of our internment in Hungary. We both
ardently desired peace. It was sad to see that Vaslav had
to be watched by detectives to assure his safety among
his own colleagues. The troupe recognised that Vaslav
only lived for his art, and was not satisfied with anything
short of perfection. They said, "One could never find a
truer artist," but thought that he was stubborn, as he
expected very exact execution. They misunderstood his
extreme reserve, and thought him snobbish. They called
him "Dumb-bell," because he was so silent. The members
of the Mariinsky Theatre were different, they loved Vaslav truly. I prayed for the end of the season.

Vaslav was dancing *Scheherazade.* He had made
changes in his make-up, which was now a deep hue of
silvery grey. Watching him, I forgot all our troubles. Once,
at the *finale,* when he made his final jump, when he is
chased by the soldier who hits him on the head, the
audience rose with a scream, and I did too, although I
had already seen *Scheherazade* more than a hundred
times. In that final jump, Vaslav, with the briefest touch
of his head on the floor, flung himself into the air by the
action of his neck-muscles, quivered, and fell. I ran
back stage, but there was Vaslav practising *entre-chats!*
So convincing had his execution been that we all thought
he was hurt.

But what I had been dreading all the time finally
happened. Since the detectives were officially admitted to
the theatre, and supervised the stage, curiously enough
no more accidents occurred. I shall never forget the astonished faces of the management of the Russian Ballet
when they asked, as they thought, some loafing strangers
to leave, and were shown the detectives' badges. One
evening when *Petrouchka* was given, during the last scene,
when Petrouchka shows himself to the magician from
the top of the Puppet Theatre, the thing happened. Suddenly the whole structure began to shake, as in an earth-

quake, and Vaslav pitched forward. He did not lose his presence of mind, and endeavoured to leap clear. From that height he would undoubtedly have injured his leg on landing, but Cecchetti, risking his own safety, sprang forward and caught Vaslav in his arms.

The investigation proved that the scenery had never been fastened. The signal had been given to begin the ballet before the stage hand could fasten it firmly enough.

In spite of all the attacks that were made on him, even now Vaslav did not complain. He merely said, "Do not blame them. They do not realise what they are doing. *Il n'y a pas des hommes méchants, seulement des hommes bêtes.*"

Our friends in Montevideo asked us to visit them again at the end of the Argentine season, which we did, and, at the request of the French and English Ambassadors, Vaslav gave an extra performance for the wounded soldiers of the Allies, Rubinstein accompanying him on the piano. The public went wild with enthusiasm at his performance, but, as I followed Vaslav's floating movements on the stage in his mazurka in *Sylphides*, little did I think that I had seen him dance for the last time in the theatre.

We returned to Buenos Aires for a few days, to arrange our departure for Europe, deciding to leave on a different boat from the troupe. But Vaslav insisted on going down to the docks to say good-bye to the artists. "They are not responsible for the actions of Diaghileff and his staff."

As we waved good-bye to the slowly moving boat from the quay of the Rio de la Plata, we knew that we had said farewell forever to the Russian Ballet.

Chapter Nineteen

HOME IN ST. MORITZ

OUR ARGENTINE friends escorted us to the dock, and Quintana promised to look after the lawsuit against Diaghileff, as the Russian Ballet had broken their contract at the very last moment by refusing to pay our passage back to Europe. Sir Reginald Tower assured us that he did not pay the slightest attention to B.'s calumnies, and that, whatever happened during the journey home, we were to remain calm. As we steamed out of Buenos Aires, it was rumoured that the Allies were looking for German spies who were supposed to be on board, under false names. Three days passed quietly. Then one evening, as I was dressing for dinner, the boat slowed down and suddenly stopped. I turned quickly to Vaslav, but he reassured me. "Don't be alarmed; it is nothing. Probably only the English cruiser we were told would stop the boat." I looked out of the port-hole. The sun was setting, and in front of its blood-red disc the shape of a swift, dark cruiser was rapidly looming upon the horizon. We went on deck. I was trembling. Some English officers came aboard. The passengers were asked to go down to the baggage-room and open their trunks. An officer went into every cabin and looked round. When he came to ours, he saluted, asked our names, and left. The search went on for three hours. I became frantic. "Vaslav, they will arrest me, take me off the boat."

"But what for, *femmka?*"

"Because I was born Hungarian."

"Now, *femmka, tu es bête.* The English are sensible people; they will not do anything to you."

Everybody was questioned; only we seemed to be left out. I rushed down to my cabin and seized the picture of the little Jesus of Prague, the one that had given Vaslav to me years before. It had always been my icon, but the prayer on the back was printed in German, so in a panic I tore it in two and threw it into the sea. As the picture floated on the waves, I could see the small head of the miraculous Jesus turned upwards, looking at me. I uttered a scream. I wanted to get it back, but it was already sinking slowly, and I had the uncanny presentiment that my happiness was sinking with it. Soon afterwards the investigating officers departed, and we resumed our journey in peace.

The homeward journey was uneventful. The only excitements were the radio reports of the war bulletin. Vaslav rested in his deck-chair practically the whole day, correcting the second revision of his system of notation. I would usually bring him a cup of beef tea and the news. One day I told him that the power in Russia had been seized by the local soviets, and Lenin and Trotsky, repatriated three days ago, had formed a Government. Vaslav was not even quite sure who they were, and remarked that it was strange that they should put somebody in power who had always lived away from Russia. We neither of us knew what this really meant for our country and the world.

On the voyage we were more reserved than ever, and did not make any acquaintances, as we had been warned by our friends in Rio of a certain Mr. R., a Belgian, who was on the boat.

In fact, this gentleman tried in every way to approach us. He was generally in the bar, or playing cards, and his wife was beautifully dressed. We were told that he was a partner in the firm of Lacloche, the best jewellery store in Buenos Aires.

On our arrival in Europe we took the Sud Express and went right through Spain. At the French frontier we had to change. It took a long time to pass the passport office. We did not like to push, and in consequence missed the connection, just seeing Mr. R. waving to us to hurry; our sleepers were in the same car as his. What were we to do? There was no other express train for two days, so we decided to put up at the local hotel and looked round for our hand-luggage. The porter who had it was supposed to wait for us on the platform, but he was nowhere to be found. Nobody knew where our luggage was, and after a frantic search we were told he had gone off duty and returned to his home on the other side of the frontier. I burst out crying, "My jewels!" and rushed to the station-master. He was no help at all. It was impossible to re-cross the frontier. The station was searched in vain. I spent a gloomy day crying for my pearls and lovely rubies, sapphires, all the bracelets, rings, which Vaslav had given me—all gone.

Next day the porter returned to duty and told us that he had put our luggage in our compartment on the express, assuming we would catch the train. "You fool!" I could not help exclaiming.

"*Tu vois, femmka,*" said Vaslav, "*tu aurais dû porter la boite à bijoux dans tes mains. En tous les cas ces choses matérielles ne sont pas importantes. Penses aux gens qui perdent leurs maris, leurs enfants, à la guerre.*"

But all this could not console me. The station-master thought the *chef de train* would put the luggage out at the next station, but I thought myself that it had been stolen by the porter.

However, we took the next slow train for Paris and inquired at each station. After a terrible journey of forty hours, in a compartment full of soldiers returning from leave, we finally arrived in Paris. No sign of our luggage. But Vaslav just said, "*Femmka, c'est perdu; n'y penses plus.* You see, you would not be worried if you did not care for that sort of thing."

But I was more worried than ever when, on trying to trace Mr. R., I found that Lacloche in Paris had no connection with the firm of the same name in Buenos Aires. All my suspicions were now turned to Mr. R. and, as it proved, correctly, only—he had not stolen the luggage, but merely deposited it safely at the office of the Wagons Lits to await our arrival in Paris!

Vaslav was full of joy as we neared Lausanne. He almost ran to the sanatorium where Kyra was. She was sitting on her bed and seemed almost as big as the teddy-bear Vaslav had given her before leaving Spain. She looked more like Vaslav than ever. He clasped her in his arms and danced round the room. Kyra screamed with joy. It was remarkable how the child changed the moment Vaslav entered the room. It seemed almost as though they had been one person split apart, and constantly wishing to be reunited. Sometimes I almost felt as if I were intruding on them. They were both essentially and fundamentally Russian—something we Europeans can never, never penetrate. They so easily adapted themselves to different circumstances, to joy, to sorrow, to luxury, to hardship.

After our bitter experiences, we realised that all association with Diaghileff and his company was over forever. Their ideas and those of Vaslav were now far apart. Diaghileff wished to go on producing sensational cubist and futurist ballets at all costs, while, much as Vaslav believed in acrobatics as an accessory to dancing, he did not see it as a final end, and did not wish the future of the ballet to follow the path of the music-hall. He greatly admired such dancers as Mitty and Tilio, but could not see them in the ballet atmosphere. He advocated that ballet-dancers should be trained as acrobats in order to give them greater power over their bodies. Diaghileff was only interested in the present, whereas Vaslav was also interested in the future.

We decided to settle down quietly somewhere, where he could compose until the end of the war. Vaslav dreamed of a return to Russia, to make his home there, to create the school, the theatre, and the artistic laboratory that he so desired. Also, he thought of having a *pied-à-terre* in Paris, so that he could keep in touch with Western ideas; and, anyhow, he adored Paris. He had already designed our future home in Russia with a special apartment for Kyra, all painted by Russian artists, with small furniture and everything in proportion for the child-mind. Now he asked me to find a suitable place to await the end of the

war. We were tired of hotels, and so I finally decided on
St. Moritz Dorf, that I had loved ever since I was a
girl. I could never forget those gigantic Alps, with the
bracing air, the dark pine-trees, and the magical sun shining on the snow. It was so like Russia that Vaslav would
surely love it. "But I hate mountains. They hide the view.
I want to see far, far away. I do not want to be shut in,"
said Vaslav. "Come and see it before you decide," I said.

So early in December 1917 we went to St. Moritz. The
place was deserted, and, as I had anticipated, Vaslav was
enchanted. We soon found a charming villa high up on
the hill on the road to Chanterella. Quickly I engaged
a staff and put everything in order. When the villa was
first heated we stood together awestruck in the clear sunshine, facing the Alp Giop, watching the smoke escaping
from the chimney of our first home. We could now live
together, undisturbed, for the first time since our marriage.

The very first night in St. Moritz I was awakened by a
terrifying noise like the roaring of guns. We were not
very far from the Austro-Italian front, and in the mountains the echo of the guns might easily have reached us.
Then the roaring became clearer, and I felt my bed shake.
"Vaslav, what is this?"

"Some new arrival at the hotel; they are pulling the
trunks about on the top floor."

But at the moment that Vaslav switched on the light
our beds were pushed over to the other side of the room
by some powerful unknown force. The lamp swung about,
the pictures fell off the walls, and the bottles and things
fell off the table, while the ground seemed to float about
under us. "Be calm," said Vaslav. "It is nothing, only an
earthquake." There was another strong shock. "For God's
sake come on, Vaslav"; and nervously I put a slipper on
one foot, a snow-boot on the other, threw a fur round
me, and made for the staircase, forgetting this time jewellery and everything else. "Vaslav, come, come!" But he
quietly began to dress.

Everyone was in front of the hotel, sitting in the snow
with chattering teeth, more from fright than from the cold.
"Let us go into the lobby, *femmka*." The telephonist was

trying to get in touch with Zürich. "In Samadan it is quite
bad . . . the Rosegthal seems to be the centre. . . . Milan
is all right. . . . Seventeen shocks already."

Vaslav was quietly watching the crooked tower. "It
will be such a pity if it collapses." Luckily very little damage was done.

Next day Vaslav left for Lausanne to fetch Kyra and
the nurse. I was rather nervous, as he could not speak
German, and was completely lost when he had to attend
to the necessities of everyday life. To book a room in a
hotel and to buy a railway ticket were experiences
unknown to him. Vaslav was very proud, and was full of
adventurous feeling starting out on his first trip alone.

Our house looked like a real home, with all our personal belongings. The entrance was full of skis and tobog-
gans, as I had decided to take part in all the winter
sports. The house overlooked St. Moritz, and the lake lay
at our feet. Opposite was the beautiful Roseg Alp and the
Piz Margna that sheltered us from the eastern winds, and
snow glittering, snow everywhere, seven feet deep, that
promised us a glorious winter. Vaslav and Kyra arrived,
and in a few days we had fallen into our daily routine.
I wanted to attend to everything for Vaslav, but he
refused. "A man should not be served by his wife,
femmka." The wardrobe of an old maid could not have
been more perfectly in order and more spotlessly clean
than Vaslav kept his things.

The balcony on the ground floor was cleared. There,
every morning, for two hours, Vaslav did his exercises, with
Kyra looking on and patiently watching Tatakaboy dance,
and when he leaped she used to cheer and clap her hands,
then often Vaslav, forgetting his iron discipline, caught her
in his arms and waltzed round singing, *"Votre amabilité,
maia Kotyik, maia Funtyiki."*

When shopping in the village, I used to signal the
latest war news up to him practising on the balcony.
There was a bulletin posted every noon in the middle of
the village, and we had arranged a code of signals with
my arms.

This winter was a very happy one. We were constantly

together undisturbed, and went for long walks all over the
Engadine. I used to practise on the Dimson skeleton run;
it was my favourite sport. Vaslav was simply worshipped
by the servants. If he met the cook on the way up to the
villa, he carried the parcels. If the coal was too heavy
to put on the fire, he helped the maid, and he even
flirted with the old laundress, bought her chianti, and
chatted to her of her native Italy. He would play with all
the children of the village. Sometimes we used to meet at
Hanselmann's for an *apéritif* before lunch, where everybody goes during the season. Hanselmann, an Austrian
by origin, the well-known *confiseur* of St. Moritz, quite a
personality, played a leading part in the life of the place.
He became a staunch friend of "Monsieur Nijinsky." Vaslav appreciated his *Käse-stängel,* gave him recipes for
Koulibjak, and sometimes discussed the political situation
with him at length.

We often went, too, to Dr. Bernhard's. His house was
the last word in Engadine style, and was the meeting-
place of many interesting Swiss and foreigners. Our neighbour, President Gartmann, also entertained us.

Kyra was developing well, and looked lovely trotting
beside Vaslav in her teddy-bear suit. They used to lunge
down the hill to Celerina at a breakneck speed. I was
scared. "Nothing will happen to my *amabilité* as long as
we are together," Vaslav used to say. The evenings we
usually spent quietly at home reading.

Vaslav accompanied me when I went skating, and,
though he did not take part in any of the winter sports,
he gave me remarkable advice on technique and balance.
His instinctive knowledge was amazing.

Then Vaslav discovered sleighs that he could drive himself, and twice a week we would go off in the morning, the
three of us, either picnicking or stopping at some roadside
inn for lunch. We explored the glaciers, passes, and lakes
of the Bernina. With the coming of the season many of
our friends arrived from Paris, and Vaslav seemed to be
quite rested and soothed by the light-hearted gaiety of
his *entourage.* As a surprise for me, he invited my sister

and my brother-in-law Schmedes. Erik was a kind soul,
and Vaslav had not forgotten his loyalty.

The spring came, and with it the foreigners departed;
we were left alone again with the natives, whose life was
quite patriarchal. It seemed remote and five centuries back
to us. The celebrated sports centre had become a very
quiet Alpine village again. In the evening, at the Hôtel
Post, the notary, the Mayor, and the doctor would meet
to discuss the welfare of their little community. Vaslav
loved to listen to their debate; it reminded him so much
of Russia. We were so much in love with St. Moritz that
we did not wish to leave it even for a day.

The first timid crocuses pushed their way up and spring
was officially here, but the torrents of melting snow kept
us indoors more, and Vaslav resumed my lessons. He
seemed lighter than ever; the number of his pirouettes and
entrechats was infinite, and, watching him make his
battements and *pliés,* it sometimes seemed to me that he
was lighter than the snow-flakes themselves. But his
strength was of steel, and he bounded like india-rubber.

Once, while reading, I remarked to him how the people
in each century seemed to resemble each other. "That is
the result of costume," he replied, "for costume determines
our movements." The idea was new to me, but, on thinking it over, I saw he was right. Vaslav was able, on seeing
the lines and materials of a costume, to reconstruct the
proper gestures of a period. He literally put bodies into the
empty costumes of any historical period.

He was full of ideas for new ballets. He composed a
delightful version of Debussy's *Chanson de Bilitis*. He
said, "I want you to dance Bilitis. I have created it for
you. It obeys the same basic choreographic laws as the
Faune." It was in perfect harmony with the movement of
the music, with all its delicate feeling and sweet perversity.
This ballet was in two scenes, the first, Bilitis and her shep-
herd, their love, their youth on the green islands of
Greece; the second, Bilitis and her girl lover, who shares
her sorrows, and her pleasures.

Vaslav's other creation was his own life put into a
choreographic poem: a youth seeking truth through life,

first as a pupil, open to all artistic suggestions, to all the
beauty that life and love can offer; then his love for the
woman, his mate, who finally carries him off. He set
it in the period of the High Renaissance. The youth was
a painter; his master one of the greatest artists of the
period, a universal genius, just as Diaghileff seemed to him
to be. He designed the scenery and costumes for it himself, modern, and yet correct to the period. "You know,
femmka, the circle is the complete, the perfect movement.
Everything is based on it—life, art, and most certainly our
art. It is the perfect line." The whole system of notation
was based on the circle, and so was this ballet. It was in
accordance with Vaslav's previous methods, but, unlike
Faune and *Sacre,* it was circular. The scenery was a design in curve, and even the proscenium opening was round.
Vaslav worked out the whole design himself to the smallest
detail, in blues, red, and gold, Raphaelistic in style.

Almost overnight our surroundings had changed. The
frozen lake began to quiver, the slopes of the Alps, covered
with fragrant flowers, had become a riot of colour, the
pink alpen-roses, the sweet-smelling purple violets, and
the cornflower blue gentians. The snow retreated to the
summits of the peaks, which were now so familiar to us
and had each its own meaning for Vaslav. We used to
run up to the Alp Giop and throw ourselves down among
the flowers. And, while lying there in the scented pasture,
we spoke of many things. I told Vaslav about my parents' unhappy marriage, and blamed my mother, but he
stopped me. "Don't be hard. You do not know the circumstances that made her act the way she did. We should
never condemn anybody, nor have we the right to judge."
I often complained about the difficult times we were
having to go through during the war, but Vaslav said, "Do
not look up to the more fortunate, look down to those
worse off than yourself, and be thankful for your destiny."

I had been suffering slightly ever since Kyra's birth,
and Vaslav urged me to go and consult a specialist in
Berne. There it was decided that a minor operation
should take place. I entered the sanatorium, and, when all

was over, wired to Vaslav. He arrived by the next train, his arms full of roses, and spent two weeks near my bedside. In Berne he saw the Sakharoffs dancing. Next day, when I complained that I could not accompany him, he said, "You have not lost anything. It is merely attitudinising, not dancing at all. *C'est du Munich.*" I saw he was disappointed, as he was ever eager to see new talent to further his beloved art.

Autumn came, the air was crystalline, the colours graded from lightest topaz to sun-burned sepia. I was not yet quite strong, and Vaslav was anxious for me to rest. Vaslav took a great interest in the household, and, in the Russian patriarchal way, saw that the house was well provided with fuel for the winter. The wood was cut in our garden, and he used to help the men in their work. He also often visited the kitchen, to the great delight of the cook. He would lift the lids of the saucepans, and, if he happened to arrive when a cake was being baked, he usually cleaned out the bowl, just as in his childhood.

I used to give Kyra's Swiss nursery governess a day off to see her husband, an employee at the Palace Hotel. One day she was called down to him urgently, and did not return for two days. When she came back, she told me of the great misfortune that had ruined her life. Her husband had suddenly become insane. He was to be sent to an asylum, and she must return to her parents. She told me of the heart-rending scene when she had seen him put into a strait-jacket. "But, Marie, didn't you notice anything before?" "No, he was always quite normal, only lately at night he used to walk round his room for hours and hours." Later, I told Vaslav that we should have to look for a new governess, and the reason why. He became strangely silent, and his face darkened. The new governess, a Swiss girl, brought up in England, had been for a long time in India, and in the evenings she would speak of her experience of fakirs and yogis. Vaslav became interested in the subject and began to study it.

This year the winter came early. When the snowing began, it went on for days and nights continuously. It was peaceful and warm; we seemed to be far away from the world, forgotten. The strange fascination of this isolated alpine village grew on us. In this sleepy whiteness, one morning the first news arrived from Bronia and *"Babouch-ka."* They were well and did not need anything. They had received the money sent by Vaslav, but when the November Revolution took place they had fled to Kiev. There was a letter enclosed to me saying that when the Bolsheviks seized power the gaols and asylums were thrown open, and poor Stanislav, left to himself, had been burnt to death. I had to break it to Vaslav; but how? I knew that he loved his brother. For days I was silent, but finally I plucked up courage and went to him. He was drawing at the time. *"Regarde, femmka, ça c'est notre Kouharka* and this is Marie." He showed me two lovely pastel portraits of the cook and the maid, transformed into Russian peasants, and a striking picture of Kyra. "This is Funtyiki; you think it looks like her?"

I hated to spoil his happiness. "Vaslav, I want to talk." He sat down in the arm-chair, and I on the edge. Petting and caressing him, I buried my face on his shoulder, and said quickly, "Stanislav is dead." A long silence, then Vaslav lifted my face and asked how it happened. I told him, and burst into tears. He looked at me smiling, but with a strange and deep quietness. "Do not cry; he was insane; it is better like this"; and he bowed his head. The same smile that he had had at his father's death came back again, and now I knew that Bolm had made a mistake, and that Vaslav was not heartless; on the contrary. But I felt it was strange—very strange.

Impresarios had heard of Vaslav's presence in Switzerland, and offers came pouring in, but I had to refuse them. One of them was bold enough to come to our home. I sent him off, but in the village he stopped Vaslav by asking for a match, and immediately began to make offers. Vaslav was so amused by the man's persistence that he asked him up to the house for tea, and promised that he would be given the first chance, when he was ready to dance again.

All this winter Vaslav was very busy composing and designing. His drawings were all based on the circle, and he developed an amazing technique of producing astonishing portraits out of a few circles.

During the long winter evenings, when it snowed and snowed ceaselessly, our little governess proposed that we should try some *séances*. We did, and it amused me, but Vaslav took everything more seriously the moment he became interested in any subject. We got some curious answers, which we wrote down and put away.

"What will happen to Hungary?" I asked.

"It will be a kingdom without a king."

"And Count Tisza?"

"He will be killed."

"And Russia?"

"Neither war nor peace. Twenty-two years of uncertainty, then a democratic confederate republic."

Many things were said about after death and the after life at these *séances*. I wondered if any of it was true.

"Of course, *femmka,* life goes on in another form. Birth and death are very similar. Both are part of a circle which goes on. We are an infinite part of God in the universe, and when we create something beautiful, we reflect Him."

Finally the day arrived when I could signal to Vaslav the unexpected news that an armistice had been declared. I ran up the stairs to the villa breathlessly to tell him the details, but he shook his head on reading the conditions. "Peace, peace. There can be no peace under those terms. War will go on, but in a hidden, different way."

We were now able to begin our excursions again. Going up to the Fexthal, we had to pass through Sils Maria, and I pointed out to him the house where Nietzsche lived and wrote his *Ecce Homo.* Vaslav liked this book. Lately he had been reading a lot of Maeterlinck's new work, *La Mort,* and meditated more than ever.

Vaslav's new ballet, a choreographic drama, was making great progress. It was to be a picture of sex life with the scene laid in a *maison tolérée.* The chief character was to be the owner, once a beautiful *cocotte,* now aged and paralysed as a result of her debauchery; but, though her body was a wreck, her spirit was indomitable in the traffic of love. She deals with all the wares of love:

selling girls to boys, youth to age, woman to woman, man
to man.

"But, Vaslav, how will you be able to express it?" He
danced, and succeeded in transmitting the whole scale of
sex life. "I want to show both the beauty and the destructive quality of love."

Speaking of his future plans, Vaslav said, "From next
autumn on, if I cannot yet return to Russia, I will form
my own company and live in Paris and dance." It was at
that time, too, that Vaslav requested me to put down in
writing his artistic ideas.

The winter season was beginning once more, and it
promised to be a record one. The war was over at last.
We decided to make our first Christmas in our own home
and in peace-time a cheerful one, and we were convinced
that after the sad, stormy years we were sailing at last
towards a calm and happy future.

Chapter Twenty

MARRIAGE AVEC DIEU

THE 24TH of December was passed in
feverish preparations. The big pine-tree, which went right
up to the ceiling, was brought into the drawing-room and
placed near the open fireplace. We adorned it ourselves;
it was a beautiful heavily laden tree, full of candies, toys,
silver nuts and garlands, and on the top Vaslav himself
placed a shining silver star—"The tree for Kyroschka."
He looked it over with a critical glance. He wanted it to
be very lovely, and so it was. We enjoyed preparing it.
Vaslav had helped me to wrap up the presents neatly in
silver paper; one for each of the household. Vaslav also

remembered many children and sick people in the village, and we went round to take them their parcels.

Our Christmas Eve was a peaceful and happy one. Kyra's eyes opened wide when she saw the beautiful illuminated tree which Tatakaboy, as she called her father, lighted for her. Next morning I slept late, and was awakened by the maid, who came in trembling and white as a sheet. "Oh, madame, as I went into the drawing-room I found the Christmas-tree fallen on the floor. It means bad luck." I shivered. *"Femmka, c'est une bêtise;* it only means that it lost balance, was overladen on one side. I can't understand it; I made it so carefully." We went down to see it. There it lay on the floor, the silver nuts all round and the silver star broken in two. We pulled it up, tied it, and I tried to forget the incident. During the last few weeks Vaslav had taken long solitary walks, which now became still longer; he seemed to be meditating. Sometimes I accompanied him, and we would walk silently through the woods, where only the murmur of the rushing glacier stream, deep covered under snow, broke the quietness.

Lately Vaslav had not asked me to dance for him as he did during the past summer and autumn, when he used to ask me to keep still for a few moments, and then to begin to dance, just trying to shut out all thought from my mind. At the beginning it surprised me; then I thought it would be a sort of improvisation, which Vaslav had always condemned as "inartistic." He assured me it was not. After a certain time I began to dance, strangely fascinated by Vaslav's oblique eyes, which he almost closed as if he wanted to shut out of himself everything else but my dancing. When I had finished, he said that I danced with a wonderful technique all the different parts of his newly composed ballet (I was not aware of it), the one he wanted Réjane to create. Each time I felt as if I were coming out of a trance, and got strangely irritable with the people around me.

I often asked how he was intending to develop the ballet, but Vaslav waved my question and sank back in one of his great silences. I did not insist, as I felt he was creating ideas that I could not always follow. He had a vision for a century ahead which I did not possess. I remembered then how he could talk, always with authority, with scientists on their own ground, and that instinctively he was right. Professor Pichler, the great Hungarian mathematician, who was living at the time in Celerina, and used to come and see us quite often, was amazed that Vaslav not only understood, but was able to discuss his problems with him. Vaslav's keen interest in mechanics had not lessened either. After having invented a wind-screen wiper for motor-cars, now he designed the then unknown eversharp pencil. *"Femmka,* send it to Laurence; he will get a patent for it."* I did not take it seriously until years later somebody else made the discovery and put it on the market. Now Vaslav was trying to solve different mechanical problems and to simplify his system of notation. He used to work until late at night, and came to sleep only towards the dawn. One day, as I was lying in bed with a slight cold, Vaslav, taking tea with me, went to the window and gazed out on the lake, which was again immobile and silent. "Vaslav, what would you do if I happened to die?" "Work, dance, create, go on with life, and bring up Kyra." "Would you not marry again?" "No." He began to speak slowly, as if he was pondering every word. "Marriage, that is when we meet the one who represents to us the fulfilment of our ideals, the truth. It only happens once in life, to some people never. No, I would not marry."

"We are so happy, I am almost afraid sometimes something will happen," I said. "Yes, sometimes it must be hard to go on with life if the one we love dies. But we have to go on. My grandfather was an awful gambler. He lost everything he owned and shot himself; it was very wrong of him. His wife died shortly after. It was a tragedy."

Lately Vaslav had been shopping. Cases of paints and pastels arrived. I thought it was more than was needed for a year, but Vaslav explained that owing to the war there was such a shortage that it was wiser to lay in a stock in time, which sounded very logical to me.

Sometimes I met Vaslav running on the road leading towards Chanterella, our favourite promenade. I did not approve of long-distance running in this altitude; I thought it would be too strenuous for him, so I made a remark. But he replied that the exercises did not provide sufficient movement for him, so that he had to find some others. He was now very silent. I tried to talk over different artistic subjects that I knew interested him, but he only gave me confused or evasive answers. But he was so much ahead in his ideas that it seemed only natural that I could not always follow. One Sunday we decided to sleigh over to Maloja. Kyra was glad and Vaslav was very gay that morning. As it took us about three hours to get there, Kyra and I got very hungry during the long drive. The road was extremely narrow during the winter, as it needed cleaning from the heavy snows and in certain parts there was always a space to await the sleighs coming from the opposite direction. Vaslav was as a rule a careful and excellent driver, but on this particular Sunday he did not wait, but simply drove on into the oncoming sleighs. We were in danger of turning over as the horses got frightened. The coachmen cursed, but this did not make any difference. Kyra screamed, and I begged Vaslav to be more careful, but the further we went the more fiercely he drove against the other sleighs. I had to clutch on to Kyra and to the sleigh to keep ourselves on. I was furious, and said so to Vaslav. He fixed me suddenly with a hard and metallic look which I had never seen before. As we arrived at the Maloja Inn I ordered a meal. We had to wait. Vaslav asked for some bread and butter and macaroni. "Ah, Tolstoi again," I thought, but did not say a word, and bit my lips. Kyra was anxiously awaiting her steak, and, as it was laid before her and she began to eat, Vaslav, with a quick gesture, snatched the plate away. She began to cry from disappointment. I exclaimed, "Now, Vaslav, please don't begin that Tolstoi-Kostrovsky nonsense again; you remember how weak you got by starving yourself on that vegetarian diet. I can't stop you doing it, but I won't allow you to interfere with Kyra. The child must eat properly." I went with Kyra to the other room to have our solitary lunch. We drove home very quietly without a word.

Vaslav suddenly threw all his reserve to the winds, and declared gaily that he would take part in all the winter sports. We attended the ski-jumps, the bobsleigh and the skeleton races. We went riding and skiing. At the first lesson Vaslav asked our teacher to show him how to brake to stop, and the same morning he made telemarks. "Well, well, the gentleman only needs a few corrections," said the teacher, as Vaslav sailed down the slopes. "He is of course a practised skier." "What do you mean? It is the first time he has had skis on." "Remember, such perfect balance; he bends his knees just perfectly, with the elasticity of a practised skier. You are fooling me." But I was not surprised that Vaslav was so good; his wonderful training helped him in all sports.

I was pleased that he had become interested in sports. We went to lunches and dinners with our friends from Spain and England who were here once more, and even attended the dances at the Palace Hotel. Vaslav took a liking to skeleton running, though I thought it was too dangerous a sport and told him so, but he was so proficient after a few hours' practice that I could not object. Skeleton running is done in a narrow ice-run built on the slopes of the Alps, with dangerous curves. The speed is terrific, as the skeleton is made out of steel and the person lies head downwards on the skeleton, which is guided by the displacing of the balance. Vaslav became brilliant in its execution. Very soon he asked me if I wanted to go down with him, lying as a dead weight on top of him. I loved it, and I had faith in Vaslav, but, even so, I had to shut my eyes when we went flying through the run. Sometimes he took Kyra down, and I could only stand and pray until they arrived safely in the valley.

Lately Vaslav had changed his manner in skeleton running, and when he fell I was alarmed. "But what are you trying to do?" "Oh, one should do sport like art, not with the intellect, but spontaneously, without knowing how it springs from the emotion. This is the way to create, to live." I did not agree.

On our walks he sometimes stopped and stood for quite a long time, not answering my questions, he seemed so far away.

Our days passed in continuous social activity. Then one Thursday, the day when the governess and maid had their day off, I was making ready to take Kyra out for a walk when suddenly Vaslav came out of his room and looked at me very angrily. "How dare you make such a noise? I can't work." I looked up, surprised. His face, his manner were strange; he had never spoken to me like this. "I am sorry. I did not realise we were so loud." Vaslav got hold of me then by my shoulders and shook me violently. I clasped Kyra in my arms very close, then with one powerful movement Vaslav pushed me down the stairs. I lost my balance, and fell with the child, who began to scream. I stood up, more astounded than terrified. What was the matter with him? I was unaware of having done anything wrong. He was still standing there menacingly. I turned round, exclaiming, "You ought to be ashamed! You are behaving like a *moujik*." A very changed Vaslav we found when we came home, docile and kind as ever. I did not speak about the incident, either to him or to anybody else.

As the days passed, Vaslav was working more and more. He seemed to make a drawing in three minutes with a lightning speed. His study and rooms were literally covered with designs; no longer portraits or scenic or decorative subjects, but strange faces, eyes peering from every corner, red and black, like a bloodstained mortuary cover. They made me shudder. "What are those masks?" "Soldiers' faces. It is the war."

They were artistic creations, even though so frightening and morbid. Then other designs came; fanciful butterflies with faces which bore a resemblance to Vaslav's and big spiders with the face of Diaghileff.

"That is Sergei Pavlovitch, and these butterflies are we, the youth of Russia, caught in his net forever."

Then his mood changed and he began to write. "It will be my diary, my thoughts." But he refused to show me.

I shrugged my shoulders. Artists had such moods, and

I remembered my mother's hysterical fits when things did not go as she wanted in the theatre.

I woke sometimes at night to find Vaslav staring at me. "I am glad you watch over me; I feel so strange, Vaslav, I don't know what I might not do. Please look after me. I have a feeling I might hurt somebody and I do not want to do it." Yes, I too felt a strange change. I could not form a judgment about anything any more. I did not know what was lovely and ugly. I had lost the faculty of distinction. I only knew that an uncanny feeling was taking hold of me, something that I felt was draining all my vital force, my will to live. "I must be getting neurasthenic; I probably need a rest." And I asked my house physician to recommend a neurologist to me, which he did. "There is nothing the matter with you, but here is the address you wish."

Then one day I really grew alarmed. It was Sunday. Vaslav went out early in the morning. I was supposed to meet him at noon. Before leaving the house, I went to the kitchen to give final instructions to the cook about lunch. Round the table were sitting the maid, the laundress, and the stoker. As I came in, they abruptly stopped their conversation and stood up. "Good morning," I greeted them gaily. They hardly replied, but looked at me with sad faces. "What has happened?"

They set their lips and became mute. "But what has happened? Are you all dumb suddenly?" Then the young man, our stoker, made a few hesitating steps and quickly said, "Madame, forgive me; I may be wrong. We all love you both. You remember I told you that at home in my village at Sils Maria as a child I used to do errands for Mr. Nietzsche? I carried his rucksack when he went to the Alps to work. Madame, he acted and looked, before he was taken away, just like Mr. Nijinsky does now. Please forgive me." "What do you mean?" I shrieked, and then Kati, the laundress, excitedly said, "Mr. Nijinsky is walking in the village wearing a big golden cross over his necktie, and is stopping everybody in the streets asking them if they have been to mass and sending them to church. He just spoke to me." I thought they were all raving, but I flew down the staircase leading from the villa to the village, where I saw in fact Vaslav stopping the passers-by. I got hold of his hands. He seemed embarrassed at seeing me. "What are you doing? What is this new nonsense? Vaslav, won't you stop imitating that old lunatic Tolstoi? You are making yourself into a laughing-stock." He looked like a punished child, very sad. "But, *femmka,* I did not do anything wrong. I just asked if they had been to church." I pointed to Kyra's big golden Florentine cross. "And what is this?" "Well, if you don't like it——" and he took it off. "The world imitates me; all the foolish women copy my ballet costumes. They make their eyes seem oblique, and it becomes the mode, only because nature gave me high cheekbones. Why can't I teach them something useful, lead them to remember God? Why can't I set the fashion, since I do set fashions, that they should seek the truth?" I was quiet. He was right. "But you have a funny way of expressing your ideas."

Then one day we went on an excursion and Vaslav again wore his cross over his sweater. On our way home he suddenly began to drive fiercely and the sleigh turned over. I really got angry, and walked home with Kyra. Of course, he was home ahead of us. When I entered the house, the servant who worshipped Vaslav opened the door and said, "Madame, I think Monsieur Nijinsky is ill, or perhaps very drunk, for he acts so queerly. His voice is hoarse and his eyes all hazy. I am frightened." "Don't be silly, Marie. He never drinks, you know. Artists have moods, but ring up the doctor and say I need him for Kyra, and put her to bed at once." I went to our bedroom. Vaslav lay fully dressed on the bed, with the cross on, his eyes closed. He seemed to be asleep. I turned cautiously towards the door, and then noticed that heavy tears were streaming down his face. *"Vatza, qu'est-ce que tu as? Vatza, ne sois pas fâché?"* "It is nothing; let me sleep; I have a dreadful headache." He had had many of those lately.

The doctor came. I took him to Kyra, and told him everything that had happened these last months. He agreed that we must pretend that Kyra had a chill and that he was attending her. Not to make the plan too conspicuous, I asked him to remain for tea, and Vaslav joined us. He showed none of his usual anxiety on hearing that Kyra was not well, but seemed indifferent.

I left them alone. Vaslav rather liked the doctor, who was not only excellent and up to date in his profession, but very musical. They had a long chat, and as I came in the doctor said, "I have just suggested to Mr. Nijinsky that you should both go somewhere in the lowlands—let us say Lausanne or Valmont—to get a real rest after all your travelling, in one of our sanatoria." Vaslav was gay and seemed rather relieved. I had no opportunity to speak to the doctor in private, but next morning he telephoned. "Mr. Nijinsky needs a rest; he has a slight case of hysteria, probably due to overwork. I would advise you to go into a sanatorium with him, and in the meanwhile I will get a nurse, so that we can have him under observation." In order not to cause him anxiety I decided to say that he was a *masseur,* as Vaslav had wanted to engage one and had already made inquiries. Next day a solid, tall, good-natured German, a native of Munich, arrived. He had been the head nurse for the last twenty years of the State asylum, and, as he was just on a vacation, he would combine business and pleasure and take over the case. He was presented to Vaslav as the *masseur,* and went up daily to give him massage. He was a remarkable actor, as nobody in the house or in the village suspected his identity. He was both amusing and clever. Vaslav gave me a long, understanding glance when I introduced him, but became very friendly, and they used to go off for long walks and drives together. His presence made Vaslav his old mischievous self again. He was full of fun, and played hide and seek happily with Kyra, and together they built snowmen in the garden. Vaslav suggested that I should invite my sister to visit us, and a week later she was on her way from Vienna.

One day at lunch Vaslav declared he had decided to give up dancing forever and to realise his ideal of going somewhere in Russia to farm.

I lost my temper. "Really, Vaslav, you should not always harp on this plan to give up your art; and, anyway, if you go, you go alone. I have had enough; I can't become a peasant. I was not born one. Even if I love you I will divorce you and marry some manufacturer." And in my bad temper I took off my marriage-ring, the heavy golden Brazilian circle, and ungraciously hurled it at Vaslav. He seemed very surprised. In the afternoon I received a huge bouquet of about five hundred carnations, with the ring in it.

My sister called me up from the first station near the border. I told her everything, almost in tears. With her arrival a whirl of entertaining began. Vaslav went everywhere—dances, dinners, races. He even began to give her dancing-lessons, and went down daily to shop for us, buying scent, shoes, and gifts in great quantities. I was rather annoyed, as he spent several thousand francs on things we did not really need. One morning he arrived with a load of sweaters, in every colour of the rainbow. "But why so many?" "*Femmka,* the shades are so beautiful. Why not?"

Our Spanish friends and also the Duc and Duquesa de Durcal arrived, and we were invited to tea. The usual crowd was present discussing lightly the armistice, the new dressmaker Chanel, the revolution in Russia, and other events.

"And you, Nijinsky, what have you been doing this year? Did you compose? Are you going to dance soon?" Vaslav leaned back nonchalantly on the couch, drinking his tea. "Well, I composed two ballets, I prepared a new programme for the next Paris season, and lately I have played a part. You see, I am an artist; I have no troupe now, so I miss the stage. I thought it would be rather an interesting experiment to see how well I could act, and so for six weeks I played the part of a lunatic, and the whole village, my family, and even the physicians apparently believed it. I have a male nurse to watch me, in the disguise of a *masseur.*" I was speechless. So it was an artistic experiment which had made us all suffer and driven me almost crazy!

The ladies got quite excited. "Nijinsky, what a delightful experiment! How ingenious, wonderful, great!" I could have boxed their ears. An elderly marquis came over to discuss the matter in detail, and there was general applause.

Only Durcal remarked, "I think, Nijinsky, it was rather a cruel experiment, very hard on your wife." "Well, I know she loves me, but I never realised she loved me so much." Vaslav had really changed. I knew that this chaffing and superficial manner was not his. It almost seemed that he was now acting the part of a *blasé mondain* aristocrat, and making fun of the others present. Mr. S., the nurse, after ten days' stay, came to me. "Madame, I am a psychiatric nurse, and have been so for thirty-five years. I know more than the greatest professors, and I have had greater experience. I nurse the patients, I live with them, while the Herr Professors only drop in for a few moments and go away. You are wasting your money in keeping a nurse. Mr. Nijinsky is the sanest person in the whole of St. Moritz Dorf." He departed, and Vaslav, who was now quite a friend, took him down to the station and saw him off.

My sister and Vaslav got on very well together. He gave her a few lessons to teach her how to walk. Vaslav said that so few people knew how to balance their bodies correctly, and showed us exercises. "Don't walk on the point of your toes, but put the middle of your soles down first." All the alarming symptoms disappeared, and I became convinced that Vaslav had fooled us. He was, thank God, all right.

The impresarios kept on writing and trying to secure his promise to dance in the spring. Vaslav seriously considered beginning in Paris. "I won't give a programme ahead. I will just put on 'Nijinsky dances'; they will have confidence in me." Also we discussed at length how to arrange our new apartment in Paris. "I think later on, *femmka,* we will build a house here in St. Moritz. It is near to Paris, to London, to Rome. Ideal for Kyra and for us to have a rest." I was pleased at these projects. How happily did I rejoin Vaslav at Hanselmann's at noon. I was training that time for the skeleton races. The season was advancing, but promised to draw out as the weather was beautiful. Some of our Viennese friends were at St. Moritz, among them Mme. Asseo, the great pianist, a friend of my sister and brother-in-law. Vaslav told them he intended to give a dance recital for all his friends present in St. Moritz. The rumour spread like wild-fire that Vaslav would dance again. He was looking for a suitable place, as all the ball-rooms in the hotels had polished floors, but in the lovely Suvretta House, the hotel in the pine forest, which looks like an enchanted castle, Vaslav discovered, with the hospitable and charming owner of the place, Hans Bon, a ball-room where the floor was suitable. He arranged to have tea served after his recital there, and everything was prepared. "What are you going to dance, Vaslav?" "You will see, all new creations." "Where will you order the costumes?" "I will make them myself, with your little Italian dressmaker. She is clever." And he began to work with her. Hundreds of yards of gorgeous coloured silks, velvets, and lamés were brought to the house.

Our intense desire all these years was to have a son, but on account of the war we waited. Ever since Kyra became Kyra instead of Wladislav we were dreaming of Borislav, as our future son would be called. Vaslav one morning suddenly declared, *"Femmka,* do you know of anybody—a great physician—who is a genius like Lombroso?" "I can inquire, but for what?" "I want to talk to somebody who would understand me, with whom I could talk over many things. I want to have a son now, and I want him to be perfectly healthy, not only physically but mentally." I was rather astonished at hearing this.

I asked Vaslav to come with me and watch my skeleton running before the races, and to give me his advice. I was in splendid form. He came, and as I ascended the steep slope he ran towards me with an excited look. "No, no, *femmka,* it is not right." "But why? I arrived in record speed." "You do it with your intellect; it must come from the emotion, and not from the brain, as all creations of art, as life, as nature." His voice sounded so

hoarse and so nervous that I gave him a side-look and did
not answer. We went to Hanselmann's. Vaslav lapsed into
a silence and fixed a gentleman opposite him with such a
glassy and disapproving look that the poor man got embarrassed and left.

The day of the recital arrived. I was kept completely
in the dark, for the first time, of what was going to be
the programme, but I did not mind this. I was sure it
would be lovely. Vaslav remarked a few days before, "I
am going to show how dances are created. I will compose
them there before the audience. I want the public to see
the work. They always get everything ready-made. I want
to show them the pangs of creation, the agony an artist
has to go through when composing, so I will even make
the costumes in front of them." He stood in the middle of
the drawing-room and draped himself in yards of material.
In a few seconds he was able to make amazing costumes
of utterly different periods. The Italian dressmaker was
kneeling down helping to roll the silks. "What a pleasure
to work with Mr. Nijinsky." Around five, the hour fixed
for the recital, we drove over to the Suvretta, Vaslav, the
dressmaker, and I. Vaslav was silent, just as before going
to the theatre. I knew this mood and respected it. Before
arriving at the Suvretta, I ventured to ask, "Please tell
me what Bertha Asseo must play for you." "I will tell her
at the time. Do not speak. *Silence!*" he thundered at me.
"This is my marriage with God." A slight uneasiness crept
over me. Vaslav looked so menacing, so dark, in his fur-
collared coat, with his Russian fur cap.

I went to receive our guests. About two hundred were
already assembled in the ball-room. Many uninvited were
also present; everybody who could get admission. Bertha
Asseo was already at the piano. We waited a few seconds.
Vaslav entered in his practice kit, and, taking no notice
of the public, went up to Bertha and said, "I will tell
you what to play." I was standing near the piano. There
was an air of great expectation. "I will show you how we
live, how we suffer, how we artists create." And he picked
up a chair, sat down on it facing the audience, and
stared at them, as if he wanted to read the thoughts of

each. Everybody waited silently as if in church. They waited. The time passed. We must have been like this for about half an hour. The public behaved as if they were hypnotised by Vaslav. They sat completely motionless. I got rather nervous as I caught a glance of Dr. Bernhard, who was standing in the background, and his expression confirmed me in the belief that my suspicion was justified. Vaslav was again in one of his strange dark moods. Bertha began as a prelude the first few bars of *Sylphides*, then *Spectre*. She hoped to call Vaslav's attention to one of his dances. Perhaps then he would begin. I felt quite upset, and wanted to relieve the tension. I went over to Vaslav. "Please won't you begin? Dance *Sylphides*." "How dare you disturb me! I am not a machine. I will dance when I feel like it." I fought desperately not to burst out crying. Never had Vaslav spoken to me this way, and before all these people! I could not bear it, and left the room. Mr. Asseo and my sister joined me. "What is happening? What is the matter with Nijinsky?" "I do not know. I want to take him home. What shall we do?" We went in again, but by this time Vaslav was dancing—gloriously but frighteningly. He took a few rolls of black and white velvet and made a big cross the length of the room. He stood at the head of it with open arms, a living cross himself. "Now I will dance you the war, with its suffering, with its destruction, with its death. The war which you did not prevent and so you are also responsible for." It was terrifying.

Vaslav's dancing was as brilliant, as wonderful as ever, but it was different. Sometimes it vaguely reminded me of that scene in *Petrouchka* when the puppet tries to escape his fate. He seemed to fill the room with horror-stricken suffering humanity. It was tragic; his gestures were all monumental, and he entranced us so that we almost saw him floating over corpses. The public sat breathlessly horrified and so strangely fascinated. They seemed to be petrified. But we felt that Vaslav was like one of those overpowering creatures full of dominating strength, a tiger let out from the jungle who in any moment could destroy us. And he was dancing, dancing on. Whirling through space, taking his audience away with him to war, to destruction, facing suffering and horror, struggling with all his steel-like muscles, his agility, his lightning quickness, his ethereal being, to escape the inevitable end. It was the dance for life against death.

Thunderous applause greeted Vaslav when he stopped, and he seemed to come back from very far. He smiled and acknowledged the compliments; he chatted with the guests. They were overcome with this dancing that was something that none of us had ever witnessed before. The first moments of terror were forgotten. Only I remembered, and Dr. Bernhard. Mme. Asseo, who played bravely through the recital, seemed to be quite exhausted from the nervous strain. We had tea together, and, as I was still trembling inwardly, she kindly patted me. "It must be very, very difficult to be married to a genius like Nijinsky. I almost wish you could be free to marry one of our nice, charming, inoffensive compatriots." Since that day I never felt the same again. What was happening to Vaslav? How could I help him? What could I do? My sister returned to Vienna, and, soon after, my parents announced their visit to Switzerland. I wished that Vaslav could have seen somebody great like Lombroso, a genius who could understand and help him. Now again he was feverishly writing his impressions in his diary every day. It was in Russian, and, as he wrote with tremendous speed, it was almost illegible, but I could distinguish that the sentences repeated themselves continuously and that the two names Diaghileff and God dominated the diary.

Vaslav spoke often of his son. So one day I gathered up my courage and said that I had found a man as great as Lombroso, Professor Bleuler, a leading psychiatrist. "Let us go and see him." In a few days' time my parents arrived, and we all four left for Zürich. I saw that Vaslav's face was drawn as we drove to the station. St. Moritz was emptying. The melting of the snow began, and our sleigh had to struggle across muddy patches.

Next day I went alone to see Professor Bleuler. Vaslav did not want to accompany me. Bleuler was an old man with an infinite understanding in his eyes. I spoke to him about Vaslav, myself, our marriage, and life for almost two hours. "Very, very interesting, all you tell me. I can assure you there is nothing the matter with you, my dear. Anyhow, we do not become insane; we are born it. I mean, the disposition is there. Genius, insanity, they are so near; normality and abnormality, there is almost no border between the two states. I should like to meet your husband; extremely interesting. If you spoke of any other man I might be worried, but the symptoms you describe in the case of an artist and a Russian do not in themselves prove any mental disturbances." I was relieved, and came home happily. I told Vaslav how nice Bleuler was and that he thought I was healthy and that we could now have a son, and that he would like to make his acquaintance. Vaslav agreed, "Of course, so would I; he seems interesting. I was quite sure everything was all right. After all, *femmka,* I was brought up in the Imperial School, and we were there under constant medical supervision. Since I left there, except for my typhoid I have never been seriously ill." In a happy mood, we went out shopping, and I noticed that Vaslav stopped before the window of a great department store where babies' layettes were exposed; he smiled, and I knew he was thinking of the son he so ardently desired.

Next day, about three in the afternoon, we drove across the bridge on the Lake of Zürich to the hilly side, where in a wood at a little distance the State asylum is built, a big, old-fashioned building with iron-barred windows. But the smiling porter and the flowers which surround the directorial building, where Professor Bleuler received, took away the disagreeable impression. We sat for a few moments and then the Professor came out. I introduced him to Vaslav, and they both disappeared in his study. Calmly I looked over the illustrated papers lying round: the *Illustration,* the latest numbers of the *Sketch* and *Graphic.* I was relieved that all this unnecessary anxiety was over; at last everything would be all right. We had had such a hard time these first six years of our marriage—the fight with Diaghileff, war prisoners, all the disillusion; but now at last the happy time would

commence. The door opened within ten minutes, and the
Professor showed out Vaslav smilingly. "All right. Splendid. Won't you step in for a second? I forgot to give you
the promised prescription yesterday." I smiled at Vaslav
as I passed him, following the Professor; what prescription
I could not remember. As he closed the door of his study
behind him, he said very firmly, "Now, my dear, be very
brave. You have to take your child away; you have to
get a divorce. Unfortunately, I am helpless. Your husband is incurably insane." I thought the sunray which
passed through the window above the head of the Professor was curiously full of dust. Why did he have that
huge green table in the middle of the room? And those
inkstands were irritatingly round—a circle; oh, yes, the
Circle. That awful, that merciless circle of misfortune. I
was vaguely hearing him ask me to forgive him for being
so hard. "I must seem to be brutal, but I have to be to
be able to save you and your child—two lives. We physicians must try to save those whom we can; the others,
unfortunately, we have to abandon to their cruel fate. I
am an old man. I have sacrificed fifty years of my life to
save them. I have searched and studied; I know the
symptoms; I can diagnose it; but I don't know, I wish I
could help, but do not forget, my child, that sometimes
miracles happen."

I did not listen; I had to get out of there quickly. I felt
the place was going round with me faster and faster in a
circle. I dashed through the door to the room where Vaslav was waiting. He stood near the table looking absent-
mindedly at the illustrated papers, pale, strangely sad, in
his Russian fur coat with the Cossack cap. I stopped and
looked; it seemed as though his face was growing longer
under my gaze, and he slowly said, *"Femmka,* you are
bringing me my death-warrant."

EPILOGUE

Fourteen years have elapsed since the day that Nijinsky's mind became shrouded in darkness, when he withdrew from this world. Fourteen years since he has been living in a world where his imaginary creations are real personalities to him, and we, the reality, are only dream-like apparitions.

He is day-dreaming unceasingly, but without the loss of his memory. He knows he is Nijinsky, and he knows his family and is aware of his surroundings. He is mute for days, for weeks, for months. He is docile, obedient, patient and indifferent, neat and as orderly as ever. His physicians and nurses adore him. His charm is still present. A lightning flash of his old mischievous self brightens up the monotony of his apparent indifference. An attention, a kind word, a compliment on his dancing, brings a smile. The music of *Petrouchka* or *Carnaval* lights up his face with joy. His memory seems to be strangely intact when a Fugue, a Prelude of Bach, a piece of Debussy's or Stravinsky's music is played to him, and if the music stops he goes on whistling correctly the bars that follow. Experiments made prove that Nijinsky still remembers. When one of his own parts is danced before him and a false step is made he corrects it; if a dancer slips, he jumps up to help. Otherwise, he has shut dancing, the most treasured thing for him, utterly out of his life. Only once in a while he leaps up and makes a *tour en l'air* or pirouette as if he had just a few moments

before finished the *Spectre de la Rose*. To the layman he
appears as a silent, quiet, indifferent man. The wild rumours that were spread of him are unfounded and false;
Nijinsky never behaved like an animal. In his insanity,
as in his health, he is the same, kindly, human. He never
attacks, only defends himself. His illness is one before
which medical science is at a loss. It is Schizophrenia—a
disease probably due to the malfunctioning of the glands;
one of which the origin is little known and the cure not at
all; one which leaves the organism intact, and is known
as a functional disease. Unfortunately it is not caused by
a germ, such as paralysis as the result of syphilis, and
therefore it is incurable.

The day when Professor Bleuler made his statement,
the day when I decided to try to save him from the fate
to which he was condemned, my frantic parents arrived
in Zürich. The idea that Vaslav was pronounced insane
made them lose their heads completely. As they were
unsuccessful in persuading me to seek a divorce, they
decided to take our lives in their hands. My mother took
me out for a walk, and, while we were away—Vaslav
being still in bed, waiting for his breakfast—the police
ambulance, called in by my panic-stricken parents, came,
and the Hôtel Baur en Ville was surrounded by the fire
brigade to prevent Vaslav's jumping out of the window,
should he attempt it. They knocked at his door. Vaslav,
thinking it was the waiter, opened, and was immediately
seized. They tried to carry him out in his pyjamas. Vaslav,
as I learned from the manager, asked, "What have I
done? What do you want of me? Where is my wife?" They
insisted that he should come, and the doctor, seeing his
quietness, asked the nurses to release him. Vaslav thanked
him, and said, "Please let me dress, and I will follow
you." When I came back at noon, I found his room deserted.

Desperately I ran to Professor Bleuler, who helped me
to find him. He was in the State asylum among thirty
other patients, but, by that time, Vaslav, owing to the
shock, had had his first catatonic attack. Professor Bleuler

deeply regretted this unfortunate incident, which brought on the acute development of the illness, which, under different circumstances, might have remained stationary. On his advice, Vaslav was taken to the Sanatorium Bellevue Kreuzlingen, where he not only found admirable care but kind-hearted friends in Dr. Binswanger and his wife. After six months, during which his physicians and myself had every hope that he would get well, suddenly he began to get hallucinations, grew violent and worse, refusing all nourishment. I took him home to St. Moritz, and, under the supervision of two physicians and three nurses, we tried to give him the illusion of freedom and domestic life. During the next seven years I attempted to rebuild, on the ruins of our happiness, a tolerable existence in St. Moritz; later, in Vienna and Paris. The greatest specialists in Europe and America were called in. They all agreed it was a case of Schizophrenia.

Professors Bleuler, Wagner Jauregg, Kreplin, Ferenczy, Freud, Jung, were consulted. "Give him the best physical care, and quiet surroundings, under the care of a psychiatrist." "Let him dream his dreams," they all advised.

Then I turned to desperate means—fakirs, healers, Christian Science—but everything failed. We took him to the theatre, to see the Ballet, to Balieff's Chauve-Souris, to clubs where Cossacks danced, and, when he saw these, his expression changed, and for a few minutes he became his old self again. But there were weeks of great violence, and then he had to be taken to a sanatorium, to which I followed him, and unfortunately found out that in all other places except Kreuzlingen he was either neglected, badly nourished, or even occasionally ill-treated.

After tremendous difficulties, Lenin was asked, by a signed petition of the attending physicians, to let Bronia and Vaslav's mother leave Russia and join him. We hoped the shock of meeting them again might help. The request was refused, but my sister-in-law, who was finally advised of what had happened, managed to dance herself through to the border, and to come to us with Vaslav's mother. But Vaslav remained impassive at the sight of them. It is

only when Kyra comes that he smiles and says, *"Attention
à l'enfant."*

The years have passed, and one day in Paris Diaghileff
came to see him. *"Vatza, mais tu es paresseux. Viens,
viens, j'ai besoin de toi; il faut que tu danses pour le
Ballet Russe, pour moi."* Vaslav shook his head. *"Je ne
peux pas car je suis fou."* Diaghileff turned away, and
burst out crying, "It is my fault, what shall I do?"

The physicians were right. The home atmosphere did
not soothe him. On the contrary, the effort to behave
normally provoked periods of violence; and then I decided to take him back to the place where he felt happy
—where he was well treated and cared for at the beginning of his illness—to the Bellevue in Kreuzlingen. He
is there now . . . dreaming. . . . His hallucinations refer
to the war. He still hears the guns which have long
ceased to echo. He still sees soldiers dying around him.
When I come to him, he approaches me with an infinitely
grateful look, as a wise dog to the master who looks after
him.

Through these fourteen years I have tried to overcome
immense difficulties, and to offer to Nijinsky what still can
remain for him—care, and a home; remembering, in the
worst moments of agony, the sentence I once uttered at
Covent Garden, seeing him dance in *Sylphides:* *"Thank
you, my God, that I have lived in this century to have
seen Nijinsky dance,"* and the promise I gave him at our
marriage—*to stand by him in happiness and misfortune.*

Through all the tragic years there have been only a
few who have proved to be true friends of Nijinsky in
disaster as well as in his days of glory. To those I want to
convey my deepest gratitude in his name and in mine:
to the late Paul Dupuy, to Mrs. William K. Vanderbilt,
Sr., to Carlos Salzedo, to Robert Alfred Shaw, and to
Tamara Karsavina. While waiting for the miracle which
could restore Nijinsky to his art, to life, and to us, in spite
of everything the loyalty of these few friends makes me
believe that Vaslav, the seeker after truth, was right when

he said, as he was taken away to Kreuzlingen for the first time, pointing to the sky, *"Femmka, courage, ne désespères pas, car il y a un Dieu."*

NEW YORK, THE HAGUE,
    1932–1933.